Before Equiano

ZACHARY MCLEOD HUTCHINS

Before Equiano

A Prehistory of the North American Slave Narrative

The University of North Carolina Press *Chapel Hill*

Set in Arno Pro by Westchester Publishing Services
Manufactured in the United States of America

Library of Congress Cataloging-in-Publication Data
Names: Hutchins, Zachary McLeod, author.
Title: Before Equiano : a prehistory of the North American slave narrative /
    Zachary McLeod Hutchins.
Description: Chapel Hill : The University of North Carolina Press, [2023] |
    Includes bibliographical references and index.
Identifiers: LCCN 2022031530 | ISBN 9781469671536 (cloth ; alk. paper) |
    ISBN 9781469671543 (paperback ; alk. paper) | ISBN 9781469671550 (ebook)
Subjects: LCSH: Slave narratives—United States—History and criticism. |
    Slavery—United States—History—17th century. | American newspapers—
    History—17th century.
Classification: LCC E446 .H93 2023 | DDC 326.0973—dc23/eng/20220707
LC record available at https://lccn.loc.gov/2022031530

Cover illustrations: *Background,* front page of the *Massachusetts Sun* on the anniversary of the Boston Massacre (Alamy Stock Photo, Image ID AC51YH); *foreground,* hand with feather and quill (© iStock.com/duncan1890).

Financial support for the research presented in this volume
was provided by the National Endowment for the Humanities.

A portion of chapter 5 was previously published in a different form as
"The Slave Narrative and the Stamp Act, or Letters from Two American
Farmers in Pennsylvania," *Early American Literature* 50, no. 3 (2015): 645–80.

for Daniel

Contents

Figures and Tables

Acknowledgments

This is not the book I meant to write when I enrolled as a graduate student at the University of North Carolina at Chapel Hill, and it is not the book I wrote during my time in Chapel Hill; its first words were not written until several years after I left that institution. But its core idea, that the words and stories of black African men and women living before the War of American Independence needed to be reclaimed from colonial newspapers, was born in the extraordinary community I found there. I am grateful for the support and friendship of Angie Calcaterra, Kelly Bezio, Allison Bigelow, Ashley Reed, Nick Gaskill, Lynn Badia, Maura D'Amore, and Harry Thomas, who welcomed me into the program and founded the Americanist writing group that helped me become the scholar I am today. Harry showed me the ropes at UNC's Center for Documenting the American South, where he and I both worked as editorial assistants for Mike Millner, writing summaries for the Center's award-winning digital archive, *North American Slave Narratives*. It was there and then, in the summer of 2008, that I began the research that would result in this book, identifying newspaper articles offering context on the events mentioned in Briton Hammon's *Narrative*.

Several years later, I returned to Hammon's *Narrative*, with the encouragement of my colleagues—especially Brian Roberts, at Brigham Young University, and Louann Reid, at Colorado State University. Early drafts of my chapter on Hammon were read by anonymous readers for *The William and Mary Quarterly* and *The Massachusetts Historical Review*, and they provided very helpful feedback, for which I am grateful. So, too, did Jane Calvert when she read a draft of my work on John Dickinson. The friends and colleagues who asked questions and offered suggestions at the various conferences where these ideas were presented are too numerous to name, but Cassie Smith was a member of the panel where I first shared these ideas, and she has been a collaborator and constant source of support ever since. Financial support for the research in this volume was provided by the College of Liberal Arts at Colorado State University and by the National Endowment for the Humanities, which awarded me a fellowship in 2016. I am especially grateful to Vin Carretta and John Ernest, who wrote in support of my applications for these and other awards. Others have helped me to locate and secure permission to reproduce the archival documents and images presented here, including Kyle Triplett, Brent Sirota, Brianne Barrett, Jay Moschella, and Andrew Williams.

At The University of North Carolina Press, I have been blessed to work with a wonderful team of editors and production assistants. This is my second go-round with Lucas Church, and although I hope this is not my last book, I would be thrilled if he were my last editor; I am grateful for his patience and diligence in seeing this manuscript into print. He helped find readers who made this volume much better than it was before they read it, and I am grateful for the pandemic-era generosity of these colleagues who remain anonymous and also to Karen Weyler, who pulled back the curtain for me. Throughout the editorial process, I was thankful for the keen eyes of Mary Caviness and Lee Titus Elliott. There are fewer errors in the book as a result of their attention to my prose; those that remain are my responsibility alone.

The encouragement and support of my wife, Alana, is the sine qua non that has made this book possible. However, in the true spirit of acknowledgments, I would be remiss if I did not note that the relationship between my family and this book is more complicated than that simple statement would suggest. On 17 February 2015, as I was carefully reading and transcribing the various materials relating to slavery found in colonial newspapers, I happened upon a 1714 runaway slave advertisement placed by a man from Rhode Island named John Scott, who was seeking information on the whereabouts of a man named Daniel. Knowing that I was the descendant of Katherine Marbury Scott, of Rhode Island, I consulted genealogical records and discovered that this slave-holding John Scott was my ninth-generation great-grandfather. When I later traveled to Newport with my brother, Richard Scott Hutchins, to conduct research on the Scott family's involvement in human trafficking, I discovered that another relative, George Scott, had made numerous trips to Africa and forced hundreds of men, women, and children to endure the Middle Passage. I was horrified to learn, for the first time, that my ancestors were active participants in the kidnapping and enslavement of other human beings. At the beginning of this study, then, I wish to acknowledge both the love and support I have received from living family members and the fact that my progenitors robbed individuals like Daniel of a similarly loving home life. It is to him, and to the unnumbered and anonymous millions like him, that this book is dedicated.

Before Equiano

Slavery and the Newspaper

A Foreign Affair

As the enslaved Eliza flies from bondage in the opening pages of *Uncle Tom's Cabin*, she makes her way across the Ohio River to the home of Senator Bird, whom Harriet Beecher Stowe introduces as a supporter of the Fugitive Slave Act of 1850. Lounging in an armchair while reading the newspaper, Bird lectures his wife on the need to protect Southern property interests by enforcing the right of slaveholders to reclaim runaways. He is willing to return such escapees to their masters, Stowe writes, "but then his idea of a fugitive was only an idea of the letters that spell the word,—or, at the most, the image of a little newspaper picture of a man with a stick and bundle, with 'Ran away from the subscriber' under it. The magic of the real presence of distress,—the imploring human eye, the frail, trembling human hand, the despairing appeal of helpless agony,—these he had never tried."[1] When Eliza arrives at Bird's door with one shoe, in a tattered dress, she is exhausted from the effort of carrying her son Harry on her back for miles; immediately after entering the home, she collapses, unconscious, in a chair. Observing Eliza's suffering firsthand, Bird realizes that the runaway slaves who would be thrust back into bondage by the Fugitive Slave Act are not abstract units of labor but human beings for whose suffering he, as a legislator, is responsible. Eliza's physical presence puts a human face on the woodcut of his newspaper, and the pathos of her story moves Bird to aid Eliza on her journey north.

Bird's abrupt about-face suggests the woeful inadequacy of newspapers, and especially the standardized language of slave-for-sale and runaway slave advertisements presenting people as property, as vehicles for communicating the humanity of enslaved men and women. If only Senator Bird had been familiar with a more personal account of slavery's miseries, Stowe hints, he never would have supported the Fugitive Slave Act. The solution, from Stowe's perspective, is simple: replace the brief, faceless, and formulaic accounts in newspapers with the vivid characters of her novel or with the detailed slave narratives on which it was based.[2] But this implicit opposition between newspaper and novel or newspaper and slave narrative obscures a long history of newspaper consumption in which readers more imaginative than Stowe's dull Senator (including Stowe herself) conjured up tales of industry, passion, and tragedy from a single sentence in the classifieds.[3] A century before Stowe serialized her novel in *The National Era*, newspapers were the primary repository for narratives of enslavement, and these abbreviated stories inspired reflection and engagement on the part of readers. Indeed, the language and thematic concerns of newspapers shaped both the form and content of the first slave narratives.

Before Equiano is, as its subtitle announces, a prehistory of the North American slave narrative, tracing the genre back to its origins in eighteenth-century newspapers and following its evolution into a literary form with well-established tropes. In doing so, this book advances and elaborates upon three basic arguments: first, that the eighteenth-century newspaper was filled with accounts of slavery, many of which should be read as slave narratives; second, that eighteenth-century men and women were actively engaged readers who imaginatively reconstructed narratives about slavery from textual fragments; and third, that throughout the eighteenth century, narratives of slavery were always implicitly—and sometimes explicitly—associated with global politics and foreign relations. These claims warrant a serious reevaluation of the slave narrative proper, and its ongoing relationship to ephemeral print forms such as the newspaper, in the nineteenth century.

Over the past forty years scholars have devoted significant time and resources to the recovery of texts written by or about enslaved African Americans, and the digital anthology of *North American Slave Narratives*, launched by Bill Andrews and curated by the Center for Documenting the American South at the University of North Carolina at Chapel Hill, now houses more than two hundred biographical or autobiographical accounts of enslaved individuals that were published in the eighteenth, nineteenth, and twentieth centuries.[4] Scholars have derived from those accounts a set of conventions for the genre and detected a shift in its form, from an early emphasis on truth telling to a stress in later works on the selfhood and subjectivity of individual men and women.[5] But as Nicole Aljoe, Eric Gardener, and others have warned, an ongoing pedagogical and scholarly emphasis on the "canonical book-length narratives" of Frederick Douglass, Harriet Jacobs, and others has relegated most of this archive to the margins of literary history—and the fragmentary, ephemeral narratives of enslavement preserved in newspapers are often ignored entirely.[6]

A widespread preference for the intentionality, structure, and thematic continuity of monographs is particularly problematic for scholars investigating the eighteenth-century Atlantic world, where the lives of enslaved individuals were more often recounted in broadsides, court records, ship logs, newspapers, and other corporately authored texts than in bound books

published for profit. In colonial North America, newspapers so dispropor-
tionately outnumbered books that, Charles Clark reports, "by 1790, it could
be said that newspaper issues had comprised 80 percent of all American publications to that point," and almost every issue contained one or more items
related to the slave trade or the enslavement of a particular individual.[7] These
notices have largely been ignored by scholars because they offer a highly
mediated perspective on the experience of enslaved black Africans. However,
as Cassander Smith argues, "If we ignore the mediated presences of black
Africans prior to 1760, we offer up what is at best a truncated African American
literary history," and recovering these newspaper records restores a richer
understanding of the ways in which black Africans intervened in American
literature years prior to the appearance of their names on title pages. Notwithstanding their difficulty in accessing pen and press, black Africans "helped
to shape the literary record of the early Atlantic world—not as passive con-
structions but as active participants."[8] Throughout the eighteenth century the
newspaper was the single most important textual form to both determine
public understandings of slavery and disseminate the literary record of enslavement, and black Africans participated in shaping and then interpreting
that record.

In preparing to write this book, I have read more than five thousand issues
of colonial North American newspapers, including every one of the 2,690 issues published before 1730 and preserved digitally in the Readex Series *Early
American Newspapers, 1690–1922*. While most of these issues were published
in Boston, they carried news from around the world and circulated throughout the Atlantic basin.[9] I have transcribed all material related to slavery in
these issues published before 1730, including slave-for-sale and runaway slave
advertisements, descriptions of transported English convicts as slaves, accounts of criminal activity by enslaved black Africans, narratives of white captivity in France or Algiers, republished excerpts from *Cato's Letters*, and other
materials too diverse to list in full. As Srividhya Swaminathan and Adam
Beach attest, eighteenth-century writers used the word *slavery* "as a descriptor for political, physical, or ideological states," and these "mutually imbricated systems of oppression" cannot be separated without compromising our
understanding of the various ways in which the inhabitants of the Atlantic
world experienced, theorized, and resisted slavery.[10] In total, I transcribed
more than two thousand unique passages having to do with the experience or
metaphorization of slavery; because many of the ads and other news items
I transcribed were published in multiple issues or updated with new information, the total number of passages related to slavery published in surviving

newspapers from this period is more than 3,100.[11] In other words, each issue contained, on average, at least one advertisement, editorial, or news item pertinent to the story of slavery in colonial North America and the Atlantic world.

Historians have long mined colonial newspapers for information about the slave trade, but Lisa Lindsay, John Sweet, and Randy Sparks acknowledge that the discipline has only recently moved beyond tracking a "flow of captives, capital, and cultures" that "often obscured the lives of individuals" to begin "populating this abstract and anonymous Atlantic" with the names and faces of those who were enslaved.[12] However well meaning, this historic focus on data—the number of enslaved persons present in a given space, the valuation of their bodies, the commodities produced by their labor—persists in the dehumanization of black Africans and their descendants. As long as the newspaper and similar archival sources are treated like a database, Jessica Marie Johnson argues, they cannot provide a meaningful perspective on the humanity and subjective experience of either the enslaved or their emancipated family members living in the diaspora. "Data is the evidence of terror," Johnson writes, but attention to the stories and lives from which we have so frequently extrapolated data "refuses disposability" and provides an opportunity to reconsider the purposes for which we have preserved colonial newspapers and other archival sources.[13] Most of these sources were written from the perspective of slavers, rather than the enslaved. Still, as Marisa Fuentes has demonstrated, it is possible—just—to recover the presence and perspective of the black Africans whose stories are excerpted in colonial newspapers: "By changing the perspective of a document's author to that of an enslaved subject, questioning the archives' veracity and filling out miniscule fragmentary mentions or the absence of evidence with spatial and historical context our historical interpretation shifts to the enslaved viewpoint in important ways."[14] We have mined the archive for data, but hidden among the slag and dross discarded in our search for facts is narrative ore, waiting to be refined and brought to a brilliant polish through rigorous and visionary scholarship of the sort modeled by Fuentes.

Why have literary scholars largely failed to regard the fragmentary accounts of slavery preserved in eighteenth-century newspapers as objects of aesthetic and cultural import? Among other reasons, our collective disinterest is, as Julie Sievers notes, consistent with a systematic bias against the collated writing and "multivocal authorship" of anthologies or newspapers.[15] One implication of this neglect is that works of nonfiction assembled by excerpting or summarizing a hodgepodge of source material cannot be objects of literary study. But the 2015 Nobel Prize for Literature, awarded to the Belarussian journalist Svetlana Alexievich, challenges that assumption. The polyphonic works of Alexievich are woven together from the oral histories of hundreds of individual men and women, drawing their diverse accounts into a single, larger narrative. The collage of advertisements, foreign bulletins, government proclamations, and domestic news in each issue of a colonial newspaper is often a jumbled mess, but readers mentally assembled that mess into larger stories of human accomplishment and suffering, à la Alexievich. The challenge for literary historians and biographers of the Black Atlantic is to employ what Andrews terms "creative hearing," through which scholars come to read these reconstructed mental narratives, rather than the banal bits of news from which they were composed.[16]

That the consumers of eighteenth-century newspapers read even the most mundane scraps of news imaginatively and expansively is a truth declared by Joseph Addison, whose *Tatler* was a standard of literary taste in the Anglophone world for more than a century. In 1710 he confessed,

> It is my custom, in a dearth of news, to entertain myself with those collections of advertisements that appear at the end of all our public prints. These I consider as accounts of news from the little world, in the same manner that the foregoing parts of the paper are from the great. If in one we hear that a sovereign prince has fled from his capital city, in the other we hear of a tradesman who hath shut up his shop, and run away. If in the one we find the victory of a general, in the other we see the desertion of a private soldier. I must confess, I have a certain weakness in my temper, that is often very much affected by these little domestic occurrences, and have frequently been caught with tears in my eyes over a melancholy advertisement.[17]

Shedding tears not for the plain facts set forth in an advertisement but for the imagined circumstances that prompted the notice, Addison conjures up a backstory compelling his sympathy. This affective response is largely a product of his imagination, but Addison also credits the compiler because "a collection of advertisements is a kind of miscellany," he writes, and the "genius of the bookseller is chiefly shown in his method of arranging and digesting these little tracts."[18] Such genius is evident, perhaps, in the visual juxtaposition of an advertisement for "several young Negro Women lately arrived from the West-Indies" and notice of a slave ship leaving Kingston, Jamaica, which, upon "saluting the Town on their departure, the third Gun set Fire to the Powder on board, blew up the Deck ... and then immediately sunk with about 60 or 70 White Men, and near 300 Negros; the Captain and 19 more White Men were saved, and about 40 or 50 Negros, tho' some with their Limbs broken."[19] Placed beside the advertisement, this tragic news out of Jamaica provides imaginative context for the journey just completed by the enslaved young women now offered for sale—who may have endured broken limbs or been rescued from the waves in that very incident. To paraphrase Henry Louis Gates Jr., reading these narrative fragments requires "the positing of fictive black selves in language," selves acknowledged via generative reading practices.[20] Through editorial intervention and creative consumption, a banal notice becomes a moving narrative and an object of literary interest.

The newspapers themselves offer hints as to the interest with which slave-for-sale advertisements and other seemingly banal bits of print were read by North American colonists. For example, in 1722, a reader of the *New England Courant* wrote to share with the paper's readers an advertisement reportedly circulating in the Massachusetts countryside, explaining that "we are now more amus'd by a single Advertisement dispers'd among us than by all the Amusements your Paper has afforded us since its first Appearance."[21] Another advertisement marketed a gazeteer as the "News-mans Interpreter, being a Geographical Index of all the Considerable Cities, Patriarchships, Bishopricks, Universities, Dukedoms, Earldoms, and such like, Imperial and Hance-Towns, Ports, Forts, Castles &'c in Europe. Shewing in what Kingdoms, Provinces and Countries they are: Very useful for to understand the several Places in the News-Letter."[22] This assertion, that understanding a newspaper requires interpretative aids beyond those provided in the text itself, both acknowledges the limitations of these textual representations and documents the practice of collation—reading the news in conjunction with additional resources to create a larger, piecemeal narrative beyond that offered on the page.

The marginalia in surviving issues offer a few additional clues as to how inhabitants of eighteenth-century North America read the newspaper, but resurrecting the readerly slave narratives for which I advocate from the archives will also require imagination on the part of scholars. Nathaniel Hawthorne modeled a fanciful approach to the archive in the opening pages of *The Scarlet Letter*, recalling the genesis of his novel: "Poking and burrowing into the heaped-up rubbish in the corner; unfolding one and another document, and reading the names of vessels that had long ago foundered at sea or rotted at the wharves . . . and exerting my fancy, sluggish with little use, to raise up from these dry bones an image of the old town's brighter aspect," he conjured into existence a story of seventeenth-century New England.[23] Although the imagination is a faculty "sluggish with little use" in some works of scholarship, it is a necessary contributor to the narratives of enslavement contained in this book because that is the approach readers of the newspaper have long taken, from Addison to Hawthorne.

The format of colonial newspapers cultivated engaged and authorly readings of the sort described by Matthew Brown, in which "readers, like bees, extract and deposit information discontinuously, treating texts as spatial objects, as flowers or hives which keep readers active but anchored."[24] Unlike the sequential and continuous narratives found in bound books, eighteenth-century newspapers required readers to collate scattered and sometimes contradictory accounts into mental coherence; they tracked stories across both space and time, connecting accounts in different sections of the newspaper and linking people or events across multiple issues. The colonial newspaper is a conglomerate such as that described by Roland Barthes, in which various kinds of writing, few of which are original, come together in juxtaposition, and because the "text is a tissue of quotations drawn from the innumerable centres of culture" we recognize "the true place of the writing, which is reading."[25] Thus, imaginative readers such as Addison or Black Peter—a literate and enslaved black African pressman who set type, cut woodblock engravings, and delivered the *Boston Evening Post* for Thomas Fleet in the 1730s— might be said to have mentally authored the first slave narratives as they consumed brief newspaper reports of enslaved individuals who joined pirate crews, committed suicide, or otherwise escaped their masters.[26] Slave narratives were read by both black and white readers, long before they were bound and sold—even before they were written.

Colonial editors assumed a black African readership for news items with a black African protagonist. In relating the story of "A Negro Man" allegedly attempting to rape "an English Woman" in Connecticut, the printer explains "a very remarkable thing fell out, (which we here relate as a caveat for all Negroes medling for the future with any white Women, least they fare with the like Treatment)" (*BNL* 1718/3/3). The Puritan minister Cotton Mather had established a Boston-area school teaching black Africans and Indians to read in January 1718, just two months before this account was printed, and his pupils may have been the intended audience for its parenthetical warning.[27] Although some colonies passed laws against teaching enslaved individuals to write, literacy was so closely linked to the Protestant emphasis on scripture that a significant number learned to read, and Jared Hardesty argues that as they learned, the enslaved "transferred what began as a religious imperative into a useful and applicable knowledge base and employed this ability to better their everyday lives."[28] Reading the Bible led to reading other texts, including the newspaper. Enslaved persons in colonial Virginia were occasionally tutored privately, and schools for the instruction of black Africans opened in New York, South Carolina, and Pennsylvania, as well as in Massachusetts.[29]

Shortly after his arrival in Philadelphia, Samuel Keimer (who would eventually be immortalized in Benjamin Franklin's *Autobiography*) opened a school for the enslaved. He advertised in the *American Weekly Mercury*, offering "to teach his poor Brethren the **Male-Negroes** to read the Holy Scriptures, &c." and promised,

> *The Great* **Jehovah** *from Above,*
> *Whose* Christian-Name *is* **Light** *and* **Love,**
> *In all his Works* will *take Delight,*
> *And wash poor Hagar's* **Black-moors** *white.*[30]

No record of the school's activity survives, but it was apparently in operation three years later, when a rival printer named Jacob Taylor asked, "Was there no Room to keep thy black School, without Letting fly thy poisoned Arrows at all Men of Learning and Professors of useful Knowledge?" The prospect of his words being read by Keimer's pupils and their kin in Africa, Taylor writes, almost persuaded him not to denounce his enemy in print at all: "What! write to those in Bedlam and in Chains, / To *Hottantots* on Afric's distant Plains?" (*AWM* 1726/1/25). But he *did* write, and surely some of those taught to read by Keimer consumed his words with indignation.

Keimer's school, like Mather's to the north, enabled members of Philadelphia's black African community to read news of other enslaved individuals and to learn about their crucial position in the world of global commerce. They might, for instance, have read of a report in the British Parliament on "the Trade to Africa, setting forth, *That all the Trade of the English Plantations to America is dependant thereon*" and felt empowered by the knowledge of their collective economic centrality, an awareness that withholding their labor could have consequences far beyond Philadelphia (*AWM* 1726/6/9). Keimer came to identify with those he taught and thought of his own life story as a narrative of slavery. Shortly before he sold his newspaper, *The Universal Instructor in All Arts and Sciences; and the Pennsylvania Gazette*, to Franklin and Hugh Meredith, Keimer declared his intention to write a memoir: "'Twould swell a Volume to a very considerable Bulk only to relate the various Scenes of Life and Circumstances the Publisher hereof has gone thro'; no History he has ever read, (keeping exactly to Truth) could ever come up to it; and as his whole Life has been truly an Original; so it has been long design'd to present the World with a true Copy thereof, for their Entertainment, under the Title of the *White Negro*."[31] Keimer promised his readers a slave narrative, an account of his labor and sufferings. His pupils, scanning the words of their teacher's newspaper, surely asked one another what Keimer could possibly know about the experience of being a black African in colonial Philadelphia.

And yet: although the slave narrative is a genre now circumscribed by race, in the eighteenth century, accounts of enslavement were not yet understood to be the exclusive province of black Africans and their descendants.[32] Brett Rushforth notes that "slavery took many forms in the early modern Americas, and this variety persisted in both indigenous and colonial settings long after the African slave trade overshadowed other slaving cultures."[33] The first mention of slavery in a colonial North American newspaper actually refers to the bondage of American Indian peoples. John Campbell published a letter written by the former governor of South Carolina, James Moore, in the second issue of his *Boston News-Letter*. In 1704 Moore led a small group of Englishmen accompanying a much larger force of Creek and Yamasee Indians, and his letter to the current governor of South Carolina, Nathaniel Johnson, recounts a series of raids "against the Spaniards and Spanish Indians." Many of the Apalachee Indians allied with the Spanish voluntarily joined Moore's expedition and resettled in South Carolina or Georgia, but those who resisted were either killed or taken as prisoners. Moore's letter explains, "The number of free *Appalatchia* Indians which are now under my protection, and bound with me to *Carolina* are 1300. And 100 for Slaves," most of whom would be transported to the Caribbean (*BNL* 1704/5/1).[34] Because the enslavement of Indian peoples in North America largely ended before the nineteenth century, when the slave narrative took shape as a literary form, their stories of bondage are generally not recognized as contributions to the genre. Neither, for that matter, are narratives of enslavement penned by Americans of European descent, such as the *Narrative of Joshua Gee* or James Riley's memoir, *Narrative of the Loss of the American Brig Commerce*.[35] The UNC database of *North American Slave Narratives*, widely accepted as a comprehensive collection, includes only texts written by or about black Africans and their descendants.

But in the first decades of the eighteenth century, years before Briton Hammon, Olaudah Equiano, and Venture Smith would publish their life stories, narratives of enslavement circulating in the public sphere more commonly featured a white protagonist than a black one. Scholars generally treat these accounts as unrelated or at best tangential to the genre of the slave narrative, a decision shaped by the primacy of the nineteenth-century narratives of Douglass and Jacobs, which have little in common with the tropes and conventions of white enslavement.[36] Yet to regard these tales of white captivity— often, but not always, in Algiers or other polities in North Africa—as constitutive of a separate genre, the Barbary captivity narrative, is to ignore the ways in which white enslavement shaped understandings of slavery as an institution and representations of slavery in the first narratives published by black Africans in North America. Paul Baepler is right: "These genres should not be examined in isolation."[37] Narratives of slavery in the early eighteenth-century newspaper feature a diverse array of protagonists, from Indian prisoners of war to white indentured servants and black African mutineers; such stories of enslavement had not yet been segregated by generic or demographic categories, and their collective influence is visible in the first book-length auto/ biographies of black Africans.

As David Waldstreicher and others have shown, colonial North America housed many different forms of freedom and unfreedom.[38] Advertisements for runaway wives, deserting sailors, transported convicts, and indentured servants often appeared in proximity to notices for runaway slaves, and the word *slavery* was regularly used to characterize each of these conditions in public discourse.[39] Acknowledging constraints on the freedom of married women and impressed sailors does not diminish the suffering or efface the unique challenges of black Africans held in chattel slavery; rather, it provides a context for the ways in which the enslaved and their contemporaries understood the institution of slavery. During this period, Katherine Hayes writes, "lines of difference and affiliation were inchoate, open to negotiation," and the enslaved often made common cause with individuals experiencing different constraints on their freedom.[40] For example, a Philadelphia advertisement announced the escape of "a Mullata slave, Named *Richard Molson*, of Middle stature, about forty Years old, and has had the small Pox, he is in Company with a White Woman named *Mary*, who 'tis suppos'd now goes for his wife, and a white Man Named *Garrett Choise*, and *Jane* his Wife, which said White People are servants to some Neighbors of the said *Richard Tilghmans*, The said fugitives are Supposed to be gone to *Carolina* or some other of his Majestys Plantations in *America*" (*AWM* 1720/8/11). This advertisement introduces at least six people to the reader, but the story it tells is clearly Molson's: he is its protagonist. The fluidity of affiliations in Molson's story illuminates the difficulties of treating slave narratives of the early eighteenth century with an expectation of the racial rigidity that characterized the genre in the nineteenth and twentieth centuries, when only black Africans and their descendants authored slave narratives.

Molson, Mary, and Garrett and Jane Choise apparently regarded their shared experience of unfreedom—varied though it may have been—as a more important marker of identity than the contrasting hues of their skin. Given his status as a "Mullata," Molson was likely the son or grandson of Thomas Molson, who emigrated from England to Maryland in 1663 and owned land in Sussex County, Delaware, just a few miles from Richard Tilghman's land in Queen Anne's County, Maryland. Like other early colonists, Thomas Molson acquired his right to land by transporting himself and others—sometimes indentured servants—to North America.[41] But neither Molson's indentured servants nor an unacknowledged black child or grandchild such as Richard Molson would profit from that land; the immediate future of white laborers like Mary, Jane, and Garrett Choise would be more similar to that of Richard Molson than Thomas. Richard Molson's biracial background may have made him a plausible or palatable "husband" for Mary in the eyes of white observers, but his choice of traveling companions speaks more broadly to the fact that slavery was not yet understood as a condition endured only by black Africans. Although scholars are careful to draw distinctions between the term-limited contractual obligations of white laborers and the indefinite, multigenerational bondage of black slaves, close-knit multiracial groups such as this one indicate that enslaved black Africans and white indentured servants often cared more about their common circumstances than racial divides. The conditions of Molson's escape make indentured servitude a necessary element in his story of slavery—an institution useful in comparison, not contrast. Accordingly, accounts of individuals like Mary and Garrett Choise are sometimes included in this study as a means of providing context for the experience of enslaved Africans and the rhetorical circumstances in which their stories were narrated.

Furthermore, some of the indentured servants in colonial North America were men and women previously emancipated from chattel slavery or the free children of enslaved black Africans—and their stories of unfreedom belong in any account of the slave narrative's history as well. Lost among the many slave-for-sale advertisements in colonial newspapers are occasional notices for the indentured labor of "a Mulatto Boy about 19 Years of Age, for the Term of 22 Years" (*AWM* 1722/8/2) or "*A Very Likely Negro Girl, in the Eighth Year of her Age, her Time of Service till she is Twenty one, to be dispos'd of*" (*BNL* 1724/10/29; see also *BNL* 1718/4/21). The most detailed early account of black

life in colonial America preserved in these newspapers is that of Elizabeth
Colson, "a Molatto Woman" executed in Plymouth, Massachusetts, for infanticide, but because she was apparently an indentured servant rather than an
enslaved chattel, her first person narrative of unfreedom and racism has long
been ignored (*NEJ* 1727/5/29).[42] That narrative, preserved only in *The New-
England Weekly Journal* of June 19, 1727, is worth reprinting here in full, as it
illuminates many of the challenges in determining which auto/biographical
records of black African experience we should read as slave narratives.[43]

The language and themes of Colson's autobiographical statement—
recounting her experience of racism, characterizing literacy as power, being
sold, identifying as a runaway, and resorting to violence as a form of self-
determination—mark it as a narrative of slavery, whether or not she herself
was ever enslaved:

> (In our Numb. 10. we mention'd the Execution of a Molatto Woman at
> *Plymouth* for the Murder of her Child, since which we have receiv'd a Pa-
> per which was found in the Prison after her Execution, supposed to have
> been taken from her own mouth by one who was in Goal with her some
> time of her Imprisonment, and is here inserted, without the Addition of
> one Word.)

> A Short Account of the Life of *Elizabeth Colson*, a Molatto Woman, who
> now must Dye for the Monstrous Sin of Murdering her Child.

> *I Was Born at* Weymouth, *and my Mother put me out to* Ebenezer Prat, *who
> was to learn me to read, but I fear they never took that Pains they should have
> done to instruct me, my Mother being School-Mistress was loth I should come
> to School with other Children, and so I had not that Instruction I wish I had
> in my Youth. I was carry'd very hardly too by my Mistress, and suffer'd hun-
> ger and blows, and at last was tempted to Steal, for which I have reason to
> lament, for although I stole at first for Necessity as I tho't, yet the Devil took
> that Advantage against me, and led me further into Sin, for one Lord's Day
> the People being gone to Meeting, I broke into a Neighbour's House, and
> stole some Victuals, and looking for more I saw a piece of Money, which I
> took, and afterwards telling a Lye, & saying I found it; so was led by one Sin
> to another.*

> *After-wards I was Sold to Lieut.* Reed, *where I had some good Examples
> set me, but having got a habit of Sin, I still grew worse & worse & worse; and
> was left to fall into the Sin of Fornication, and after my Time was out with
> Master* Reed, *I was in great distress what to do with my Child, but carried it
> about from place to place, till I left it at* Dighton, *and ran-away from it, and*

soon fell again to that shameful & Soul-destroying Sin of Fornication the Second time; and not having the Fear of God before my Eyes, I was justly left of God to this horrid Sin the Third time, that led me, together with the Instigation of the Devil, and the wretchedness of my own Heart, to that monstrous Sin for which I must now Dye: And so I have not only brought my Body to dye a shameful Death, but my Soul in danger of Death & Damnation.

O that all People would be Warned to flee from the Sins I have been Guilty of, least they run themselves into more terrible Distresses than they can easily imagine, amongst their ungodly Companions, who will not be able to help them out of their Distresses, when they have left God and God hath left them. I would therefore earnestly intreat all Young People to watch against the beginnings of Sin in themselves, for you know not where you will stop this side Hell if once you allow your selves in Sin, tho' you may think you can: For I remember that when I was Young I heard of a Woman that Murdered her Child, and I said, I never would do so. I may say to you as my Mistress did to me, you do not know what you may be left to. Therefore I would intreat all Young People to beware of Stealing, Lying, and especially that shameful Sin of Uncleanness, which hath been the leading Sin to that horrid Sin for which I must Dye. O then take this Advice from a poor Dying Malefactor, who must suffer a Shameful Death as the just demerits of a sinful Life.

O that all People would take Warning by me, of grieving the Holy Spirit of God by sinning against the light of their own Conscience, and of Prophaning the Sabbath-Day, and not regarding the Warnings of Christ's faithful Embassadours, but be now advised to take fast hold of Instruction, and let it not go, keep it for it is thy Life: And let them then that think they stand, take heed lest they fall.

The key phrase suggesting that Colson was an indentured servant and, therefore, unqualified to write a slave narrative, is her simple declaration that "*my Time was out with Master* Reed."[44] However, that phrase hardly rules out the possibility of slavery. The legal status of enslaved men and women could and did change; slavers often promised the enslaved their freedom at a specified future date and occasionally signed papers making that agreement binding. To wit, an execution notice for "One Joseph Hono, Negro," explains that Hono "had been in the Country about 44 Years, and about 14 Years free for himself" before running afoul of the law (*BNL* 1721/5/29).[45] Hono was almost certainly brought to North America in chains before coming to an agreement with his enslavers and setting a date for the end of his bondage. Quock Walker (whose case helped abolish slavery in Massachusetts) similarly won his freedom after a slaver modified the terms of his bondage from chattel slavery to a form of indenture.[46] Yet even if Colson was always "only" an indentured servant, her narrative asks the reader to think of her experience as a form of slavery. "*I was Sold,*" she declares. The language of indentured servitude was not that of selling an individual but disposing of his or her time. Advertisements announced, "A Very likely Indian Woman's Time for Eleven Years and Five Months to be disposed of" (*BNL* 1720/3/21; see also *BNL* 1718/8/4) or "a Servant Woman's Time to dispose of, being near five Years to come; and likewise three Negroes to be Sold" (*AWM* 1729/9/4). Colson identifies with Negroes sold, not with servants whose time is disposed of, and whether or not she was an indentured servant, Colson uses the language of slavery: she insists on the commodification of her person and not merely a claim on her time. As Jordan Stein argues, "reducing the experience of black Americans to the condition of being enslaved . . . creates the impression that slavery only matters when it's being recounted."[47] This overdetermined interpretive framework leads to the marginalization of writers like Colson, who occupy a hazy middle ground between bondage and freedom.

Colson was likely affiliated in some manner with the family of John Colson, who was born in Bermuda in 1681 and emigrated to Weymouth, Massachusetts in 1700. John Colson married the white Susannah Lincoln in 1705, but Elizabeth might have been the product of an earlier marriage to an unknown Afro-Bermudan woman who died between 1700 and 1705, or she and her mother might have arrived as human cargo, part of John Colson's larger household, which included his mother Mary. Susannah bore John eleven children and may have inherited a twelfth, Elizabeth, to raise as her own.[48] The rapidly increasing size of the Colson household likely accounts for the decision to "*put me out to* Ebenezer Prat," a local man seven years John's senior, who had only four children at home and who had probably welcomed the prospect of domestic help, until he found the hungry Elizabeth supplementing her diet with food from a neighbor's larder. But Pratt failed to provide the education that Elizabeth's mother—whether her stepmother Susannah or, perhaps, a black Bermudan governess for Colson's children—hoped she would receive and that the enslaved inhabitants of Boston acquired at Mather's school. Racism, presumably, kept Elizabeth from joining her mother and the "*other Children*" at school, so Pratt kept her until he or John Colson sold Elizabeth to Captain-Lieutenant William Reed, who moved from Weymouth to Abington, Massachusetts in 1708.[49]

Elizabeth Colson seems to have regarded the Reed family highly, and so did the people of Abington. Reed was the town clerk and firmly ensconced at

the center of the town's social life; his funeral in 1753 was, one witness reported, "the largest I have ever seen in town."[50] Caring for Reed's eleven
children and helping to entertain those who called on the Captain would
have brought Colson into contact with the region's most august personages.
The social promiscuity of Reed's household apparently helped Colson find
comfort in a lover's arms, but Colson's entangled legal status and her position
as a racial outsider likely persuaded the father of her first child that she was
not marriageable. Colson gave birth in Abington, and she may have tried,
like other enslaved women, to keep both the pregnancy and birth a secret
during the term of her service.[51] Eventually, of course, the Captain set her
free—perhaps to avoid the gossip and public scrutiny that her behavior had
provoked among the local white residents. On her own, with no social or economic capital, Colson made her way further south, to Dighton, Massachusetts, where she left her child *"and ran-away from it."* Again, Colson uses the
language of slavery, of an escaped slave, and well she might, because there was
no guarantee that her abandoned black baby would grow up in freedom. Her
child might have been one of several advertised in Boston papers: "A young
Negro Child to be given away, and Forty Shillings with it" (*NEC* 1724/5/18);
or *"Any One that would take a black Child, at 6 Weeks Old, may inquire of the
Printer"* (*BNL* 1726/4/21). Colson's decision to run away left the future legal
status of her child ambiguous. As the offer of forty shillings suggests, the
guardians of such a child would want compensation for the time, money, and
effort it would take to raise him or her and might decide to extract that compensation through the enslavement of her baby or, at best, a prolonged period of servitude. Colson became a runaway not only to secure her own
freedom but also to forget that she had likely sacrificed her child's. "What ultimately matters" in asking whether Colson wrote a slave narrative is, as Katherine Fishburn wrote, "whether the metaphors by which you choose to write
your life become literalized in the next generation."[52] Colson understood her
own life through the language and metaphors of slavery, and she knew that
those metaphors could well become reality for her child.

When a second baby was born, Colson killed it. She recalls, *"when I was
Young I heard of a Woman that Murdered her Child, and I said,* I never would do
so. *I may say to you as my Mistress did to me,* you do not know what you may be
left to." Perhaps she had heard word, thirteen years earlier, of an execution in
New York, where "a Free Negro Woman was Hang'd at Jamaica on Long-
Island for Murdering her Bastard Child" (*BNL* 1714/1/17). For that woman,
as for Colson, infanticide might have seemed a mercy. Though black Africans made up only a fraction of the population in colonial New England,

Catherine Adams and Elizabeth Pleck note that "there were more black than white or Indian women accused and punished for infanticide."[53] This disparity likely reflects a bias in how the deaths of infants in the care of white and Indian or black African mothers were treated. However, Terri Snyder writes that African cultures such as the Igbo and Akan "viewed self-destruction as a permissible response to enslavement," and Colson may have killed her baby to save it from what she saw as an even worse fate. For enslaved persons and indentured servants alike, the power of self-harm was one of the only means by which they could deny their labor to those who claimed it and regain a measure of self-determination. "Stories of slave suicide accentuated similarities between blacks and whites," and Colson's infanticide must be read alongside accounts of self-harm by indentured servants and enslaved Africans alike.[54] The story of "a poor Negro Man" who "laid his Head down on a piece of Timber, and with a Sythe cut the back side of his Neck to the Bone" (*BNL* 1722/3/19) is of a piece with an account from Maryland of "an idle Servant" who ran away "but being brought home again . . . chose rather to disable himself, than be oblig'd to Work, and accordingly about a Fortnight ago, he took a Broad Ax, and chopt off one of his Hands."[55] Distinctions between the experience and status of free blacks, indentured servants, prisoners of war, impressed sailors, transported convicts, and chattel slaves were less clearly defined in the eighteenth century and its records than they are in nineteenth-century slave narratives and other long texts challenging specific forms of unfreedom, such as Herman Melville's *White-Jacket* (1850), a polemic against naval impressment and flogging. The genre was porous in its earliest manifestations, representative of a more diverse cross section of the colonial world.

Another difference between nineteenth-century slave narratives and narratives of slavery from the early eighteenth-century newspaper is evident in the conjectural geography of Molson's escape to the Carolinas. Just as the genre's racial boundaries became more rigid in the nineteenth century so, too, did the moral valence of its geography. In the nineteenth century, those fleeing chattel slavery journeyed north, to the freedom of Canada; only Mark Twain's fictional runaway Jim, in the parodic *Adventures of Huckleberry Finn* (1884), travels south to escape from bondage. But Molson and his companions "are Supposed to be gone to *Carolina*" because freedom had yet to align itself with the compass rose. Before his flight in 1720 Molson likely would have heard the persistent rumors of Spain's plans to join forces with Florida Indians and raid the South Carolina coast to kidnap enslaved black Africans (*BNL* 1719/2/4). Weeks later, word traveled up the coast "by Letters from South Carolina . . . that the threatned Danger we were apprehensive of by an

TABLE I.1 Uses of the word "slavery" in colonial newspapers, 1704–1729

Uses of the word slave	Runaway Ads	Slave-for-Sale Ads	Domestic News	Editorials	Foreign News	Total
# of uses	7	24	29	35	203	298
%	2.3%	8.1%	9.7%	11.7%	68.1%	100%

The category "Domestic News" encompasses items reported in British North America; the category "Foreign News" encompasses items from the British West Indies, South and Central America, and the Old World, including England.

invasion from the Spaniards is well over" (*BNL* 1720/3/21). Thus, his travel south with three white companions might represent a calculation that South Carolina was no longer at risk of invasion by foreign powers. Alternatively, his journey south might signify a preference for a living environment in which black African bodies were more prevalent, a place where he could blend in more easily with the general populace.[56] In either case, Molson's escape represents a complicated geographical gambit, a bet on his understanding of local politics in another British colony, as well as the likelihood that that colony would be safe from attacks by European and Indian nations. The geographic and political calculus undertaken by Molson, before his journey south, was far more complicated than the decisions of Douglass and Jacobs, to travel north. Nineteenth-century slave narratives are enmeshed in the geography and domestic politics of the United States, but eighteenth-century narratives of slavery, particularly those narratives surviving in newspapers, were often composed in response to international politics.

Indeed, most newspaper readers would have understood an eighteenth-century narrative of slavery to be the personalization of foreign policy, rather than an account of racial oppression. The word *slave, slavery,* or some other variation appeared in 298 advertisements, editorials, or news reports between 1704 and 1729 (see table I.1). By far, the word *slave* or *slavery* was most likely to be used in foreign news bulletins; while it appeared fairly frequently in slave-for-sale ads published before 1709, it was used only rarely in advertisements published during the following twenty years, as enslaved black Africans were increasingly described as servants. And the word's use in editorials rarely referenced the experience or persons of black African men and women.

As noted previously, the word *slave* or *slavery* was used to characterize a wide variety of conditions, from the experience of political or religious tyranny to the oppression of women, but it most often referred to individuals

TABLE I.2   Referents for the word "slavery" in colonial newspapers, 1704–1729

	Personal Relationships	American Indians	Religious Oppression	Political Tyranny	Black Africans	Foreign Relations
# of uses	6	20	24	27	69	173
%	2.0%	6.7%	8.1%	9.1%	23.2%	58.1%

Because a news item might use the words "slave" or "slavery" to refer to more than one group or context, the sum of these percentages exceeds 100 percent. Items included in the "Personal Relationships" category dealt primarily with romantic relationships between men and women. The "Religious Oppression" category refers exclusively to the perception of Catholicism as a form of ideological slavery; it does not include the many references to "Christian slaves" taken by Islamic polities because those conflicts are most frequently framed as political, not religious, conflicts. Items subsumed under the category of "Political Tyranny" most frequently refer to the condition of England under the rule of James II, prior to the Glorious Revolution. Many descriptions of slaves or slavery are not included in this accounting; galley slaves, for instance, were forced to labor for various reasons, so references to these laborers are not included unless the reason for their punishment is clear. Notably, accounts of slavery drawn from the classical period were very infrequent, appearing only four times in the twenty-five years surveyed.

taken captive in a conflict between two sovereign nations (see table I.2). Some passages used the words *slave* or *slavery* to describe multiple groups or contexts, as in the case of published city ordinances establishing patrols "after 9 at Night . . . to see if after that time, any Indian, Negro or Molatto Servant or Slave is found abroad" (*BNL* 1705/9/3) or an announcement that Queen Anne would award "the Assiento, or Contract for supplying the Spanish West Indies with Slaves" to the South Sea Company (*BNL* 1713/8/10). The first example refers to enslaved people of two different racial or national groups, while the second characterizes the sale of enslaved Africans as a tool of foreign policy, a concession won by England from Spain during negotiations after the War of the Spanish Succession. In a majority of instances, the words *slave* or *slavery* referred to foreign relations between two sovereign nations. Newspapers reported "that the Persians have made an Irruption into the Kingdom of Astracan, from whence they have carried away a great Number of People into Slavery" (*BNL* 1719/4/6) and "that the Tartars have made another Excursion, and carried off the Horses of 4 Polish Troops, whom they killed, and carried a great Number of People into Slavery" (*AWM* 1722/1/16). Most often, in newspaper discourse, slavery was a condition imposed upon or removed from individuals in the course of a larger conflict or agreement between two sovereign powers, and the lives of the enslaved were, thus, understood to be personal and domestic extensions of an international incident. The predominance of newspaper entries associating slavery with relations between foreign countries produced a rhetorical context in which even local interactions between the enslaved and their masters or neighbors might be thought of as enmeshed in geopolitics.

To wit: when Black Peter began setting type for *The Boston Evening-Post* in 1735, he first composed the word *slaves* in the paper's second issue, where it appeared in an announcement of war between two sovereign peoples: "*Charlestown,* (in *South Carolina,*) *June 18.* This Day a Proclamation was Published, wherein War is declared against the *Tuscareers* Indians, promising 50 l. for each of them that shall be brought in dead, or 50 l. if alive, they having killed several of the English and carry'd off Slaves and Cattle."[57] This notice clearly identifies English victims of Tuscarora violence as slaves but declines to label Tuscarora captives—worth "50 l. if alive"—with the same status. The English are rhetorically cast as victims enslaved by the unjust aggression of a foreign power, but the bodies of Tuscarora Indians (dead or alive) are made a righteous recompense for the loss of English life, liberty, and property. The relevance of this national appropriation of slavery, as an evil suffered primarily by the English rather than the peoples against whom they defined themselves, to Peter's own status in the household of Thomas Fleet cannot have escaped the black pressman. The very next piece of news—perhaps placed intentionally by Peter in this sequence as a demonstration of the organizational genius touted by Addison—is an analogous case of English engagement with national and racial others that situates black Africans, like the Tuscarora, as aggressors whose lives and bodies are forfeit to an aggrieved English community: "*New York, August 18.* On the 12th Instant a Brigrantine arrived here in 21 Days from *Jamaica,* the Master whereof says, the Day before he sailed it was reported, that the Forces which were out after the Rebellious Negroes had killed and taken about 25 of them and taken about Forty fire Arms. That the Government was about making Roads clear thro' the Island, for the better suppressing those Negroes; and Marshal Law to be continued" (*BEP* 1735/8/25). These news items establish the logic of Peter's bondage: the possession of racialized foreign bodies and the profit of their labor are due to Englishmen such as Fleet as the just compensation for injuries sustained by the state through unprovoked foreign aggression. The newspaper taught readers to think of Peter, and taught Peter to think of himself, not as a slave but as a spoil of some international conflict.[58]

Under this narrative framework, the emancipation of any enslaved person—including Peter—should be a matter of national concern. Just as enslavement was a product of foreign relations, so, too, was emancipation. Thus, less than two months after Peter began work on *The Boston Evening-Post,* he helped publish notice that King George II would authorize the collection of monies "to be applied for Redeeming all such of his Majesty's Subjects as are or shall be taken Captives and carried into Slavery" (*BEP* 1735/10/13). Where, Peter might have asked, were the Guinean funds dedicated to his own repatriation? For Fleet and other English subjects, the absence of a comparable outreach from African states on Peter's behalf only worked to legitimize his bondage.[59] This absence also threw the burden of freedom back onto individual black African men and women. While English "slaves" awaited state-sponsored redemption monies, black "servants" had to work towards self-emancipation and then repatriate themselves. Peter published evidence of this truth in the *Post's* sixth issue, which relates the story of "a Negro Man and Woman belonging to *Rhode Island*, who have been free several Years, and by their Industry and Frugality scrap'd together two or three hundred Pounds, [and] having a Desire to return to their own Country to spend the remainder of their Days, sail'd from *Newport* for *Guinea* about a Fortnight ago" (*BEP* 1735/9/22). Perversely, their prototypically American story of self-reliance served to further identify this "Negro" couple as foreign bodies: bodies lacking the right to state-sponsored repatriation and other protections of English subjects.

Like this couple, or the "rebellious Negroes" of Jamaica, Peter traveled English roads and English waters as a foreigner, in need of a pass to legitimize his presence on lands and seas claimed by a sovereign state that did not acknowledge him as a subject. Beginning in 1690, laws were passed in the North American colonies forbidding the enslaved from travelling without written authorization from their enslavers; those without a pass could be beaten by any English—that is to say white—traveller who found them.[60] These pass laws providing enslaved foreigners with a limited, conditional right to travel across English territory resemble nothing so much as the treaties guaranteeing English ships with passes the right to travel in Mediterranean and Atlantic waters without fear that their sailors would be enslaved by North African pirates. Throughout the seventeenth and eighteenth centuries, the British government warned sailors that "our Ships must have Mediterranean Passes, otherwise they will be made Prizes" (*NEC* 1721/8/14), and often, when a British vessel sailed without appropriate travel papers, "The Ship was lost for want of a Mediterranean pass" (*BNL* 1718/9/22). Failure to obey international pass laws resulted in slavery, and local laws requiring the enslaved to travel with passes suggested that slavery was, fundamentally, a matter of regulating foreign affairs and foreign bodies in a domestic space.[61] Attempts by Massachusetts legislators to constrain the movements of "*any Indian,*

Negro or Molatto Servant or Slave ... unless upon some Errand of their Masters or Owners" treated foreign bodies as though they were ships passing through the Mediterranean: subject to lawful punishment and captivity unless in possession of proper documentation (*BNL* 1705/9/3).[62] Peter's status as an easily identifiable foreign national limited his ability to travel, and those limitations, in turn, shaped the very nature of the newspaper he helped bring into being each week.[63]

The birth of *The Boston Evening-Post* is inextricably linked to the narrative of Peter's enslavement, and that narrative illustrates the three foundational arguments of this book, which are, in review, as follows. First, because eighteenth-century newspapers were the source of the period's most numerous and popular narrative materials on slavery and because their language and ideas shaped the first book-length, stand-alone auto/biographies of enslaved Africans, they should be read as slave narratives. Second, because eighteenth-century readers were accustomed to consuming corporately authored, discontinuous texts, they responded to narrative fragments both by associating them with related but disconnected fragments and by imaginatively reconstructing circumstances and events missing from the extant narrative; thus, eighteenth-century newspapers and the slave narratives they contain must be recovered by scholars through the same processes of collation and imagination by which they were first read. Third, because slavery was a condition rhetorically and philosophically associated with war, eighteenth-century stories of slavery were always embedded in a global political context, linking domestic labor to foreign affairs even when an explicit connection was absent. Peter's participation in the production and distribution of the *Post* made the paper a partial, fragmentary record of his life story, and reclaiming his life from its pages through collation and other imaginative reading practices attests to the ways in which eighteenth-century readers regarded slavery as a foreign affair.

When the paper launched on August 18, 1735, as a replacement for Thomas Fleet's prior paper, *The Weekly Rehearsal*, it included a notice to his subscribers and other interested parties announcing the policies by which the *Post* would be produced and distributed. Fleet declared:

> *... That he intends for the Future to print it every* Monday EVENING;
> *(having the Approbation and Advice of several Gentlemen in Town, who are his Customers) and will take Care to collect and publish not only the most fresh and authentick Advices from abroad, but also what occurs among our selves or Neighbours, worthy the publick View; and all the Readers in Town may*

depend upon having it left at their Houses some Time before Dark, (unless upon extraordinary Occasions) which may be a Diversion after the Business of the Day, now the Evenings are grown pretty long. (BEP 1735/8/18)

The paper's name was a promise that the news would be delivered each Monday before dark, so that its readers would have "*a Diversion*" to fill their nighttime hours. This association with a particular temporal period—the evening—differentiated the *Post* from its competitors and might be thought of as a marketing strategy. But it is also a product of Peter's involvement in the paper's production and delivery.

Because Peter's black skin identified him as a foreign body, he was subject to Massachusetts pass laws prohibiting him from traveling more than an hour after sundown.[64] Thus, if Peter was to deliver Fleet's papers after the Monday news had been collected and set into type, he had to do it in the twilight hours, before dark. Both the name of the paper and Fleet's delivery strategy were shaped by the constraints of Peter's enslavement. Reciprocally, the newspaper created constraints on Peter's time, a frame within which he was forced to live his life; every Monday evening, Peter carried copies of the paper through the streets of Boston while Fleet and his customers ate their suppers. Projecting backwards from that Monday deadline, Peter would have spent all day Monday composing type, blocking it into forms, inking the type, pressing it onto paper, and blotting the finished product before carrying it into the streets. His Saturdays might have been spent mixing ink, purchasing paper, and organizing type in preparation for this frantic day of labor. Tuesday through Friday, Fleet would have sent Peter to collect news from the captains of ships arriving in Boston Harbor; to collect payment from subscribers and advertisers; and to work on other projects, from carving woodcuts to hawking broadsides. The language of the *Post* filled his hands and his eyes and his ears. The production and delivery of the *Post* determined his schedule. As Peter persisted in composing, pressing, and delivering the paper over the course of years, their stories merged and intertwined, mutually determined.

The ramifications of that intertwining became legible quickly. Just four weeks after the *Post* launched, Fleet published an advertisement announcing a change in Peter's life: "*To be sold by the Publisher of this Paper, a young likely Negro Woman, of an excellent Temper, who is season'd to the Country, speaks good English, and can do all sorts of Houshold Business*" (BEP 1735/9/8). The precise identity of this young woman is unknown; she might have been Peter's daughter, wife, sister, or friend. But whatever their relationship, Peter had to bring word of her pending sale to each of the paper's subscribers, for their "*Diversion.*" Of course, his own experience of this advertisement and its unspoken promise of familial and social alienation must have been anything but diverting—distressing, heartbreaking, numbing, perhaps, but not diverting. Even if the young woman was a housemate with whom he was on poor terms, her departure would have been an unwelcome reminder to Peter of his own precarious legal status. If the plight of an enslaved individual facing forcible relocation through a slave-for-sale advertisement sometimes escaped the attention of white readers, surely this particular notice and this particular piece of suffering did not, as the young woman's plight was communicated both textually and physiologically, by Peter's countenance, when he delivered that issue of the *Post*. If the paper's recipients did not already know of this anonymous maiden's commercial availability and immediately recognize her pending departure as the reason for Peter's long face, they would have made the connection soon after reading Fleet's advertisement. The story of Peter's compulsory participation in the sale of a fellow sufferer was easily read by his contemporaries and has been preserved for our witness in the pages of the *Post*. On this occasion, as on many others, and for this enslaved person, as for many others, a life story was memorialized in the newspaper.

The stipulation that this young woman is "*season'd to the Country*" was a reminder of her foreign status—that she, like Peter, belonged to another continent and another racial group, with bodies that supposedly required acculturation to the North American climate. Although we do not know whether Peter was born in Massachusetts or Jamaica or Guinea, we know that he was always recognizably other; his racial, and therefore his national, status was always visible. Even as he made his regular delivery rounds to drop off copies of the *Post* at households where he was well known, Peter's foreign identity was foregrounded by the paper he left behind.

Perhaps the best illustration of how Peter's domestic chores and his domestic identity were shaped by foreign affairs came in the spring of 1741. By late April, Peter and the other inhabitants of Boston were beginning to read rumors of racial unrest in New York. The governor's residence in Lower Manhattan, Fort George, had been damaged in a case of arson, and several other buildings had been burned to the ground. These arson attacks were attributed to the city's enslaved black residents, and because England was then embroiled in the War of Jenkins' Ear, links between the supposed black African arsonists and foreign states caused additional concern, as colonists worried that the enslaved might conspire with their enemies to overthrow English defenses from within.[65] In response, the New York militia acted as though it

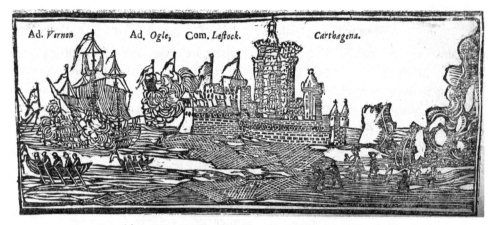

FIGURE 1.1 Detail from *Some Excellent Verses on Admiral Vernon's Taking the Forts and Castles of Carthagena*. Image courtesy of the Rare Book Collection at The New York Public Library and the Astor, Lenox, Tilden Foundations.

faced an existential threat and might be overrun: "There being some suspicion of the Negroes, a military Watch is kept every Night" (*BEP* 1741/4/20). But at the same time that enslaved black Africans in New York were being interrogated as potential enemy combatants, black Africans living in the Caribbean were being recruited as allies in the war against Spain. British naval officers traveled "to *Jamaica* for what Men they could spare, upon which 4 or 500 of the Mountain Negroes (formerly Rebels) offer'd to go Volunteers, which were accepted, and the Press was very hot for White Men" (*BEP* 1741/4/27). Later reports describe what seems to have been a second wave of recruitment, as a correspondent in Kingston wrote that "Eight Transports with a Convoy are sail'd from hence, in which we have furnish'd One Thousand sensible Negroes for the Use of the Expedition" against Spanish forces at Cartagena de Indias, on the coast of present-day Colombia (*BEP* 1741/5/4). Both the black arsonists in New York and the black recruits in Jamaica were understood to be foreigners; whether they cooperated with or conspired against the British state, black Africans and their descendants in the New World were regarded as ineluctably alien.

Evidence that Peter read these news bulletins and thought carefully about how they might impact his own status in Massachusetts has been preserved in a broadside published by Thomas Fleet, memorializing Admiral Edward Vernon's seizure of the Spanish forts overlooking Cartagena. The broadside features a woodcut done by Peter and a poem entitled, "Some Excellent VERSES On Admiral VERNON's taking the Forts and Castles of

Carthagena, In the Month of *March* last."[66] It is possible that Peter authored the poem, but what is certain is that Peter's artistic vision was the driving force behind this broadside—that his woodcut preceded and shaped the text. Vernon's success against the Spanish was narrated in the *Post*, and the poem clearly draws on that news report in its recounting of events. (This poem and another for which Peter provided a woodcut, discussed subsequently, have been reproduced in full in the Appendix.) Several factors are cited for Vernon's success, including "the Cowardice of the *Spaniards*" and "the Fury of our Soldiers," but reports of the battle also acknowledged the crucial part played by the black African recruits of Jamaica. Before sending ground troops to assault the Castle of San Luis de Bocachica, British forces established their artillery "behind a Wood, and when all was ready the Wood was cut down and clear'd in one Night by 1500 Negroes, so as to leave the Walls open to the Cannon" (*BEP* 1741/5/18). Clearing the field of fire allowed British cannon to blow a hole in the castle wall so that British grenadiers would not have to take fire in a prolonged assault; as a result of black African labor, the operation concluded with a minimum of casualties and was long heralded as a signature success of the larger war.[67]

Peter's broadside celebrates Vernon and mocks the Spanish Admiral Blas de Lezo, but it also memorializes the contributions of the black men who cleared the way for British soldiers. After an account of naval conflict, in its final stanzas, the poem relates,

> While these brave Things were done at Sea,
> Our Soldiers work'd for Blood,
> Built on the Land a Battery,
> Behind a hideous Wood.
>
> *Wenworth* commands, down go the Trees,
> With horrible Report;
> Agast, the trembling *Spaniard* sees
> The Negroes and the Fort.
>
> Our Picture shows all this with Art,
> (Was ever Work so pretty!)
> And soon you'l see the second Part,
> When we have took the City. (lines 61–72)

This allusion to Peter's woodcut, which depicts bodies (presumably black bodies, though the figures are so small that it is difficult to tell) approaching the castle by land, indicates that his image predates the poem's composition and that the poet writes, at least partly, in response to Peter's art, narrating the image's component parts. That Peter's picture is referenced as the poet's inspiration immediately after the introduction of "Negroes" into the story of Bocachica's fall further suggests a link between their inclusion in this account and Peter's participation in the poem's composition. It would seem that Peter began cutting the image of his own volition, emphasizing the role of black African troops with whom he identified, and that this woodcut then served as the poem's raison d'etre.

In the spring of 1741, Boston was bubbling with news, and Peter chose to accentuate, through art, the positive contributions made by black African soldiers in Cartagena de Indias as a counterpoint to the narrative of black African malfeasance making its way north from New York. In a news environment where Peter would inevitably be identified as a foreigner, because of his skin, he attempted to push public opinion towards a belief that black Africans were allies, not adversaries. This poem—perhaps the first in English prompted by a black artistic vision of the Americas—constructs the identity of black Africans in British colonies through foreign affairs reported in the newspaper, responding to New York's reports of betrayal and criminality by establishing a link between Boston's black African population and the men who helped Vernon at Bocachica.[68] As Peter delivered the *Post* and offered a copy of his broadside for sale at each of the households he regularly visited, his body served as a sign visibly associating black Africans and their descendants living in Massachusetts with the foreign rebels-turned-allies recruited from Jamaica.

This broadside is part of a larger pattern, as Peter used his art on other occasions to comment on the news and celebrate the good deeds of other black Africans. Eight years before his broadside on the battle of Cartegena de Indias, he carved a woodcut to illustrate a broadside commemorating the execution of an enslaved Indian man named Julian. Peter likely sympathized with Julian who, "By his Account he first was sold, / When he was not quite three Years old."[69] Fleeing from slavery, Julian ran fifteen miles, from Bridgewater to Braintree, before a runaway slave advertisement facilitated his capture. Because "Advertisements were issued out after him, and a Reward to take him up, and bring him home, one Mr. *Rogers* of *Pembrook*, being at *Weymouth*, on his way home happen'd to see one of the Advertisements, took it, and returned back to look for the said Indian, and on Monday Evening last, after some enquiry, found him." Stopping at the home of a man named Scot, on his journey back to Julian's enslaver, Rogers lost track of his captive. Confronted by Rogers in a cornfield, Julian "suddenly turn'd about, and

FIGURE 1.2 Detail from "Advice from the Dead to the Living; or, A Solemn Warning to the World," Boston Public Library, H.90.104 no. 2. Image courtesy of the American Antiquarian Society.

made up to him, and then stab'd the Knife into his left Breast" (*BNL* 1732/9/14). While most execution broadsides feature a stock image of an individual being hung, Peter's woodcut portrays this unique, climactic scene of conflict. He carved it to illustrate the act for which Julian would hang but also, I believe, because the aftermath of this murder presented the black African community of greater Boston in a positive light to their British enslavers, as allies rather than adversaries.

There are four figures in Peter's woodcut: Julian, Rogers, Scot, and an unnamed African man responsible for Julian's capture. After Julian had stabbed Rogers, "Mr. *Scot* and a Negro in the House seeing Mr. *Rogers* assaulted, ran up to assist him" and disarm the murderer. However, when Julian fled the scene as Scot and his black African companion attempted to save Rogers's life, "the Negro pursu'd him, and soon catch'd him and held him, till Mr. *Scot* went and brought others, and then secur'd him" (*BNL* 1732/9/14). Each of these figures appears on the broadside. Rogers is prone on the ground between two figures with weapons, likely Scot on the right and Julian on the left. A fourth figure, framed in what looks like a window or door, occupies the visual space between Scot and Julian but clearly stands at some distance from the murder scene. This fourth figure—situated at the woodcut's center, but visually constrained by the thick black lines that surround him on all sides—is likely the anonymous African responsible for Julian's capture. At first glance, the black man in a box appears to be inanimate, a picture on a wall, and his confinement within an enclosed space away from the action suggests the fundamental nature of slavery as a series of limits on the movement and agency of its victims. Only escape and violence have liberated Julian from a similar condition of confinement, and even in Peter's woodcut, he remains surrounded by the thick black lines that mark the image's edge. But the very existence of this image suggests the possibility of agency and self-determination for the enslaved.

Despite his own status as an enslaved person, Peter literally carved out space for public advocacy. His woodcut inserts a black African body missing from the broadside's poem back into the narrative of Julian's capture, redirecting public attention to the civic contributions of black Africans in North America and away from the prior week's news, "That Cap. *John Major* in a Schooner from this Place (*Portsmouth*) was treacherously Murdered, and his Vessel and Cargo seized upon by the Negroes" of Guinea.[70] Peter created art in response to the news, choosing to illustrate stories that cast Africans as allies of the British rather than those that identified them as foreign adversaries. Although *The Weekly Rehearsal* and *The Boston Evening-Post* published many runaway slave advertisements, Peter never carved a woodcut of a runaway slave to accompany them. Still, for readers more discerning than Stowe's Senator Bird, Peter's story—and the story of other enslaved black men and women—was clearly legible in their pages.

IN THE CHAPTERS THAT FOLLOW, I recover the stories of many other enslaved individuals whose experiences have been preserved in the newspaper and other eighteenth-century textual fragments. Chapter 1 revisits the lives of Basilio, Scipio, Boston, and other enslaved men who crossed paths with Judge Samuel Sewall, author of *The Selling of Joseph* (1700). Although Sewall has often been hailed as the first advocate for abolition, he was an active participant in the slave trade for at least a decade and likely much longer. Because of his hypocrisy, black arsonists tried to burn down his home, and attacks on Sewall became the justification for Boston's oppressive 1723 slave code. I argue that Sewall's complicated relationship with slavery—his advocacy for its abolition and his simultaneous participation in the slave trade—resulted from his belief that slavery was a product of foreign affairs and foreign wars. His opposition to slavery made Sewall famous, but a broader picture of Sewall's views on slavery has been preserved in the newspaper and necessitates the reevaluation of his legacy.

If Sewall won fame by advocating for the emancipation of the enslaved, the men and women who emancipated themselves won infamy through the runaway slave advertisements published in newspapers and circulated throughout the Atlantic world. A handful of scholars have advocated for treating these advertisements as early slave narratives, but the broader academy has been slow to give these texts the attention offered to more substantive and developed biographical accounts. Reading a single runaway slave advertisement with the same sustained attention we habitually offer book-length works of prose is taxing work; repeatedly extrapolating forward and backward from a single point in time might strain even the imagination of an Addison or a Peter or a Hawthorne. But many enslaved individuals ran away over and over again, and newspaper readers accustomed to reading discontinuous narratives over the course of years likely found these serial accounts of flight enthralling opportunities for imaginative reconstruction. Chapter 2 argues that these recurring escape attempts make the work of reconstructing a runaway's narrative more feasible, particularly for students or nonspecialists, and provides a model for reclaiming the biographical accounts preserved by their determination to run.

Runaways were something like accidental celebrities, but the first Africans to have their life stories published in stand-alone, extended prose narratives were actual celebrities—princes whose enslavement was retrospectively acknowledged to be a mistake of foreign relations. Thus, in chapter 3, I read the narratives of Ayuba Suleiman Diallo, William Ansah Sessarakoo, and other princes, with the recognition that these accounts were authored more for political purposes than an interest in their biographies. I argue that the freeing of Diallo and Sessarakoo, and the publication of their life stories, signified the integration of both these princes and their peoples into a global Protestant coalition. Their life stories build on an interest in celebrity, and enslaved celebrities, which was cultivated by the newspaper. Slavery, both in the eighteenth-century newspapers that made royal figures into global celebrities and in the earliest book-length accounts of slavery, was a matter of diplomatic relations conducted by princes.

The subject of chapter 4, Briton Hammon, is not a prince, but he is a man who clearly understood that his life and his experience of enslavement was imbricated in global political systems. Hammon's autobiography, *A Narrative of the Uncommon Sufferings, and Surprizing Deliverance of Briton Hammon, a*

Negro Man,—Servant to General Winslow, of Marshfield, in New England (1760), has frequently been described as the first slave narrative, and it presents the genre as the personal application of foreign affairs. Hammon interacts with officials of the Spanish government and the Catholic church as well as British and French naval forces, in an attempt to stay alive and to secure his own liberty. His tumultuous journey through the contested diplomatic space of the Atlantic world suggests that surviving slavery and achieving a measure of self-determination in the eighteenth century required the enslaved to become adroit political actors capable of carefully positioning themselves as the allies or adversaries of multiple international coalitions.

The political implications of slavery—and the use of slavery as a political metaphor—came to greater prominence in the War of American Independence, and chapter 5 investigates how the enslaved and others came to terms with that usage. In response to the Stamp Act, the white inhabitants of North America increasingly referred to themselves as slaves oppressed and held captive by a foreign state. As John Dickinson and others appropriated this term—divorcing it from the conditions of bondage suffered by prisoners of war or human chattels kidnapped in Africa—they drew criticism from supporters of Parliamentary oversight of the colonies, including J. Hector St. John de Crèvecoeur. This chapter reads *Letters from a Farmer in Pennsylvania* and *Letters from an American Farmer* as an epistolary conversation about the right to describe political oppression and foreign rule as slavery, drawing their work into conversation with the poetry of enslaved writers like Phillis Wheatley Peters and Caesar, the son of Black Peter.

Citizens of the newly declared United States of America greatly reduced their use of slavery as a descriptor for the political oppression of foreign states. And the slave narratives produced in the long nineteenth century similarly shifted away from an eighteenth-century link between enslavement and foreign affairs. This shift occurred for multiple, interrelated reasons: because the U.S. Constitution set a date for the abolition of the slave trade; because an increasing number of North America's black residents had been born in the Western Hemisphere, weakening their identity as foreign nationals; and because both the emancipation of individual persons and the abolition of slavery as an institution became domestic political matters, rather than international ones. For these reasons, *The Interesting Narrative of the Life of Olaudah Equiano, or Gustavus Vassa, the African* (1789) was the last of its kind—the last narrative of slavery to frame itself as an intervention into foreign affairs. Thus, the book concludes by arguing that we must read this seminal text not as a beginning of the slave narrative tradition but rather as an inflection in its development or the end point of an earlier genre. Only by treating Equiano's work as the bookend for a prior conception of bondage will the narratives of slavery that preceded and shaped his autobiography be fully integrated into our conception of the American literary tradition. The study of these eighteenth-century narratives will facilitate our collective acknowledgment that enslaved black Africans were political actors at the center of international disputes. These men and women leveraged their position into power, but that power and their agency in its exercise only becomes visible when we see the enslaved as they were seen and as they saw themselves in the eighteenth century: as expatriates whose bondage was a function of foreign relations reported in the newspaper. The newspaper continued to shape narratives of slavery in the nineteenth century, but those well-known works of African American literature were composed with different aims and rhetorical conventions than the narratives of enslaved black Africans circulating before Equiano.

Some may, with Melville, contend that "it is not the purview of literature to purvey news," and so dismiss the newspaper accounts from which this book has been written out of hand, on aesthetic grounds.[71] But as Ezra Pound once wrote, "Literature is news that STAYS news," and today—when racism still plagues the United States; when the first hundred and forty years of black Africans' presence in North America still passes without comment in many courses on American literature; and when publishing basic facts about the origins of slavery in the US elicits outrage of the sort with which the 1619 Project was met—the stories of these enslaved individuals remain news.[72] Even if we regard these newspaper accounts as devoid of beauty, each of us might still become "a beautiful reader of a newspaper" and so recover the lives of the black African men and women preserved in their pages.[73]

CHAPTER ONE

Sewall's Secret

The Selling of More than Two Dozen Black Africans

Among the heroes of American abolitionism, colonial judge Samuel Sewall is often revered as the first to commit himself to the cause of universal emancipation. Sewall earned this reputation with *The Selling of Joseph*, a small pamphlet he published in 1700, which argues from the biblical example of Adam "that Originally, and Naturally, there is no such thing as Slavery."[1] Reading these words, John Greenleaf Whittier declared,

> Honor and praise to the Puritan
> Who the halting step of his age outran,
> And, seeing the infinite worth of man
> In the priceless gift the Father gave,
> In the infinite love that stooped to save,
> Dared not brand his brother a slave! (lines 50–55)[2]

But Whittier and the numerous scholars who have burnished Sewall's abolitionist credentials over the centuries are wrong; Sewall did dare to buy and sell slaves.[3] *The Selling of Joseph* was not Sewall's final word on the topic of slavery, and his views on the matter were far more complicated than most have acknowledged.

In the three decades after he wrote *The Selling of Joseph*, Sewall placed at least fourteen slave-for-sale advertisements in the *Boston News-Letter* and the *Boston Gazette*, announcing his intention to sell more than two dozen enslaved black Africans to the inhabitants of Boston. These fourteen advertisements are typical of the period; their language suggests a casual regard for the breathing bodies to be seen and sold at Sewall's warehouse, conflating dry goods and human lives. Yet for those who have hailed Sewall as an advocate for emancipation, the advertisements constitute an extraordinary counter-narrative that must be weighed in opposition to the sentiments expressed in *The Selling of Joseph* and are, accordingly, reprinted here in full.[4]

> To be disposed of by *Mr. Samuel Sewall* Merchant, at his Warehouse near the Swing-Bridge in Merchants-Row Boston, several Irish Maid Servants time, most of them for Five years, one Irish Man Servant, who is a good Barber and Wiggmaker, also Four or Five likely Negro Boys.[5]

A Negro Boy and Two young Negro Women to be Sold by *Mr. Samuel Sewall* Merchant, and to be seen at his Ware-House by the Swing Bridge in Merchants Row Boston. (*BNL* 1715/4/18)

A Very likely young Negro Wench that can do any Houshold Work to be Sold, inquire of Mr. *Samuel Sewall* at his Ware-House on the Dock in Boston. (*BNL* 1716/4/9)

Two fine lusty Negro Men to be Sold by Mr. *Samuel Sewall* Merchant, and to be seen at his Warehouse at the Swing-Bridge in Merchants-Row Boston. (*BNL* 1716/6/18)

A Lusty Negro Woman, that can do any Houshold Work and speaks good English, to be Sold by Mr. *Samuel Sew*, Merchant. Enquire at *Mrs. Flints* in Queen-Street, Boston. (*BNL* 1716/10/15)

A Likely Negro Boy about Twelve Years of Age, to be Sold by Mr. *Samuel Sewall*, Merchant, Inquire at his Store-House near the Swing-Bridge, Boston. (*BNL* 1716/12/17)

Very good Loaf Sugar to be Sold by the parcel or Single Loaf, on Reasonable Terms: And a likely Negro Woman that can do any Houshold work, by Mr. *Samuel Sewall* Merchant at his Ware-house in Merchants Row, *Boston*. (*BNL* 1717/9/2)

A Likely Negro Boy about Fifteen Years Old, speaks good English, to be Sold by Mr. Samuel Sewall Merchant, Inquire at his Warehouse, No. 24 on the Long-Wharff. (*BNL* 1719/5/25)

Two Likely Young Negro Men, to be sold by Mr. Samuel Sewall at his Warehouse No. 24 on the Long-Wharff, Boston. (*BNL* 1719/6/8)

A Fine Negro Man and Two Young Negro Women, to be Sold by Mr. Samuel Sewall Merchant, Inquire at No. 24 on the Long Wharff. (*BNL* 1722/6/25)

To be Sold by Samuel Sewall Merchant, Three Likely Negro Women, Just Arrived, To be seen at his house in Winter Street.[6]

To be Sold by Mr. Samuel Sewall Merchant, a Young Likely Negro Man and a Young Negro Woman, just Arrived, to be seen at his House in the Common. Also good Spanish Iron to be Sold by Messieurs Richard Bill & Samuel Sewall at their Warehouse on the Dock. (*BG* 1725/8/2, 8/9)

A Likely Negro Man that can speak very good English, to be Sold by Mr. Samuel Sewall *at his House on the Common.* (*BG* 1726/5/30)

To be Sold by Mr. Samuel Sewall *at his House in the Common,* Boston, *several likely Young Negro Men & Boys, Just Arrived.* (*BNL* 1726/6/23)

The number of advertisements and the regularity of their appearance demonstrate that Sewall participated in the slave trade as a matter of course; a single advertisement might be explained away as an exception or the outgrowth of some extraordinary circumstance, but these notices indicate that he participated in human trafficking throughout the last two decades of his life. Sewall's slave-for-sale advertisements suggest that we have badly misread *The Selling of Joseph*. As Elisabeth Ceppi contends, "Sewall's argument against holding black people as slaves promotes an ideal of white self-mastery that is compatible with slaveholding," and Sewall clearly believed his ownership of other human beings was compatible with his tract's arguments against slavery.[7] Careful readers will find that *The Selling of Joseph* argues not that slavery must be abolished but that colonists are wrong to participate in the slave trade naïvely, without investigating the circumstances—the stories—behind the bondage of individual men and women.

Casuistry, or the investigation and resolution of specific cases of conscience, is the dominant principle of Sewall's treatise, which takes as its title and aegis the case of Joseph's biblical enslavement at the hands of his brothers.[8] In placing Joseph's narrative at the center of his argument, Sewall characterizes slavery as an international affair; foreign relations between sovereign peoples shape the local drama of Joseph's story and the stories of other individual slaves. Those stories, in turn, come to define the contours of trade and diplomacy between nations. Given Sewall's own involvement in human trafficking, his celebrated declaration of

Caveat Emptor!

amounts not, as sometimes thought, to a warning against purchasing any and all slaves but to a call for participants in the slave trade to evaluate the morality of each transaction, each chattel's story of enslavement, through the lens of foreign policy and the standards established in the 1641 *Massachusetts Body of Liberties*: What were the particular circumstances leading to this individual's enslavement? Did an international conflict bring about this human being's bondage? Was the conflict just? Was the enslaved individual treated with "a Respect agreeable" to his or her status as "the Offspring of GOD" during the transatlantic crossing?[9] In other words, Sewall's casuistic approach to slavery calls for the collation of information gathered from foreign bulletins in the newspaper, the captains of slave ships, and the enslaved themselves into discrete narratives of slavery. Only by compiling these narratives could a buyer such as Sewall beware the moral hazard of enslaving individuals who, like Joseph, may have been kidnapped and sold without cause. Sewall's emphasis on the idiosyncratic circumstances of enslaved persons was likely an outgrowth of his approach to jurisprudence, where he similarly struggled to distinguish between personal interest and moral principle. Casuistic reasoning, John Lund argues, often left Sewall "conflicted or, less charitably, susceptible to self-deception."[10]

Because many of the surviving issues of colonial newspapers were once owned by Sewall, these issues and the marginalia preserved in them— together with Sewall's diary, letter books, and other papers—can be used to reconstruct his experience and interrogation of individual slave narratives. These artificial and synthetic narratives of slavery never existed on the printed page; they were created mentally, by Sewall and similarly invested readers, to evaluate the morality of slavery on a case-by-case basis. Thus, it might be said that the first slave narratives, or at least the earliest precursors to the slave narrative, were not written at all. In the eighteenth century, the print record preserving the speech and deeds of black Africans and their descendants was always shaped by a white editorial hand, and Marion Starling has characterized records from the 1703 trial of "Adam Negro" as the "first slave narrative."[11] In 1694 John Saffin promised Adam his freedom after seven years' service; when Saffin reneged on his promise in 1701, Adam sought his freedom through Judge Sewall and the judicial system. Adam's words are present only in the testimony of others, so if a narrative exists—and Frances Smith Foster questions that assertion—it exists only in "a conglomeration constructed from a series of personal and public documents."[12] However, this fragmentary and synthetic account of Adam's bondage and resistance typifies the generic pattern identified by John Sekora, in which each enslaved man or woman is both an "eyewitness to a system that must be exposed, and witness called before abolitionist judges and jurors to reply to specific questions—no more, no less. Once again, white sponsors compel a black author to approve, to authorize white institutional power. The black message will be sealed within a white envelope."[13] Within the curated white envelope of slavery, Adam's subjectivity is demonstratively extant only in snippets of speech reporting his indignant response to white abuse. Nonetheless, a "black message" of resistance and selfhood is accessible in the synthetic narrative of Adam's struggle for freedom, and similar messages might be reclaimed from the other unpublished, synthetic narratives that Judge Sewall constructed in his casuistic evaluation of each enslaved man or woman's plight.

Sewall's participation in the slave trade for three decades after his guarded criticism of human trafficking in *The Selling of Joseph* suggests that he and others searched for the fragmentary but compelling narratives of slavery to be found in newspapers and on the lips of both slavers and the enslaved. Too often, the stories that Sewall pieced together about the enslaved led him to conclude that their bondage "was lawful and good."[14] Ignorance of his protracted involvement in the buying and selling of human beings has long led abolitionists and historians to burnish his reputation, as an advocate of liberty, more brightly than his deeds deserve. This recovery of Sewall's slave-for-sale advertisements should complicate the way in which we teach and talk about *The Selling of Joseph*, but it is also an opportunity for scholars invested in the slave narrative's origins and evolution to resurrect and reconstruct the synthetic narratives that Sewall pieced together in evaluating the desire of Adam and other enslaved individuals for freedom. Though inconsistent in his self-proclaimed "Antipathy against slavery," Sewall cared at least enough about the lives of the enslaved to seek out their stories.[15]

The Circumstances of Composition

The Selling of Joseph has often been linked to the contest between Saffin and Adam, and Sewall's frequent invocation of the biblical Adam's name can make it seem as though the judge wrote his pamphlet as a preemptive assault on Saffin's right to void the indenture. But Saffin's agreement with Adam ran through 1701, and the case was not resolved until 1703, so Sewall's sentiments in *The Selling of Joseph* were unlikely to have been prompted by the suit. More recently, Gloria Whiting has argued that Sewall's pamphlet was conceived in response to another battle over the rights of local black Africans, contending that Sewall wrote *The Selling of Joseph* as part of his campaign to effect the marriage of Sebastian and Jane, two enslaved Bostonians who surface often in Sewall's diary.[16] John and Eunice Wait, who claimed Sebastian as a chattel, first visited Sewall to ask for his help in arranging the marriage on March 27, 1699, and after protracted negotiations with Nathaniel and Deborah Thayer, who claimed Jane, he finally performed the ceremony on February 13, 1701.[17] The struggles of Adam, Sebastian, Jane, and other black Bostonians undoubtedly played some part in Sewall's decision to write *The Selling of Joseph*, but at the turn of the eighteenth century, his pen and his checkbook were employed far more frequently in the service of white slaves held in captivity across the Atlantic.

On October 30, 1695, Samuel Sewall sent John Ive, in England, the first of many letters soliciting his aid on behalf of two white New England sailors held captive in North Africa, at Mequinez—a Moroccan port.[18] Sewall had already worked with Ive to secure the release of Bostonian Joshua Gee, who returned from bondage in 1688 and who, Sewall wrote, "thanks for my kindness to him when Captive in Algier."[19] Seven years later, Gee and his wife, Elizabeth, solicited Sewall's help in raising money for the redemption of Elizabeth's brother, Thomas Thatcher of Yarmouth, and James Bull, a Boston native who had settled in Bristow, England. In 1698, Sewall forwarded to Bull and Thatcher, through Ive, Cotton Mather's "Pastoral Letters which He has written to direct and comfort them" together with "about 60 pounds of N.E. Money." Hearing a rumor that the Crown might intercede on their behalf, Sewall declared, "Twould be a very noble undertaking for the English Nation for to Redeem these miserable Slaves," and begged Ive "that if there be any publick method taken for the Redemption of Slaves out of Africa, you would strenuously move that ours may partake in the Benefit." He continued to raise money for and correspond with Ive about Thatcher and Bull in 1699, as he drafted *The Selling of Joseph*. His advocacy on their behalf continued until he heard word from Ive in 1702 that Bull had been ransomed and Thatcher had died in captivity.[20] He, along with many other Massachusetts residents, celebrated news of Bull's release with a public day of Thanksgiving on January 15, 1703.[21]

Sewall hints that his thoughts on the enslavement of black Africans were, in fact, prompted by the sufferings of Thatcher, Bull, and others. *The Selling of Joseph* attempts to draw a line between their captivity and the importation of chattel slaves from Africa: "Methinks, when we are bemoaning the barbarous Usage of our Friends and Kinsfolk in *Africa:* it might not be unseasonable to enquire whether we are not culpable in forcing the *Africans* to become Slaves amongst our selves. And it may be a question whether all the Benefit received by *Negro* Slaves, will balance the Accompt of Cash laid out upon them; and for the Redemption of our own enslaved Friends out of *Africa*."[22] The "barbarous Usage" of Bull and Thatcher prompted Sewall's thinking in *The Selling of Joseph* and shaped his inquiry into the justice of chattel bondage. Although many scholars now emphasize the differences between the experience of white sailors held for ransom in North Africa and the black Africans who endured or heard from relatives about the Middle Passage, Sewall and his contemporaries used the same word to describe both groups: slavery. And Sewall's advocacy, on behalf of New Englanders held in North Africa, for two decades before the publication of *The Selling of Joseph*, suggests that he thought of its call for emancipation as the solution to an international crisis in which the "Negroes" of North Africa were pitted against Englishmen on both sides of the Atlantic, more than a local dispute between the Thayers and Waits or Saffin and Adam.

Enslaved Africans living in Boston were largely from Senegambia and the Gold Coast, not Algiers, but the differences between Igbo, Akan, and Algerian peoples were often and easily obscured in the discourse of white colonists (not to mention the differences between Morocco, Tripoli, Algiers, and Tunisia).[23] Sewall speaks of New Englanders in Africa and black Africans in New England as though a bilateral exchange of human property might satisfy both sides. And when Cotton Mather celebrated the release of Bull, he quoted liberally from several accounts of English captivity in North Africa describing "Negroes" as the oppressors of English prisoners. These white "Slaves, in Cruel and Inhumane Bondage," are "kept at Hard work, from Daylight in the Morning till Night: carrying Earth on their Heads in great Baskets, driven to and fro, with barbarous Negroes by the Emperours Order; and when they are drove home by the Negroes at Night, to their Lodging, which is on the cold Ground, in a Vault or hollow place in the Earth, laid over with great Beams athwart, and Iron Bars over them; they are told in there like Sheep."[24] The effect of such rhetoric is to equate the condition of Adam, Sebastian, or Jane with that of Thatcher and Bull. If anything, Sewall and his contemporaries surely thought that enslaved black Africans in Boston were better off than their countrymen, who were often paraded "chained and nearly naked, having been robbed of their clothes," when they first arrived in a North African port.[25] While it would be an exaggeration, Paul Baepler argues, to claim that "the American slave narrative is derivative of the writings of white slaves in Africa," Sewall's familiarity with the sufferings of Gee, Thatcher, and Bull surely influenced his interactions with Adam and the narrative of his struggle for freedom as preserved in Massachusetts court records.[26] The manifest injustice of white captivity led Sewall, over the course of many years, to recognize that many of the black men and women he interacted with on a daily basis were similarly innocent victims of international conflicts.

Sewall concedes, in *The Selling of Joseph*, that lawful captives may justly be sold as slaves, yet he warns that New England colonists can have no assurance the black Africans arriving on their shores are, in fact, lawful captives. The problem, Sewall writes, is a deficit of knowledge: "For ought is known, their Wars are much such as were between *Jacob's* Sons and their Brother *Joseph*. If they be between Town and Town; Provincial, or National: Every War is upon one side Unjust. An Unlawful War can't make lawful Captives." In the absence of knowledge about the circumstances in which each imported black African was made a chattel, Sewall insists that he and his fellow colonists cannot assume the men and women sold on Boston's docks have forfeited their right to freedom by resisting lawful authority. When Sewall and other Massachusetts officials could verify that the enslaved had been taken in an unjust war or otherwise kidnapped, they attempted to restore these unfortunates to free-dom.[27] Yet Sewall also insists on the theoretical legality of slavery, citing the biblical patriarch Abraham as an example of a slaveholder whose participation in the slave trade was justified by his knowledge of particulars. "Until the Cir-cumstances of *Abraham's* purchase be recorded," Sewall contends, "no Argu-ment can be drawn from it. In the mean time, Charity obliges us to conclude, that He knew it was lawful and good." Casuistry, or the investigation of specific circumstances, excuses Abraham's involvement in human trafficking, and Sewall presumably thought of his own participation in the slave trade as simi-larly justified by his knowledge of slavery's contexts.[28]

Although *The Selling of Joseph* was penned more than a decade before Sewall's first surviving slave-for-sale advertisement appeared in the *Boston News-Letter*, he continued to espouse its views publicly, lamenting the en-slavement of black Africans and American Indians. He reaffirmed his views in a 1706 letter to Nathanael Byfield, a judge for the Court of Vice-Admiralty, and in December 1714, three months after his notice for "Four or Five likely Negro Boys" appeared in the paper, Sewall sent a copy of *The Selling of Joseph* to Henry Newman, a colonial agent in London and secretary of the Society for Promoting Christian Knowledge (*BNL* 1714/9/13). He also asked New-man "to do somthing if it fall in his way, towards taking away this wicked prac-tice of Slavery. Will be no great progress in Gospellizing till then."[29] Sewall regarded the institution of slavery as an obstacle to the conversion of black African and American Indian peoples, and he objected to laws characterizing the enslaved as personal property. In one of the best-known passages of his journal, Sewall "essay'd June, 22, [1716] to prevent Indians and Negros being Rated with Horses and Hogs; but could not prevail. Col. Thaxter brought it back, and gave as a reason of the Non-agreement, They were just going to make a New Valuation." Scholars have long cited this passage as evidence of Sewall's advocacy for the enslaved, but placing Sewall's unsuccessful argu-ment in a broader context creates a more nuanced picture of his aims.[30] The rhetorical circumstances of this debate matter, just as Sewall believed that the circumstances surrounding an individual's enslavement mattered.

Sewall's argument against tax laws treating the enslaved as possessions rather than people may seem to anticipate the outrage expressed by Frederick Douglass in his *Narrative*. Douglass recollects his experience at a slave auc-tion, when "we were all ranked together at the valuation. Men and women, old and young, married and single, were ranked with horses, sheep, and swine. There were horses and men, cattle and women, pigs and children, all holding the same rank in the scale of being."[31] But where Douglass wrote to abolish slavery, Sewall likely wrote for other, quite different purposes. Just four days earlier, on Monday, June 18, 1716, he had placed an advertisement for "Two fine lusty Negro Men" to be seen and sold at his warehouse on Merchants Row in Boston (*BNL* 1716/6/18). No one in the General Court would have understood Sewall's objection to rating humans and hogs together as an attack on slavery; such language was quite common in the evaluation of estates, and certifying wills which listed human beings, animals, and other items of value promiscuously was an essential part of Sewall's legal work. For example, Sewall transcribed the will of his son Samuel's father-in-law, Massachusetts governor Joseph Dudley, into his personal records, noting that Dudley left "to Rebekah my dear wife, my servants, Houshold Goods, Plate, and Two Hundred pounds in money."[32] This conflation of enslaved humans and animals or goods also appeared in slave-for-sale advertisements announcing, "*There is to be Sold on the 28th of June next at Vendue, a like Negroe Woman, Horses, Cattle, Hogs, a new Cart, and Houshold Goods.*"[33] Sewall saw similar language every month in the wills of New England colonists, and his objection on this particular occasion likely had more to do with transatlantic politics than the transatlantic slave trade.

In the days before Sewall made his objections to the conflation of slaves and swine, John Campbell—Boston's postmaster and the publisher of its only newspaper—received a record of Governor Robert Hunter's latest speech to the General Assembly of New York. News of the Jacobite rising of 1715 was circulating widely in the colonies, and Hunter's speech disavowed the Pretender James Stuart (son of James II) as a would-be tyrant attempting to enslave the inhabitants of England with the support of France and the Vatican. Collapsing the distinction between human and animal is, Hunter alleges, the key to Stuart's tyrannous aims; he asks, "is there a Man who has the least Concern for Humane Nature it self, who is not fill'd with Joy to find the Essential Differences betwixt that and the Subordinate Species of Animals refixt and maintain'd, which must have been entirely Cancelled by that sort of Power which alone could have given Success to and have supported the Cause of a Popish Pretender"? Hunter concludes this stirring rebuke of foreign powers by asking the Assembly to fund "an augmentation of the Troops here," reminding his listeners that "the Subject here is less loaded with Publick Taxes than any of their Neighbours" (*BNL* 1716/6/25). Both his own slave-for-sale advertisement, published four days earlier, and the timing of Sewall's objection to valuing the enslaved as animals for tax purposes—when the bill in question had passed more than a week earlier, on June 11—suggest that Hunter's speech, and not the suffering of the enslaved, likely prompted his complaint.[34] Sewall sought to strike any association between people and property from the law because that association was, ostensibly, a plank of the Pretender's "Popish" platform: best to distance a colony whose relations with the Crown had often been troubled from any hint of Jacobite leanings.[35] Sewall's approach to slavery was likely more opportunistic than principled, his opposition to the institution a product of diplomatic and personal circumstances.

Both *The Selling of Joseph* and Sewall's well-known diary entry on lumping horses and human chattel into one category of property were probably written in response to the dangers, real and perceived, posed by foreign powers seeking to enslave English subjects. The condition of slavery was, in the minds of Sewall and his contemporaries, a byproduct of international disagreements, whether those disagreements were between two anonymous kings in Africa, the Dey of Algiers and Queen Anne, or George I and Catholic supporters of Stuart succession. Thus a 1727 declaration of Scotland's royal burghs scored in the margins by a colonial reader declares, "*In some other Kingdoms, the oppressed Subjects have no Comfort for the lavish wasting of their Blood & Treasure against foreign Enemies, but the ungrateful View of the confirming that Power, which (designed for defending) is unnaturally employed to subdue themselves, & governs Freeborn Subjects as if they were the miserable Slaves of a conquered Country.*"[36] Slavery was first and foremost a tool of foreign policy in the eighteenth century, a legitimate exercise of power between nation states occasionally misapplied in domestic contexts or, as Sewall knew, in the coercion of innocent foreign citizens. In 1710 the colonists of New France were warned by British officers that "*the Chief Inhabitants of this Country, shall in same manner be made slaves amongst our Indians*" unless they arranged for the return of Eunice Williams, daughter of the well-known minister John Williams, whose Mohawk captivity became the subject of an early American best seller (*BNL* 1710/11/6).[37] Sewall objected to slavery because he believed that some of the black African inhabitants of Boston had been made chattels unlawfully, like Thatcher, Bull, and Williams; in the absence of information about the circumstances of their enslavement, he intimates that all must assume the enslaved have been wrongfully coerced to labor. But Sewall also believed that slavery could be "lawful and good" if individuals were captured during the course of a just war, and he defended Abraham's involvement in chattel slavery. Sewall's participation in the slave trade suggests he concluded on more than one occasion that the circumstances of enslavement permitted him to profit from human trafficking in good conscience. Scanning the newspaper for word of wars in Africa and Europe, Sewall constructed a backstory for the black Africans brought into his warehouse and sat in judgment of their circumstances.

The Liberation of Basilio

In December 1709 Boston dignitaries paid their respects to Charles Sucre, governor of the colonial city of Cartagena de Indias on the coast of South America (whose conquest at the hands of Edward Vernon would be celebrated thirty years later by Black Peter), and Sewall presented their visitor with a gift. He gave Sucre a commentary on the biblical book of Job written by Gaspar Sanctius, sending his offering in the hands of Immanuel Basilio, "who was born in Margarita Taken at La vera Crux, and wrongfully made a Slave and is now waiting on the Court's Judgment to declare him Free."[38] Basilio had arrived in Boston at least one year earlier and in January 1709 sent Governor Dudley a petition protesting that he had been wrongfully enslaved.[39] Sewall was present for Dudley's deliberations on the matter and recorded in his journal, "a Spaniard's petition is read praying his Freedom. Govr refers it to the Judges. Mr. Cook notifies Capt. Teat to appear to morrow." When Captain Matthew Teate of the *HMS Reserve*, either Basilio's current enslaver or the contracted recipient of his labor, heard the petition read, he "pleads the Govr told him he was a slave; Capt. Teat alledg'd that all of that Color were Slaves: Obliges to have the man forth-coming at Charlestown Court."[40] In his petition Basilio self-identified as a Spaniard, but Teate argued that the pigmentation of Basilio's skin was too dark for him to plausibly claim to be of European descent. Perhaps Basilio was a descendant of the Guaiqueríes who lived on Isla Margarita when Christopher Columbus claimed it for Spain in 1498, or he may have been the descendant of black African slaves brought to the island for labor. Whatever his parentage, Basilio's skin color confirmed, in Teate's mind, his status as a slave. Sewall was not so sure. His evaluation of Basilio's case demonstrates that Sewall acted on the casuistic principles of *The Selling of Joseph*, considering the stories of individuals enslaved in Boston as a way of determining whether their bondage was "lawful and good" or an injustice to be remedied.

Over the next year, as Basilio waited for a decision, Sewall formed his own opinion—and that process illustrates the judge's casuistic approach to questions of slavery and freedom. Basilio's case called up, for Sewall, earlier arguments against the purchase of slaves in Boston; his view of Basilio's suit was shaped by his observation of the institution in local settings. Just a day after he heard Teate's testimony, Sewall lamented the death of a friend, Joseph

Bridgham, and noted parenthetically, "Mr. Bridgham buried a Carolina Indian Man last Monday; and another the Monday before; One about 30. the other 40 years of Age, which he bought not a year ago."[41] Basilio's suit made the deaths of these enslaved Indians more notable in Sewall's mind. Each had previously passed unremarked, but he now found their abbreviated lives relevant to the legal question occupying his thoughts.

Bridgham's dead Indian servants were likely those advertised in April 1708, "To be Sold at the Sign of the Blue Anchor in Boston; Four Carolina Indians, viz. A Lad, Two Men and a Woman" (*BNL* 1708/4/19; see also *BNL* 1708/4/5). In May 1708, one month after these foreign nationals were sold into servitude and as they were becoming acclimated to life in New England, Sewall met with Governor Dudley to consider the complaints of Mohegans living in Woodstock. Together they deliberated over a letter "concerning Nenemeno, an Indian that went away ten years ago; He said the Govr has a Crooked heart, he has taken away our Land, and now would send us to Salt Water. He first enquired after Ninequabben, who it seems was sent to sea upon Wages with his own Consent, and Taken."[42] Sewall, Dudley, and the other members of the council reviewed requests such as Basilio's on a regular basis, evaluating claims of wrongful enslavement. In this case, Sewall and Dudley concluded that Ninequabben sailed voluntarily before being taken by foreign privateers. However, Sewall's silence with respect to Nenemeno may suggest that he had been wrongfully sold. When he met his friend Bridgham in August 1708 and interacted with Bridgham's new chattel servants, Sewall might have wondered whether Dudley would similarly present their protestations of freedom to the council on some future day.

No petition from Bridgham's servants ever came to Sewall. They may have lacked the necessary language skills, and their sudden deaths—just eight months after arriving in Boston—cut short any opportunity for civil action. In noting their untimely passing, Sewall may have recalled an argument made in the *Boston News-Letter* two and a-half years earlier against chattel bondage: "*If a White Servant die, the Loss exceeds not 10l but if a Negro dies, 'tis a very great Loss to the Husbandman; Three years Interest of the price of the Negro, wil near upon if not altogether purchase a White Man Servant. . . . A certain person within these 6 years had two Negroes dead computed at 60l which would have procured him six white Servants at 10l. per head*" (*BNL* 1706/6/10).[43] While considering Basilio's plea for freedom, Sewall likely remembered earlier arguments against enslaving people of color and considered the case of Bridgham's servants a relevant precedent.

Sewall's key question, in *The Selling of Joseph*, is how an individual came to be enslaved, and both Basilio and Bridgham's Indian servants were enslaved as a result of the War of the Spanish Succession. The most important question of the war was whether a French noble (Philip, Duke of Anjou) or an Austrian (Archduke Charles) would inherit the throne of Spain. England joined Austria in its fight against France, and colonists read with interest of battles fought across the Atlantic. But the inhabitants of North America and the Caribbean also experienced this global power struggle locally, through the lens of slavery. For English colonists and their correspondents in Whitehall, the war became a referendum on France's ability to fulfill the terms of the *assiento*—a contract authorizing its holder to sell black African slaves in Spain's North American colonies.[44]

Throughout the war, Sewall and other Bostonians read of assaults on Antigua, St. Christopher's, and South Carolina, as the French attempted to supply Spanish officials in Central America with human chattels.[45] Editorials explained, "The reason of the Frenches Effort thus, is said to be, That the French King at the beginning of this War borrowed a considerable Sum from *New-Spain*, with the Engagement in 5 years to furnish them with 50000 Negros for their Mines, which time of Contract being out, and his necessity requiring another Borrow; The *Spaniards* were Crusty, and would not Lend till the first agreement was answered; so he thought an Attack on these Islands to be the readiest way to accomplish his bargain" (*BNL* 1706/5/6). The inhabitants of Massachusetts took up a donation for the people of St. Christopher's, where privateers regularly landed "to get off negroes," and they read of raids conducted on the island of Nevis (*BNL* 1706/4/22, *BNL* 1706/11/11).[46] French forces sacked Nevis and "took also 3200 Negros"; an additional six hundred "Negros that were in the Mountains," upon learning that the French planned to sell them in Spanish mines, attacked so fiercely "that the French durst not move half a Mile out of Town for fear of the Negros" (*BNL* 1706/5/20).[47] Any encounter with French forces during this period represented a risk of enslavement or, for those already enslaved, a transfer to Spanish mines. If Basilio was taken on the coast of New Spain in Vera Cruz and unjustly made a slave, the French were likely to blame—French ships made port in Vera Cruz to take on supplies throughout the war.[48] And Bridgham's servants would have been swept up in a local skirmish between South Carolina militia and a multinational coalition of Spanish, French, and Indian forces.

Sewall read about the skirmish in which Bridgham's servants were probably enslaved. In August 1706, five French privateers sailed from Havana for South Carolina. They stopped briefly at St. Augustine to take on additional

Spanish and Indian crew and made for Charlestown, which they had heard was devastated by sickness. However, when they landed, they found a healthy and well-armed military force awaiting their arrival. English forces captured a raiding party sent to harass estates on the outskirts of Charlestown, and as the French flotilla departed, "two Sloops under the Command of Col *Rhett* returned from *Seway-Bay* in *Charlstown* Harbour, and brought with them the *French* Ship their Prize, with their Land-General and several other Officers on Board" (*BNL* 1706/10/14). During King William's War, French prisoners had been sold to work alongside enslaved black Africans in Barbados sugar fields, but prisoners of European descent taken during this skirmish were luckier.[49] The first reports from South Carolina indicated "we have in all about 230 Prisoners *French* and *Spaniards*" (*BNL* 1708/10/14). That number apparently included Indian captives allied with the European powers because a later update indicated "that the Government of *South-Carolina* had sent all the *French* and *Spanish* Prisoners whom they had taken in the Invasion, to *Virginia*, in order to be transported to *England*, except about 90 or 100 Indians, who they have Sold for Slaves" (*BNL* 1708/10/28).[50] American Indian— and perhaps also black African—captives were first identified by their affiliation with European nations before being separated into racial categories; nationality trumped race as an initial marker of identity. Basilio's self-identification as a Spaniard makes perfect sense in this context: Spaniards would be exchanged for English prisoners and freed, while Indian and black African captives could expect to be sold into slavery.[51] Bridgham's servants, taken in this or another comparable skirmish, were a reminder to Sewall that even "lawful Captives" could be "unjustly dealt with" by captors who, like Captain Teate, used skin color to discriminate between prisoners to be exchanged and prisoners to be sold as chattel.

In a desperate search for fifty thousand bodies to fulfill their agreement with New Spain, French privateers imported black Africans from Guinea and stole those already enslaved from English and Dutch enemies. They also, presumably, captured and enslaved more than one free person of color living in the Caribbean. Basilio claimed that he had been kidnapped in Vera Cruz, and Sewall—who anticipated precisely such a scenario in *The Selling of Joseph*— was undoubtedly sympathetic to his claim. Sewall asked each of his readers to imagine "if some Gentlemen should go down to the *Brewsters* to take the Air, and Fish: And a stronger party from *Hull* should Surprise them, and Sell them for Slaves to a Ship outward bound: they would think themselves unjustly dealt with," as Basilio did.[52] Sewall's hypothetical was set in England because he aspired to a transatlantic readership but also, perhaps, because he had heard of attempts to enslave white servants kidnapped and sent to the Caribbean.[53] Whether Basilio was of Spanish, Indian, or African descent, Sewall would have recognized that his kidnapping in Mexico was exactly the scenario that he had imagined, substituting Vera Cruz for Brewsters and France for Hull.

Rather than attempting to sell Basilio in Vera Cruz, where he might have been recognized by an acquaintance as a freeman, the French would have taken Basilio to another harbor, where he would not be recognized. But his presence in Boston suggests that before Basilio came to his fate and was sold in Spanish mines, the vessel he sailed on was taken by an English privateer or man-of-war. Perhaps Basilio was captured in a battle Sewall had read about four years earlier, when ships from New York reported, "Admiral Whetston has taken a French Ship of 44 Guns on the Coast of New-Spain; she went from Guinea to New-Spain with Negro's, and there disposed of them" (*BNL* 1705/8/6). Two tick marks in the newspaper's margins demonstrate that at least one reader (Sewall?) found Whetston's victory a story of interest.[54] Or Basilio might have been on a French vessel that left Vera Cruz to raid the North American coastline and steal away those already enslaved, as in the skirmish that brought Bridgham his American Indian servants.

In 1707, a French sloop was sighted in the Atlantic off Block Island, just south of Rhode Island, and negotiations with these raiders were reported in the newspaper. Sewall's copy of this story is annotated, and the markings that were presumably made by the judge radically alter the meaning of this story for the two enslaved black Africans involved.[55] The original story explained "that there was a French Privateer Sloop (said to be taken from Pensilvania) that came from Placentia with 75 men, who Landed on the Island, and took several of the Inhabitants Prisoners; but another Party of 9 English and 7 Indians gathered in a Body, drove the French to the Water-side, who came upon Articles with them to restore their Prisoners and what they had taken for 20 Sheep and 2 Cheeses which they did except 2 Negroes and so stood off to Sea" (*BNL* 1707/9/1). The story seems fairly simple, notwithstanding a few confounding details. (How did seven Indians and nine English colonists drive off seventy-five French pirates?) The pirates landed, took hostages, and traded the English hostages for food but kept two black African hostages as chattels. However, the insertion of handwritten punctuation and the revision of one word in Sewall's copy call that narrative into question. Sewall's copy, with additions and revisions bolded, contends "that there was a French Privateer Sloop (said to be taken from Pensilvania) that came from Placentia with 75 men, who Landed on the Island, and took several of the Inhabitants

Prisoners; but another Party of 9 English and 7 Indians gathered in a Body, drove the French to the Water-side, who came upon Articles with them to restore their Prisoners and what they had taken, for 20 Sheep and 2 Cheeses, which they did; accept 2 Negroes and so stood off to Sea" (*BNL* 1707/9/1). Inserting a semicolon after the word *did* and changing *except* to *accept* opens up this narrative of negotiation to multiple readings. Rather giving the raiders two enslaved black Africans, did the Indians and English, demanding value in exchange for their sheep and cheese beyond the return of hostages taken, accept "2 Negroes" from the French in payment? If Basilio came to Boston through such an exchange, Sewall might have learned the truth of this affair firsthand and edited his record of the event accordingly. Or even if he was not sold by the French to the inhabitants of Block Island, Basilio might have arrived in Boston when the privateer was taken days later, in waters off Martha's Vineyard (*BNL* 1707/9/15).

The truth of Basilio's path from Vera Cruz to Boston is likely lost irrevocably; his name does not appear in the official colony records or in the muster books of the *Reserve* and the other men-of-war that visited Boston in 1708 and 1709. He may have been enslaved after a confrontation with French and Spanish privateers on the beaches of South Carolina (*BNL* 1706/10/14), or he could be the "lusty Negro who is a very good Trumpeter" taken from a French privateer in the waters of Jamaica (*BNL* 1708/3/29; also *BNL* 1704/7/31, *BNL* 1704/8/28). But his narrative of slavery, along with the narratives of other enslaved individuals, circulated in colonial North America and were heard and read and pieced together from multiple sources by Sewall. Annotations to the Block Island hostage story and other newspaper stories dealing with slavery or the enslaved demonstrate a readership engaged not only in the consumption of stories but also their creation and elaboration beyond the printed page (see *BNL* 1708/3/29; *BNL* 1718/3/3; *BNL* 1719/2/9). The first slave narratives—Adam's, Basilio's—were related aurally or synthesized mentally from a hodgepodge of source material, and their echoes remain in court documents, journals, and newspapers.

If Basilio told Sewall a story of captivity at the hands of French slave raiders, he could have been confident that the judge would respond sympathetically. Even Boston and Newport, Rhode Island, with their relatively small populations of enslaved Indians and black Africans, had been rumored to be the target of French raiders from the West Indies (*BNL* 1706/6/3, *BNL* 1706/6/17, *BNL* 1706/8/19).[56] Reading about the fate of wealthy merchants and landowners in Nevis, who were bankrupted by French privateers, Sewall and the other leading citizens of Boston imagined their own fates. The threat was real enough that they devoted a thousand pounds and many more hours of labor to fortifying the city, so Basilio's story would have reminded Sewall of his own sense of vulnerability.

And if Basilio was born a Protestant—possible, though not likely, given his birth in lands controlled by Spain—or converted in New England, his enslavement at the hands of the French might have drawn additional sympathy from Sewall and Dudley. Other prisoners of war who converted to the Protestant faith were freed and permitted to remain in Massachusetts as English subjects. In 1706 a French prisoner named Timothy LeFebre "declared him self to have Embraced the protestant religion & prayed leave to Dwell in this province." Hoping to prompt other prisoners to convert, Dudley asked LeFebre to announce his decision in front of the departing French prisoners; he granted LeFebre's plea and expressed satisfaction with his naturalization a year later.[57] Conversion was a potentially liberating experience for individuals enduring different forms of unfreedom; while enslaved black Africans in Boston were rarely emancipated after their conversion to the Protestant faith, Jared Hardesty attests that religious affiliation granted slaves "the material and educational benefits provided by churches."[58]

The suffering of an enslaved Protestant on board French ships would have recalled, for Sewall, the captivity and torture of Huguenots on board the king's galleys. In 1701 Sewall received a letter from Cotton Mather describing the suffering of French Protestants sentenced to labor as galley slaves—a fate even worse, writers agreed, than captivity in North Africa.[59] Sewall published the letter and distributed it to his friends, urging them to pray for the relief of those condemned to the gallies.[60] Colonists searched the foreign bulletins for information about the condition of these galley slaves, and more than two dozen updates on their struggle for personal and religious liberty were published in colonial newspapers during Sewall's lifetime.[61] In 1713, Sewall or another anonymous colonist rejoiced, marking in the *Boston News-Letter* with an X the "Order given by the French King upon the Pious and Generous Instances of the Queen of Great Britain, to set at Liberty a great number of Protestant Slaves on Board the Gallies upon account of their Religion" (*BNL* 1713/12/28). The suffering of Protestants aboard French ships was an ongoing concern for Sewall, and his sympathy for Huguenot galley slaves may have predisposed him to hear Basilio's narrative sympathetically.

Teate sought bodily possession of Basilio's labor because the sailors of the *Reserve* were deserting in droves, and a law known colloquially as the Sixth of Anne made it illegal to impress colonists, who compared impressment to slavery.[62] Dudley tried to address the problem by declaring that sailors

traveling without a pass could be held until Teate verified they were not de-
serters, but the *Reserve* continued to hemorrhage men (*BNL* 1708/12/27).[63]
A year earlier, when Charles Stucley of the *HMS Deptford* had similarly struggled to man his vessel, he requested Dudley's help in filling his complement:
"I must begg your Excellcy will Secure for her Majties Service on board me,
what Foreigners you can."[64] Stucley asked Dudley to send him men like
Basilio—a foreign prisoner of war—because he could not impress colonists,
and Teate had likely done the same. Teate's declaration that "the Govr told
him he was a Slave" suggests Dudley thought Basilio was a slave and sent him
to the *Reserve* as a gesture of goodwill. With Sewall's help Basilio escaped service in the navy and was still in Boston when Teate left New England on February 26, 1710; the *Reserve*'s captain complained, in a letter to the Admiralty,
"I cannot Prevail wth the Governour to Suply me wth one man."[65] Instead of
additional sailors, Dudley sent Teate four passengers—Mohawk and Mahican
leaders sent to London on a diplomatic mission. Teate, who thought "all of
that Color were Slaves," must have found the exchange of Basilio for these
Indian dignitaries a particularly bitter pill to swallow.[66]

Basilio's story of wrongful enslavement ultimately persuaded Sewall and
Dudley to save him from service on the *Reserve*, but neither could know the
truth of Basilio's narrative. That Basilio was enslaved—if only briefly—is certain. That he was born free in Margarita or emancipated prior to being enslaved in Vera Cruz is an assertion beyond our knowledge and also, almost
certainly, beyond Sewall's. Who could verify his story but a resident of Vera
Cruz or Margarita? And how was Dudley, Sewall, or anyone else in Massachusetts to communicate with those distant cities held by a foreign power at
war with England and her colonies? As David Waldstreicher attests, the enslaved often used "the assumptions of resource-rich whites to get what they
want[ed] and need[ed]," deploying a "knowledge of the developing colonies"
and their unique geopolitical biases to advance personal interests.[67] Basilio
must have known that Sewall and his associates would have to take his word
on several key points, and at least one confidence man had already passed
through Massachusetts searching for sympathy with false stories of captivity
on a French privateer and coerced labor.

One Henry Burch, a white convict escaping from servitude in Philadelphia, passed through Boston in 1705 with his own narrative of slavery, and his
story was snapped up by the *News-Letter*. Burch told the inhabitants of Boston that he was sailing to Barbados in 1696 with his uncle when "they were
taken by a *French* Privateer near *Barbadoes*, and one of the Privateers took a
dagger and run thorow the young Lads Cheek and Jawbone, and struck out

two of his Teeth, cut his Left hand thorow 3 fingers, the prints whereof are still to be seen." Burch eventually escaped the French and sailed to Virginia in 1700, where "his Uncle sold him a Servant unto one *Richard Skinner* a Planter for 6 years, & gives him a large Sum of Money to murder him when he was gone.... And as soon as his cruel Uncle was gone, his Master *Richard Skinner* sent him out to the [*Hope*], where he continued 3 years, along with his Negro's and Indian Overseers" (BNL 1705/11/5). Burch's story was fabricated: he had never been abused by French pirates or forced to work on a Virginia plantation alongside enslaved black Africans under an Indian overseer. But he told these stories of slavery, recalling the plight of Bull and Thatcher in Mequinez and Huguenot martyrs aboard French gallies, because he knew that they would touch the heartstrings of colonists in Massachusetts. Burch's gambit gave him access to the "money and other purloinables" of "Charitable Gentlemen, who treat all Strangers with the Civilities at their Houses," and he left in a shirt stolen from one of those men (BNL 1705/11/12). Whether Burch stole the shirt off Sewall's back or lifted it from another of Boston's leading citizens, he left behind an atmosphere of suspicion, as well as a blueprint for preying on the sympathies of Boston's inhabitants.

If Basilio was a free man enslaved by the French during the War of the Spanish Succession, he was fortunate to find a home in Boston, where his circumstances would naturally elicit the sympathy of Sewall and other powerful individuals. But he may well have been more politic than fortunate. Douglass describes the ignorance of African Americans enslaved in the nineteenth century—denied knowledge of their age, parentage, and other information—as a crippling form of bondage.[68] But in the early eighteenth century, individuals taken on board a captured vessel or runaway slaves and convicts like Burch came to see ignorance as a form of empowerment, exploiting the absence of efficient communication networks to assume new identities. Because slavery was still primarily an international affair in which human chattels passed through the hands of foreign nationals from multiple countries, the enslaved could and did use their knowledge of global politics to play on antipathies between English and French, Catholic and Protestant.

Basilio's narrative is fragmentary, a product of collation and imagination. It is also tantalizingly present and specific, as tantalizing as Adam's. Both the story that Basilio told Sewall and the stories that Sewall pieced together, relying on newspapers and oral testimony, attest to the ways in which international power struggles stimulated the slave trade and, occasionally, provided the enslaved with opportunities to escape or ameliorate their bondage. French participation in the War of the Spanish Succession fueled an increased demand for human labor, but it also provided savvy black Africans in North America with an opportunity to exploit the nationalism of Englishmen like Sewall.

Stories without Faces

Immanuel Basilio's brief appearance in Sewall's records provides a focal point around which textual fragments relevant to his circumstances might have been collated by Sewall into a larger, synthetic narrative that can still be read today. Notice of a black trumpeter taken on board a French privateer captures one possibility for Basilio's past, and aggregating multiple accounts—of the *Reserve*'s staffing, of enslaved black Africans taken off board French privateers, and of other individuals who petitioned Dudley for their freedom—allows readers to identify common elements in the experience of those similarly situated. This conglomeration of sources is, like the documents produced during Adam's trial, a synthetic slave narrative outlining the contours of one man's quest for freedom. But Sewall and his contemporaries—including the literate black Bostonians educated in Cotton Mather's school for the colony's colored community—often read the dozens and even hundreds of textual fragments reprinted in colonial newspapers without a name or face around which a biography could coalesce. In the absence of a known protagonist, these faceless narratives of slavery established a baseline against which the idiosyncratic cases of Adam or Basilio would be measured. Sewall's casuistry required an understanding of slavery's role as a tool of war and diplomacy, and the stories of anonymous black Africans whose lives and deaths were glossed in the newspaper created a rhetorical and moral context for the more accessible lives of individuals like Basilio and Adam.

When Sewall advertised, in 1726, that he would sell "*several likely Young Negro Men & Boys, Just Arrived,*" he did not specify where they had arrived from (BNL 1726/6/23). But these faceless men and youths likely made their way from Africa to Boston by way of the Caribbean; Gregory O'Malley estimates that 15 percent of the black Africans who finished the Middle Passage in a British port promptly boarded a second ship bound for another city on the Atlantic coast.[69] Because Sewall likely purchased these individuals from a middleman and because they presumably spoke no English (Sewall, like other slave traders, advertised language skills as a selling point whenever possible), the only clues Sewall could have had about the genesis of their captivity would have been found in the newspaper, where foreign bulletins shared updates on politics and military actions in Africa and other distant locales.

Sewall complained, in *The Selling of Joseph*, that buyers of slaves could not know the details of how each enslaved black African came to be a captive because, although the newspapers were filled with reports from Algiers, Morocco, and other North African states, word of political and military affairs from Senegambia, Sierra Leone, the Gold Coast, and southwest Africa was scarce. Reports of European and Moroccan pirates harassing slave traders off the African coast were plentiful, but word from the continent's black inhabitants was far more difficult to come by. John Campbell began publishing the *Boston News-Letter* in 1704, and the first surviving account of African politics to appear in a North American newspaper was printed seventeen years later, in 1721. Correspondents in Lisbon reported, "Letters from Angola (Southward of Guiney) say, that several Chief Lords in that Country had rebelled and committed Hostilities, to the number of Sixteen Thousand in Arms, but that the Governour Don Henriques de Lignoredo de Alarcon, assisted with the others that continued Faithful to the King, about Six Thousand Men, attacked the Rebels and defeated them, killing and taking about Eight Thousand, and among the Prisoners, four of their Chief Leaders and Fomentors" (*BNL* 1721/4/24). Administrative reforms passed in 1720 forbad Portuguese governors from pursuing private business interests or engaging directly in the slave trade, but it seems likely that some of the eight thousand prisoners taken in this conflict were eventually sold as slaves.[70] Reading such a notice, Sewall might have felt confident that the Luso-African rebels resisting Lisbon's rule were in the wrong and concluded that human chattels imported from Angola could lawfully be sold as slaves.[71]

But subsequent reports of colonial governors treating Africans disingenuously should have reminded Sewall of the need for narrative particulars beyond the labeling of "Rebels" and "Fomentors." When a white surgeon at the Cape of Good Hope "murdered one of these Hottentots," the Dutch governor there devised a scheme "in order to elude their severe tho' just Demand" for his execution. On a stage "not unlike that of a Mountebank's," the surgeon drank a bowl of flaming brandy "with counterfeit Symptoms of Terror and Confusion. . . . A few Minutes after he was pleased to die, and his Carcase was carried off in Pomp into the Factory to be buried, where he soon came to Life again" (*AWM* 1721/5/4). And in Sierra Leone an Englishman named Walter Charles, appointed chief factor or governor of Bunce Island by the Royal African Company, demonstrated a similar disregard for the local Luso-African community. Tired of routing trade through a prominent middleman named José Lopez de Moura, Charles "thought proper to treat this Man ill; and, on several Occasions, with infinite Contempt and Rigour; having seized his

Effects, surprized his Relations, and made Slaves of them." In response, Lopez and three hundred Africans "took the Factory without any Resistance, which they pillaged, and afterwards burnt to the Ground, carryed away all the Slaves that were in the Factory, as likewise the White People, whom they used with great Civility; and upon Application the latter were all released" (*BNL* 1729/5/29).[72] These detailed stories demonstrated, for a careful reader such as Sewall, the pitfalls of assuming that European governors sent to supervise trade could be trusted to act uprightly or that all those enslaved in Africa were lawful prisoners of war.

Of course, not all foreign bulletins were so fulsome as these; many provided only vague notices of important events, leaving readers to parse opaque phrases. For instance: if Sewall had somehow missed that first notice of war between the Portuguese and Luso-Africans at Angola or if his knowledge of African geography was incomplete, he might not have realized that a bulletin printed one year later, informing readers "that the Portuguieze and Natives of Gabenda were at War, and gave no Quarters on either Side," was an update on the same conflict (*BNL* 1722/4/23). Portugal had established trade relations with Cabinda, a coastal city just north of the Congo River and modern day Angola, at the end of the fifteenth century, but by the early eighteenth century, English and French traders offering superior goods and prices had displaced their Portuguese rivals. Portugal, in response, sent military expeditions to the coast, attempting to reassert its influence.[73] But this mention of hostilities at Cabinda would have told Sewall almost nothing useful about whether or not slaves arriving in Boston from southwest Africa had been taken lawfully, in a just war, unless he had some prior knowledge of the civil war at Angola.

Still, subsequent updates on the conflict between Cabinda and Portugal might have persuaded Sewall that slaves bought in the region were "*lawful Captives taken in those Wars.*"[74] In 1723 Portuguese forces persuaded their allies in Sonyo, a city in the Kingdom of Kongo just south of the Congo River's mouth, to join them in an assault on the Royal African Company's fort at Cabinda. Word of the impending attack reached Nurse Hereford, the Company's governor at Cabinda, from "the Mussuca" of Malimba to the north, who was "a Friend of the English." This Malimban leader warned Hereford that three hundred Portuguese sailors would "be joined by 150 Negroes from the Kingdom of Soana, who together with the Cabenda Indians, were to destroy the English Settlement." While negotiations between the English and Portuguese were still ongoing, "the Fort was attack'd by Land, and overpower'd with Numbers, insomuch that . . . the Fort was enter'd and plunder'd, the Portuguese Colours hoisted, and the Royal African Company's Ship stripp'd of all that was valuable, and then burnt." When Sewall learned, in 1724, that Hereford and thirty-six Englishmen who escaped this attack "would otherwise have been cut to pieces by the Negroes," he might have concluded that slaves imported from Cabinda could justly be sold as chattels, having attacked English nationals without warning and during the middle of peace negotiations (*AWM* 1724/8/20).[75] Hugh Thomas estimates that despite this setback for the Company, "English colonies, including those in North America, were probably getting a fifth of their slaves from this region," so knowledge gleaned from the newspaper of attacks on the English at Cabinda might have allowed Sewall to rationalize the sale of slaves imported from southwestern Africa.[76] Although he could not know the specific circumstances behind the enslavement of any single African imported from Cabinda, the newspaper provided Sewall with a narrative of unprovoked violence, allowing him to imagine that the otherwise anonymous men and boys arriving on Boston's docks had committed, of their own volition, a wanton act of war against Englishmen.

The story of Hereford's expulsion from Cabinda provided enslaved black Africans from the region with a history when they arrived in British colonies, but it also provided them with a character. The story casts residents of Cabinda and Sonyo as bloodthirsty—"would otherwise have been cut to pieces by the Negroes"—and untrustworthy, stereotypes perpetuated in other representations of black Africans. When Morocco descended into civil war in 1727, during a family dispute between two brothers named Abdelmalek and Ahmed ed-Dehebi over the throne, a division of black soldiers loyal to ed-Dehebi was often identified as the most potent and fearsome fighters on either side. They reportedly dispeopled an entire city, "all the Inhabitants having been put to the Sword" (*BNL* 1728/4/25). News reports emphasized the indiscriminate killing of these fighters: "the Blacks having taken Miquinez by Storm, and in the Action kill'd 300 Christian Slaves, 500 Jews, and 2000 Moors, that Muley Abdimeleck had fled towards Fez, but the Bashaw of the Blacks, with part of his Army were gone after him to cut off his Head, and present it to the Emperor Muley Hamet Deby" (*NEJ* 1728/11/4).[77] News from Africa made black men seem prone to gratuitous violence and deceit, and some in the Americas embraced that reputation. When forty-eight pirates "who were all Molattoes" were sentenced to death in Jamaica, they told stories of their exploits on the gallows, boasting "that they had eaten Eleven white men's hearts; and that they had 7 or 8 Prisoners taken out of Trading Vessels, whom they set in a Rank as close as they could stand together, to try how many they could kill with a Shot, who declared, They kill'd 3 men at a

Shot" (*BNL* 1723/4/11). Volunteering up tales of excessive violence and cruelty, these black pirates perpetuated a stereotype, and that stereotype gave every African arriving in the Americas an implicit backstory marked by hatred for white men and women.

Unfortunately, this reputation was also perpetuated in domestic news reports. During Sewall's lifetime, North American newspapers carried more than forty accounts of crimes committed in the colonies by Africans or their descendants.[78] These descriptions of criminal behavior were counterbalanced by just four news items representing black men and women as positive community influences.[79] In other words, the most widely distributed public record of black life in Sewall's lifetime suggested that Africans were almost ten times more likely to commit a crime than they were to promote social welfare. The black African inhabitants of Boston generally, and those newly arrived from Africa in particular, inherited from the public discourse a reputation for violence and deceit, a backstory over which their individual claims to humanity and freedom would be narrated.

From Abolition to Arson

Although Sewall enjoyed cordial relations with many of the city's black African residents, both bond and free, he was also the target of crimes attributed to black Bostonians; because the perpetrators remained largely anonymous, he could only imagine a motive for the attacks on his person and property. In the spring of 1723, arsonists fired several buildings in Boston and attempted to burn many more. The first blaze was lit in the predawn hours of Saturday March 30, when "a Fire broke out in the Buildings of *Elisha Cooke*, Esq; at the lower End of King-Street, which consumed 4 or 5 Tenements. And about the same time on Tuesday Morning, a House in Leverett's Lane near the Quaker's Meeting House, was set on Fire by a Negro Man Servant, of this Town, who, upon examination, own'd, that he had twice attempted to burn the said House" (*BNL* 1723/4/4). A rash of fires followed, and the very next one threatened Sewall's home. Two weeks after the first fires, on April 13, 1723, "a Fire broke out in the Barn of Mr. *David Deming* Collar maker, about 77 Feet to the Eastward of the Wooden part of Judge *Sewall's* dwelling House." Fruit trees growing between the two structures helped preserve Sewall's home, but the author of this news report—probably Sewall himself—declared, "Chiefly the Divine MERCY delivered us, from Unreasonable and Wicked men" (*BG* 1723/4/15). Sewall noted in his journal that the "Progress of the fire is mercifully staid" but said nothing of its origins; perhaps he wondered whether the fire was meant to threaten his home and whether the arsonist was one of the three black Africans he had sold on the docks just nine months earlier (*BNL* 1722/6/25).[80]

The threat of black African arsonists was familiar to Sewall and other Bostonians. Enslaved black Africans in New England set fire to their enslavers' homes and outbuildings throughout the seventeenth and eighteenth centuries: three Massachusetts homes were burnt by arsonists in 1681, and a Westfield barn full of livestock was set ablaze in 1754.[81] Fire was a convenient and often anonymous weapon easily accessible to the enslaved. But this rash of attacks brought to mind events that had taken place to the south a decade earlier, when arsonists attempted to burn down the city of New York in 1712. On that occasion, "Some Cormentine Negroes to the number of 25 or 30 and 2 or 3 Spanish Indians having conspired to murder all the Christians here, and by that means thinking to obtain their Freedom, about two a clock this morning put their bloody design in Execution, and setting fire to a House, they stood prepar'd with Arms to kill every body that approach'd to put it out, and accordingly barbarously murdered the following persons that were running to the fire, Viz Adrian Hoghland, Adrian Beeckman, Lieut. Corbet, Augustus Grasset, William Echt, —Marschalck Jun. —Brasier Jun. Johannes Low" (*BNL* 1712/4/14). When Boston began to burn in 1723, newspapers reported, "about 50 Men of the Militia are order'd to be ready with their Arms upon the Cry of Fire, least the Negros should make an Attempt upon the Lives of People who go to Extinguish it" (*NEC* 1723/4/15). Sewall and others in the city thought about their own experience of arson through the lens of this earlier incident in New York and took appropriate precautions to prevent a similarly fatal outcome for first responders.

Although the initial report out of New York in 1712 only implicated some thirty black African and Indian conspirators, the number of suspects ballooned rapidly. The next update indicated, "We have about 70 Negro's in Custody, and 'tis fear'd that most of the Negro's here (who are very numerous) knew of the Late Conspiracy to Murder the Christians." Some of these suspects were executed—burnt alive, hung, or broken on the wheel—while others committed suicide to escape torture (*BNL* 1712/4/21). The conspirators' attempts to win their freedom through violence cast suspicion on all the Indian and black African inhabitants of New York, leading to a figurative witch hunt; the last update published in the *News-letter* announced that "Nineteen Negroes of the Conspirators, who lately design'd to Murder the Christians here, have received Sentence of Death, and most of them are already Executed: There are several others of them in Custody to be Tryed next

Week" (*BNL* 1712/4/28). As an officiant in the 1692 witchcraft trials at Salem, where nineteen people were hanged, Sewall knew the dangerous power of a faceless narrative that could turn stereotypes into a sanction for violence against broad categories of people. He publicly repented of his role in the Salem executions, yet Sewall still contributed to the criminalization of race, prioritizing his own house and life over the rights of Boston's black African and Indian inhabitants.

After his house was threatened in 1723, Sewall participated in the public response to the fires. As a member of the Superior Court, he may have helped to question the first black African man imprisoned, who "accus'd 5 more of being concern'd with him, who were all examin'd and committed to Prison last Week"; two more were arrested on suspicion of setting a fire at a tanning yard, bringing the total number of incarcerated black African servants to seven (*NEC* 1723/4/15). Then, in response to the continued threat of arson, Sewall advised Governor William Dummer to offer a reward for information leading to the capture of the "*villanous & desperate* Negroes" responsible, lest they "burn and destroy" all of Boston. On April 16, the proclamation was read publicly, declaring "*whosoever shall discover the said Offenders so as that they be rendered to Justice, and by Law convicted of the said Crimes, such Persons shall have as a Reward for their good Service therein the Sum of* Fifty Pounds, *to be paid to them out of the Publick Treasury; and if any Person who has been concern'd in the said Facts or an Accomplice therein, (whether Negro or otherwise,) shall make Discovery as aforesaid, He shall be pardoned & indemnified as to his said Offence, and notwithstanding entitled to the above-mentioned Reward*" (*BNL* 1723/4/18). Black Bostonians present when the bill was read took umbrage and were arrested. On the corner of School Street, "a Negro who stood to hear it, cry'd out, *A Bite, a Bite* and was immediately seized"—eight were now imprisoned for the fires, and the burning would not stop.[82] The following evening, on Wednesday April 17, a brand was thrown into Bartholomew Green's printing house; the *News-Letter*, which published Dummer's proclamation, had become a target of the unrest (*NEC* 1723/4/22). Green's office was located on Newbury Street, a short distance from Sewall's home, and the judge must have wondered when his home would again be targeted.

Sewall would not have to wait long. The next evening his son, the Reverend Joseph Sewall, addressed the crisis publicly during his Thursday night lecture at Old South Church, and his remarks were inflammatory enough that a black African arsonist attempted to burn down his father's home in response. Another minister, Samuel Dexter, attended the lecture and wrote in his diary, "18. I went to B: Lecture—Mr. Sewal preached from ye 4 Psal: 4.

Stand in Awe & sin not. He made an Excellent discourse, particularly Occasioned by ye Late fires yt have broke out in Boston, supposed to be purposely set by ye Negroes. Ye Lord seems to have a Controversy with his People & is makeing some of ye vilest Instruments a scourge to us. Do we do our duty to ym. The Lord make us more watchfull & Carefull."[83] Although Dexter heard a sermon exhorting the white inhabitants of Boston to be more dutiful in their care for "ye Negroes," his diary also preserves the racially charged language used by Joseph Sewall to describe black Bostonians. Sewall may have intended his sermon to be a conciliatory gesture acknowledging the grievances of enslaved black Africans, but at least one of his auditors thought the preacher's words offensive.

Joseph Sewall's sermon survives, and it dwells at length on both the duties incumbent on white Christian slave owners and the bodily labor of their black African servants. Recognizing that enslaved black Africans have been burdened with a weighty physical and spiritual load, he questions why God must ask "ye soul to bare so much burden," before concluding that "thus he might help make the soul to brake of [off] from sin."[84] Joseph Sewall characterizes the bondage and burdens of black Bostonians as inducements to repentance, citing Matthew 11:28, "Come unto me, all ye that labour and are heavy laden, and I will give you rest."[85] Throughout the sermon, he calls on enslaved black Africans to lay down the burden of sin and look forward to a day when they will, through God's mercy, be freed of their loads.

Those loads are associated by Joseph Sewall with the black body. He suggests that the black bodies of enslaved Africans are themselves burdens to be cast aside in a spiritual and physical whitewashing; anticipating the confession of the arsonists or their conspirators, he writes,

> thar is or may be [that] God may
> haste mercy and recovery—
> thar is a hope maintained in sum Ne
> gro or other that day [uphold] the soul
>
> 3 the experiences of other day helps
> much to serundur them.
>
> [symbol] The riches of the grace of X is
> a s[u]pport unto the soule 1 isah 18 tho[86]

This passage of the sermon points to the proclamation published by his father and Dummer the "other day" as an inducement for "sum Negro" to confess ("serunder" or "surrender"), promising that all who do admit their guilt will be forgiven of their sins. But the terms of forgiveness are framed by Joseph Sewall in the racialized language of Isaiah 1:18—"Come now, and let us reason together, saith the Lord: though your sins be as scarlet, they shall be white as snow; though they be red like crimson, they shall be as wool." Implicit in his promise of whiteness is both a condemnation of blackness as well as an offer of racial ascension, by which confessing black African sinners might transcend the limitations of their stigmatized physiques.[87]

This sermon, like Dummer's proclamation, was meant to be understood as an offer of emancipation. In a city where enslaved black Africans were valued at thirty pounds a head, a reward of fifty pounds meant freedom—the chance for a man and a woman to redeem themselves from servitude with enough money left over to purchase passage for Africa, England, or any other port in the Atlantic world.[88] So Joseph Sewall used words like *freedom* and *liberty* often in his sermon, reminding his black auditors of what was at stake. Paraphrasing Philippians 2:6, he describes Jesus in terms that foreground the possibility of emancipation and social ascension: "Tho he was in a form of a servant he thought it no robrey to be equal with God." Christ ascended through the resurrection, and he suggests that the slave who informs will likewise be transfigured. Joseph Sewall quotes Philippians 3:21 to argue that, like Jesus, servants may become physiologically empowered—white—through the mercy of Christ "who shall change our vile body, that it may be fashioned like unto his glorious body."[89] This passage is, presumably, one of the reasons Dexter's sermon notes refer to black Bostonians as "ye vilest Instruments"—his offer of physical and spiritual freedom is predicated on a worldview that treats black African bodies and souls as liabilities, handicaps in the search for civilization and salvation.

Joseph Sewall probably considered his sermon a diplomatic overture to the black Africans of Boston, and surely some regarded his sermon as an expression of pastoral concern. On two separate occasions, in 1748 and then in 1764, black African women named Phillis Cogswell and Flora used the Isaiah passage cited by Sewall to describe the color of their own sins and, presumably, to express their desire that they be made white. Phillis declared that "come now and let us reason together saith the Lord tho' your sins be as scarlet, seemed to be comforting Texts," and Flora mourned that "as to my Sin . . . I have seen it to be of a Crimson Colour & of a Scarlet Die."[90] And at Joseph Sewall's death in 1769, the enslaved Senegambian poet Phillis Wheatley Peters wrote, "I too have cause this mighty loss to mourn, / For he my monitor will not return" (lines 48–49); the reverend was her trusted advisor, and undoubtedly other members of the black community in Boston thought of him in similar terms.[91] But on April 18, 1723, at least one of his listeners took offense at the racialized language of his sermon and expressed contempt for Sewall's message by attempting to burn the minister's childhood home. After the Thursday lecture ended, Judge Sewall retired to his house on Newbury street, where "a Negro was seen attempting to set Fire to Mr. Holbrook's House" (*NEC* 1723/4/22). The would-be arsonist was forced to flee before he could accomplish his purposes and was never captured, but the Sewalls—and not Holbrook—were likely the intended targets. Samuel Sewall lived next door to "neighbour Holbrook"; he was also a member of the governor's council that had established a reward for capture of the arsonists and the father of a tone-deaf preacher who had just promised the physical and spiritual benefits of whiteness to any black African informant willing to betray the arsonists.[92] For at least a few of Boston's black African residents, Samuel Sewall was not the famous abolitionist we know from *The Selling of Joseph* or the friend of Sebastian, Jane, Adam, and Basilio—he was a slave trader and the public face of an oppressive legal system.

That legal system would only become more oppressive in response to this attempt on the judge's life. The next day, Friday April 19, 1723, the city of Boston adopted new laws regulating the behavior of "Indians Negros and Molattos within this Town." Among other provisions, this new code prohibited meetings between free people of color and the enslaved; outlawed their possession of firearms; required free black Africans and American Indians to bind out their children as servants; instituted a curfew for servants and the enslaved; and made gatherings of two or more enslaved persons a punishable offense. Most important, with respect to the recent rash of fires, the new laws made it a crime for black African and Indian servants to be seen in the street after a fire alarm sounded. The official justification for these laws echoes Dexter's notes from the previous evening's sermon, declaring that they were drafted because "Sundry fires haue of late broke out among us to the great Terror & Affrightment of the Inhabitants, which we haue too Just grounds to beleiue were wickedly contrived and Designed by Some Evel Instruments."[93] Evil instruments, vile instruments, vile bodies—the black African inhabitants of Boston had been judged by Joseph Sewall, and the attack on his father only consolidated public opinion against both free and enslaved communities of color.

In a real though figurative sense, Samuel Sewall was the author of Boston's oppressive 1723 slave code as well as *The Selling of Joseph*. Sewall pushed the governor to establish a reward for the arsonist's capture, and that reward provoked an attempt to burn down the printing house that published it. Then he sat in the pews and watched as his son used the reward to provoke the arsonists with promises of whiteness. His home was threatened after the sermon, and the next day a new slave code was passed. Sewall was at the center of events culminating in those new laws criminalizing the routine movements and gatherings of black Africans and American Indians.

The arsonist who tried to burn down his home was never identified, never caught—and the threat of an anonymous black African criminal willing to attack Sewall in his home led Boston's most prominent citizens to pass laws governing the travel and interactions of all nonwhite residents. In the absence of a protagonist who could be imprisoned and executed, this faceless slave narrative became a backstory attributed to every black African and Indian inhabitant of Boston. A tenth servant was imprisoned in May, and two of the ten were executed that month (*NEC* 1723/5/6; *NEC* 1723/5/27; *BG* 1723/5/13). Of the remaining eight black African suspects, seven were cleared and the eighth was executed in July (*NEC* 1723/6/17; *BNL* 1723/7/11). The fires stopped burning when the executions began, but their impact—in the form of the new slave code and a new fear of the city's colored residents—would be felt by both the black and the white inhabitants of Boston for years to come. That slave code is a part of the narrative, the story of the arsonist who threatened Sewall's life and lived to tell about it. This fractured, synthetic, faceless narrative—compiled from the newspaper, Dexter's diary, Sewall's sermon, and city ordinances—is a story that lived in the imagination of Sewall and every other white Bostonian during the spring of 1723, and it preserves the struggle of at least one man for revenge, for his own freedom, and for the freedom of Boston's black community.

Scipio's Emancipation

Sewall's legacy as an abolitionist is fraught with exceptions and complications. He participated in the slave trade, and he was at the center of arson cases leading to the rollback of civil rights for Indians and black Africans, yet there is no evidence he ever held enslaved persons for their labor, and he helped more than one win his freedom. In 1714 Sewall wrote in his journal that an enslaved black African named "Cophee tells me he gives Mr. Pemberton £40. for his Time, that he might be with his wife. I gave him 5ˢ to help him."[94] The case of Adam is well known and oft discussed, but his kindnesses to Coffee and Basilio are less frequently cited, and in addition to his efforts on behalf of these three enslaved men, Sewall played a part in the emancipation of Scipio—a black African servant who appears frequently in the pages of his journal.

Because Scipio ran errands for Sewall so frequently, Margaret Newell and others have argued that he was owned by Sewall.[95] But Scipio was actually the legal property of Sewall's son-in-law, Grove Hirst. The first mention of Scipio in Sewall's journal comes on December 15, 1708. Inclement weather led the judge to extend a visit to the Hirst family, and when Sewall left, he gave a small remembrance to Scipio and to each of the other servants who helped to care for him during his stay.[96] Five years later, Sewall recorded that "Scipio comes and tells me that my daughter Hirst is brought to Bed of a son. I give him a good shilling."[97] But Sewall's daughter Elizabeth died in 1716, and Grove Hirst followed her to the grave a year later, on October 28, 1717. Three days before his death, Hirst dictated his last will and testament to Sewall, specifying "That my Negro Man Scipio shall have his Manumission or freedom at the Expiration of Four years after my decease, at which time my desire is That my Exocrs give him twenty Pounds out of my Estate."[98] Dictating his will to a father-in-law who was both a slave trader and Boston's leading antislavery activist, Hirst may have felt some pressure to emancipate Scipio. The will does not specify who was to receive the benefit of Scipio's labor during his remaining four years of indentured service, but Sewall became the executor charged with delivering Hirst's bequest to Scipio, and the judge took on the enslaved human property of his son-in-law as a servant after Hirst's funeral.

For the rest of his life, Scipio lived with and worked for Sewall. He traveled with him regularly and occasionally ran errands. Four years after Hirst's death, Sewall "delivered Scipio his Money which he delivered me to keep for him: and gave him my Bond to pay him £20. with Interest at 5 per Cent" a year later. Sewall delayed discharging his debt to Scipio, but that may well have been done at his servant's request—Scipio had saved enough money over the years that he asked Sewall to hold his funds and likely felt little immediate need for twenty pounds. Indeed, he was probably glad for the chance to improve upon his capital. After Scipio's formal manumission in 1721, he continued living in the garret of Sewall's home; together, the two looked up at the skies on November 27, 1722, and observed an eclipse of the moon.[99] During the fires of 1723 Scipio, along with Sewall, probably breathed a sigh of relief each time a Newbury Street blaze was extinguished, and in the aftermath of that crisis, Scipio probably ran Sewall's errands with more caution, careful to carry a pass from Sewall if he was out alone at night or visiting other free black Bostonians. And then, on January 6, 1725, Scipio died; his errands for the judge and his travels across the Massachusetts countryside came to an end. Sewall mourned the death of a servant and friend who had been "a Staff to Support me in my age"; he probably "made a good Fire, set Chairs, and gave Sack" to those paying Scipio their last respects, as he did when another free black African named Boston passed away.[100]

The story of Scipio's journey to freedom is written in Sewall's own hand: first in his probate records, where the will of Grove Hirst is recorded, and then in his diary. Although the narrative of Scipio's emancipation is less dramatic than Adam's or Basilio's, Scipio was no less free at its end, and all three stories survive in a tangled web of documents that must be collated by readers before they become legible. This process of discontinuous reading and the piecing together of narratives is today the province of scholars, but in the eighteenth century it was commonplace. Every day Sewall and other North American colonists compiled reports in the newspaper, snatches of gossip in a letter, and information gleaned from other texts into a larger story. In the case of enslaved individuals such as Adam, Basilio, Scipio, and the anonymous arsonist who made multiple attempts to burn down Sewall's home, that larger story was a slave narrative. Sewall constructed synthetic slave narratives for slaves like Basilio petitioning for their freedom. And *The Selling of Joseph* suggests that he investigated, as best he could, the particulars of the black Africans he bought and sold in the marketplace, laboring to convince himself that their bondage, like that of Abraham's servant, was "lawful and good"—because the enslaved were imported from Cabinda or because they had committed crimes in another colony. The slave-for-sale advertisements placed by Sewall in the newspaper are a counternarrative calling the judge's abolitionist bona fides into question, but they are also an invitation to recover the narratives of slavery that he and other colonists preserved in court records, diaries, letters, ship logs, and annotated newspapers.

CHAPTER TWO

Daniel and the Scotts

The Serialized Stories of Serial Runaways

Samuel Sewall's diary, letter books, court records, and other papers provide multiple mentions of enslaved individuals such as Scipio and Immanuel Basilio, enabling imaginative readers to track their lives and their experience of bondage across time and space. But these two men are exceptional cases; most mentions of the enslaved in documents surviving from the early eighteenth century are singular and anonymous. In many cases, the language of one slave-for-sale or runaway slave advertisement is the only surviving record of an enslaved man or woman's life.

The slavers describing these individuals occasionally wrote with enough specificity that colonial readers, who examined the newspaper thoughtfully and with enough attention to detail that they sometimes altered the language or corrected the grammar of a slave-for-sale advertisement, could imagine with some vividness an enslaved individual's present circumstances and past misfortunes. Evidence of colonists reading the classifieds closely lingers in their marginalia. One painstaking reader inserted a comma after the word *Child* in this advertisement from the *Boston News-Letter*: "A Lusty Young Negro Woman aged about Eighteen Years, and her Child[,] to be Sold at Mr. Adam Beath's in Union Street, Boston."[1] Both child and mother would, apparently, be sold—a fact important enough to the reader that she felt a need to intervene textually. When Sewall read of "A Very likely Negro Lad, aged about Fifteen Years, to be Sold by Messieurs Whittemore and Willard," he crossed out the first two letters of the word *Negro* before stopping his pen; perhaps he knew that the youth had a white father and thought him too fair skinned to be described in that way (*BNL* 1716/12/3).[2] Another reader, likely interested in purchasing a black African servant advertised by John Frizel "and to be seen at his House in Fleet-Street, Boston," underlined the words *Fleet-Street*—a reminder to stop at Frizel's home on his way to Old North Church or the shipyards, perhaps (*BNL* 1720/10/17). Eighteenth-century readers combed through advertisements with the same care that they read notices of foreign politics, and sometimes they were rewarded with a compelling story. While scholars have mined these advertisements for quantitative data, their moving narrative depths have in large part been left unplumbed.[3]

TABLE 2.1 Slave-for-sale advertisements in Massachusetts, 1712–1714

	1712	*1713*	*1714*
# of Advertisements	25	31	40
# of Slaves Advertised for Sale	28	50	77

Most slave-for-sale advertisements are terse communications of essential economic facts, but the prose sometimes grows more magniloquent, and a biography—a narrative of slavery—emerges from the classifieds. This 1728 advertisement, for example, strays well beyond essential economic facts: "*A Negro Man, about twenty five years old, that has been in the Country about fourteen years, and has had the Small Pox: A strong fellow for any Work without doors, and excelling in all manner of houshold Work; washing, baking, dressing meats or rooms, waiting, &c.: Only given to drink, and wanting a severe Master, not us'd to the whip: To be Sold: Enquire of the Printer hereof.*"[4] Although he is unnamed, the protagonist of this life story is otherwise knowable in a way that most inhabitants of the eighteenth-century Atlantic world—whether black or white—are not. His narrative was penned by a man now even more anonymous than he is, and the survival of his story, rather than his enslaver's, is itself a mark of the success with which this man contested the terms of his bondage.

Although we know that this young man was born in approximately 1703, the advertisement offers readers no clue to the location of his birth or the origin of his ancestors; he may have been born free in Africa or into captivity in the West Indies. Whether he was kidnapped during childhood or raised a chattel, he arrived at Boston in 1714 as an eleven-year-old boy and a stranger to New England. His arrival coincided with the end of the War of the Spanish Succession, at a moment when Britain—now in possession of the *assiento* from Spain—had a greater incentive to participate in the slave trade than at any point in its history. An increase in the volume of the British slave trade is evident in the number of slave-for-sale advertisements placed in Boston between 1712 and 1714 and the total number of slaves offered for sale in those advertisements (see table 2.1). Either directly or indirectly, this boy arrived in Massachusetts as a result of the War of the Spanish Succession—a truth that colonial newspaper readers would have understood intuitively. More important, because of that global conflict, he arrived as part of the largest cohort of imported black African adolescents in Massachusetts history to that point. In 1714, twenty-seven "Negro Boys" were sold by Sewall, Frizell, and other Boston merchants (*BNL* 1714/9/13). This young man may have been the "Pretty

Negro Boy aged about Twelve years" (*BNL* 1714/1/17), or the boy sold in conjunction with the ship *Hanover* and its inventory, or any one of the other two dozen young men sold that year (*BNL* 1714/9/27). His story was a subplot in the larger narrative of Boston's booming trade in human chattels.

Those who read the slave-for-sale advertisement would have dated his experience of smallpox to the outbreak of 1721, which drove Boston to a frenzied debate over the efficacy and ethics of inoculation. Perhaps he knew Onesimus, the freeman once enslaved by Cotton Mather, whose descriptions of smallpox inoculation in Africa persuaded Mather of the practice's efficacy. However, unlike Onesimus, this young man was never inoculated and so contracted smallpox along with many others in the city.[5] After catching the disease he spent days isolated from all human contact, scratching at red pustules, and when he finally emerged from quarantine, he bore visible scars attesting to his suffering on his cheeks and on his arms. Like the Huguenot galley slaves in France who were forced to bury victims of the plague, his new immunity to smallpox and his status as a bondsman probably meant that he was called upon to bury Boston's dead and to care for those enduring quarantine.[6] Alternatively, handling the recently dead may have been the reason he caught the disease in the first place.

By the time he contracted smallpox he had already learned to bake and was accustomed to a variety of household chores; he waited at table and then washed the dishes or clothes that were dirtied there before eating his own meal, separately. He also spent enough time working outdoors, whether in a garden or as a hired laborer, to win the reputation of a "*strong fellow.*" At age twenty, only recently recovered from his brush with smallpox, this nameless young man watched Boston burn in the arson attacks of April 1723. The timing of those fires—which were kindled just as the cohort of adolescent boys that was sold in 1714 reached adulthood—is suggestive; he likely knew one or more of the arsonists and may have participated in the attacks himself. Here, again, his story blends into the larger tale of slavery's expansion in Boston, because whether he helped to start the fires or merely watched them rage, he, like the rest of Boston's black African population, suffered the consequences. With the passage and enforcement of Boston's 1723 slave code, he found whatever autonomy he had previously enjoyed curtailed. Unable to socialize with his peers or move freely, he undoubtedly experienced a heightened sense of depression. Drinking, perhaps to escape the difficulties of his situation, he eventually discovered that his master was reluctant to dispense corporal punishment and, emboldened, found new ways to resist his authority. All of this larger life narrative was accessible to thoughtful readers living in Boston, who had lived through the smallpox epidemic and the fires and the influx of black African bodies after Great Britain secured the *assiento,* and who would not have needed to consult the archive in reconstructing his life.

This man's biography, though brief, demanded the pathos of such readers, at least some of whom, like Joseph Addison, were predisposed to shed a tear over advertisements recounting the sufferings of servants and slaves. And yet: engaging as his story may be, it is also fleeting and ephemeral—the anonymous individual memorialized in this advertisement never resurfaces in the public record. His story ends, abruptly, almost before it began. Colonial newspapers generally reported on the movements and deeds of celebrities— royals, pirates, captains, and preachers—whose life stories could be traced by readers across multiple issues over the course of years. But most of the anonymous black African men and women whose actions are reported in a colonial newspaper never resurfaced in the print record; like this "*strong fellow*" who escaped the whip, they disappeared into the margins of a weekly paper published for white subscribers.

Only a few who endured slavery managed to achieve a degree of local celebrity, allowing those who read the newspaper or listened while it was read aloud to follow their stories across the weeks, months, and even years. For example the escape, capture, trial, and execution of "the Negro Cora, (who kill'd Mr. Aquilla Hall)" in Maryland was described over a matter of six months in newspapers up and down the coast (*NEJ* 1729/6/23). Cora shot Hall with a gun in 1728, "on Christmas Day in the Morning, as he was walking in his Orchard." He had escaped from Hall some time earlier, but rather than running to freedom, Cora "lay in Ambush" and took revenge on his master. In a previous, unsuccessful attempt on Hall's life, Cora had "struck at him with an Ax, which cut him over the Eye brows, and had certainly split his Skull, if he had not suddenly mov'd his Head"; this time, he succeeded in killing his former captor.[7] Three months later the newspaper reported that Cora had been caught and that he had confessed to murdering Hall (*MG* 1729/4/8). Sentenced to have his body hung in chains after his execution, Cora's death was made "a Means to terrify such wicked Wretches from the like Practices for the future" (*MG* 1729/4/22). His notoriety was so great that when Cora's brother, "the Mulatto Man Joe," ran away twenty years later and shot his own enslaver, Edward Taylor, as Taylor pursued him (*MG* 1751/1/2), the newspapers identified Joe as a "brother to him who was hang'd some Years ago for shooting Mr. Aquila Hall, in Baltimore County" (*MG* 1750/12/19).[8] A memory of Cora's life lingered in the colonial imagination long after his execution because the serialized stories of runaways, and especially the stories of serial runaways, who escaped from their masters repeatedly, captured the attention and imagination of readers, who remembered these local celebrities for decades.

By publishing the serialized stories of these serial runaways, newspapers encouraged readers to trace the lives and movements of enslaved individuals over time in the same way that they followed the exploits of infamous pirates or the movements of royalty. David Waldstreicher has argued that individual runaway slave advertisements ought to be recognized as slave narratives because each memorializes moments of black African agency and resistance in print.[9] However, despite a widespread interest in reproducing runaway slave advertisements, scholars have been relatively slow to give these texts the interpretive attention that Waldstreicher suggests they deserve, perhaps because the narrative arc of any single newspaper advertisement is necessarily limited by the medium's brevity.[10] But serial runaways provided colonial readers and, now, modern scholars, with multiple installments in the narrative of their lives, and the advertisements themselves often encouraged newspaper subscribers to link one escape attempt with another. These serialized stories of resistance provided many colonial readers with their first sustained narrative encounters with slavery, and they offer scholars new opportunities to trace the representation of bondage, resistance, and black African agency across time and space. Newspaper readers exercised their imaginations in reconstructing the life and movements of these individuals from sequential but disconnected textual fragments; if scholars are to profit from their example, we must learn to do likewise.

Finding a Runaway (Again)

The serialization of these stories demanded discontinuous reading, as narratives were suspended and then resumed at irregular intervals, when news reached the publisher. For instance, the escape of "a Negroe Man Named *Stephen,* a Cooper by Trade" unfolded over the course of five weeks (*MG* 1728/12/24). Seven days after word of Stephen's escape appeared in the *Maryland Gazette,* a second advertisement was published:

> Stolen out of the Stable of Mr. *Geo. Neilson,* in *Annapolis,* this Day Fortnight at Night, a Bay Horse, about 14 Hands and a half high, branded on the near Shoulder and Buttock, with the Letters AP joyn'd close together, with a Sprigg Tail, and his Fore Feet newly shod. Whoever secures the said Horse to Mr. *Neilson* aforesaid, shall have Half a Pistole *Reward;* paid by *Geo. Neilson.*

> N.B. *'Tis suspected he was taken away by a Negro, belonging to* Cha. Carroll, *Esq; who ran away about the same Time, and was advertis'd in the last Week's Gazette.* (MG 1728/12/31)

The next chapter in Stephen's story appeared in an unexpected place—as an addendum to an advertisement for a missing horse. Its placement there presumes that readers will consume the entire newspaper and recognize seemingly unrelated snippets of news as continuations of an earlier narrative. When Stephen was discovered, four weeks later, "harbour'd at the Plantations of the Hon. *Charles Calvert,* Esq; in *Prince George's* County, by the Negroes there, and the Overseer (who is a Negroe)," the conclusion of his story was narrated with only a passing reference to previous events (*MG* 1729/1/21). The reader's familiarity with earlier chapters in Stephen's escape from slavery is taken for granted: readers are expected to retain Stephen's anecdotal history in their memories for a month or twelve months or more, until his story can be continued or concluded. In this way, serialization cultivated a narrative and imaginative awareness of black African lives, asking readers to anticipate the next installment in an indefinite series of updates on the adventures of each runaway.

A desire for freedom brought serial runaways into the public gaze again and again, but these recurring cameos in the public spotlight did not always translate into the celebrity enjoyed by Stephen or Cora. Many runaway slave advertisements never mention the escapee's name, and even when an enslaved person is identified by name, it can be difficult to determine whether the recurrence of that name indicates a continuation of an earlier story or the arrival of another, a different black servant similarly called Caesar or Pompey or John by his white enslaver.[11] To wit: in June 1724, John Gibbs placed the following advertisement: "*RAN-away from his Master, Mr.* John Gibbs, *Painter in Boston, A Negro Boy named* Jemy Conungo, *about Twelve Years old, well set. He had on when he went away, a Speckled Linnen Shirt, a pair of Canvas Breeches, open at the Knees, without Shoes or Stockings. He caried with him a Canvas Jacket, and a Cotton Shirt*" (BG 1724/6/29). The advertisement ran for a month, and Gibbs eventually raised the proffered reward from forty shillings to the princely sum of ten pounds—much more than was typically offered for the return of a runaway (BG 1724/7/6). Jemy might have escaped permanently, but another advertisement, published a year later, suggests that he was likely recaptured and sold to another local artisan: "RAN away on the 7th of this Instant June, from Mr. Henry Lawson, of Boston, Taylor, a likely Negro Boy, named Jemmy, about 14 Years old: He has on a dark Frize Jacket, Leather

Breeches, and Leather heel'd Shoes, but no Stockings, Hat nor Cap."[12] Since both runaways hail from Boston, both are named Jemy [Jemmy], and both were born in approximately the same year (1711 or 1712), it seems likely the two advertisements narrate the resistance of a single enslaved boy over the course of a year, during which he escaped twice and was sold once.

Jemy's case is fairly clear-cut, if ultimately impossible to resolve definitively; that of his companion, Caesar, is more complicated. Two weeks after Jemy ran from Gibbs, another enslaved young man ran from the painter: "*RAN away on the 6ᵗʰ Instant, a Negro Man, named Cesar, about 22 Years of Age, of a middle Stature, and well set. Had on a dirty Cotton and Linnen Shirt, and Ozenbriggs Breeches, open at the Knees. He took with him an old Cherridery Jacket a striped red and White Woollen Cap, without Shoes or Stockings. Note, He is wont to hid on board Vessels, unknown to the Commanders, in order to get off*" (*BG* 1724/7/13). Caesar's escape from Gibbs provides additional context for Jemy's decision to run away. As the two lived and worked together, Caesar certainly told the younger man of his multiple escape attempts, and Jemy's decision to run away—repeatedly—can probably be traced back to Caesar's tutelage. Both Caesar and Jemy were serial runaways, but was the Caesar who left Gibbs in 1724 the same man whose disappearance was advertised in Boston by the royal customs collector John Jekyll four years earlier? Jekyll's Caesar was seventeen, so as in Jemy's case, the age, location, and name of each runaway matches; but Caesar was a far more popular name than Jemy, so the likelihood that both advertisements describe a single man is slightly lower (*BG* 1720/1/18). In addition to Jemy and Caesar, there are three other pairs of colonial newspaper advertisements between 1704 and 1729 that probably describe the iterative escape attempts of a single individual: Jack (described as a short well-set fellow in both *AWM* 1720/7/21 and *AWM* 1722/9/27); Timothy ("*Named* Jupeter, *but calls himself by the Name of* Timothy" in *BNL* 1726/12/29 and "*Named* Timothy, *commonly called* Tim" in *BNL* 1727/8/24); and Peter (a Philadelphia-area runaway around thirty years old in *AWM* 1728/3/14 and *AWM* 1729/12/23).

Each of these five probable matches provides a two-part narrative that invites imaginative readings. Jack, for instance, escapes the second time with "a brindled Dog," perhaps because he thought the dog would provide protection in fighting off the dogs that tracked him down during his first escape or as a help in hunting game, for food (*AWM* 1722/9/27). Both of the advertisements for Timothy call attention to the authority exercised by those who styled themselves masters, in naming the enslaved, and the resistance of an enslaved man who insisted on his right to self-determination, forgoing the name imposed by his enslaver for one of his own choosing. And Peter apparently acquired a "Scar of a Cut over his Left Eye" between his first escape attempt in March 1728 and his second, in December 1729 (*AWM* 1729/12/23). A runaway who was caught could acquire several new distinguishing features as masters beat or branded runaways like Peter for their disobedience, hoping that the resulting scars would facilitate identification in the event of a second or third escape attempt.

In addition to these five probable repeat runaways, another eight individuals definitely escaped on multiple occasions between 1704 and 1730: Daniel (*BNL* 1712/9/29, *BNL* 1714/5/24, *BNL* 1714/8/23); Harry (*BNL* 1711/12/31, *BNL* 1713/6/29); Jack (*AWM* 1723/8/8, *AWM* 1725/6/3, *AWM* 1726/9/22); Jethro (*BNL* 1719/9/28, *BNL* 1720/9/5); Lester (*BNL* 1712/2/9, *BNL* 1713/6/29); Peter (*BNL* 1705/12/10, *BNL* 1714/6/14); Quam (*AWM* 1722/6/21, *AWM* 1723/6/13); and Zipporah (*BNL* 1717/5/6, *BNL* 1718/10/6, *BNL* 1720/6/9). In other words, notice of a second or third escape attempt was fairly commonplace in colonial newspapers, regularly providing readers with the opportunity to read narratively across issues, in the same way that they were already accustomed to following the movements and exploits of a single runaway like Stephen or those of public figures in Europe—anecdotally, over the course of years, and with significant gaps in reporting. These serialized narratives of slavery featured unlikely alliances, the promise of violence, and unresolved endings, so they often made for compelling reading.

Runaway slave advertisements engage readers because they are narratives in search of both a beginning and an end, so they naturally generate questions about why the enslaved person is running and where—as well as other, more particularized inquiries.[13] Zipporah, an enslaved Indian woman about thirty-five years old, fled with an Irishman twelve years her junior on her third escape attempt, and readers must have wondered if the pair was romantically engaged. Quam persuaded three different white men to run with him on two separate occasions and took several guns with him on his second attempt; whether and how those guns would be used, in the event his party was overtaken by their enslavers, was an open question. In many cases, of course, readers never learned the end of the story, much less its beginning; they probably never discovered whether Zipporah and her Irish companion formed a lasting attachment or what became of Quam and the guns he took with him. An occasional well-publicized capture (as in the case of Stephen) notwithstanding, the runaway slave advertisement is typically an open-ended narrative form. Serial runaways provided readers with a unique sense of both closure and continuation. The second and third advertisements necessarily offered an update or end to the story of the first escape attempt, satisfying the reader's curiosity about earlier events even as they tantalized with the possibilities of a new chapter in the life of a runaway.

Narrated in the classifieds of the *Boston News-Letter* over the course of a decade, the serialized story of Peter's life illustrates the way in which serial runaways provided readers with both the excitement of an unresolved storyline and a sense of narrative continuity. Peter's entrance onto the public stage was announced on December 10, 1705: "RAN-away from his Master William Pepperil Esqr. at Kittery, in the Prvince of Maine, a Negro Man-Slave named Peter, aged about 20, speaks good English, of a pretty brown Complexion, middle Stature."[14] This particular advertisement provides relatively little in the way of a narrative, but it is immediately followed by a second notice, informing readers that "an Indian Man (under the Command of Cap. Joseph Brown) named Isaac Pummatick, was seen at Newbury, in Company with the above Runaway Negro." Together, these two, deserter and runaway, escaping from different forms of unfreedom, provide a more interesting array of narrative possibilities: Did one persuade the other to flee, or did they meet on the road, after each had escaped of his own volition? Would Pummatick's knowledge of local American Indian communities provide Peter entrée into Indian villages or access to their paths through the woods as the two sought their freedom? However they managed it—perhaps by stowing away on the *Thomas*, which left Boston for Currituck in the Province of Carolina a few weeks later (*BNL* 1705/12/17)—Pummatick and Peter made their way to South Carolina, where they discovered that local readers were familiar with their story and eager to write its ending. There, Governor Philip Ludwell secured the runaways and sent notice of their capture to the readers (and slavers) anxiously awaiting the next chapter in their adventure: "In *December* last, There was Advertisements of a Negro man Slave, and an Indian's Running away from Mr. *William Pepperil* of Kittery in the Province of Main, desiring they might be apprehended where ever they came, and by vertue of said Advertisements coming (in the News Letter) to *South-Caralonia*, whither the said Negro and Indian had travelled, The Governour of said place has secured the said Runaways for the Owner" (*BNL* 1706/4/22). The story of Pummatick and Peter's partnership came to an abrupt end after four short months, almost before it began.

But in the years that followed, Peter—who would attempt to escape from bondage at least twice more—authored new chapters in his narrative for the *News-Letter*'s patient and far-flung readership. In the summer of 1712, he attempted to run from Ebenezer Hubbard of Middletown, Connecticut. Once more, he seems to have made his escape as part of a group, leaving Middletown at approximately the same time as three other servants: "Two Negro Men" and "A Spanish Indian Man." But Hubbard's description of Peter provides a coda to the story of his escape with Pummatick; he writes that Peter possesses "a Skare on the back of one of his hands near the Nuckles, with a Slit on one of his Ears"—the former injury possibly suffered in self-defense while running, and the latter meted out as a punishment for his first escape attempt (*BNL* 1712/8/18). Readers might have imagined a South Carolina fistfight in which Peter resisted recapture and the angry response of Governor Ludwell, who ordered his ear slit in retaliation.[15]

This third installment in Peter's history also left readers waiting, again, for a resolution to Peter's story: Would he find freedom in this new, collaborative escape attempt? If recaptured, what injuries would he sustain this time? Answers arrived with the June 14, 1714, issue of the *News-Letter*: Peter had escaped a third time and was, yet again, worse for the wear. The man from whom he ran this time, Joseph Tuck of Beverly, warns readers that Peter "goes a little Lame, lost his Fore-upper Teeth" and fills in missing chapters from his history, reminding readers that Peter "was formerly Servant to Mr. *Pepperel* of Kittery, Mr. *Boreman* Tanner in Cambridge, Mr. *Morecock* in Boston, and Mr. *Hubbard* of Middleton." This list of those who previously claimed a legal right to Peter's person, which includes two men potentially unknown to the *News-Letter*'s readership, invites subscribers to remember and reconstruct Peter's past; his newest description is a forecast of the future. Already bearing scars on his hand and ear, he now walks awkwardly and in pain. Having lost his teeth—perhaps to the butt of a gun, after another desperate struggle with the men who recaptured him—every word he utters is a lisping testament to his struggle for freedom. Broken in body but not in spirit, Peter ran away a third time. Readers could not know it, but his narrative—at least so far as it was authored in these irregular installments—had come to an end. They would wait in vain for the continuation or conclusion of Peter's story.

The serialized stories of runaways like Peter and Cora provide a valuable perspective on the experience of slavery in colonial North America and in the evolution of resistance by enslaved individuals. To cite just one lesson implicit in the discontinuous narratives of Jemy, Caesar, Zipporah, and Peter: runaways who lived in a colonial city often seem to have been sold or transferred to a new owner after their recapture. This was also true of another serial runaway, a man named Daniel who ran on three separate occasions—and apparently succeeded in his final attempt:

RAN away from his Master *Edward Wanton* of Scitu[ate] Ship Carpenter, the Second of this Instant Septemb[er] A Molatto Man Servant, Named *Daniel*, about 19 years [of] Age, pretty Tall, speaks good English, thick curl'd Ha[ir] with a bush behind, if not lately cut off, black Hat, cot[ton] and linen Shirt: he had with him two Coats, one a ho[me] made dy'd Coat, the other a great Coat dy'd a muddy col[our] strip'd home spun Jacket, Kersy Breeches, gray Stocki[ngs] french fall Shoes.

Whosoever shall take up said Runaway Servant and [him] safely Convey to his above-said Master at Scituate, or [give] any true Intelligence of him, so as his Master may have [him] again, shall have Satisfaction to Content, besides all neces[sary] Charges paid. (*BNL* 1712/9/29)

RAN-away from his Master *John Scott* of Newport Rhode-Island, a Molatto Man named *Daniel* born in New-England, and by Trade a Ship Carpenter, formerly belonging to *Edward Wanton* of Situate, he is about 20 years of Age, indifferent tall, and slender bushy hair, carried with him white and speckled Shirts, Sea Cloaths and Bedding, and other good Cloaths as a Cinnamon coloured Broad-Cloath Coat trim'd with Froggs, Ticking Breeches, Worsted Stockings &c. Whoever shall apprehend the said Run-away and bring him to his said Master, or secure him and give notice to his Master aforesaid that he may have him again shall have reasonable Satisfaction and Charges paid. (*BNL* 1714/5/24)

RAN away from his Master *John Scott*, the 17th of this Instant August, A Molatto Man named *Daniel*, formerly belonging to *Edward Wanton* of Situate; he is indifferent Tall and Slender, by Trade a Shipwright, but 'tis thought Designs for Sea. Whosoever shall stop, take up, or secure the said Run-away, and bring him or give Notice of him to his said Master at Newport, Rhode-Island, shall be well rewarded, and reasonable Charges paid. (*BNL* 1714/8/23)

These three advertisements, detailing Daniel's appearance, origins, livelihood, and movements over the space of two years, provided the public with a record of his life; the second and third advertisements, which allude to the first, encourage readers to draw upon their past knowledge of Daniel, assuming a familiarity with his story and person—so much so that the final notice does not even mention the color or composition of his clothes, an omission otherwise unheard of in runaway slave advertisements. By the autumn of 1714, Daniel was a local celebrity whose slender build, bushy hair, and personal history were well known to New England readers. His story, reconstructed with aid from both the archive and the imagination, suggests the outer limits of what might be done with and gained from these serialized narratives of serial runaways; the balance of this chapter is, accordingly, dedicated to his experience of and resistance to slavery.

Daniel's remarkable history illustrates the way in which eighteenth-century narratives of slavery were frequently interwoven with competing claims of bondage. His life in the households of John Scott and Edward Wanton thrust opposed theories of slavery into conflict, and Daniel's experience of chattel slavery is best understood in contrast to an account of bondage authored by the master for whom he labored. Moreover, Daniel's narrative illustrates the imaginative expanse of a genre defined by the desire for freedom. As a shipwright Daniel built sloops and snows and ketches that would traverse the Atlantic, hauling dry goods, foodstuffs, and human cargo; as a sailor he made voyages to the West Indies and along the New England coastline. These voyages—both those he made personally and those undertaken by vessels he built—provided Daniel with an imaginative universe through which he could travel vicariously or in retrospect from the shores of New England. The story of the sloops he built and the snows he sailed on is his story, and so, too, is the tale of those enslaved persons left behind in the Scott family after Daniel's escape attempts. Their varied fates populate a constellation of alternative futures imagined by Daniel before and during his attempts to flee, attempts whose shifting focus (from an escape by land to an escape by sea) demonstrate his investment in imagining a range of possible outcomes after slavery.

At stake in the work of recovering Daniel's story is the matter of imagination's role in the work of literary and historical recovery—the imaginations of modern scholars and historical subjects alike. John Sweet and Lisa Lindsay have advocated for "inventive research strategies" in auto/biographical studies of subaltern peoples: seeking fragmentary sources and "developing creative ways of analyzing them."[16] But scholarly creativity is more frequently concealed than celebrated, as claims of causation or authorial intent are flanked with citations meant to obscure the imagination's role in historical and literary reconstructions. Hesitance to openly embrace imagination's role in the recovery of black African stories may stem from the pressures felt by the authors of antebellum slave narratives who, James Olney and Mitch Kachun have argued, "needed to exercise caution in calling attention to potential flaws in their memories or their use of imagination in constructing their narratives."[17] However, to "make vivid the lived experience of individuals" who experienced slavery, Martin Klein calls for the investigation of "tracks that have been left by the people we study. In some cases, they do not exist. In others, they are buried in missionary archives and occasionally in colonial archives," but in every case this work of recovery is an exercise of imagination.[18] The archives have hardly been exhausted; however, they are finite repositories long committed to preserving the lives of those who exercise power, rather than those who resist it. Only an embrace of innovative and creative scholarship will restore Daniel—and the particularized humanity of similarly forgotten black African men and women—to our collective consciousness. Daniel's journey to freedom began with an act of imagination, an attempt to conceive of life as a free man, and if eighteenth-century black African lives are to matter, they cannot only be counted; they must also be imagined.

Enslavers Who Resist

Daniel's first known enslaver, Edward Wanton, considered himself a slave, and Daniel's fight for freedom is best understood within the context of Wanton's own struggle for liberty. Born in England during the reign of Charles I, Wanton was reportedly the son of Valentine Wauton, the regicide who married Oliver Cromwell's sister Margaret and participated in the overthrow of the English crown. Both Wauton and his son fled England to escape the retribution of Charles II during the Restoration. Edward apparently changed his last name after arriving in New England, but a document in the Wanton family papers at the Newport Historical Society insists, "We always cling to the family name of Wauton. . . . The tradition of this fact seems to have always existed privately amongst us in America: yet we cannot now prove legally (in spite of much research & trouble) that Edward Wanton of Boston was the son of Col Valentine W."[19] No proof of Wanton's parentage survives, but his arrival in Boston during the late 1650s, just before Charles II returned to power, is consistent with the timing of Wauton's departure from England. The first person to claim Daniel as a human chattel was probably the son of a man who committed his life to the overturning of tyranny and arbitrary power, and the son would follow in his father's footsteps.

In 1661 Wanton removed from Boston to Scituate, where he would establish the shipyard that Daniel later worked in.[20] Wanton arrived in his new home as a member of the Society of Friends; he joined the Quakers on June 1, 1660, after serving as an officer of the guard during the execution of Mary Dyer. Convinced that she had been wrongly executed, Wanton spent the rest of his life promoting Quaker principles and interests in New England.[21] To join the Society of Friends in colonial Massachusetts was to risk corporal punishment, death, and enslavement. When the family of Lawrence and

Cassandra Southwick adopted the Quaker faith in 1657, they were jailed and fined repeatedly. These fines impoverished the family, and in 1659 the Secretary of the Massachusetts Bay colony, Edward Rawson, ordered that two of the Southwick children be sold as chattels to compensate the state for their unpaid debts: "Whereas Daniel Southwick, and Provided Southwick, son and daughter of Lawrence Southwick, absenting themselves from the publick ordinances, have been fined by the courts of Salem and Ipswich, pretending they have no estates . . . the treasurers of the several counties are, and shall be fully impowered to sell the said persons to any of the English nation, at Virginia, or Barbados, to answer the said fines." No captain would accept Rawson's commission to transport and sell the Southwicks, and one reportedly asked if he was serious: "will you offer to make slaves of such harmless creatures?"[22] Nevertheless, Rawson's order established a precedent for treating Quakers as human chattels; when Wanton converted, he knowingly risked his life, property, and freedom.

Quakers represented the abuse they suffered at the hands of colonial administrators as a form of estrangement—what we would now term racialization.[23] George Bishop argued in 1661 that Puritan magistrates who banished and sold Quaker missionaries or converts wrongfully treated these English subjects as foreigners. Puritan officials had warned that exiled Quakers who returned to Massachusetts Bay "*shall incur the Penalty of the Laws formerly made for Strangers*" even though, Bishop insisted, the "Law for Strangers did not concern them."[24] The 1641 *Massachusetts Body of Liberties* stipulated that only strangers (a term used to describe both foreign nationals and non-Christian peoples) could be sold as slaves.[25] In seventeenth-century Massachusetts, before the establishment of race as an immutable phenotypical category, black Africans and Indians were sold as slaves not because of their race but because they were considered foreigners, and Puritan magistrates who applied laws governing the treatment of strangers to the colony's interactions with Quakers lumped these individuals into a group whose members would eventually be stigmatized as racial others. Bishop laments the conflation of Friends and enslaved black Africans in his discussion of Robert Hodgson, a missionary examined by the magistrates of New Amsterdam. There Governor Peter Stuyvesant sentenced Hodgson to "*work two years at the Wheel-barrow with a Negro, or pay, or cause to be paid Six hundred Gilders*." Although chained to a wheelbarrow, Hodgson refused to work out his sentence, "Upon which they caused a *Negro* to take a *Pitch'd Rope*, nigh *four* Inches about, and to beat *him* . . . about *One hundred* blows." On two other occasions they "set a strong *Negro* with *Rods* to whip *him*" and "forced another *Negro* to lay many more stripes upon him." Fed with "such as they gave their Slaves," Hodgson suffered for weeks until Stuyvesant's sister begged for his freedom.[26] Bishop uses Hodgson's story to demonstrate that Quakers faced the threat of enslavement and suffered corporal punishment similar to that endured by enslaved black Africans and Indians.[27] He and other Quakers wrote narratives of slavery to appeal for the protection of the law and to insist that they should be treated as subjects, not strangers.

When Wanton fled for the second time, to Scituate, he left the jurisdiction of the Massachusetts Bay Colony and entered Plymouth Colony, where Friends enjoyed a less antagonistic relationship with local authorities. Wanton's first recorded encounter with Plymouth officials came some seventeen years later when, after being made a widower for the second time, he remarried. In February 1678, while protesting an injustice done to a Quaker neighbor, Wanton was informed that his September 1676 marriage had not been solemnized in accordance with colonial law. Over the next two decades, Plymouth officials levied numerous fines against Wanton for this and other, related offenses; when he refused to pay those fines, they seized his property. Wanton kept several informal records of the goods and livestock that were taken, noting in one characteristic entry, "in the 3 month 1685 I edward wanton being from home Samuell Studgon cunstable of Sittuate came to my house & tooke away a cow for the preists rate." On other occasions the magistrate seized fabric, sugar, a brass kettle, and other livestock.[28] The list of items seized and Wanton's calculation of their value resembles the lists published in Bishop's exposé of Puritan injustice, and Wanton may have had those precedents in mind as he compiled a record of his sufferings at the hands of Plymouth officials.

Whether or not he thought these informal records might someday be of use to another Quaker apologist, Wanton certainly intended that his 1679 narrative of enslavement at the hands of Puritan magistrates be read by and preserved for posterity. In his finest hand, with a number of typographical flourishes and on a full folio sheet, he recorded the details of his suffering:

Of Scituate in Plemplimouth

Edward Wanton being maried at A generall meeting Amongst ye people of god called quakers in the seventh moneth 76, About a yeare and five monethes afterward having a notion to speake to the governour & Maiestrates Consarning A cow & A calfe taken from A poore man for A fault which was Said to his charge Committed foureteene yeares before did say unto them that the children that were Born to him ten yeares after ye fault

was committed should have eaten the milk that the cow should have
given: In replie to this they Answered that I had Married contrarie to
theire Law And I must Look to heare of it and ye next day they fined me
Ten pound and told me yt if I would not put in securitie I must goe to
prison, I told them againe I should put in noe securitie; I am not afraid to
goe to prison for it is not the first time yt I have beene in prison upon
truths account: but so be it known unto you: the Lord would deliver us
out of your hands and we shall be A free people as sure as ever he delivered his people out of Egypt and And if this must be overcomd through
sufferings I feare not to goo to prison. Soe the court removed from yt
place I waited upon them; almost half a day and i went to them and asked
whither I was A prisoner or noe and the governour answered 'noe,' thou
hast an estate and thou may goe About thy Bisniss; soe they sent theire
marshel when I was not at home twice and he tooke it not away, but they
send A warrant to Another Cunstable and he Carried me to court againe;
they told me they sent there officers twice to my house; and could finde
nothing but A Ship upon the Stocks and they did not know whether it
was mine or noe, Soe if I would not pay it or Show my Estate; they would
put me in prison and keep me there till I was willing to pay it or show my
goods or Estate; I told them yt if they kept me seven yeares there I should
be of the same minde or if I were to marrie againe I should marrie in the
same manner for I did beleeve yt there were severall of them yt were convinced by the witniss of god in them in theire sconcience that I had don
noe evill nor had not sined against god in the thing the governour said he
did beleeve yt my Marriage was Lawfull Before god but I had broken
theire Law then the next day they called me and said they had considered
my bisiniss and would not keep me noe Longer nor put me in prison then
theire Constable Thomas Hudson came and past by my house in the
morning and asked me how I did and Som houres after came and som
other and took out of his field two oxen and A cow which by theire own
account as I heard were price At Eleven pound ten Shillinges this was don
ye 21 of ye 8 month 79 yet never since they were taken away have I at all
heard what they have done with them neither did any of my familie know
of theire goeing till afterward they were told by other people[29]

Drawing on a biblical account that would be widely deployed by enslaved
African American writers in the nineteenth century, Wanton compares himself to the children of Israel, who were held as slaves in Egypt and forced to
manufacture bricks.[30] The Israelites briefly apostatized after their escape into

the wilderness and worshipped a golden calf, but in this playful adaptation of scripture Wanton suggests that it is his oppressors who value cows and gold more than God, not him. Wanton's conversion to the teachings of George Fox resulted in religious persecution, and he internalized the message of Bishop's *New England Judged*: that Friends in colonial America were no better than strangers in a strange land, slaves who would soon be condemned to labor beside—or beneath—the foreign bodies of black African and American Indian servants.

Although Wanton's account does not conform to all the generic conventions of texts we now refer to as slave narratives, he clearly thought of himself as a slave, and that self-conception shaped his interactions with the authorities of Plymouth. Surely his disregard for authority and his self-identification as a slave also shaped his interactions with Daniel and provided a model of resistance for the young man who would eventually flee his shipyard. As a man who resisted the imposition of legal authority even as he relied on the law to justify his power over black African bodies, Wanton was hardly singular. In the early eighteenth century two other colonial slaveholders taught their enslaved servants to resist and escape when they themselves turned runaways. In a rare runaway master advertisement, James Lubbuck's creditors promised, "*Whereas James Lubbuck of Boston, Chocolate-maker, has lately Absconded & Carried away with him Four Negro's, and sundry other Effects to a Considerable Value, and his Creditors having met on said Occasion, do Promise to Reward any Person who shall Secure said Lubbuck, Negro's &c. with Twenty Pounds, Money*" (BNL 1728/5/2).[31] Lubbuck demonstrated, for the "*Four Negro's*" he took with him in his flight, how to react when they found his demands unreasonable. And Lubbuck himself had been taught how to resist and run from lawful authority by one of his own servants—just eight months earlier Lubbuck had placed his own advertisement: "Ran-away from his Master Mr. *James Lubbuck* of Boston, Chocolate-Grinder, on the 28th of last Month, A Young Negro Man-Servant, about 20 Years of Age, a short Fellow, speaks pretty good English, has thick Lips, battle-ham'd, and goes something waddling" (NEJ 1727/9/4). Enslaved individuals like Daniel and this anonymous "battle-ham'd" young man resisted their enslavement and ran away, but so too did their enslavers, Lubbuck and Wanton. The slave narrative in colonial North America is a story of individuals who, experiencing various forms of unfreedom, taught one another strategies of resistance and retreat. Most often, this meant an enslaved black African or American Indian man fleeing from a white English master. Occasionally, it meant that white English master fleeing creditors with the enslaved members of his household. When Daniel left Wanton's shipyard, he left behind a man who had himself risked enslavement and resisted racialization. He fled Scituate and Newport just as Wanton had fled London and Boston.

Slavery in Scituate

Daniel's mother was enslaved and, in all likelihood, a native of Africa. His father was probably a white English colonist, perhaps Wanton himself or one of his sons. It is possible that their coupling was voluntary; enslaved black women chose to have sex with white men for a variety of reasons, including love, pleasure, preferment, and compensation. Jessica Marie Johnson notes that some "black women sought out profane, pleasurable, and erotic entanglements as practices of freedom."[32] Describing one such instance in his petition for divorce, an enslaved black African man known by the names Jethro and Boston attested in 1741 that ten years earlier his wife, Hagar, had pursued the attentions of "one William Kelly (then a Soldier at St. Georges River)" and was subsequently "delivered of a Female Molatto Child" as a result. The temptation of a uniform was not experienced exclusively by the white heroines of Jane Austen novels, and Hagar reportedly sought a soldier's bed for reasons of her own. While the affair was "instigated by a white man," Jethro/ Boston believed Hagar was a willing participant "not having the fear of God before her Eyes" and obtained permission to divorce her.[33] Daniel's mother could similarly have chosen a white partner for reasons of her own, only to be left—like Hagar—without the support of her child's father.

More likely, Daniel was the product of rape, as a white man used his social power and physical strength to sate his lust on the body of an enslaved woman. Nine months later, in 1693, a baby boy was born. It is possible that Daniel's mother spoke English well enough and was familiar enough with the Bible to name him Daniel, after the boy prophet who rose to power and prominence in captivity, far from his ancestral homeland. But it seems more likely that he was given the name of Daniel by the white man who claimed him as property. That choice would have been cruelly ironic; the Daniel of scripture was a youth renowned for preserving the modesty and freedom of Susanna, a young woman living in captivity who was threatened with sexual violence. When, as Daniel grew older, he heard this story—and anyone living in the home of Edward Wanton would have heard biblical texts read and discussed often—he must have realized that his very existence evinced an inability to protect the innocent, as his namesake had. In more ways than one, his name was a testament to the oppressive power of slaveholders.

A few months earlier, in 1692, another black baby had been born in Massachusetts, only to die. An unwed black African woman named Grace birthed the child, and after its death, she was accused of infanticide.[34] Grace was executed around the time of Daniel's birth, in the summer of 1693, alongside a white woman named Elizabeth Emerson who had confessed to infanticide and who acknowledged from the gallows "thy Black Fellow-Sufferer there!"[35] Emerson had languished in prison for two years before her execution, but Grace sat in jail for just four months, "from Jan 13th 1692 unto May ye 2d 1693" before suffocating in the hangman's noose.[36] Their public deaths were a warning to the community of the consequences of sin, and Daniel may have survived to see his first birthday only because, after witnessing Grace's death and the penalty for infanticide firsthand, his enslaved mother decided not to kill the baby fathered by her rapist. Instead, she delivered him up to the custody of that peculiar American institution: chattel slavery.

Born into a community that stigmatized interracial sex, Daniel's presence in New England was a silent, implicit rebuke to the region's religious aspirations. In 1706, some thirteen years after Daniel's birth, Massachusetts Governor Joseph Dudley would sign into law "An Act for the better preventing of a Spurious and Mixt Issue," stipulating that "any English Man, or Man of other Christian Nation" who "shall commit Fornication with a Negro, or Molatto Woman" be whipped and fined and the woman sold out of the province.[37] Daniel's body was an unwelcome reminder of what Cotton Mather had termed, in his discussion of Elizabeth Emerson and Grace, *uncleanness*; his life was a testament to the moral failings of the region's religious seekers.

Daniel may have been raised in the Wanton home from infancy, or he may have arrived in his youth. But he had worked in Wanton's shipyard (run by a son, Michael Wanton, during the eighteenth century) long enough to earn the title shipwright by age twenty, so he probably spent his adolescence in Scituate. While Boston housed most of the five hundred black residents of Massachusetts, Scituate's location on the coast made it a relatively cosmopolitan municipality. The seven children of James Newell and Mary White, who "had the singular fancy to marry her slave," were born in Scituate between 1691 and 1706, so Daniel would have grown up interacting with other girls and boys who understood the anxieties attached to the offspring of illicit interracial sex in colonial Massachusetts.[38] Yet White, who was descended from Scituate's first settlers and owned substantial property, provided her children with social status and wealth that Daniel would never enjoy.[39] The children of White and Newell were born free, but Daniel knew, from his youth, that enslaved black Africans in New England could obtain their freedom through other means.

In Scituate, enslaved individuals regularly and successfully sued for their freedom in court. The best-known case is that of Adam, a man claimed as property by colonial judge and Scituate resident John Saffin, who in 1694 pledged to release Adam from bondage in seven years' time.[40] After promising Adam his freedom, Saffin rented his labor to Thomas Shepard, a tenant on one of Saffin's farms in Bristol County, so Daniel would have seen Adam only on the occasions when the enslaved man came to visit friends or family in Scituate. But in 1701 Daniel—and other members of the local black community—would have listened with interest to the news that Saffin had refused to honor his agreement with Adam. Shepard accused Adam of "having been a very disobedient, turbulent, outragious and unruly Servant in all respects these many years, and hath carried himself so obstinately both to my self, Wife & Children, that I cannot keep him nor bear with his evil manners any longer; and therefore request Mr. *Saffin* his Master to take him again into his Custody and Release me of him."[41] Saffin, in turn, claimed that Adam's behavior violated the terms of their agreement, and he asked the Superior Court to acknowledge his continued claim of ownership. The case dragged on for two years before, in 1703, Sewall persuaded the Court to grant Adam his freedom.

Other local enslaved men and women won their freedom at the turn of the eighteenth century. Saffin's neighbor, Walter Briggs, left "Mariah ye little neger girle" to his wife Frances in a 1676 will, and after Frances's death eleven years later, Maria, or Meriah, became the legal property of their son, Cornelius.[42] Maria gave birth to her own son, Will Thomas, in 1689, and in 1693 Cornelius, like Saffin, agreed to emancipate Maria after she had served him for a set period, declaring "*it is my will that thirteen years after the date hereof my Negro Servant woman named Maria shall be set free and at liberty to be at her own disposing.*" Ten years later, before Maria had fulfilled the prescribed term, her son was sold; she had escaped slavery herself but was forced to watch her son labor in perpetuity as a chattel.[43] Still, her other children would be free: Maria gave birth to two daughters after her emancipation. The first, a daughter named Mary, arrived on May 4, 1708, two years after she was emancipated. However, when Cornelius Briggs learned of that birth, he took possession of Mary and claimed her as his own, arguing "that Mariah is not a free Negro Woman"; again like Saffin, Briggs attempted to renege on the agreed-upon terms of manumission. Maria and her husband, Anthony Sisco, sued for their daughter's freedom and eventually won Mary back from Briggs in an extended legal battle.[44] Slaveholders like Saffin and Briggs were not above breaking the law to make a profit—Saffin smuggled slaves into Massachusetts illegally, and Briggs rescinded his promise of freedom to an aging slave when the opportunity to claim that woman's more valuable child presented itself.[45] But enslaved black Africans in Scituate sought their freedom tenaciously, and seized every opportunity to secure their liberty. As Daniel watched Adam and Maria battle for their freedom, he determined that he too would one day be free.

Daniel belonged to the black African community of Scituate, but as he labored in the shipyard of Edward and Michael Wanton, he was also immersed in the town's Quaker culture. The Wantons were themselves Friends, and Joseph Cullon suggests that most of their apprentices were too; as Daniel worked and ate and roomed with Quaker men and boys on a daily basis, he may even have adopted their characteristic speech patterns, using *thee* and *thou* instead of the singular *you*: a pattern of speech widely associated, in colonial New England, with a disrespect for lawful authority.[46] When Daniel answered one of Edward Wanton's inquiries with the words *thee* or *thou*, he might have thought of himself as inhabiting the very antislavery rhetoric of resistance that his own master had deployed in his fight with Puritan magistrates.

In 1706, when the Scituate Quakers outgrew the meetinghouse they had used since 1678, Edward Wanton built a new church on his property. No records of its erection survive, but a teenaged Daniel probably contributed to its construction, alongside each of the other carpenters who worked in Wanton's yard.[47] During the construction of the meetinghouse, or perhaps in the Wanton home, he heard stories of Quaker suffering—heard the tale of Robert Hodgson, as well as Edward Wanton's own account of enslavement at the hands of Massachusetts magistrates. These stories would have been well received by Quaker auditors, but they did little to persuade Daniel of the sect's claim to truth. He lived with Quakers and helped to build a house of worship for the Society of Friends, but Daniel never joined them—the religious movement that would eventually help to abolish slavery was, at that point, still led by hypocritical slaveholders like Wanton and held little appeal for him.[48]

Still, the shipyard was likely an agreeable place to work, and Daniel cultivated skills there that would serve him in good stead as a runaway sailor. Shipwrights worked most intensively during the winter, when the fields of neighboring farmers lay dormant and spare labor could be bought cheaply. At their busiest, Cullon estimates that the Scituate shipyards employed a hundred or more laborers, and as he grew older and more experienced, Daniel would have supervised the seasonal labor of farmers-turned-carpenters who were less familiar than he with the trade. By his late teens, Daniel could "saw and lay plank, shape timber with an adze, drill tunnels by the dozen, and perform a myriad of other tasks."[49] He returned to the Wanton home each evening covered in sawdust and small woodchips, walking from the shipyard past the church he had helped to raise. There he would collect his evening meal and eat, though not, in all likelihood, at the family table.

At the Wanton home he was only a servant, but in the shipyard he was a craftsman and could earn the respect of all with a job well done. The easy camaraderie that likely characterized his work environment is suggested by this anecdote from a Scituate shipyard during the second half of the eighteenth century:

> There used to be a Weymouth man who carted lumber to the ship-yard, and "Uncle" Sam Silvester, as he was called, was one of the workmen who was considered good at telling stories. One day, when the Weymouth man came, the carpenters got him to tell some stories, to see if he could get ahead of Uncle Sam. He tried to make out the Scituate people quite ignorant compared with the people of Weymouth. He said that on his way over to Scituate, the Sunday before, to hear old Dr. Barnes preach, he called at a house on his way across lots to get a drink of water, and, finding the lady of the house washing, said, "Do you wash Sundays?" "No," she replied, "I do not intend to; I did not know it was Sunday." Uncle Sam heard the story through, and then said, "I knew that woman; she was a Weymouth woman."[50]

No mention of Uncle Sam's race appears in the story, and he could have been white, but his title and his role as a sly storyteller conform to stereotypical nineteenth-century portrayals of African American men as tricksters.[51] Daniel may have taken on such a persona himself, or he might have joined with the other carpenters in encouraging another laborer to entertain them with stories. The yard was likely a congenial workplace, where his work was valued and labor was interspersed with stories of local prejudice and foreign travel.

Voyages, Real and Imagined

However pleasant his work in the Wanton shipyards may have been, Daniel never lost sight of status as a slave, and the stories of voyages to the West Indies, Africa, and Europe brought to the shipyard by sailors and ship captains reminded him of the constraints placed upon his own movements—his

TABLE 2.2 Vessels built in the Wanton shipyard during Daniel's working life

Date	Name	Tonnage	Rigging
1698	*Benjamin*	20	Sloop
1699	*Unity*	30	Sloop
1699	*Dove*	100	Ship
1699	*Hopewell*	30	Sloop
1700	*Mary*	20	Sloop
1700	*Sarah & Isabella*	50	Brigantine
1700	*Hannah*	60	Brigantine
1701	*Margaret*	20	Sloop
1701	*Hopewell*	30	Sloop
1702	*Adventure*	40	Brigantine
1702	*Expenditure*	40	Sloop
1702	*Adventure*	40	Brigantine
1705	*Endeavour*	80	Brigantine
1706	*Hopewell*	20	Sloop
1707	*Mary*	20	Sloop
1707	*Adventure*	50	Brigantine

This list of vessels is taken from data in Briggs, *History of Shipbuilding on North River, Plymouth County, Massachusetts*, 393–407.

inability to travel anywhere outside of Scituate without the express permission of Edward Wanton. As a youth, Daniel was likely contented with hearing about the journeys undertaken in vessels he helped build.

Surviving records indicate that the Wanton Shipyard launched at least sixteen vessels during the period when Daniel likely worked there, but the number may have been much larger (see table 2.2). These sloops, ships, and brigantines made port locally, on the North American coast, in Newfoundland, Piscataqua, Rhode Island, Connecticut, New York, New Jersey, Pennsylvania, Virginia, and North Carolina. They also visited more exotic shores, entering harbors in Madera, Fyall, London, Barbados, Antigua, St. Christopher's, and Jamaica.[52] Daniel sent a piece of himself in every vessel, and as he learned of happenings on board these ships or in the port communities they visited, he must have imagined what would have occurred if he had been present.

In May of 1704, for example, when the sloop *Unity* left Boston for Barbados, an eleven-year-old Daniel might have wondered whether its master, Captain James Bridgham, would return to Boston with a cargo of human chattels (*BNL* 1704/5/1). Most enslaved black Africans arriving in New England during the early eighteenth century came from Barbados, and in the early eighteenth century Rhode Island slavers imported more black Africans to the Americas than all other North American colonies combined.[53] Perhaps he was envious of the men and boys on that expedition and wished for the opportunity to visit an island where most of the residents were black Africans or perhaps he wondered whether life in the warm West Indies might be preferable to his experience of cold New England winters. But when he learned, five months later, that Bridgham and the *Unity* had been taken by French privateers, Daniel probably experienced rather different emotions (*BNL* 1704/10/2). Primarily, he must have felt grateful that he was not, in fact, on board the *Unity*. Bridgham would be released by the French almost immediately and would take his new vessel, the *Hampton*, on future voyages to Barbados (*BNL* 1705/11/19). But any black African sailors or human cargo on board would have been seized by the French and sold in Spanish mines, claimed as spoils in the War of the Spanish Succession. Daniel knew, better than most in Massachusetts, that the primary objective of French privateers was to capture enslaved persons; members of the Wanton family were in key military leadership positions and helped defend the coast of Rhode Island and Cape Cod from the threat of French raiders. The French capture of the *Unity* and other vessels that Daniel helped build must have registered as both insult and threat: the sloop he helped build would certainly, now, be used as a transport shipping enslaved black African bodies to Spanish mines, and Daniel knew that he or even a free black African resident of Scituate like Jerusha Newell could potentially be taken by French privateers aboard the *Unity* at any time.

Two of Edward Wanton's sons, each of whom would go on to serve as the colonial governor of Rhode Island, acted as New England's first line of defense against foreign naval threats. William Wanton and his brother John each captured several French privateers, and when the French seized thousands of enslaved black Africans on Nevis, one of the Wanton sons carried the news from Antigua (*BNL* 1706/5/13).[54] A number of thrilling sea adventures published in the *Boston News-Letter* were credited to intelligence received from one or another of the Wantons, and Daniel surely heard stories that were never published when the sons visited their father in Scituate. As he listened to John Wanton or another of the local captains speak, he would have inhabited those stories, imagining himself at sea, confronting danger, just as twenty-first century youth have imagined themselves at Hogwarts, facing Voldemort. When, for example, John Wanton returned from Montserrat in the spring of 1705 with the story of "a Boy bound for Montserat, had a hot dispute the 12th of February last, with a French Privateer of 6 great Guns," the twelve-year-old Daniel must have listened with rapt attention. On a ship of "8 Guns, with 8 men," that boy would have been an indispensable part of the fighting force that killed twenty-two French sailors before succumbing to overwhelming numbers; the French privateer shipped ninety-four men and eventually triumphed (*BNL* 1705/4/16). With his intimate knowledge of sloops and ships and brigantines, Daniel could picture the part that boy had played more vividly than most, as he ran below decks, from gun to gun, replenishing stores of powder, lighting fuses, and watching as the French vessel absorbed his shot. This narrative of adolescent heroism and maritime peril brought to New England by John Wanton shaped Daniel's perceptions of the Atlantic world and populated his imaginative universe.

By the time of his final escape attempt in 1714, Daniel felt more comfortable and safe at sea than on land. He had probably been on several voyages in his youth and by that point had ready access to "Sea Cloaths and Bedding" (*BNL* 1714/5/24). Like an adolescent Benjamin Franklin whose reading of *Robinson Crusoe* left him "Hankering for the Sea," Daniel also desired the adventure of maritime life; "living near the Water," he too "was much in and about it, learned to swim well, and to manage Boats."[55] Tales of boyish bravery might have excited that desire, but he also would have seen firsthand the ways in which naval life worked to blur social boundaries of race and class. Life at sea represented an opportunity for Daniel to escape the certainty of his future as a chattel, to rise above the unfortunate circumstances of his birth in Puritan New England.

He may have taken his first voyage with William or John Wanton, who made frequent trips to the West Indies. Perhaps Daniel successfully passed through the French blockade of Antigua with William in March 1705, only to learn, upon his return, of the brave cabin boy who had been less fortunate and now found himself a prisoner of war (*BNL* 1705/4/9). But at some point he sailed for another member of the Wanton family: Edward's son-in-law, John Scott. Scott was a merchant, a ship captain, and the grandson of Richard Scott and Katherine Marbury, who helped found Rhode Island in the seventeenth century. He married Edward Wanton's daughter Elizabeth in 1685, and the two purchased a plot of land in Newport, Rhode Island, in 1696; they would buy a "mantion hous" on the Sakonnet river ten years later, in 1706.[56] After Daniel's first escape attempt, in 1712, he left Scituate and the Wanton shipyard to live in Rhode Island with the Scotts. This transfer of custody was to be permanent; in his last will and testament Edward Wanton wrote, "I do Give Will & bequeath to my Daughter Elisabeth Scott over and above what I have formerly Given her, my molatto boy called Daniel if he may be found he being now run away."[57] Daniel's move from Scituate to Newport entailed a change in profession; no longer a shipwright, he became the carpenter on John Scott's ship *William*.

In the eighteenth-century Atlantic, where wooden vessels were frequently damaged—by pirates, privateers, lightning, hurricanes, unknown reefs, and the attentions of marine life—a good ship's carpenter was indispensable to the safety of any voyage. In extreme circumstances, a carpenter like Daniel might repair or replace the main mast after damage in a storm; on a more regular basis, he would monitor the vessel's leaks, as well as the integrity of its long boat or yawl. A ship's carpenter was deemed more valuable and indispensable than its pilot; only the captain and his mates occupied a higher position in the social hierarchy of a merchantman.[58] When pirates raided a commercial vessel, they often forced the carpenter to join their crew because his labor was necessary to keep a vessel afloat. Pirates "forced *Edward Cheeseman* Carpenter of *Phillips* to go with them" (*BG* 1724/5/4), and one year later a different crew "forced out of the said Brigantine one *George Whiteborn*, a Carpenter belonging to the said Brigt. . . . & one *Ralph Hew* Carpenter . . . very contrary to their Wills" (*BG* 1725/5/17). Carpenters were valued craftsmen, and Daniel's skills provided him with a measure of social power during his service to John Scott and other captains; they also made it economically impractical for Scott to seriously consider freeing him.

New England slaveholders occasionally attempted to coax their slaves into compliance by consulting their preferences, so Daniel's move from Scituate to Newport may have been a mutually agreed-upon outcome—an attempt on Wanton's part to reconcile the captured runaway to his fate and on Daniel's part to secure more favorable working conditions. Because most first person accounts of running away are found in narratives published by formerly enslaved individuals and because they detail successful escape attempts, the practice is commonly understood to be just that: an escape attempt. But running away was not always meant to result in complete and permanent freedom. In some instances, it was an act of protest meant to persuade the slaveholder to sell or otherwise accommodate a dissatisfied slave.[59] In December 1767, the Reverend John Ballantine, of Westfield, recorded the dissatisfaction of an enslaved black African woman named Sylva or Sylvia, who left the home of Elnathan Bush in Sheffield to seek sanctuary with Ballantine. A Congregational minister named Ebenezer Gay claimed the legal right to Sylvia, but she "lived at this time with Mr. B[ush]." When Gay paid Ballantine a visit, "Sylva, his Negro, came here" too; she left Bush's custody to take refuge with Ballantine and appears to have stayed there for several months. In February 1768, Ballantine wrote, "Mr. Elnathan Bush of Sheffield here to talk about buying Sylvia ... Mr. Bush went to Suffield and agreed with Mr. G[ay]. but Sylva is so averse and takes on so bitterly, the bargain is given up."[60] Sylvia's flight to the Ballantine home was an act of protest, rather than an escape attempt, and it resulted in a return to her preferred home, a move from Bush to Gay. Given his subsequent history, Daniel probably hoped to secure his freedom when he left the Wantons in 1712. But upon his capture, he might well have used his escape as an occasion for negotiation, to obtain a more favorable living situation. Although slaveholders were not required to consult the preferences of those they enslaved, sometimes they did; thus, one slave-for-sale advertisement describes "*a Lusty Negro Man, fit for Country Work, and inclines to Live there*" (BNL 1725/3/11). Wanton's decision to send Daniel to work for Scott was likely an attempt to appease a young man dissatisfied with life as a chattel, and his first escape attempt may have been a pretense for bargaining rather than a serious effort to win his freedom.

Scott made multiple voyages down the Atlantic coast to the Caribbean every year. He sailed to Barbados in 1704, to Jamaica in 1707 and 1708, and to Antigua in 1710 (where he would have heard fairly sensational stories about the assassination attempt of a runaway, who tried to shoot the island's governor, Daniel Parke).[61] Like other Rhode Island merchant ship captains, Scott carried lumber, beef, pork, butter, cheese, onions, horses, candles, and cider to the Caribbean, supplying the planters there with food and livestock. They, in turn, sold Scott slaves, sugar, molasses, cotton, ginger, indigo, rum, and English textiles.[62] In 1712, shortly after Daniel ran away and was recaptured, Scott made a voyage to colonies on the mainland, stopping in New York and South Carolina (BNL 1712/10/6, BNL 1712/11/17). On this trip, if not earlier—to Antigua, perhaps—Daniel likely shipped with Scott in the *William*. He listened to firsthand accounts of the recent arson attacks on Long Island and there experienced for himself the lingering distrust of a white populace that looked at every black African face with distrust. In South Carolina he saw Indian prisoners taken in the Tuscarora War sold as slaves and watched them loaded onto vessels bound for the Caribbean. When he returned to Newport, in 1713, it was with a more perfect understanding of the struggle for power between English colonists and the racialized peoples with whom they shared the North American continent, a realization that his personal struggle for freedom was one manifestation of a larger conflict between the English and those they thought of as foreigners or heathen—a continuation or evolution of the conflict in which the Quakers and Edward Wanton were caught during the seventeenth century.

His voyages throughout the Atlantic basin, both bodily and imaginative, also provided Daniel with a sense of the possibilities open to a man of his talents if only he could escape from bondage. To remain with the Wantons or Scotts was not only to linger in slavery himself but to tacitly support the slave trade as he built or maintained the vessels that transported human cargo throughout the Atlantic. Dissatisfied with these truths, Daniel ran again in 1714—and this time, he ran without any thought of return.

Futures Lived and Imagined

In his first effort to run away, Daniel apparently fled on foot. He gathered several changes of clothes, which represented a significant quantity of capital in colonial North America, and walked out of Scituate. But this effort and his subsequent attempt were short lived. His distinctive "bush" of hair and dark skin made Daniel conspicuous on the roads of New England, where the vast majority of travelers were white and wore hair that lay flat. On his second and third escape attempts, therefore, Daniel adopted a new strategy; at sea, he could disappear into a promiscuous mix of ships from every nation, with crews far more diverse than the inhabitants of a typical Massachusetts town.

Daniel acquired significantly better clothes during the interval between his first and second escape attempts, suggesting that his time with John Scott provided the carpenter with new economic opportunities. He may have been allowed to hire out his time while on shore in Rhode Island or found occasion to invest in goods for trade during Scott's trips to other British colonies. Instead of the homespun coats he took on the road with him in 1712, he left in May 1714 with a "Cinnamon coloured Broad-Cloath Coat trim'd with Froggs" (BNL 1714/5/24). This new prosperity probably opened up new possibilities for evading his pursuers, but another change also made his escape by sea more likely to succeed: the end of the War of the Spanish Succession. During this global conflict, New England mariners were united by their fear of French naval power, and many captains found employment as privateers. However, after the war ended, these British privateers were often stripped of the royal letters of marque that had authorized their attacks on French vessels, and the demilitarization of colonial ports left thousands of sailors searching for a new way to monetize their skills. Many decided to turn pirate, plundering British coasts and ketches, as well as the French ships they had targeted during the war; the years following the War of the Spanish Succession, from 1713 to 1726, produced one last major surge in early modern piracy.[63] The war's end meant that more of the vessels in any colonial port were captained or crewed by men considering piracy and other illegal activities as a means of economic support, so Daniel's pivot to the sea as an escape route was opportunistic—far more likely that he would find a captain willing to sail with a runaway slave during this period of piracy than during a war in which many of those captains were representatives of the British government.

The year 1714 was thus an ideal moment for Daniel to stow away, and the large number of Massachusetts residents who likewise saw this period immediately following the War of the Spanish Succession as an opportunity to seek freedom at sea is suggested by the passage of a 1718 law fining ship captains who knowingly accepted runaway minors, apprentices, servants, or slaves into their crew the hefty sum of fifty pounds. Legislators cited complaints "that persons under age, apprentices and servants, within this province, do oftentimes get on board the outward bound vessels, and are there entertained by the masters or mariners"; Daniel was one of many individuals who decided, after experiencing some form of unfreedom in Massachusetts, to stow away.[64] Some captains and crews welcomed runaways onto their vessels during this surge of piracy; all Daniel had to do was offer a story plausible enough to provide cover for the captain, should he be caught on board. Daniel might have claimed, as other runaways did, that "he was a free Negro and lived at *Bristol*" (BNL 1704/7/17); that "*he had found a Body of Ore for his Master, and that his Master had given him free*" (AWM 1722/11/15); that "his former Master Capt. *Palmer* had Sold him to a Person in the Great Valley, who had given him his Freedom (AWM 1723/7/11); or that "*he was Freeborn, and the Son of* John Mallott *a Free Negro in Jamaica, and ship'd by the way of* Barbados *here for his Education*" (NEJ 1729/3/24). For an unscrupulous captain in need of a carpenter, all Daniel would have had to do is offer an explanation for how he came to be free.

But if he thought that a ship captain might not accept him as a hand, Daniel also could have used his knowledge of life at sea to find a suitable hiding place onboard a vessel without its master's knowledge—as Jemy's friend Caesar tried so often to do. The experience of a runaway who called himself John Williams and who fled from bondage in 1724 is illustrative of this practice. Williams arrived in Plymouth harbor in the shallop *Ann* belonging to his enslaver, Richard Trevett of Marblehead, Massachusetts.[65] When Williams disappeared, those in Trevett's shallop asked for permission to search the *Morehampton*, a ship captained by John Moffat. Moffat, who knew he could be fined if Williams escaped with his help, authorized Trevett's representatives to search his vessel twice. Neither search discovered evidence of Williams on board, and Moffat was allowed to sail for his destination: Oporto,

Portugal. A sailor later testified that two days after they set sail, in the middle of the Atlantic, "some of the people found the said Negro on board stowed away in the Fore Castle behind some Wood and Covered up with some things to conceal him."[66] Williams had buried himself in a pile of firewood and lay quietly long enough to escape detection until it was too late for Moffat to turn back for Plymouth. When Moffat discovered the stowaway, he questioned him in front of the ship's crew to establish that he had arrived on board the *Morehampton* without the aid or encouragement of any of its men. Daniel, who had helped to build several of the ships that sailed from New England, would have known even better than Williams where the best hiding spots would be on any given vessel.

Like Williams, Daniel would have known that escaping into the Atlantic was no guarantee he would remain free indefinitely. When Moffat discovered Williams, he resolved to return him to Trevett and, thus, avoid any accusation of aiding and abetting him in his escape. But Williams ran a second time and shipped from Bristol with Captain Francis Thorne as a "Foremost Man" on board the *Clapham*. Williams might have breathed a sigh of relief in eluding Moffat; the *Clapham* sailed for Cadiz, and the Iberian Peninsula is literally an ocean away from New England. But it was Williams's misfortune to be recognized in Cadiz by one of Trevett's friends, a ship captain named John Hastie who sent him back into bondage on the first boat to Massachusetts. "Must [I] stay with [my] Master all Days of [my] life?" Williams sadly asked Hastie.[67] Even after running away, a lifetime of servitude was a very real possibility for the self-emancipated individuals who moved within the expanding British empire and its expatriate communities in Spain or colonies governed by other European nations. Escaping from Wanton and Scott was a start, but Daniel was acquainted with many in the New England maritime community, and a chance encounter on the Atlantic with any of these acquaintances could have sent him back to Newport in chains. Daniel knew, when he left Rhode Island, that he was choosing a life of anxious uncertainty, a life that could be interrupted at any point by a chance encounter with someone who recognized him as the legal property of John Scott.

And because of his skin color, Daniel faced the prospect of kidnapping and reenslavement at the hands of anyone unscrupulous enough to take advantage of his racial status. When the ship *Adventure* wrecked and an enslaved black African named Titus was cast away on Hispaniola in 1714, its former captain, a man named Zachariah Fowles, sold him illegally. Titus was the legal property of Boston resident Edward Lyde, and Lyde had sold his labor to Fowles, but when the two washed up in Santo Domingo, Fowles secured passage to St. Thomas. There Fowles "Affirmed the said Negro to be his slave and pretended he wanted money and therefore he sold him" to a local merchant named Anthony Fay for forty-one pounds. Fay, in turn, "sent him to Martinique for sale among the French, but the fellow feigned himself sick which Prevented his being sold there." Titus may not have been happy with his life of servitude in Boston, but he preferred life with Lyde to working on a French sugar plantation and escaped that fate through artifice. Titus eventually returned to Lyde's custody in Massachusetts (though not before he had "played several rogue tricks" on those charged with returning him), but his misadventures with Fowles illustrate the danger facing any black African man or woman traveling in the Atlantic world, whether bond, free, or runaway.[68] Even if Daniel never again met someone who recognized him as the property of John Scott, he might, because of his skin color, be reenslaved by someone like Fowles. Running away—even running away successfully—did not guarantee Daniel freedom or a happy ending.

Rather, in running away, Daniel rejected a known evil in exchange for hope: hope he would find the freedom that escaped John Williams, Titus, and other enslaved indviduals who ran away or were separated from their enslavers. He could not know what the future would hold, but surely, as Daniel prepared to run, he tried to imagine the possibilities of life with the Scotts and of life as a free man. Our imaginings, then, of what Daniel's life would have been like had he stayed with the Scotts and of what it was, on the run, are in a real sense an extension or recovery of his mental experience. Daniel disappears from the historical record in 1716, when Edward Wanton noted, in his will, that he was still missing. But his absence in the archive need not signify the end of his story because he, when he ran, imagined a better life than any he could conceive of with the Scotts, and both of those imaginary lives are part of Daniel's story.

Daniel was one of three enslaved carpenters to seek an escape by sea in as many years, and all three probably counted on their skills as a carpenter to win them a place on a vessel.[69] But those same skills would have made it quite difficult to leave a life on the ocean. With pirates kidnapping white carpenters at every opportunity, a skilled runaway such as Daniel would have been too valuable for a captain to willingly part with his service and, because of his history, too vulnerable to insist on the right to be discharged. The only place he might find himself accepted as an equal was among others who had renounced the protections and demands of European colonialism: pirates. We cannot know what Daniel did with his life after escaping, but before he left, he must have considered the possibility of joining—whether by choice or by force—a crew of pirates.

Pirate crews were notoriously diverse and democratic in a discriminatory and hierarchical age, relying on the assistance of men like Daniel in their raids on coastal communities.[70] When pirates abducted and recruited individuals from merchant vessels, those captives were often of black African or American Indian descent. Black African captives were sometimes used by white crew members as a form of currency with which to purchase clemency (*BNL* 1718/10/20) or as a form of compensation for those they robbed (*BNL* 1725/1/28), but they were also welcomed as members of a crew. The pirate Don Benito shipped a crew "of about 60 Spaniards, including the Negros and Molattos; 14 English, and 18 French" (*BG* 1724/7/13), while other vessels were similarly stocked with black African crewmen, "having fourteen White Men and Nine or Ten Negroes & Molattoes on Board" (*BNL* 1725/8/5). Black African pirates who had escaped from slavery sometimes served as pilots, helping the captain navigate waters they grew familiar with during the period of their enslavement. When the French raided English settlements on Nevis, they did so with "a Barbados molato, James Johnson, for their pilot," and an anonymous Rhode Island runaway-turned-pirate returned to wreak vengeance on the New England coastline a decade after Daniel's disappearance.[71] In 1728 "A Spanish Pirate, a Schooner of 6 or 8 Guns, and 80 Men" attacked the inhabitants of Gardner's Island, "carried away the Houshold Stuff, as Beds, Pewter, Brass, Iron, &c," and butchered the livestock. One of the island's residents managed to raise the alarm in Rhode Island, and two sloops were sent to capture the pirates, just as Joseph and William Wanton had been called out against the French twenty years earlier. One of these sloops caught up with the pirate vessel "and engaged for some time." They failed to capture the schooner but learned, during the fight, that "the Pilot of her [was] a Negro Man, who sometime since belonged to Rhode-Island" (*BNL* 1728/9/12). If, when Daniel escaped the Scotts, he hoped someday to take revenge on those who had been his masters, he might have imagined returning some day in this fashion, as a pirate—to seize the goods of those who had taken his labor without his consent.

Of course, if Daniel had come to the Rhode Island coast in the fall of 1728 to take his revenge on John Scott, he would have arrived too late: Scott died on April 12, 1728. Scott's will provides a window into the future Daniel ran from, the life he might have endured had he given up his dreams of freedom. Scott left to his wife, Elizabeth Wanton, "three Slaves To her own use and behoof (Vizt.) one Negro Man named Gery, one Negro Woman named Jenny & One Negro Boy Named Codando."[72] Daniel would have spent the remainder of his life in her service or, more likely, as a carpenter in the service of their son George, who carried on the family business. Like his father, George Scott sailed for Antigua and other Caribbean islands often. But rather than buy human chattels in Antigua, for resale in New England, George cut out the middleman and sailed directly for Africa, where he traded dry goods for human cargo that he personally sold to Antigua plantation owners. Had he remained with the Scott family in Rhode Island, Daniel might have had the chance to see the continent from which his mother or her ancestors had been stolen.

Enslaved sailors who traveled with George Scott to Africa endured peril but also enjoyed better opportunities for escape than they typically found in colonial North America; tropical disease and slave revolts left many dead, but they also created a chaotic environment in which opportunistic individuals could win their freedom. During a 1740 voyage Scott and most of his company fell sick at one point or another. In an April letter he reported "we have now five people Sick & bonner so bad I beleive will not recover."[73] Two months later he wrote again, to confirm that "My Negro Bonner is dead."[74] The black servant he brought from Newport to Africa saw his ancestral home but succumbed to disease before he could secure his freedom. Others, though, were luckier. While Scott remained ill, in bed, his second mate went ashore with a canoe, and an enslaved person "gott out of ye boat with two ounces of gold & has gott clear off."[75] The illness that attacked visitors to the coast of Africa could kill, but it also, occasionally, created opportunities for escape.

On another voyage George Scott survived a slave revolt off the African coast. Some of the recently enslaved managed to free themselves from the shackles chaining them to the deck and seized control of his ship, the *Little George*, killing its physician and two sailors. The surviving slavers—Scott, four men, and a boy—retreated to his cabin, where they barricaded the door and fought off further attacks with a pistol. Discovering gunpowder and a swivel gun in the hold, the freed slaves threatened to turn it on Scott and his crew; Scott, in turn, cut a hole in the hull and threatened to sink the ship. After nine days at an impasse, the slaves ran Scott's ship aground on the African coast and fled into the mainland. Rather than attempt to repair the *Little George* while holding off attacks by the local populace, Scott and his crew abandoned his ship and rowed a longboat up the coast until they found a Montserrat slaver willing to aid them (*BNL* 1731/5/6). Scott never elaborates on the racial identity of his fellow slavers, but a black crew member who survived the first onslaught of the emancipated slaves would have had multiple opportunities to escape or defect. Daniel's future with the Scotts would have been just as dangerous as the life he likely cobbled together as a carpenter aboard a pirate ship; the difference is that he could choose, after escaping from John Scott's Newport mansion, which risks to run. Having weighed an imaginary future of service to the Scotts and the slave trade against a life on the run, with pirates and other fugitives from the law, Daniel chose to run.

Restorers of Readings

Daniel's name appears in just four documents, one of which was never seen by the general public: the three runaway slave advertisements published between 1712 and 1714 in the *Boston News-Letter* and Edward Wanton's 1716 will. However, his story—the story read today by scholars searching through the archive, as well as the story understood by those who learned of Daniel's escape attempts in real time—is far more expansive than those documents might suggest. For example: John Scott and the other inhabitants of colonial Newport might have read this 1715 runaway slave advertisement as a sort of coda to Daniel's narrative: "RAn away from his Master, *William Burden* Ship-Carpenter of Newport on Rhode-Island, on the 23d of April last, a very likely Spanish Indian Lad, without any Marks on his Face, had long Hair, looks very like our Indians, named *Caesar*, speaks Indifferent good English, aged about Eighteen Years, had on a brown Kersey Jacket, a pair of old Broad-Cloth Breeches pretty near the same Colour, an old Beaver Hat, and a course Linen Shirt" (*BNL* 1715/5/9). Just as Jemy was induced to run away by the influence of Gibbs's black servant Caesar, so the Indian man enslaved by Burden and called Caesar was likely moved to escape by Daniel's success. Working in the same industry and in the same community, Daniel and Caesar surely knew each other—and Caesar's disappearance a short eight months after Daniel vanished suggests that Daniel inspired those who knew him to follow his example. Burden's advertisement for Caesar is just as much a part of Daniel's story as the advertisements published by Scott or the memorial detailing Wanton's suffering at the hands of Plymouth magistrates.

The narrative of slavery assembled here from archival research, imagination, and surmise might seem like the artificial construct of a scholar, and it is. But it is also a fair approximation of the narrative experience originally created by the serial publication of the three relatively terse advertisements introducing Daniel to a reading public. When a Massachusetts colonist picked up the *Boston News-Letter* and read of Daniel's third escape attempt, she would have known or intuited far more about his life than was explicitly stated. John Scott and the Wanton family were well-known public figures whose names appeared in the newspaper and other public communications regularly. The Wanton connection to both maritime defense and Quaker dissidents was well established, and every time Scott left for or returned from the Caribbean, a notice of his trip was published in the paper. Daniel's ancestry and early life would have been more vividly imagined by such a reader—who may have remembered his birth or the birth of similar children—than they can be in the twenty-first century. And his futures—both the future of bondage he ran from and the life of freedom he ran to—would have been similarly detailed in the imaginations of readers intimately familiar with the realities of slavery and maritime life. Thus, although this narrative of slavery is admittedly artificial, its artifice likely reflects the experience of an eighteenth-century reader better than the bare text of the runaway slave advertisements memorializing Daniel's life. The careful readers who corrected grammar errors in slave-for-sale advertisements and found serialized biographies in the classifieds read slave narratives long before they were written, and the recovery effort of scholars imaginatively piecing together the history of enslaved local celebrities like Daniel restores the humanity of those whose stories have long been forgotten.

Daniel's life was movingly replayed in the minds of some who read the fragmented story of his escape, and the story of enslaved individuals in colonial North America may once again be narrated if only we dare to imagine the lives of serial runaways such as Jemy, Cora, Peter, and Zipporah. Ralph Waldo Emerson famously disparaged "restorers of readings," but that work, of restoring the serialized narratives once read in colonial newspapers, is both the duty and the privilege of American scholars who study the history and literature of a country that was built on the backs of enslaved laborers like Daniel.[76]

CHAPTER THREE

Royalty Enslaved
Of Princes, Pretenders, and Politics

The local celebrity of a serial runaway like Daniel stemmed from the success—and then the failure—of his attempts to escape. His notoriety was fragile and circumstantial, contingent upon the outcome of his actions. But another class of celebrities whose movements attracted the interest of eighteenth-century newspaper readers enjoyed fame that was far more durable because it was a product of birth rather than achievement: royalty. News about the health, nuptials, and negotiations of royalty filled the pages of colonial newspapers. For example, on July 13, 1713, the *Boston News-Letter* relayed word from a Madrid correspondent that the "Prince of Austria, who for some time was indisposed of a Cold, attended with a Fever, is now perfectly recovered. The Queen hath declared, that she is three Months gone with Child, which hath occasioned great Joy here, and the Principal Nobility have complimented her Majesty upon that occasion." The sniffles suffered by Charles VI and the pregnancy of his wife, Elizabeth Christine, made headlines: their health was the opening story in that week's issue. Daniel's desperate struggle for freedom was recounted in the classifieds, and many readers would have sympathized more with an enslaver than with the enslaved. A prince and a slave might seem to have little in common, yet immediately after noting the compliments paid to Elizabeth, the Madrid correspondent continued with this news, "A Courier from Carthagena hath brought an Account, that the Persons who went from thence on the 2d of February last, to redeem the Captives at Algiers, were returned on the 6th Instant, with two hundred and eight Slaves."[1] Sovereigns and slaves shared the paragraphs of eighteenth-century newspapers, and their stories intertwined in ways that make visible both the political import of early slave narratives and the bondage inflicted by princes upon their people.

The two hundred and eight white captives taken at sea and then ransomed from their bondage in Algiers by friends and family members in Spain were seized by Algerine rovers. These state-sanctioned pirates plundered any vessel flying a Spanish flag because Philip V of Spain had been at war with the Ottoman regencies of North Africa for the entirety of his reign.[2] In the absence of a treaty between Philip and the Dey of Algiers, Ali Chauch, Philip's subjects were regarded by Algerine corsairs as property afloat, in search of a new owner. Hostility between royals, or even the mere absence of a treaty, rendered their subjects vulnerable, liable to be taken captive as slaves in what Samuel Sewall and other eighteenth-century jurists might have termed a lawful and just war.[3] For this reason, a discussion of the Austrian king's health and of Algerine captives returning home to Spain might be thought of not as two different subjects but as different vantage points on the question of how best to secure the liberty of various European peoples.

Kings and queens, princes and princesses embodied the rights of their eighteenth-century subjects. The monarch, Thomas Hobbes stipulates in *Leviathan*, acts on behalf of each member of the body politic. Thus, "of the Act of the Soveraign every one is Author, because he is their Representative unlimited; . . . every member of the Body is Author of it." Accordingly, a monarch's interactions with another state could result in the forfeiture of his subjects' rights: "If a Monarch subdued by war, render himself Subject to the Victor; his Subjects are delivered from their former obligation, and become obliged to the Victor."[4] Only the health and freedom of a benevolent monarch stood between his subjects and the prospect of enslavement, so the juxtaposition of news about a monarch's well-being and news of slaves redeemed from their bondage to a foreign prince provides two different perspectives on the liberty of a people. Slavery was a condition imposed on foreign subjects by princes in the course of war but also, potentially, a condition suffered by princes—and the subjection or enslavement of a prince presaged the impending bondage of his people. The prince and the slave were often linked in the early modern imagination, and not only in a romance like Aphra Behn's *Oroonoko: or, the Royal Slave* (1688); the fear that individual subjects might be made chattels by a foreign ruler was surpassed only by the prospect of an entire nation being enslaved upon the subjugation of its prince.

This figure of the enslaved prince was not, for eighteenth-century readers, a purely fictional or philosophical construct. In 1713, newspapers reported that Charles XII, King of Sweden, had been captured and his people enslaved by Janissaries of the Ottoman Empire:

> They attack'd the 12th of February the Intrenchments that Prince had caused to be made about his House, and after an incredible Resistance, forc'd the same, and afterwards set the House of Fire, which obliged the King of Sweden to surrender. His Majesty was carried away for Adrianople or Salonica, under a Guard of 200 Turkish Troopers, followed by about 100 Swedes, but they can give no further Account of his Majesty for

whom they are in great Pain, not only because of his dismal Circumstances of being a Prisoner amongst the Infidels, but because he was very
much indisposed when he was carried away. These Gentlemen add, that
all the Swedes were made Slaves, and that the Seraskier of Bender has
bought those that fell into the Hands of the Tartars. (*BNL* 1713/6/15)

Charles XII was, in 1713, living as a refugee in Bender, Turkey, because he had lost
a decisive battle in the Great Northern War to Russian forces at Poltava in 1709.
During his four years as an exile, Charles borrowed heavily from Ahmed III, the
Ottoman Sultan, to support himself and his men; when the Swedish king demanded yet another sizable loan in December 1712, the Sultan decided that
he had overstayed his welcome and ordered the Seraskier of Bender, Ismail
Pasha, to expel Charles and his followers from Turkey. On February 1, 1713,
Pasha commanded his forces to attack, and Charles was injured: a bullet
grazed his nose, cheek, and ear, and he broke his foot in two places during the
battle. Charles was kept under house arrest in Pasha's home, while his companions were stripped of their clothes and held for ransom. Ahmed subsequently disavowed Pasha's attack on the Swedes and received the wounded
Charles at Adrianople in honor; any discomfort or curtailment of liberty endured by the King was relatively minor and fleeting. Still, the prospect of
Turkish forces enslaving a Christian prince and his people fascinated readers
on both sides of the Atlantic, who struggled to make sense of conflicting reports from writers half a world away, in Turkey.[5] Drawing on a steady stream
of updates from correspondents in England, the *Boston News-Letter* provided
coverage of the king's capture over the course of six weeks. The denouement
for colonial readers came in July 1713, as they read of the Sultan's formal apology to Charles; in proof of his sincerity, "the Grand Vizier and two Bashawn
were Executed in the Presence of the King of Sweden" on Ahmed's orders
(*BNL* 1713/7/27). Readers learned only in retrospect that reports of Charles's
enslavement had exaggerated the extent of his unfreedom.

Stories such as this one, of a prince and his people enslaved without warning, provided fodder for the fears of British subjects on both sides of the Atlantic, who worried—particularly after the death of Queen Anne, in 1714—that
the Stuart Pretender would return to claim his father's throne. Upon Anne's
death, the throne was to pass from the house of Stuart to Sophia of Hanover
and her heirs, excluding many closer relatives because of their adherence to
the Catholic faith. Among those excluded from the monarchy by the 1701
Act of Settlement was the son of James II: James Stuart, or the Old Pretender. Supporters of the Pretender and the house of Stuart rioted when

Sophia's son was proclaimed King George I after Anne's death, and in 1715 many took up arms to fight for the Jacobite cause.[6] Correspondents loyal to George framed this conflict as an attempt to overthrow the king and, thus, enslave his people. For example, the officials of Limerick, in Ireland, voiced their objections to the Pretender in terms that resonated across the Atlantic, expressing their "*Opposition to our Grand Enemy the Pretender, a Person that has been bred up in intire Aversion to Her Majesties Person and Government; and fully instructed by frequent Examples in the Arts of Slavery and Oppression, and how to extirpate our most holy Religion by the Sword and Faggot*" (BNL 1714/1/17). George is consistently described as "*our strongest Bulwark against Popery and Slavery*" (BNL 1715/12/5) while the Jacobites "*Court Captivity and Chains!*" (BNL 1716/3/5). The Pretender was a symbol of slavery for British Protestants on both sides of the Atlantic. An exiled prince purportedly eager to impose the yoke of bondage, he would remain an oft-invoked threat to British liberty throughout the first half of the eighteenth century.

Most colonists in North America supported George I and the House of Hanover, but they were not reflexively opposed to the cause of princes exiled for religious reasons; deposed rulers interested in reclaiming their thrones were not automatically denounced as instruments of oppression. In 1737 and 1738 a Lebanese nobleman named Sidi or Sibi toured colonial North America, stopping in Boston, Newport, New York, and Philadelphia.[7] Honored with the title of sheikh, Sidi was a Christian whom the Massachusetts physician John Ballantine described in his diary as "a Grecian Prince, much persecuted by ye Turks for his religion, recommended by some Noblemen in England as an object of charity."[8] Because Sidi was a Christian prince driven out by a Muslim majority, he was to be regarded sympathetically, a champion of truth and liberty wrongfully expelled; because of his Catholic sympathies the Old Pretender was, in turn, a caricatured enemy of English Protestantism and an instrument of papal oppression. Eighteenth-century British newspaper correspondents defined slavery as oppression suffered at the hands of religious and political others. The word was used most frequently to describe a condition imposed on Protestants by Catholic oppressors or, more generally, on Christians by Muslim oppressors.[9] Thus, most discussions of slavery in the early eighteenth century advanced an implicit diplomatic agenda predicated on the enmity of theologically and politically opposed princes. The Catholic Pretender threatened to enslave because he sought to replace the Protestant George I, while the Christian Sidi was a victim of persecution because he challenged the tyrannical rule of an Islamic empire. The identity of a prince and his place in an eschatological struggle between Protestants and Catholics,

Christians and Muslims, determined whether he was a potential tyrant threatening to enslave a free people or a judicious prince preserving them from bondage.[10]

As foreign dignitaries like Sidi—including several enslaved black African princes— arrived in Britain and its colonies, their stories of oppression and their claims on the sympathy of British colonists were accordingly evaluated through this interpretive framework. English subjects might not have cared about the rights or well-being of the average enslaved black African, but as Wylie Sypher observed, "your free-born Briton could feel for a prince, particularly a prince in distress."[11] Individual slave owners and corporate bodies, such as the Royal African Company (RAC), liberated captive royals in order to advance Britain's imperial Protestant cause. Accounts of these enslaved princes and their liberation, which were the first book-length biographical accounts of black African life in the Americas to be published, promoted the diplomatic efforts of political and religious leaders. Concerned more with advancing British and Protestant interests abroad than the art of biography, *Some Memoirs of the Life of Job, the Son of Solomon, the High Priest of Boonda in Africa* (1734) and *The Royal African: or, Memoirs of the Young Prince of Annamaboe* (1750) took their cue from newspapers, framing slavery as an outgrowth or expression of British foreign policy. Ayuba Suleiman Diallo and William Ansah Sessarakoo, the royal protagonists of these early slave narratives, were freed because their emancipations would strengthen weak alliances between African states and Britain's Protestant coalition.

The Ottoman attack on Charles and the enslavement of Swedish forces surprised outside observers because the two powers were supposedly allies in the Great Northern War against Russia; the Swedish King's emancipation and Ahmed's subsequent apology to Charles reinforced their alliance. So, too, with the liberation of Diallo and Sessarakoo. Slavery was, in the understanding of most eighteenth-century British readers, a condition imposed on theological and political opponents in the eschatological struggle between Christian and Muslim, Protestant and Catholic. Therefore, the freeing of these enslaved black African princes signified their incorporation (and, thereby, the incorporation of their peoples) into a coalition opposing papal aggression and the bondage threatened by tools of Rome, such as the Pretender. The story of slavery, as told in both early eighteenth-century newspapers and the early book-length biographies of Diallo and Sessarakoo, was a story of diplomatic relations between foreign powers—the story of princes enslaving and enslaved.[12]

The experiences of Diallo and Sessarakoo were not unique; narratives of enslaved black African princes and their emancipation by magnanimous

Englishmen abounded in the eighteenth century. Assessing these narratives, William Pettigrew has argued that "hospitality to and friendship with African royalty would become a trademark protoabolitionist gesture for the remainder of the eighteenth century."[13] However, this anticipatory approach to the stories of enslaved black African princes is mistaken: the Englishmen who honored these princes and participated in the creation of these narratives often profited directly from slavery, and the princes themselves—including Diallo and Sessarakoo—were generally slavers who continued to buy and sell human chattels after their return to Africa. Neither enslaved royals nor their enslavers wanted to abolish the trade in human property. English sympathy for enslaved royalty was not a harbinger of nineteenth-century abolitionism but an outgrowth of the early modern view that slavery was a byproduct of wars between ideologically opposed alliances. Freeing and befriending these princes furthered England's global interests in the promotion of Protestantism and English commerce, strengthening the British empire and reducing the likelihood that English subjects would themselves be enslaved. But this emphasis on foreign relations reflected African, as well as English, priorities. The princes who collaborated in the creation of these narratives frequently came to be enslaved as a direct result of their efforts to cultivate a closer relationship with English officials, and after their betrayal, they doubled down on that strategy. Their alliances with English clergy, traders, and nobility, both those that led to their enslavement and those that liberated them from bondage, were generally intended to reinforce and expand lucrative commercial partnerships predicated on the slave trade. Thus, narratives of enslaved royalty were less records of resistance than personal perspectives on the expansion of global alliances and the inner workings of a slave trade that made those diplomatic relationships both profitable and a source of security.[14]

Diplomatic Failures and the Delagoa Princes

The returns of Diallo and Sessarakoo to their African homes were publicity triumphs for the crown, for Protestant evangelists, and for the RAC. *The Royal African*'s narrative of British beneficence proved particularly popular, running through three editions in five years. But these diplomatic triumphs celebrated with biographies were preceded by another, much less successful effort to repatriate enslaved royals. Two brothers from Mozambique's Baía da Lagoa or Maputo Bay—known to British sailors in the eighteenth century as Delagoa—became celebrities in the 1720s when they arrived in London and were introduced to well-connected officials of the RAC, the Society for Promoting Christian Knowledge (SPCK), and other organizations. Like Diallo and Sessarakoo these two siblings, known as the Delagoa princes because a third brother was acknowledged as "the Indian King" by a captain trading for the East India Company (EIC), were enslaved and then sent back to their homes with apologies and trade goods, just as Diallo and Sessarakoo would be.[15] However, their story is preserved only in contemporary newspaper accounts, archival records, and correspondence. No triumphal biography commemorates the repatriation of James Chandos Mastoon and John Towgood Mastoon because James, the elder brother, hanged himself in England, and John cut off all communication with the British as soon as he returned to Delagoa.[16] Their enslavement and emancipation was a story deemed worthy of public attention only until the Mastoon brothers rejected British diplomatic overtures.

Colonel John Towgood of Jamaica, who brought the Mastoons to London, wrote an account of their kidnapping for the EIC. He explained that in 1716 a Captain White, sailing "in the Companys Service or by permission" to Delagoa, entertained the king and his brothers on board ship. These visits with White left John and James with "a desire to see England," and when White left Delagoa, those two sailed with him. In exchange for the safe passage of his brothers and their attendants to England, Towgood alleged, the king offered "great Quantities of Elephants teeth and Ambergreese." White accepted these valuable goods but reneged on their bargain; after making port in Madagascar, to purchase human chattels, White sailed for Jamaica, where he sold the princes and their attendants as slaves.[17]

In 1717, when the Mastoon brothers reached Jamaica, the colonial government in Spanish Town was composing punitive legislation in response to a recent rash of maroon uprisings; liberating the enslaved was not a priority for local leaders. Black Africans forced to work Jamaica's sugar plantations regularly defected to maroon strongholds in the mountains, and in order to curb these rebellions, Governor Peter Heywood signed into law "An Act for the more effectual punishing of Crimes committed by Slaves." One year later, a second attempt to staunch the loss of enslaved laborers resulted in "An Act for the Encouragement of voluntary Parties to suppress rebellious and runaway Negroes." And in 1719, the government passed legislation forbidding the practice of allowing the enslaved to work for hire or rent their own houses.[18] However, these punitive measures, designed to discourage and forcibly prevent the escape of enslaved black Africans like James and John Mastoon, failed to deter the brothers in their quest for freedom. After approximately eighteen months in Jamaica—months spent, presumably, sweating and bleeding in the sugar cane fields or at a local refinery— "these two young princes learn'd so much English as to Discover the Villainy and Treachery of the S^d Capt White." When finally they could speak in the language of their captors, the story told by James and John, of a privileged upbringing in Delagoa and the shock of being sold as slaves when they reached Jamaica, was so moving that "their Case was recommended to one Mr. Bowles who sued for their Liberty and obtained a sentence."[19] Notably, there is no mention of the attendants who accompanied the Mastoons and who were similarly betrayed into bondage. Most slaveholders in Jamaica and throughout the Americas were primarily concerned with the retention of their human property, not the recognition of injustices by which the enslaved came into their hands.

Notwithstanding the structural disadvantages they faced as human chattels in Jamaica, James and John Mastoon secured their freedom for two reasons. First, they were able to verbally compose a narrative of slavery that persuaded Bowles and others of the essential injustice of their legal status. Because of our familiarity with nineteenth-century slave narratives, scholars generally regard the genre as a vehicle for documenting systemic injustices with the purpose of instigating broad social change. But many of the earliest slave narratives, including those delivered orally by Adam and Basilio to Judge Sewall or by James and John Mastoon to Bowles, were not meant to bring about the end of slavery or the slave trade. Instead, these eighteenth-century accounts of captivity generally sought a more local end: personal emancipation through persuasion. When slavery was still broadly understood as a condition imposed upon foreign nationals rather than a condition inherited by birth and merited by race, individuals in bondage might plausibly hope to convince their captors of the wrongfulness of their enslavement. No matter the horrors related by Frederick Douglass, Harriet Jacobs, and other nineteenth-century chattels, no nineteenth-century slaveholder would have ever considered releasing enslaved African Americans after hearing their tales of hardship: they had been born and frequently bred into bondage, and their captivity was justified by a belief in racial inferiority. James and John Mastoon, on the other hand, began life in freedom, and slaveholders understood that their captivity was a product of circumstance; if enslaved persons could convince eighteenth-century slaveholders that they had been kidnapped unjustly, they might plausibly hope for freedom. Some of the earliest, oral slave narratives were prepared by those still in bondage, so their function understandably differs from those prepared in the nineteenth century by freed men and women longing for the liberation of the friends and family members they left behind during their escape.

Second, the Mastoon brothers escaped from slavery because their emancipation would plausibly advance British foreign policy interests and the personal fortunes of those who liberated them. Their status as princes made it more likely that James and John Mastoon would be freed, but British slavers would free anyone if they thought his or her liberation would bring economic or political benefit. To wit: during a 1709 dispute between the RAC and independent slavers, the "separate traders" alleged that "the Company has raised the price of negroes, which is more than double what it was before the Trade was laid open, in order to outdo and ruin them." The Company, in response, alleged "that one of the separate traders having made a bargain for some negroes, carry'd them to Barbadoes without paying for the same, but that the Company, in order to secure peace and a friendly correspondence with the negro Kings, sent to Barbadoes and bought the said negroes and returned them to the King from whom they were so taken."[20] In order to win preferential treatment from the black African leaders for whose custom it was in competition, the RAC returned a number of enslaved persons to Africa; their deliverance from Barbados was motivated by the prospect of an economic advantage. Since the enslaved were foreign subjects, their emancipation was a potential bargaining chip in negotiations between British entities and foreign governments—especially when the enslaved were members of a foreign ruling family.

A desire to rectify the injustice of their kidnapping may have motivated Bowles to agitate for the Mastoons' freedom, but the significant sums he spent afterwards, to keep them in comfort, suggest that he viewed his advocacy and care for the brothers as an investment on which he intended to capitalize and not only a matter of rectifying wrongdoing. Towgood writes that after their emancipation, Bowles "took them into his protection and maintained them handsomly." Bowles hoped to realize a profit on his care for the princes, and so did Towgood. However, when the ship carrying Bowles and the Mastoons to England capsized off the coast of Cuba during a hurricane, Towgood explains, "Bowles was unfortunatly Drown'd and Yo^r Memorialist took them from the S^d Rocks and hath brought them to England and ever since Subsisted them at his own Private Expence." By stressing costs incurred for the transportation, feeding, and clothing of the Mastoons, Towgood makes an appeal for generous compensation from the East India Company. He believes that their restoration will facilitate "the Carrying on and Selling a trade to Delago" and represents himself as a key to "Securing to you the trade in their Brothers Dominions." In exchange for his aid in bringing James and John Mastoon to the EIC in London, Towgood requests "such Considerations as the said Service deserves And the great advantages that may acrow to Your Company thereby."[21] And if the EIC was unwilling to recoup his expenses, Towgood later wrote, he would be willing to bring James and John Mastoon home himself, if only the board of directors would "give him Yo^r Licence to send a ship to Delago at his own Expence."[22] A narrative of injustice helped win their freedom, but in recounting their sufferings, the Mastoons also clearly intimated that their emancipation and their return to Africa would result in economic opportunities for whoever brought them home, as well as a stronger political tie between England and Delagoa.

In his memorial, Towgood claimed to have the brothers' best interests at heart, but others familiar with their treatment believed that the Mastoons effectively remained in bondage during their first few months in England. Henry Newman, secretary of the SPCK, wrote an account of the Mastoons for the archbishop of Canterbury, in which he describes Towgood as "a Rattle & a Rake" whose interest in the princes was purely pecuniary. For "the first 6 months that they were in London," Newman explained, "they were kept like Prisoners at the Spread Eagle Inn in Grace [Church] Street where they saw none but those who by chance found 'em out" and thus had "no body near 'em to hinder their Learning to Swear & Curse &c." Towgood's ill treatment of the princes was problematic, from Newman's perspective, primarily because it reflected poorly on "the Honour of the Nation, and the Religion we profess."[23] The diplomatic and evangelical implications of Towgood's conduct and the brothers' education mattered more to Newman and others involved in their care than the actual state of their bodies and souls.[24]

Towgood retained custody of the Mastoons while the EIC considered his memorial. At first, the EIC proposed sending the brothers home by way of Bombay, but Towgood objected that such a course would subject the princes (who had already endured the Middle Passage and been shipwrecked by a hurricane), "to too many calmaties in passing so many Climates," so the EIC turned the affair over to the RAC, which interrogated the brothers to ascertain whether their repatriation would actually advance its economic interests.[25] Their deliberations focused on the question of whether it would "be for the Service of the Royall African Company of England to take care of these two African Princes, and Provide in the best manner they can for Conveying them to their own Country." RAC officials questioned the Mastoons about the location of their own country with respect to the kingdom of

Monomatapa, where the RAC hoped to trade and "w[h]ich these Princes represent to be a Moon from their own Capitall." The relative proximity of Monomatapa led the RAC to conclude that the brothers "in all probability . . . cannot but be known to some or other of" its rulers. The repatriation of these formerly enslaved men was contingent on a political calculus tracking at least four different polities: England, Delagoa, Monomatapa, and Portugal— England's rival for custom in the region. When considering whether to aid the princes, the RAC considered "the nearness of Situation to the Portuguese." The Mastoons' repatriation was treated not as a matter of establishing a bilateral trade relationship but as a game of multidimensional chess complicated by unknown variables: Did they live close enough to the location where the RAC wished to establish a new fort? Would James and John have the standing to persuade other royals to favor the English over the Portuguese in trade? If their relationships with royalty were not strong enough, would "the relation of their Case and treatment . . . conciliate the Affections of the Natives to the Company's Interest"?[26] This last question is particularly telling, as it foregrounds the function of narrative in eighteenth-century diplomatic relations. In its final calculations, the RAC hoped that the Mastoons' slave narrative would sway the affections of a foreign people and create custom. When they read Towgood's memorial and listened to the brothers' account, RAC officials attempted to assess its affective potential as a diplomatic tool for establishing trade.

Although Towgood's petition to the EIC/RAC was not publicly available, eighteenth-century readers followed this account of enslaved royalty secondhand, in newspaper reports. Eventually, after the princes had languished in London for months, it was determined that the RAC—and not the EIC— would oversee the expedition returning James and John Mastoon to their homeland. Colonists learned of the Mastoons and their plight in September 1721, when it was reported that "Two Indian Princes, who were sold into Slavery some time since, are daily attending the Directors of the African Company, in Order to be sent Home. And tis said the Company expect a very beneficial Trade to their Father's Dominions by their Means. And we hear that the East India Company have presented the Gentleman that has the Care of them with Five Hundred Pounds" (*AWM* 1721/9/7). Towgood received the reward that he sought, and the RAC made clear its view that enslaved individuals should be manumitted if their release might facilitate foreign trade.[27] In this way, both the RAC and the EIC communicated to slaveholders and those held as human chattels, across the empire, that they viewed enslavement as a tool and product of foreign policy. The stories and the lives of enslaved persons were framed in the terms of international economic interests.

But in the case of James and John Mastoon, as with black African princes who would be wrongfully enslaved and then emancipated in the decades to come, religious bodies worked closely with officials overseeing trade to promote Protestantism as well. While the RAC and the EIC were still negotiating over the right to trade in Delagoa, the SPCK educated the Mastoons with a hope that their repatriation might lead to evangelical opportunities. That hope was spurred by a misrepresentation of the reason for the Mastoons' presence in London; minutes of an SPCK meeting held on February 2, 1721, note that these "Black Princes and their Retinue lately come from the Southern Coasts of Africa, and to the Eastward of the Cape of Good Hope from a Place call'd Delago with a design to inform themselves of the Religion and Customs of England."[28] This misconstruing of the Mastoons' motivation presents them as pilgrims, rather than captives seeking escape through whatever means necessary—including their conversion to and promotion of a foreign religion. In their focus on the expansion of Protestantism, the SPCK turned a blind eye to the precarity with which these recently enslaved brothers negotiated their freedom. This willful ignorance should not surprise; as Edward Andrews notes, the Protestant desire for native missionaries was so great that some even suggested that black Africans and American Indians be kidnapped for the purpose of indoctrinating them as emissaries for the faith. This proposal was intended to "give Anglicans the opportunity to strike back at Catholics and provide an institutional framework for competing against Spanish, Portuguese, and French rivals" for imperial control of the Americas, Africa, and elsewhere.[29] The Mastoon brothers were viewed as pawns of economic and religious imperialism, the means by which English Protestantism would triumph spiritually and financially over the specter of Catholic tyranny.

Notwithstanding their emancipation, the Mastoons were never free in London. James and John Mastoon wanted nothing more than to return to their homeland, but their dependence on a rake like Towgood or even the self-interested benevolence of the RAC and the SPCK left them at the mercy of groups committed to the conversion and economic exploitation of Delagoa. Their sense of living under the duress of constraint is evident in one of their only recorded speech acts. At a meeting of the SPCK on October 5, 1721, more than a year after their arrival in London, James and John were introduced to Society members who inquired "whether the African Company wuld be dispos'd to send any Person or Persons over sea with the Princes capable of Instructing them." In response, the Princes "signify'd that if any

Persons would go over with them to instruct them they should be kindly receiv'd, and if they did not like the Country they should be at Liberty to return to England in the same ship that carry'd 'em over."[30] This invitation from the Mastoons also functions as an implicit rebuke, contrasting the faux hospitality of Englishmen, who had held them in London for many months after their supposed emancipation, with the simple hospitality of their own country, where visitors would be free to leave immediately if Delagoa did not suit. Their offer is a plea for help, an expression of their desire to return to home. Until they could make this choice, James and John Mastoon would continue to regard the increased mobility and improved treatment offered them as a counterfeit or partial liberty.

As with Towgood's memorial, this account of the Mastoons' interactions with the SPCK was not available to a broader public, but the narrative that did circulate reinforced the message that accounts of slavery were to be read as extensions of English foreign policy. Newspaper readers who had previously learned that James and John were freed to advance RAC trade interests in Africa now read that "the two Princes, brought hither from the Eastern Coast of Africa, having been instructed in the Principles of the Christian Religion, were Baptized at Tuddington, in Middlesex, by the Rev. Dr. Pratt, Dean of Rochester; the Duke of Chandois and the Ld Visc. Fane, standing Godfathers and the Lady Pope Blunt Godmother" (*BNL* 1722/2/5). Notice of their baptisms and a reminder of their bondage, when the Mastoons were "brought hither," are flanked with announcements of new affiliations in this newspaper report, which frames the baptism as both a sacred ordinance and a de facto treaty. Although their conversion to Christianity may have been sincere, it was also strategically advantageous. As John Catron observes, "By embracing Christianity in the eighteenth century, blacks were not simply accommodating white culture and the social realities of a brutal system of coerced labor; they were, rather, attempting what became resistance within accommodation."[31] For the Mastoons, baptism was a step towards self-determination and repatriation; for the RAC, the SPCK, and the readers of English newspapers, their baptism represented an ecclesiastical and commercial alliance. By stressing the creation of new, symbolic relationships between English and Delagoan royalty, this account subordinates both slavery and sacrament to the more pressing concerns of English nationalism and militant Protestantism.

Eventually, with support from the RAC, the SPCK identified an instructor willing to travel with the Mastoons to Delagoa and continue their religious education in Africa. A missionary named Marmaduke Penwell agreed to accompany the brothers, and in March 1722, more than eighteen months after they first arrived in London, preparations for their journey home began in earnest. Penwell, James, and John were to sail on the *Northampton* under the command of Captain Sharrow, who was given £100 to provision his passengers. But their voyage got off to a rocky start; the brothers, who had already endured the Middle Passage and shipwrecked in a hurricane on their journey from Jamaica to England, were delayed in their return home when the *Northampton* ran aground at Exmouth on March 24, 1722. Reporting this misfortune to the SPCK, Penwell estimated that the *Northampton* would be seaworthy again in two weeks, but he and the Mastoons were still in Exmouth more than a month later, when tragedy struck.

During their time in Exmouth, James Mastoon struggled to behave in the disciplined, Christian manner that Penwell expected: he swore and drank and slept in, neglecting his assigned devotional readings. He behaved, in other words, as he had grown accustomed during his time with Towgood, only reforming when Penwell threatened to report his behavior to John Perceval, his SPCK sponsor. While Newman saw the SPCK as an organization freeing the Mastoons from vice, James experienced the prohibition of vice as a form of bondage. When he attempted to join two men from the *Northampton* on a stroll, "they was not willing he should go along with them so out walk'd him," abandoning him in the English countryside. After this slight, James tried to run away to London, "but was prevented by the Mate of the Ship going after him & brought him back."[32] Notwithstanding their emancipation, their baptisms, and the patronage of royalty, including the Duke of Chandos and the Earl of Egmont, the Mastoons were still not free. Their stigmatized black bodies made them unfit company in the eyes of their benefactor captors, but if James was not welcome to walk with them, neither was he welcome to walk away from them. Although they were no longer enslaved, the Mastoons were still constrained by racism and an expectation that they embrace the conventions of Christianity and English manners.

The strain of living in this liminal state of nonfreedom culminated in suicide two weeks after this escape attempt, on May 1, 1722, when James Chandos Mastoon ended his own life, hanging himself near the midnight hour. Newman, explaining this incident to the Archbishop, blamed his death on "the disorder in his head [which] he has discover'd at certain times [which] makes this accident the less surprising to his friends."[33] James may have behaved in ways that we now associate with mental illness, but the trauma of his various ordeals—his misfortunes at sea, the violence he endured on the sugar plantations of Jamaica, the strain of living abroad—was more likely to blame for his demise than a genetic or preexisting psychological condition. Recounting his death to Perceval, Penwell wrote that "James & his brother had some words, from words to blows. I hearing an unusuall noise came down stairs & saw Catpn Sharrow a beating Prince James. As soon as he saw me, he called me a Presbiterian rogue & said he wou'd use me like a Scoundrell when he got me on board." Penwell, cowed by this threat, retreated to his room, leaving James to his fate. The elder Mastoon refused to sleep under the same roof as Sharrow and sought refuge at two different houses but was turned away by a housekeeper and then a maid before wandering off into the night. When Sharrow was told of James Mastoon's disappearance and asked to order his retrieval, "Capn Sharrow asnwer'd that he might go & hang himself for he wou'd not send after him."[34] Sharrow's curt rejection proved prophetic. In the morning, James was found in an apple tree, hung among its blossoms by his own garters.

James was not lynched, but his untimely death was a product of racial violence and slavery-related traumas. Although Sharrow was charged with returning the Mastoons to their homeland in relative comfort, he was also a professional slaver in the employ of the RAC, who purchased human chattels after his visit to Delagoa so that he could bring them through the Middle Passage to be sold in the West Indies. Beating James Mastoon may conceivably have been well intentioned, an attempt to protect John Mastoon from future assaults, but it may also have been an inadvertent expression of Sharrow's true feelings or a reversion to his habitual treatment of black Africans. Whatever Sharrow's motive, this violence from a man he was supposed to trust, who was supposed to transport him safely over the ocean, probably recalled, for James, his betrayal and suffering at the hands of White, as well as the beatings he endured in Jamaica. He likely took his own life to prevent a return to slavery, forestalling future violence from Sharrow and others. Suicide, as Terri Snyder laments, was sometimes the last meaningful choice left to the enslaved and has accordingly been framed reductively as "the ultimate act of resistance."[35] Mastoon was not legally enslaved at the time of his death, but his suicide is a reminder of the ways in which slavery's dehumanizing brutality effected psychological violence and mental instability. This dehumanization was perpetuated after emancipation, when the Mastoons continued to endure unfreedom, held in London while the EIC, the RAC, and the SPCK treated the brothers like poker chips in their promotion of English and Protestant interests.

When John Towgood Mastoon finally returned to Delagoa, he rejected Penwell, Christianity, and the English. Upon his return home, John rushed into his mother's home and slammed the door in Penwell's face; Penwell waited outside for six hours, at which point the surviving brother reappeared and, with surly treatment, persuaded the missionary to leave.[36] This rejection of Penwell and England may have been a political calculation, as "the Dutch had settled a Factory there," and John would have been able to see that the Dutch would be more useful to his family and friends in Delagoa going forward than the English. But it might also have been a straightforward and sincere expression of his feelings. Finally free, in his homeland, to demonstrate what he really thought of English and Christian culture without having to worry that the RAC or the SPCK might send him back into slavery, John spurned his captors. This rejection may be the reason why Penwell reported to Perceval that "a commander of a Ship that was lost here July last past knew Prince John & told him he was a villain to impose so much upon the African Company in telling them that he was a Prince."[37] As long as the Mastoons might be useful ambassadors for the SPCK or the RAC, it was to the advantage of all—Towgood, the Mastoons themselves, Sharrow, Penwell, and the organizations depending on their influence—to inflate their social standing. Once John had rebuffed the English, their status as princes was no longer advantageous; indeed, characterizing them as rude or relatively lowborn might help to mitigate any negative news arising from their rejection. John Towgood Mastoon made it home alive because he understood that his survival was a matter of foreign relations, of posing as an ambassador of goodwill for his captors. But because his professions of friendship—and, perhaps, his claims of social prominence—were exaggerated, the narrative of his personal diplomatic success and of his brother's tragic end was buried: in letterbooks, the SPCK minutes, and other private manuscripts.

Diallo and the African Endorsement of Slavery

Because the Mastoon brothers eventually spurned Penwell and England, this failure of foreign relations never received the same publicity that their initial cooperation with the RAC and conversion to Christianity did. The lessons of their baptism and of Towgood's compensation were absorbed by a colonial population whose knowledge of the Delagoa princes came primarily through the newspaper. So when, a decade later, the noble-born Diallo arrived in Maryland wearing chains, these colonists knew just what to do. Like Towgood, they sent word of Diallo's condition to the RAC in London, where James Oglethorpe—a Member of Parliament, director of the RAC, and founder of the colony of Georgia—was so interested in Diallo's story and his potential utility as an advocate for the RAC that he arranged for the purchase of Diallo's freedom and his passage to England.[38] There Diallo, like the Mastoons, was fêted by the English nobility until he could be sent back to his father in Africa. Since Diallo spoke highly of England and promised to promote English trade after his return, this triumph of diplomacy was publicized in a narrative penned by Thomas Bluett, who met Diallo in Maryland and accompanied him across the Atlantic to London.

Even though Bluett's *Some Memoirs of the Life of Job* was written a generation before works such as *A Narrative of the Uncommon Sufferings, and Surprizing Deliverance of Briton Hammon, a Negro Man,—Servant to General Winslow, of Marshfield, in New-England* (1760) and so might warrant a claim of primacy in the field of African American literature, it is often neglected by scholars.[39] This neglect may be a function of Bluett's mediating white hand and its visible presence on the title page, whereas the influence of white editors, amanuenses, publishers, and readers is largely implicit in the *Narrative* of Hammon or the poems of Phillis Wheatley Peters and Jupiter Hammon. Or perhaps our collective disinterest has more to do with the fact that Diallo unapologetically practiced slavery both before and after his own experience of bondage. Scholars have devoted significant resources to *A Narrative of the Life and Adventures of Venture* (1798), who purchased two enslaved black Africans after his emancipation, but they frequently gloss over the implications of his status as a dealer in human chattels.[40] To dwell on the participation of Diallo and Venture in the bodily subjugation of other human beings even after they had themselves endured the Middle Passage and the rigors of enslavement is to separate the slave narrative from its identification with slavery's abolition. Indeed, to acknowledge and think carefully about their unabashed acquisition of other human beings as property is to risk implying that a slaver might author a slave narrative—that a genre we associate with resistance might be complicit in the work of oppression. Small wonder, then, that Bluett's *Memoirs* and Diallo's story have been marginalized in discussions of the earliest African American literatures.

Neither Diallo nor Venture express any interest in abolishing the institution of slavery, and neither conceived of his life story as a vehicle for social reform. Diallo told his story in order to secure his freedom and viewed his experience of enslavement as an object lesson in foreign relations. For him, for Bluett, and for the readers who considered his experiences, enslavement was a matter of politics, borders, war, and diplomacy. As James Campbell notes, Diallo's enslavement was likely a function of "the emergence of the Bambara empire in the interior [which] unleashed a flow of captives and war prisoners to the coast."[41] Both Bluett's *Memoirs* and the denouement of Diallo's story, which was recorded by Francis Moore, attest to the fact that narratives of slavery served to delineate lines of allegiance and enmity between sovereign peoples and their princes. Whereas slave narratives of the nineteenth century stress the common humanity and universal rights of all people, whether enslaved or free, their precursors in the eighteenth century worked to divide one group from another and to clarify which of those groups deserved their freedom.

Diallo's story of captivity begins with an acknowledgment of international borders and African politics. Born into a wealthy Fulani family of Muslim imams in the Kingdom of Futa Toro, Diallo was sent in 1730 to sell two of the family's human chattels to an RAC slave ship moored on the Gambia River. Before Diallo left home, his father warned him "not to venture over the River, because the Country of the *Mandingoes*, who are Enemies to the People of *Futa*, lies on the other side."[42] This question of boundaries is one on which Diallo dwells at some length, because in his experience, borders beget bondage. Bluett writes that Diallo "was born at a Town called *Boonda* in the County of *Galumbo* (in our Maps *Catumbo*) in the Kingdom of *Futa* in *Africa*; which lies on both Sides the River *Senegal*, and on the south Side reaches as far as the River *Gambia*. These two Rivers, Job assured me, run pretty near parallel to one another, and never meet, contrary to the Position they have in most of our Maps. The Eastern Boundary of the Kingdom of *Futa* or *Senega* is the great Lake, called in our Maps *Lacus Guarde*."[43] Diallo—or Job, as Bluett rendered the name Ayuba—lingers over the geography of Futa Toro because, as his father warned, his person was secure only so long as he remained within its limits.

Near Fort James and the village of Joar, Diallo met with Stephen Pike, who captained the *Arabella* for the RAC and who would be Diallo's captor during the journey across the Atlantic. However, during this first meeting they conferred on an equal footing, as Diallo sought to sell his chattels to Pike. When Pike refused to pay Diallo's asking price, the African slaver "crossed the River *Gambia*" and sold two humans for twenty-eight cows.[44] Slavery was, for Diallo, an international affair of boundaries negotiated by buyers, sellers, and human cargo alike, so his own story of bondage begins with an accounting of the multiple national interests present at the site of his enslavement. The "Negroes" he bartered were almost certainly not natives of Futa Toro, and after attempting to sell them to an Englishman, Diallo and an interpreter named Loumein Yoai traversed the Mandinke border to complete the sale; at least three and probably four different nations were involved in this transaction.

On his return journey home, Diallo and Yoai laid down their weapons at the home of a friend, where they stopped for a meal, only to be kidnapped by a company of Mandinke bandits "who live upon Plunder." Their status as foreigners made Diallo and Yoai vulnerable; like ships in the Mediterranean, whose passengers were enslaved by North African corsairs simply because they were in foreign waters, Diallo and Yoai lost their right to freedom as soon as they were beyond the protection of their prince. In an effort to further distance Diallo and Yoai from the protections of a prince and nation-state, the Mandinke raiders shaved their beards and hair, "to make them appear like Slaves taken in War."[45] Because Samuel Sewall and others around the world accepted slavery as an ethical consequence for captives taken in a just war, their Mandinke captors sought to disguise Diallo and Yoai as enemy combatants. But as I observe in chapter 1, this sleight of hand was precisely the problem outlined by Sewall. If slavery may be justified by a war, only someone with a comprehensive knowledge of international affairs and foreign peoples could begin to assess whether a particular individual had rightly been made a captive, and even then, the particulars of an enslaved person's history might be falsified, as in the case of Diallo and Yoai. Their shaved heads and faces were narrative props meant to tell a story of just enslavement to Englishmen whose grasp of African languages and whose interest in the means by which the enslaved came to wear shackles were equally suspect.

Ironically, Diallo was brought back to Fort James and sold to Pike, who initially failed to recognize him as the slaver whose offer of human cargo he had recently rebuffed. While he was held there, Diallo's presence may have been recorded by Moore, a clerk for the RAC who noted the *Arabella*'s departure for Maryland and who would welcome Diallo back to Africa four years later. Eventually, Diallo managed to communicate his status as a member of the Futa Toro ruling class, and a message was sent to his father, pleading for his redemption; Douglas Grant notes that Pike's asking price for Diallo's redemption was set at two slaves—or the exact cargo that Pike had refused to purchase from Diallo, days earlier, and that Diallo had subsequently exchanged for twenty-eight Mandinke cows.[46] But Pike, Moore, and other representatives of the RAC at Fort James were unwilling to wait indefinitely for Diallo's ransom to arrive, so Diallo sailed with Yoai, aboard the *Arabella*, to Maryland.[47] Only years later would Diallo learn that his father tried to secure his freedom by sending two enslaved individuals to take his place in bondage; neither Diallo nor his father objected to slavery itself, only to their personal subjugation within that dehumanizing system. Since his father's offering did not arrive until after the *Arabella* had sailed, Diallo endured the same journey on which he had sent so many others, arriving in Annapolis as human cargo.[48]

Although he offered a verbal slave narrative of sorts to Pike, Moore, and others at Fort James, the full benefit of Diallo's facility with language only came to bear after his arrival in Annapolis. Vachell Denton, an American agent for William Hunt who served as a director for the Bank of England and had helped to fund the voyage, arranged for Diallo's sale to a tobacco planter named Tolsey. But Diallo—whose life as a member of the ruling class in Futa Toro had not prepared him for the strenuous labor of growing and harvesting tobacco—soon proved a poor investment. Bluett writes that "he every Day shewed more and more Uneasiness under this Exercise, and at last grew sick, being no way able to bear it; so that his Master was obliged to find easier Work for him" herding cattle.[49] However, even this respite resulted in trials, as a white youth persecuted him whenever he left the herd to pray. Eventually, unable to communicate his dissatisfaction in English, Diallo ran away from Tolsey and was taken up by a magistrate unable to determine, initially, where he had escaped from. Although I have been unable to locate a notice published by Tolsey or the magistrate, an advertisement printed two years earlier describes the predicament in which Diallo found himself:

> *New-Castle* County, ss.
>
> ON the 31th Day of *October* last, a Strange Negroe Man, was taken up as a Run-away in *Miln Creek* Hundred in this County; He is a Low sized Slender and nimble Fellow, seems to be about Twenty five Years old; has a large Head, small Hands and Legs, looks Wild and Staring, wears a Brown Jacket, ragged black Shirt, short Ozenbriggs Trowsers, with a Pair of Leather Breechces underneath; he seems, as if he cannot Speak, or understand English, or the Language of any of the Negroes of this Place; so that 'tis not yet known here to whom, or where, he belongs. Whoever knows the said Negroe, or his Owner; are desired to make the same known to the Sheriff of the said County, *Wm. Read* (*AWM* 1729/11/13)

William Read understood that communicating with an enslaved person who knew no English would require locating a second enslaved black African with the right language skills to act as a translator. For this reason, slave owners and officials had to track, as best they could, the region in Africa from which each of their chattels had been kidnapped. In the nineteenth century, enslaved individuals often lamented that their African heritage had been forgotten or deliberately concealed by owners who wished to keep them ignorant, but in the early eighteenth century—when holding slaves required communicating with individuals from a wide range of linguistic backgrounds—that knowledge was potentially valuable.

Luckily for Diallo, Bluett took an interest in his case and attempted to communicate with him, allowing Diallo to demonstrate his literacy and awaken Bluett's curiosity. Grant notes that Bluett was both an attorney and a clergyman, whose affiliation with the Society for the Propagation of the Gospel likely led to his recognition of Diallo's Islamic faith.[50] When Bluett attempted to communicate by "Talking and making Signs to him, he wrote a Line or two before us, and when he read it, pronounced the Words *Allah* and *Mahommed*; by which, and his refusing a Glass of Wine we offered him, we perceived he was a *Mahometan*, but could not imagine of what Country he was, or how he got thither." Crucially, Diallo's verbal slave narrative activated both the imagination and the active participation of his audience, who responded to a brief, partially understood account with interest and a desire to flesh out the narrative. Bluett's two primary lines of inquiry are interrelated; in the eighteenth century, the questions of which country Diallo had come from and how he had become a slave were, in some sense, merely different facets of the same question. In their eagerness to expand the narrative, Bluett and his companions sought nonlinguistic evidence, deducing "by his affable Carriage, and the easy Composure of his Countenance" that "he was no common Slave."[51] Even though his audience understood only two words of his written narrative—a far more fragmentary account than even the most abbreviated texts treated in this study—Diallo excited sympathy and communicated the message that he had been unjustly enslaved.

Only after Diallo had endured "some time" as a captive was he able to communicate through a translator and prepare a second, more detailed and moving slave narrative. When an old black African who spoke Joloff, one of the languages with which Diallo was familiar, visited him, the runaway explained that he had fled from Tolsey and expressed a desire for religious accommodation. After Tolsey came to reclaim him, Diallo received "a Place to pray in, and some other Conveniencies" but continued to seek his freedom.[52] Writing a letter to his father in Arabic, he sent it to Denton, who forwarded it to London in the hope that it might eventually make its way to Fort James and his father in Futa Toro. But this second slave narrative found an intermediate audience in Oglethorpe, who arranged for its translation into English. Oglethorpe found the letter so compelling that he made arrangements for Denton to purchase Diallo back from Tolsey for £45 and send him to London.[53] Even though he could not communicate in English, his narrative prowess won Diallo concessions from Tolsey and, ultimately, his freedom.

Upon his arrival in England, Diallo worked to establish relationships and skills that would strengthen the relationship between England and Futa Toro. Just as he had instructed Bluett in the political boundaries of his own country, Diallo quizzed the sailors who brought him to England on the geographical features of their homeland. They taught him of "the Head Lands and remarkable Places" they passed, and he wrote down their accounts so that he could reference them "if he met with any *Englishman* in his Country." Diallo's interest in topography, and his description of the English coastline, might seem unrelated or ancillary to the narratives he wrote. However, he and Bluett and others who recorded stories of enslavement in the eighteenth century understood that accounts of bondage were always imbricated in a geopolitical matrix, such that situating human beings within landscapes real and figurative often determined whether or not they were identified as slaves or freemen. Diallo believed that his knowledge of English geography might protect him from being enslaved a second time, in the future; the only Englishmen he was likely to meet in Africa were slavers, and he likely hoped that a knowledge of the English coast—as well, presumably, as a new respect for Mandinke borders—would preserve his liberty in the future.

In addition to his study of geographical features, Diallo spent time cultivating relationships with English gentry. His status as a member of the ruling class in Futa Toro helped him secure the sympathy of Bluett, Oglethorpe, and others who identified with Diallo because they saw him as a peer.[54] Indeed, Grant reports that Diallo applied for and received membership in the Gentlemen's Society of Spalding. His own literacy, as demonstrated in a letter of application—and in yet another narrative of his enslavement, penned by the tradesman and antiquarian Joseph Ames—was deemed sufficient evidence of his status as a master, not a slave.[55]

During his time in Hertfordshire, Diallo "had the Honour to be sent for by most of the Gentry of that Place," and those members of the ruling class purchased his freedom. English gentry sought Diallo's acquaintance, but also Diallo reciprocally sought the acquaintance of English royalty. When Diallo "expressed his great Desire to see the Royal Family," a meeting was arranged. With the support of his benefactors, "he was soon cloathed in a rich silk Dress, made up after his own Country Fashion, and introduced to their Majesties, and the rest of the Royal Family. Her Majesty was pleased to present him with a rich Gold watch; and the same Day he had the Honour to dine with his Grace the Duke of *Mountague*, and some others of the Nobility, who were pleased to make him a handsome Present after Dinner."[56] Among the gifts made to Diallo were a number of agricultural implements and other

goods intended for use in Gambia. While some of these presents—the clothing, for instance—were largely gestures of goodwill, many were clearly meant
to demonstrate the utility and desirability of English technology to a visitor
who would soon be in a position to influence trade negotiations. When English nobility fêted Diallo, they sought to establish a relationship that would
bolster foreign trade in the future and not merely to apologize for or rectify
his wrongful enslavement.

Bluett saw Diallo embark for Africa in July 1734, so his narrative concludes
with the "hope he is safely arrived, to the great Joy of his Friends, and the
Honour of the *English* Nation."[57] But because Moore welcomed him back to
Gambia and penned an account of his time with Diallo, we have a denouement to *Some Memoirs* in which Diallo confirms his appreciation of England
and English traders while also demonstrating his continued belief in slavery
as an institution. Indeed, because Diallo uses the gifts given him by English
gentry to purchase human chattels, his affirmations of a special regard for
England might be seen as synonymous with his implicit affirmation that slavery is just and that the slave trade is sound policy.

After Diallo's arrival at Fort James, he and Moore traveled together to Joar.
En route, they met with six of the Mandinke slavers who had captured Diallo
three years earlier, which prompted him to reflect on both his experience of
enslavement and his relationship with the English. Hearing from the slavers
that the pistol which Pike had traded to the slavers as compensation had mis-
fired and accidentally killed the Mandinke king, Diallo remarked to Moore,

> you see now God Almighty was displeas'd at this Man's making me a
> Slave, and therefore made him die by the very Pistol for which he sold
> me; yet I ought to forgive him, *says he*, because had I not been sold,
> I should neither have known any thing of the *English* Tongue, nor have
> had any of the fine, useful and valuable Things I now carry over, nor
> have known that in the World there is such a Place as *England*, nor such
> noble, good and generous People as Queen *Caroline*, Prince *William*, the
> Duke of *Montague*, the Earl of *Pembroke*, Mr *Holden*, Mr *Oglethorpe*, and
> the Royal *African* Company.[58]

According to Moore, Diallo holds Pike, the RAC, and England blameless, but
he condemns the Mandinke and suggests that they incurred divine wrath for
kidnapping him. Slavery writ large causes no divine displeasure, only his personal enslavement. That he praises the RAC—whose presence in Gambia
spurred the demand for slaves—speaks to Diallo's comfort with human bondage
as a source of labor and his prioritization of personal and national economic

interests over any reckoning with the moral and social implications of slavery. More important than the prospect of men and women undergoing the Middle Passage in the future were his relationships with English royalty and the prosperity that an improved trade relationship with the RAC might bring to Futa Toro.

Indeed, in his eager promotion of English interests, Diallo worked to make the transatlantic slave trade more acceptable to his countrymen. Moore reports that because no enslaved black African sold to the English had ever returned to the continent, Diallo's peers believed that "all who were sold for Slaves, were generally either eaten or murdered." But since "he spoke always very handsome of the *English*, and what he said, took away a great deal of the Horror of the *Pholeys* [Fulani] for the State of Slavery amongst the *English*," his countrymen were more willing to participate in the trade. In other words, the slave narrative Diallo shared verbally in Gambia actually promoted trade with English slavers like Moore and Pike. And with the trade goods given him in England, Diallo "bought a Woman-Slave and two Horses."[59] This purchase represented an endorsement of chattel bondage, as Diallo converted his social capital among both the Fulani and the English into human capital.[60]

Diallo's only interest in the curtailment of slavery and the slave trade concerned the bondage of other Muslims. Grant writes that in his bargaining with the RAC, Diallo persuaded them to agree that "whenever a Mohammedan was bought as a slave by the Company's agents in the Gambia, he should be allowed to redeem himself upon application, in exchange for two other good slaves."[61] This provision, of course, expands the scope of slavery; in the place of one enslaved person, two—a bargain that the RAC and other traders would have been all too happy to accept, whether or not the captive identified as a Muslim. In seeking to establish his own people as a privileged class, Diallo only underscores the social divisions that made slavery possible in the first place—identifying all non-Muslims as potential bondsmen.

Diallo's rhetorical prowess won privileged status for his kinsmen, strengthened economic ties between the English and Fulani peoples, and provided additional support for the slave trade. After his return, Diallo both purchased a human chattel himself and promoted the sale of African peoples to English traders. His narratives of enslavement, both those he shared himself in Joloff and Arabic, as well as those prepared in English, on his behalf, fostered systems of bondage and oppression.[62] Because they prop up slavery and the slave trade and because Diallo seemingly always self-identified as a master, readers might reasonably object to any characterization of these relations as slave narratives. As James Olney attests, the genre has long been identified with a group of texts with "very specific motives, intentions, and uses under-stood by narrators, sponsors, and audiences alike: to reveal the truth of slav-ery and so to bring about its abolition."[63] To acknowledge Diallo's story as a slave narrative is to recognize the inadequacy of this foundational assump-tion about the motives, intentions, and uses of the genre. By the nineteenth century, abolition had become the purpose for which black writers and narra-tors told their stories of bondage, but in the eighteenth century, the enslaved and their allies were more concerned with personal emancipation and with the promotion of national interests than with dismantling a dehumanizing global system.

The Standardization of Royalty

Although Diallo was not, strictly speaking, a prince, he was recognized as a religious and civic leader with the standing of a nobleman by Bluett, Oglethorpe, and the English gentry. By contrast, the Mastoons were com-monly accepted as princes, but when Penwell saw how they lived in Dela-goa, he declared that their political power and influence had been overstated. The problem for Penwell, Bluett, and others who wanted to assess the social status of enslaved black Africans was that they could not map African claims of power and influence directly onto Western systems of governance. Diallo's place in the theocratic society of Futa Toro, for example, had no clear analog in the parliamentary monarchy of Great Britain. This problem might have seemed idiosyncratic when RAC and SPCK officials considered the case of the Mastoons or when Bluett published *Some Memoirs*, but as enslaved indi-viduals continued to self-identify as princes and request repatriation, it came to seem more pressing, and in 1750, the RAC published another account of royalty in bondage that doubles as a primer on how to process both claims of royalty and the slave narrative as a genre.

The Royal African: or, Memoirs of the Young Prince of Annamaboe was pub-lished in 1749 to document the experiences of William Ansah Sessarakoo, who in 1747 was taken from his home in Annamaboe on the Gold Coast of Africa and sold as a chattel in Barbados before being redeemed and returned to his home by way of England. At least, the book bills itself as a biography of Sessarakoo. However, readers who opened it expecting the life story of a ce-lebrity were likely disappointed; Sessarakoo, who is never identified by name, makes no appearance until two-thirds of the way through the book. Instead of focusing on Sessarakoo's life, *The Royal African* considers the status of en-slaved black African princes and the stories of enslaved people more broadly, detailing the diplomatic, political, and economic history of Annamaboe in an attempt to hammer home the point that readers must consider each slave narrative as an extension of foreign relations, rather than a biography.[64] As Ryan Hanley notes, "Readers of *The Royal African* were reminded constantly that Sessarakoo's status as the legitimate son of and—as it was incorrectly assumed—heir to a powerful trading partner made him an object of significant diplomatic utility."[65] The book's primary purpose is to establish Annamaboe's significance as an English trading partner and Sessarakoo's standing in Annamaboe society.

The book opens with a letter, written by the anonymous author of *The Royal African* to an unnamed nobleman, that acknowledges the influence of newspaper slave narratives on global perceptions of England and English character. Because the story of Sessarakoo's betrayal by an Englishman was publicized in newspapers throughout Europe, the nobleman had lamented that "*all* Europe *should be informed of a Fact that does us so little Honour.*" The *Royal African*, then, was written to restore the esteem of readers in Europe and throughout the world for English probity and policies. Although newspapers carried the initial, disgraceful story of Sessarakoo's enslavement, there was no guarantee that each paper would print word of his redemption, honorable reception in England, and repatriation. So the author,

> *not being perfectly satisfied with the Narrative in the News-Papers, and having had always a Curiosity to learn, with as much Exactness as my be, the Circumstances that attend such extraordinary Events as happen in our own Times, I have been, perhaps, more diligent and nice in my Enquiries into the Matter of Fact, and whatever relates to it, than many People, and finding my Pains rewarded by some Acquisitions of Knowledge, which I thought considerable, it appeared to me worth employing a few leisure Hours, in reducing what I have learned into some Kind of Order, that the Facts and Observations might not escape my Memory.*[66]

In other words, the author writes to correct and augment an abbreviated, fragmentary slave narrative he found in the newspaper, conducting research and collating multiple sources to create a more expansive account of Sessarakoo's life in precisely the manner that I have suggested other readers consumed newspaper accounts of slavery. This new, enlarged narrative aimed to improve England's international standing by demonstrating the nation's respect for the royalty of other nations.

Patrick Dwyer, the slave captain who betrayed Sessarakoo and sold him into slavery, allegedly planned to hold him for ransom until he could be

redeemed by Sessarakoo's father, John Corrantee, but Dwyer died unexpect-
edly just after his ship, *Lively*, arrived in Barbados and Sessarakoo had been
sold.[67] Friends of Dwyer defended his abuse of Sessarakoo by "*denying that
the Person so treated is a* Prince," so the author of *The Royal African* takes up the
broader question of how to consider claims of black African royalty such as
those forwarded by Sessarakoo, Diallo, and the Mastoons. Acknowledging
that the titles of "*Emperor, King, and Prince*" have been applied to black African rulers "*with visible Impropriety upon some Occasions*," the author nevertheless insists that such honorifics are appropriate. "*It is no Matter*," he
writes, "*what his* Title *be in* Africa, *or what the Nature of that Government
which he administers; for if he be at the* Head *of it, can assist, or injure us in our
Trade, he is strictly speaking a* Prince; *and his Children may be so stiled by Cour-
tesey without any Solecism.*"[68] The real task, he proposes, is not mapping European political titles onto black African leaders but assessing the power of
those leaders to influence trade, either directly, by shifting their custom to rival nations, or indirectly, by impugning the character of Englishmen. This
flexible approach to identifying black Africans with a claim on English respect would enlarge the number of enslaved persons who might plausibly
identify as princes. *The Royal African* thus codifies an earlier RAC emphasis
on treating black "Africans with humanity, hospitality, and dignity, a dignity
that remained attached to royalty," as Pettigrew attests.[69]

The ultimate effect of this more humane view of black Africans is to regard
more and more of the enslaved as worthy of royal treatment. Relating the
story of an Englishman who won the confidence of his Senegambian hosts
"*by his Kindness and good Usage*" and so "*was by them directed to a* Gold Mine,"
Sessarakoo's biographer condemns the racism engendered by slavery and
proposes that all black Africans be regarded as potential diplomatic allies. He
writes

> that it is from an humane and generous Treatment of Negroes, and indeed of
> all barbarous Nations in general, that we must expect such Discoveries, as well
> as reap greater Advantages in Trade, than other Nations. For whatever some
> Men may think, human Nature is the same in all Countries, and under all
> Complexions; and to fancy that superior Power or superior Knowledge gives
> one Race of People a Title to use another Race who are weaker or more igno-
> rant with Haughtiness or Contempt, is to abuse Power and Science, and in
> spite of both to shew ourselves worse Men than those who have neither.[70]

Given that the humane and generous treatment extended to princes generally
involved emancipation, this proposal is tantamount to calling for abolition,

but the author never takes the argument to its logical conclusion. It might seem surprising that the RAC would sponsor a publication that even hints at abolition, but this proposal actually doubles down on the cold, greedy logic that spurred slavery in the first place. The only reason given to treat black Africans generously is a desire for "*greater Advantages in Trade, than other Nations.*" If humanity had proved more profitable than cruelty, the RAC undoubtedly would have been happy to operate with a spirit of generosity—but in practice, only an acutal prince was worth more when he was free.

The author's history of Annamaboe, which forms the bulk of the book, serves to foreground the role of diplomacy in securing the right to African trade and, therefore, in the experience and narration of enslavement. He traces the role of diplomacy in securing the African slave trade back to the reign of Edward IV, who received "a solemn Embassy" from John II of Portugal in 1481, requesting that the English monarch prevent his subjects from traveling to Guinea. Almost two centuries later, in 1679, shortly after English merchants had established the RAC, they built a fort in Annamaboe "with Consent of the Natives, who received an annual Rent for the Ground upon which it stood."[71] From the beginning, then, English access to African goods and human chattels required negotiation both with European monarchs and with black African potentates, who could dicker with the representatives of multiple countries in order to drive a better bargain.

The presence of multiple European suitors willing to compete for the right to buy human chattels meant that black African leaders such as Sessarakoo's father enjoyed a degree of leverage in these negotiations. *The Royal African* documents that power imbalance, crediting the good government of Corrantee and the freedom of his people as the reason they could pit European powers against one another: "The Liberty which these People enjoy makes them both powerful and rich; so that the *English*, the *Dutch*, and the *French*, neither have, nor pretend to have any coercive Power over them, nor ever had." Because the merchants of Annamaboe could easily "transfer their own Trade which was very considerable either to the *Dutch*, or to the *English Interlopers*" who competed with the RAC, "they were at all times obliged to live upon good terms with the inhabitants and *Braffo of Annamaboe*," and the slave trade was contingent upon the Company's ability to cultivate goodwill with Corrantee, who Randy Sparks describes as a "wily diplomat." The burden of diplomacy and courtesy thus fell on European traders rather than black African princes, who could find other slavers with relative ease. Conscious that this state of affairs would surprise English readers, the anonymous author notes that "for a hundred and fifty Years past several Nations have been bidding one against another; and . . . one need not wonder that the Negroes, dull as they are (nor are they near so dull as they are represented) have been sufficiently taught to avail themselves of their own Power, and of the Follies and Vices of the *Europeans*."[72] The power to purchase enslaved black Africans was contingent on the cultivation of goodwill with black African princes, and their favor could be won or lost in accordance with the stories told by and about the enslaved.

Both Sessarakoo's kidnapping and his emancipation were byproducts of a diplomatic arms race in Annamaboe, as French and English traders competed for influence with Corrantee; his narrative of enslavement is an account of failed foreign relations and their subsequent repair. Wishing to curry favor with Corrantee and to become "the most favoured Nation at *Annamaboe*," French traders proposed taking one of his sons to France, where he would be educated, fêted, and shown the magnificence of the court.[73] Consenting to this proposal, Corrantee gave the French a son named Bassi, and he "was received with all the Honours due to a Prince," returning clothed in "fine laced Cloaths to dazzle the Eyes of the Negroes, and to draw the Father over entirely to the *French* Interest." Although Corrantee continued to trade with the RAC, the stories told by his son of French finery led him to increase the volume of Annamaboe's trade with France. English traders, who wished to diminish French influence and custom, acknowledged that France was a country of greater splendor than their own but insisted that England possessed greater naval power and a more robust economy. Corrantee, eager to profit from this rivalry, proposed that a second son—Sessarakoo—be educated in England just as the first was in France. An independent slaver in competition with the RAC offered to make all necessary arrangements and transported the young prince to Barbados before betraying him. Sold and subjected to "rough Usage," Sessarakoo was made a slave at the expense of English interests in Annamaboe, which suffered when Corrantee learned of his fate.[74] Sessarakoo boarded a boat to establish stronger ties with English merchants and nobility, but his enslavement caused a rupture in the relationship between the RAC and Corranteee.

Because slavery was a condition brought about—at least theoretically, if not always in practice—as a result of war, Corrantee and the RAC fell into hostilities over the kidnapping of Sessarakoo.[75] At Corrantee's behest, "the Commerce of *Annamaboe* fell almost wholly into the Hands of the *French*," and RAC officials were told in plain terms that they should not expect to trade with Corrantee for the foreseeable future. British officials responded to this declaration of a trade war with physical violence: "as the News of the

War between the two Nations [England and France] was arrived, and one of his *Britannick* Majesty's Ships was actually upon the Coast . . . the King's Frigate stood in as near the Town of *Annamaboe*, as could be done with Safety, and began to fire upon it." Cannonballs brought Corrantee back to the negotiating table, and he made a show of banishing the French from Annamaboe, but all involved understood that their exile and his reconciliation with RAC officials were no more "than a temporary Expedient." Tensions and violence between the two countries had been produced by Sessarakoo's enslavement, so only his emancipation and repatriation could possibly restore good feelings between the parties involved. The trade war—and the "brisk cannonading" which concluded that conflict—would only cease when Sessarakoo was returned in good health to his father.[76]

This link between war and slavery in Sessarakoo's narrative reveals the shifting logic of eighteenth-century human trafficking. Ostensibly, the trader sold Sessarakoo in order to extort a ransom from Corrantee, who had borrowed significant sums from him. But the author of *The Royal African* notes that this purpose might have been accomplished by other, less drastic means—such as holding him captive—and that if he really intended to redeem the boy, he likely would have shared this information with Sessarakoo's Barbadian purchaser, who was not told of Sessarakoo's status. Instead, the author suggests that Sessarakoo's betrayal is evidence of the trader's racism: "that, in his Opinion, all Blacks were destined to be Slaves." Sessarakoo's enslavement and redemption are framed as a contest of sorts, between two competing views of slavery. For the trader who sold Sessarakoo, slavery was a matter of race, while the author characterizes slavery as an outcome of international conflict whose victims were occasionally freed during the course of diplomatic reconciliations. The enslaved, he writes, come into that condition as a result of military expeditions, "For the kings of the interior Countries in *Africa*, are continually at War with each other, and Prisoners taken in Flight, or surprised in sudden Excursions, are sold by both Parties."[77] Both rationales for slavery were based in reality, and in the middle of the eighteenth century, they coexisted. But as slavery in the Americas shifted from a system supported primarily by the importation of black Africans to a system supported primarily by the breeding and rearing of human chattels who inherited their status from a prior generation, on the basis of race, the stories told by and about the enslaved necessarily changed. Sessarakoo would be returned to Annamaboe and Corrantee, but only because a race-based justification for slavery had not yet fully displaced a belief in slavery as an outgrowth of failed foreign relations.

The international crisis spurred by a single English trader was eventually resolved by a promise from the RAC to redeem Sessarakoo, educate him in England, and return him to Corrantee in a lace coat at least as fine as the one his brother brought home; the cannonading of Annamaboe ended as a result of statecraft, not war. If the stipulation that Sessarakoo come home clothed in lace seems frivolous, *The Royal African* notes that diplomacy often hinges on matters of style, rather than substance: "other Nations are as much affected by Things which are at the bottom of as little Significance; for what are those great Points, of Stile, Rank, and Ceremony in all publick Negotiations, but *laced Coats*, if beheld in a critical and impartial View?" Sessarakoo's story of slavery both began and ended with a lace coat because lace was a symbol of French and English esteem for Annamaboe. Colonel Edward Hamilton, who sailed with Sessarakoo on his return to Africa aboard the *Surprise*, a twenty-gun frigate, reported that Sessarakoo debarked "magnificently equipped in a full-dress scarlet suit, with gold lace à la Bourgogne, point d'Espagne hat, handsome white feather, diamond solitaire buttons, &c."[78] This splendor and an accompanying royal salute from the English men of war in attendance, like Sessarakoo's earlier introduction to George II, was a sign of favor from the crown and a resumption of diplomatic relations between England and Annamaboe.

In his negotiations with the RAC, Corrantee always understood that the slavers spoke on behalf of English royalty and Parliament. Corrantee and other black African leaders knew that the company was "at all Times answerable to the several *Negroe* Governments upon the Coast for the Conduct and Behaviour of the *British* Nation."[79] Because English slavers were understood to be an extension of the British government, the author insists that their actions were always freighted with diplomatic import. Each human chattel exported on English ships signified the strength—or in Sessarakoo's case, the weakness—of a bilateral trade relationship. Thus, *The Royal African* taught its eighteenth-century readers both to believe in war as the rationale for enslavement and to think about the narrative of every enslaved person to endure the Middle Passage as a commentary on the status of foreign relations between trading partners.

The Other Princes

Sessarakoo, Diallo, and the Mastoon brothers were among the most famous eighteenth-century princes to be enslaved, emancipated, and repatriated, but many others were betrayed into bondage. This proliferation of enslaved princes may have been a result of what Philip Curtin describes as a demonstrable preference, on the part of English slavers, for human chattels "thought to have had high status in their own societies."[80] In 1759, the London papers announced that an unnamed

> young *African* prince appeared publickly at the Theatre Royal in *Drury Lane*. This youth was committed some time since to the care of an *English* captain to be brought over for education, but the captain, instead of performing his promise, sold him to a gentleman in *London*. The father of the prince being lately dead, and the captain being upon the coast, was at that time desired by his subjects to bring young prince home; but he giving them no satisfactory account, was seized, imprisoned, and ironed, and then confessed the truth; upon which an order was sent to a merchant in that trade to procure the prince's enlargement, which was done by purchasing him of the gentleman who bought him; and he is soon to return to his native country.[81]

Eight years later, in 1767, two young men—Little Ephraim Robin John and Ancona Robin Robin John—were kidnapped by slavers in Old Calabar on the Guinea Coast and brought to the Caribbean, Virginia, and England before returning to their homeland with the help of a Bristol trader, who expected the brothers to direct trade to him after their return, and the Wesley brothers, who later sent Methodist missionaries to Calabar.[82] Enslaved black African royalty continued to be celebrated and emancipated regularly, throughout the eighteenth century, inasmuch as their freedom would serve British and Protestant imperial interests.[83] For these princely protagonists, the experience and narration of enslavement continued to revolve around diplomatic matters.

Stories of enslaved princes awakened the imaginations and sympathies of many, but they did little to change the general perception of enslaved black Africans unable to claim noble birth or, perhaps, unable to communicate their royal descendancy in English.[84] Joseph Warton, in his "Ode to Liberty," described how "Guinea's captive Kings lament / By Christian lords to labour sent, / Whipt like the dull, unfeeling ox," but the plight of enslaved persons whose suffering was not ennobled by a claim to royal birth was largely ignored.[85] Although Samuel Johnson lamented that "Princes have been sold" and "when once they were brought to a market in the plantations, little would avail either their dignity or their wrongs," he also argued for the continuation of slavery, noting that abolition "would not only be *robbery* to an innumerable class of our fellow-subjects; but it would be extreme cruelty to the African Savages, a portion of whom it saves from massacre, or intolerable bondage in their own country, and introduces into a much happier state of life."[86] Johnson's sympathy for enslaved black African royalty and callous disregard for the distress of the average black African suggest that class trumped race in English evaluations of social status. But race still mattered, and the goodwill extended to black African royalty seemingly exhausted the store of sympathy available to black Africans as a group; their stories preemptively displaced auto/biographical narratives featuring enslaved men and women without a claim to fame.

In other words, lengthy works of prose featuring enslaved black African princes both normalized the idea of the slave narrative and, paradoxically, helped forestall the genre's launch by monopolizing the attention and sympathy of the reading public. As Barry Weller has argued, accounts featuring enslaved royalty make "a genealogical claim, addressed in large part to whites of European descent, for the human value and dignity of those whom European society has enslaved and degraded, but by definition it is not a claim which can be deployed on behalf of all those whom the society has oppressed."[87] Advancing such a claim only reinforced the need to identify special merit in black Africans before they could be worthy of an English reader's esteem, and Randy Sparks observes that slavers' efforts "to liberate members of the African slave-trading elite who had been wrongfully enslaved actually served to legitimate the enslavement of other Africans and reinforced their own reputation for fair dealing."[88] Stories of enslaved black African princes thus exaggerated the difference between these princes and the people they ruled, reinscribing the degradation and marginalization of black Africans unable to advance a claim of nobility.

Nevertheless, these narratives provided a blueprint for all seeking emancipation. Hanley is right that "popular British representations of African nobility emphasized their protagonists' intrinsic similitude to Europeans at the same time as pointing out the all-important differences between them and the vast majority of Africans."[89] And yet these stories also taught enslaved black African readers in North America how to position themselves in a Protestant world defined by the English fear of Catholic and Muslim nations seeking to subjugate all free peoples. Enslaved princes could not protect their people from bondage, but princes like Diallo or Sessarakoo, who profited from the slave trade, also could not sell their subjects or their enemies into slavery. What they could—and did—do is demonstrate the emancipatory power of diplomacy. Enslaved black Africans living in colonial North America learned, from the liberation of these princes and from newspaper accounts circulating throughout the Atlantic, of the global power struggles in which English slave-holders were embroiled and how to leverage those international conflicts into improved living conditions—and even, occasionally, freedom.

CHAPTER FOUR

Fighting for, and against, the British

Briton Hammon and the Power of Enslaved Black Africans' Allegiance

The Royal African Company emancipated enslaved black African princes under the assumption that these potentates would feel a sense of gratitude towards the British empire after their repatriation, directing trade to RAC vessels and welcoming Protestant missionaries into their homelands. Enslaved black Africans without a familial link to royalty could not offer their captors the benefits of an alliance, but they understood the symbolic power of their own personal acts of allegiance to a nation state. Ryan Hanley has argued that "we must situate African agency back within the specific material and political contexts of the period," and doing so will require acknowledging the investment of enslaved black Africans in foreign affairs.[1] As Britain struggled with Spain and France for imperial dominance in the Western Hemisphere, the enslaved chose sides, attempting to leverage international conflicts into personal liberty, or at least improved living conditions. And news of these conflicts, whether it was read silently or aloud in public spaces, was communicated through the newspaper.

During the first half of the eighteenth century, British forces fought in a number of wars against Spain and France, most notably the War of the Spanish Succession and the War of Jenkins' Ear, which was eventually folded into the War of the Austrian Succession and its North American front, King George's War. Enslaved black Africans were cognizant of these conflicts, and some saw this perennial enmity between Protestant and Catholic nations as an opportunity to liberate themselves by entering the conflict and tipping the balance of power away from their captors.[2] In the spring of 1741, as the British residents of North America read newspaper reports warning about the threat of Spanish and French marauders attacking the coastline, a series of fires broke out in New York City, and colonial officials accused the city's black African residents of arson. Thirteen were burned at the stake, seventeen hanged, and more than a hundred imprisoned. Those brought in for questioning who confessed to plotting arson and murder repeatedly declared that their actions had been motivated by a belief that French or Spanish troops would arrive soon thereafter to help them hold the city. In other words, free and enslaved black Africans reported participating in the uprising of 1741 because they believed that demonstrating their allegiance to foreign powers, by committing an act of war on behalf of those powers, might result in improved living conditions and, potentially, their liberation. They saw themselves as political agents who wielded real political and martial power at a global scale.

Although historians have attended to this uprising and crackdown, literary scholars have largely ignored the record of courtroom testimony produced by Daniel Horsmanden and the dozens of embedded autobiographical narratives embedded in his *Journal of the Proceedings* (1744).[3] Horsmanden's manifest racism made him a biased evaluator of what eighteenth-century jurists called "Negro evidence." His transcript appears to be an accurate account of the courtroom's oral exchanges, but these narratives produced by black Africans under threat of torture and execution were coerced and therefore suspect confessions.[4] Their testimonies outline a plot remarkably like earlier conspiracies of the enslaved, to burn Barbados in 1676 and Antigua in 1736; noting similarities in the rebellion outlined by Horsmanden and these prior schemes, Jill Lepore calls the confessions "formulaic" and "utterly conventional."[5] And yet: to reject these accounts because of Horsmanden's mediating hand and the threats of violence that preceded their speech is to abandon the men and women who tell their stories in Horsmanden's *Journal* as unknown and unknowable ciphers. Given the implicit presence of a white editorial hand in all eighteenth-century records of black life and experience, the academy's collective acceptance of a highly mediated text like Briton Hammon's *A Narrative of the Uncommon Sufferings, and Surprizing Deliverance of Briton Hammon, a Negro Man,—Servant to General Winslow, of Marshfield, in New-England* (1760) would seem to leave little excuse for dismissing these testimonies or other similarly problematic texts.[6] Notwithstanding scholarly suspicions that the testimony of black Africans in Horsmanden's record is of questionable verity and historicity, the voices of these witnesses preserve irreplaceable perspectives on how free and enslaved black Africans conceived of their place in the broader Atlantic world, and their testimonies anticipate Hammon's message: that black Africans are, and should be seen as, pivotal figures in international affairs.

Throughout the *Journal*, black witnesses speak of enslaved Africans as political actors seeking power through foreign alliances. A connection between the fires and Spanish interests is repeatedly established by the testimony of black Africans on the witness stand, who identify "*Spanish* negroes" as prime movers in this affair and express their understanding of the war as an extension of extant international conflicts. The first to give evidence, a young man named Sandy, testifies that "*William* (Capt. Lush's Spanish Negro) told him, that if they did not send him over to his own Country, he would ruin the City." Framing himself as a voice of restraint, Sandy tells the court that he encouraged agitators not to attack their masters directly, but to run away and enlist in the Spanish navy: "if you want to fight, go to the *Spaniards*, and not fight with your Masters."[7] This comment, which positions the New York rebellion as a conflict analogous to the ongoing War of Jenkins Ear, characterizes the arsonists as undeclared Spanish agents; Sandy asks only that they declare their allegiance to foreign powers openly, rather than acting as sleeper cells. Sandy, and the black African witnesses who would testify after him, identify the rebellion as a new, New York front in the war with Spain, opened by independent, black African actors.

Subsequent testimony expresses the belief that Spanish and French forces would eventually arrive to support the arsonists in their assault on New York. A witness named Jack reports hearing "*there were Spanish Negroes at Hughson's*, who told him, they had designs of taking this Country against the Wars came" to New York. The later stipulation that, "*if the* Spaniards *and* French *did not come, they were to do all themselves*," only underlines the belief that foreign reinforcements would support their offensive. When Bastian takes the stand in the *Journal*, he places this expectation of foreign aid within a broader context, suggesting that the conspirators took their cues from a close reading of the international news. He reports "that they expected *that War would be proclaimed in a little Time against the* French," who only became involved when the War of Jenkins Ear was subsumed by the War of the Austrian succession, "*and that the* French *and* Spaniards *would come here; and that they* (meaning the Negroes present and the Hughsons) *would join with them to take the Place*."[8] The rebellion's success is predicated on the arrival of reinforcements who will fight alongside the city's free and enslaved black Africans against their British oppressors. This belief—that the enslaved could assess the course of foreign affairs and play a decisive role in shifting the balance of North American power, from British Protestant colonists to French and Spanish colonists united by their Catholic faith—speaks to their self-conception as empowered political actors on an international stage.

Evident throughout this testimony from black African witnesses is an immersive awareness of foreign affairs and a careful attempt to formulate plans and alliances in response to international events reported in the newspaper. Even if the statements of Sandy and Jack and Bastian are false, coerced confessions extracted by Horsmanden's threats of violence and his promises that confessors would receive the court's leniency, their ability to provide testimony along these lines demonstrates their investment in global politics and a prior consideration of their standing in the conflict between Britain and Spain. For example, when white witnesses testified that a black African identified as Quack had boasted the recent fires were insignificant in comparison to the violence that would soon be visited on the city, Quack countered with a claim that they had misunderstood him. Acknowledging that he had spoken the words in question, Quack insisted that he had been talking about fires in a different city, which he had learned of through the newspaper. He,

> by his Excuse admitted he had spoken the Words he was charged with; but it being soon after we had the News of Admiral *Vernon's* taking *Porto Bello*, he had contrived a cunning Excuse, or some abler Heads for him, to account for the Occasion of them, and brought two of his own Complexion to give their Words for it also, *That they were talking of Admiral* VERNON's *taking* Porto Bellow; *and that he thereupon signified to his Companions, that he thought that was but a small Feat to what this brave Officer would do* by-and-by, *to annoy the Spaniards;* or Words tantamount; *so that it happen'd Quack* was enlarged from his Confinement for some Time.[9]

When called upon to explain words that could have been construed as a declaration of war upon the British, Quack flipped the script by reframing his comments as a celebration of the most recent British military success, calling upon two other black African witnesses to give particulars about their response to this victory. They, like Black Peter in Boston, followed the exploits of Edward Vernon closely, conscious that their social and legal standing might hinge upon battles fought in the Caribbean. So adroit was their digestion, reformulation, and deployment of the "News" that Horsmanden could not believe a black African "Complexion" capable of the task. But black Africans like Peter and Quack understood that their bodies and sociopolitical identities were always under discussion in the newspaper's accounts of wars, negotiations, and international commerce, so of course they could situate their speech with respect to Vernon's victory over the Spanish.

To be familiar with the news was, for enslaved individuals living in the eighteenth century, to be armed with information that might lead to their emancipation, or at least to improved living conditions. The War of Jenkins' Ear was fought, in part, over the *assiento*: a contract allowing and sometimes obligating its possessor to provide human chattels for sale in Spanish ports.[10] In other words, the enslaved were already at the center of the hostilities between

Britain and Spain; if black African conspirators plotted to burn down the city of New York, they simply took on a more active and agential role within a conflict in which they were already implicated. Andy Doolen argues that these links in the *Journal* between enslaved black Africans and international events were a product of "white war panic, caused by conspiracy and war," but black African princes clearly thought about themselves—their bondage, freedom, and personal interests—in the context of global events, and so did their countrymen without a claim to noble birth.[11] The black African testimony preserved in Horsmanden's *Journal of the Proceedings* repeatedly attests to this fact, and so, too, does Hammon's *Narrative*—a text published in the absence of war panic, as British colonists celebrated the crippling of the French navy and anticipated a final victory over their enemies. In his *Narrative* Hammon, like the black African witnesses in Horsmanden's *Journal of the Proceedings*, identifies as a political actor whose choices have the power to shape global events; he describes himself fighting *for* the British, rather than *against* them, but for similar reasons: to secure increased personal liberty and to improve his quality of life.

When Briton Hammon left Marshfield, Massachusetts, on Christmas day in 1747, he embarked on a voyage that would take him to British settlements in Jamaica, logging camps off the Yucatan peninsula, the Indian-controlled coast of southern Florida, Spanish Cuba, and imperial London, before he finally returned to Massachusetts in 1760. In his account of these travels Hammon dives overboard to escape an Indian assault, shoulders the litter of a Catholic bishop, and fights the French on board a third-rate British ship of the line. Despite the exotic and engaging character of his personal history, this brief text likely would have languished in relative obscurity except for one fact: Briton Hammon was a black African.

Only the extended title of his *Narrative* reveals Hammon's racial identity; there are no other clear signs that he was of African descent in the text. Although scholarly readers have disagreed as to the meaning of Hammon's status as a servant, most now accept that he was enslaved. His apparent liberty to enter into a labor contract taking him to the Caribbean might suggest that Hammon was a freeman who received wages from General John Winslow, but Robert Desrochers Jr. explains that enslaved black Africans living in New England frequently received permission to enter into such arrangements during the winter months.[12]

While Vincent Caretta and others have hailed Hammon's autobiographical adventure story as the first slave narrative, some readers have questioned the extent to which Hammon actually controlled the published content of the work.[13] Tracing Hammon's account to the Boston publishing firm of Green and Russell, John Sekora documents similarities between the title page of Hammon's account and that of another 1760 narrative describing the experiences of a white youth named Thomas Brown, who was taken prisoner during the French and Indian War.[14] Parallels between the two texts indicate that editors likely manipulated the first and last paragraphs of both accounts in order to make them more marketable to the public. But Rafia Zafar has argued that "oral narrators are not quite so powerless as Sekora and others have assumed," and the strategic political work performed by Hammon throughout his *Narrative* attests to his savvy control of its core elements.[15]

Hammon—like the black African witnesses in Horsmanden's *Journal of the Proceedings* and other enslaved persons—presents his story in a way that emphasizes his participation in pivotal international events. During most of the twentieth century, readers accepted *The Interesting Narrative of the Life of Olaudah Equiano, or Gustavus Vassa, the African* (1789) at face value, assuming that he was born in Igboland and that he endured the Middle Passage, as he claimed. But in 1999, Carretta publicized manuscript records of Equiano's baptism and enlistment onboard the *Racehorse*, both of which identified his place of nativity as South Carolina:

> The parish register of St Margaret's church, Westminster, records the baptism on 9 February 1759 of 'Gustavus Vassa a Black born in Carolina 12 years old.' . . . The muster book of the *Racehorse* records the entry on board, as of 17 May [1773], of 'Gustavus Weston,' identified as being an able seaman, aged 28, and born in South Carolina. Given the approximate phonetic spelling of Vassa, and given that the rating or rank, age and birthplace match those of Vassa found in earlier muster lists, in the *Narrative* itself, and in the parish register of St Margaret's, and given that [the ship's captain, Lord] Mulgrave was one of the original subscribers to *The Interesting Narrative*, 'Gustavus Weston' was certainly Gustavus Vassa.[16]

Carretta has argued forcefully that Equiano's personal experience of the Middle Passage was central to the commercial and rhetorical success of *The Interesting Narrative*. The motive for a mature Equiano to fudge the details of his birth in the service of a greater moral good—the abolition of the slave trade—seems clear.[17] Comparing Hammon's *Narrative* to contemporary newspapers and other historical records indicates that he also may have deliberately misrepresented his experiences for rhetorical purposes; editorial intervention seems inadequate to explain at least two instances in which his account diverges from other sources. These divergences suggest that while Hammon's

Narrative may not be a wholly accurate account of his adventures, its rhetorical prowess foregrounds both the textual plasticity of history and the intentionality of black African voices widely assumed to have been muffled by editorial intervention. As Randy Sparks has argued with respect to such texts, "inaccuracies and deceptions are themselves important to an understanding of the narrators and their life strategies."[18] In both instances where Hammon's *Narrative* differs from the historical record, the effect is to promote his centrality in the global power struggles between British Protestantism and its Catholic enemies.

Exploring Hammon's representational strategies highlights his self-conception as a political actor on a global stage and the benefits of using historical methodologies to assess the rhetorical achievements of enslaved black Africans. Daniel Vollaro raises important questions about Hammon's description of his encounter with a large group of American Indian inhabitants of South Florida, where Indian populations had been declining for decades; he notes that "modern writers have expressed little skepticism over the details of Hammon's story, treating the *Narrative* as an unvarnished accounting of events witnessed by its author," even though this "deference to the 'documentary' value of the *Narrative* runs against the grain of a literary analysis, which would suggest that we *not* so readily trust Hammon's witness to history."[19] Jeffrey Gagnon has since argued for the factuality of Hammon's encounter with Indians, contending that he met with the Calusa, "a powerful tribe of skilled boatmen," but the apparent fabrication of later events in the *Narrative* indicates that Vollaro's suspicions are likely well-grounded.[20] The opening paragraph of Hammon's *Narrative* promises to "*only relate Matters of Fact as they occur to my Mind*," but Vollaro's analysis and a review of previously unexamined eighteenth-century newspapers suggest that Hammon incorporated stories that "*occur to my Mind*" as well as "*Matters of Fact*."[21]

Acknowledging that the historical record does not always corroborate claims made in Hammon's *Narrative* provides an opportunity to celebrate his creative response to the international power structures of slavery. This approach to the *Narrative* enables its readers to move from "*Matters of Fact*" to Hammon's motives and "*Mind*," foregrounding the dominant social incentives and strictures that shaped the lives of enslaved black Africans in the Atlantic world. Hammon may have exaggerated or fabricated his account of captivity among the American Indians of South Florida, as Vollaro suggests, to emphasize his common humanity with white readers in opposition to the supposed "savagery" of his Indian assailants. His *Narrative* also seems to exaggerate the nature of his participation in a naval battle and other matters,

perhaps in the hope that his account would result in more favorable treatment from his military-minded "Master" at their reunion after thirteen years
apart. Whatever the motivations behind Briton Hammon's *Narrative,* his account of adventure and bondage deserves closer scrutiny than it has hitherto
been given. It may not be a completely accurate history of Hammon's travels,
but it is a work of literature that illuminates the geopolitical thinking of enslaved black Africans in the eighteenth century and anticipates the rhetorical
sleight of hand literary scholars appreciate in later texts, such as the *Narrative*
of Frederick Douglass.[22]

Sixty Indians in Twenty Canoes

After leaving Massachusetts, Hammon sailed to Jamaica in thirty days aboard
the *Howlet,* arriving near the end of January in 1748.[23] He arrived in Jamaica at
a time of rough justice for sailors of black African descent. Newspapers record that on January 6, 1748, the local courts convicted "a Negro fellow named
Ben (belonging to Capt. Jennings of Old Harbour) for robbing Mr. Ely Flowers" and sentenced him to death. Less than two weeks later and just days before Hammon made port, a man named Hector stabbed his enslaver, one
"Captain Hussey," and the court decreed that he should be "immediately
hanged"—after his left hand was cut off, presumably both to inflict additional
pain and to provide local officials a trophy with which they might warn other
enslaved persons contemplating rebellion.[24] Jamaica's harbors would have
been bustling with activity as the governor, Edward Trelawny, and Admiral
Charles Knowles, the colony's ranking naval officer, prepared for a March assault on French and Spanish forces at Hispaniola and Cuba, respectively.
Commanding a fleet that included at least eight ships of the line, Knowles
took the French fort at Port Louis "with some of [Jamaica's] Land Forces,
and a great Number of Voluntiers and Negroes," before being rebuffed by
Spanish defenses at Santiago de Cuba.[25] In Jamaica, Briton Hammon entered a bustling community of black African sailors, soldiers, and agricultural
workers.

Of course, Hammon was lucky simply to have arrived in Jamaica at the end
of an uneventful voyage. The Caribbean was a dangerous body of water
during the eighteenth century and sailing to Jamaica without encountering
and engaging French or Spanish privateers was itself an accomplishment.
When he wrote the *Narrative* in 1760, Hammon recalled these dangers, re-
membering that during his brief five-day stay in Jamaica he had met a man
named Romond, the captain of a Spanish schooner taken prisoner by British

privateers. Perhaps Romond's ship was one of the "three valuable Prizes" that Black Peter and the *Boston Evening Post* reported taken by the brig *Defiance* and Captain John Sweet, then sent by him to Jamaica in the first two months of 1748.[26]

Hammon's meeting with Romond is a critical, if fleeting and critically ignored, moment of the *Narrative* because Hammon explains that Romond would eventually resume command of a sloop and rescue Hammon from captivity among the Indians living on the Florida coast. Hammon recalls that Romond "asked the *Indians* to let me go on board his Vessel, which they granted, and the Captain knowing me very well, weigh'd Anchor and carry'd me off to the *Havanna*" (*N* 22). Hammon never explains why or how he and Romond become intimates, but this is the first of many occasions when Hammon self identifies as a focal point in international conflicts—a diplomatic envoy in communication with both British Protestants and their Catholic foes. Perhaps Hammon's allegiance was the subject of their initial conversations; if Romond offered to help him escape from slavery, Hammon might have been more than willing to enlist in the Spanish navy.

Hammon's close relationship with Romond merits critical scrutiny for at least two reasons. First, as the captain of a Spanish sloop, Romond presumably spoke Spanish as his primary language, while Hammon presumably spoke an African dialect or English as his primary language. Unless Romond spoke English or Hammon had learned substantial Spanish on a prior voyage, it seems unlikely that the two would have been able to communicate effectively. Second, according to the *Narrative*, Hammon spent only five days in Jamaica, and Romond reportedly arrived on the island at some point during that period. It is difficult to imagine the circumstances in which a Spanish prisoner of war and an enslaved New England sailor aboard a logging vessel, both newly arrived in a large, bustling harbor, would spend enough of the overlapping four days they were in Jamaica together that they would know each other "very well." If, during his brief stay on Jamaica, Hammon fortuitously met an imprisoned, bilingual, Spanish captain and developed a bond deep enough that the man would put forth some effort to save him from Indian captivity when they met again six months later, then Hammon was a very lucky man indeed.[27] However, the historicity of Hammon's acquaintance with Romond is almost irrelevant; the larger point here is that Hammon encourages his readers to think of him as a man invested in foreign affairs who naturally bridges political, martial, and linguistic divides.

After this encounter with Romond, Hammon sailed from Jamaica in early February for either the Bay of Campeche or the Bay of Honduras (located to the west and east of the Yucatan Peninsula, respectively), where he spent three months cutting logwood and loading it onboard the *Howlet*.[28] In harvesting logwood, a source of red dye, from the coast, Hammon entered an ongoing international dispute between Britain and Spain. When colonial newspaper readers learned of Knowles's assault on Santiago de Cuba in March 1748, they cataloged it as one more in a string of the battles comprising the War of Jenkins' Ear. British access to Caribbean shipping routes, Spanish ports, and Central American commodities such as logwood were at the center of this dispute. When Knowles ordered a British fort in the Bay of Honduras destroyed in 1747, then removed the soldiers and cannon housed there to the south and the British-controlled Mosquito Coast, he hoped to appease the Spanish; the question of whether British vessels such as the *Howlet* could be in the Bay was one of the issues that the war was meant to resolve. Prior to Hammon's departure from Massachusetts, he or Winslow might have read in Boston newspapers that although the Spanish refused to allow permanent British fortifications in the Bay, they were currently "willing to permit us to cut Log-wood," and Hammon's ship left the Yucatan on May 25, 1748, loaded with as much as 400 tons of the stuff.[29] After skirting enemy territory along the western shores of Hispaniola and Cuba, the *Howlet* ran aground a sandbar off the coast of Florida. The crew urged Captain John Howland "to heave over but only 20 Ton of the *Wood*, and we should get clear," but Howland refused, and Hammon made for shore with eight other members of the crew (*N* 21). En route, they encountered sixty Indians in twenty canoes.

Hammon's account of an unprovoked assault by these American Indian raiders, who reportedly murdered the rest of the crew, burned the *Howlet*, and took Hammon captive, is the portion of his *Narrative* that first aroused scholarly suspicion. Vollaro suggests that modern readers ought to treat this history of Indian aggression with skepticism because a 1743 report by two Jesuit missionaries to a Miami River settlement near the reported location of Hammon's shipwreck found a village of only 180 people, with approximately forty-five adult males. Furthermore, Vollaro notes that when the Spanish evacuated southern Florida in 1763, they removed just eighty Indian families from the region—"the entire Indian population of South Florida." These accounts of an Indian population decimated by disease and war with northern nations make it difficult to envision a raiding party of the size Hammon describes.[30] Moreover, Vollaro objects that Hammon's recollection of Indian captors taunting him in "broken English . . . telling me, while coming from the Sloop to the Shore, that they intended to roast me alive" is problematic for the same reason that a deep friendship with Captain Romond seems unlikely (*N* 22). Because Florida had been under Spanish control for two centuries, many of its indigenous inhabitants spoke Spanish, as well as their own languages. But these Florida Indians would have been even less likely to know English than Romond.[31] Still, notwithstanding Vollaro's objections to specific details of Hammon's account, it seems reasonable to assume that Hammon was, in fact, stranded off the Florida coast. During hurricane season in the fall of 1747, newspapers reported that more than thirty vessels were lost in the vicinity, and two other vessels were wrecked on Florida's shores at approximately the same time that Hammon was marooned in June 1748.[32] Ships frequently foundered in the area.

However, several scenarios other than the one given in the *Narrative* might explain the destruction of Hammon's ship and crew. First—and perhaps most likely—Hammon or his editors may simply have exaggerated the number of Florida Indians who killed the rest of the crew, burnt the *Howlet*, and took Hammon hostage. Three newspaper accounts of Indian raiders attacking British ships off the Florida coast during the early 1750s support Vollaro's skepticism regarding the number of Indians described by Hammon. Whereas Hammon describes twenty canoes and sixty Indians, these reports suggest much smaller groups of raiders. One sailor describes being "boarded by two Canoes full of Indians"; another account describes a longboat "surrounded by 7 or 8 Canoes full of Indians"; and the third account, a letter by one Captain Crauford, assures the reader that Indians "were very numerous about" his onshore encampment but gives no indication that Crauford or his men actually saw the Indians supposedly surrounding them. In Crauford's letter, as in Hammon's *Narrative*, the report of "numerous" Indians may mask a reality more in line with the handful of canoes reported elsewhere. As Vollaro suggests, Hammon or his editors may have sensationalized a true account of aggression and captivity in order "to satisfy the genre expectations of his readers," who expected captivity narratives to include violence.[33]

Vollaro also advances a second possibility: that Hammon may have been taken captive by "Creek or Yamassee slave raiders from the English-speaking territories to the north," supported by British plantation owners seeking to recover Black slaves escaped into Florida.[34] This theory would account for an "English Colour hoisted in one of the Canoes" that eventually attacked the *Howlet* (*N* 21). However, Indian peoples allied with Britain during the War of Jenkins' Ear likely would not have followed Hammon to Cuba and sought reparations from the Spanish governor, Don Francisco Antonio Cagigal de la Vega, as Hammon reports. Furthermore, official British sanction for Creek slaving raids in Florida seems to have been suspended between 1743 and 1756.

A third explanation is that Hammon's shipmates perished during a shipwreck and that Hammon was rescued or taken captive by Florida Indians without a militarized encounter. None of the three accounts of Florida Indians raiding shipwrecked vessels during the early 1750s report Indian-induced fatalities. Indeed, the most violent act recorded in these reports—the burning of a marooned ship and abandonment of its crew—is perpetrated by Spanish privateers. Sailors reportedly fear "losing our Lives by the Indians" who are "so eager to kill them," but newspaper reports of these encounters portray Indians who seem content to appropriate shipwrecked cargo and profit from the labor of castaways.[35] If indeed Hammon fabricated or embellished his tale of "barbarous and inhuman Savages . . . hallowing like so many Devils," he may have done so in order to shift the weight of racial prejudice from his own shoulders to those of the Indians, implicitly inviting readers to understand a civilized "*Negro Man*" such as himself in opposition to Indian savagery and allying himself with the white sufferers of Indian captivity narratives (*N* 21-22).

Reading Hammon's Indian captors as allies, rather than adversaries, Gagnon proposes that Calusa raiders attacked to free another person of color, who they viewed as a fellow sufferer. As Gagnon notes, the Calusa may have thought they were liberating Hammon, and Hammon himself might have agreed; it is possible that "the Calusa rescued Hammon because they perceived him to be a victim of British slave traffickers who had historically captured and enslaved the Calusa as well" as black Africans. If Hammon welcomed their intervention, he "forged transnational bonds" of precisely the sort that New York's enslaved black Africans allegedly sought to establish by burning down the city.[36] Navigating the Atlantic without the support of a national sponsor, Hammon needed to create networks of alliance and allegiance in order to survive. Whether he saw the Indians with whom he lived as benefactors or enemies, he surely understood his encounter with them as a reminder of his own fragile and unmoored social status.

One final possibility is that the *Howlet*—like the marooned vessel of Captain Crauford and so many other British ships during the War of Jenkins' Ear—may have been attacked by the *guarda costa*, a fleet of independently owned and operated privateers manned by multiracial crews who plundered British vessels with the tacit sanction of the Spanish Crown. A 1738 account of shipwreck off the Florida coast tells of the ship's captain rowing for shore in a longboat only to encounter "a Spanish Sloop and Scooner, with several Spaniards and one of the Florida Indians painted on board." Spanish forces likewise fought with Florida Indians against British forces in defense of

St. Augustine in 1740.[37] In addition to employing Indian sailors, the *guarda costa* also employed Indian tactics, using canoes to seize larger merchant vessels. William Finks, captain of the sloop *Experiment*, gave legal testimony to the effect that he saw "two large Canoes giving Chace to a small Schooner." Finks's own sloop "was then forcibly taken Possession of by one of the large Canoes, which he then found to be a *Spanish* Guarda Costa, or rather a Pirate." These Spanish pirates were always eager to take black African sailors and passengers prisoner, whether they were enslaved or freemen. At approximately the same time that the *Howlet* foundered, newspapers reported that a Spanish privateer took "the Schooner of Capt. Ingram, belonging to Virginia, out of which they took several hundred Pounds in Cash, and great Numbers of Negroes." Finks, for his part, testified that "there were on board his Vessel three Negro Freemen, named *Benjamin Brooks*, *Robin* and *Joseph*, as also an Indian Boy, named *Pompey*, all subjects of his *Brittanick* Majesty, and a Negro Man Slave, named *Isaac*," who remained in captivity even after the pirates had released their white prisoners.[38] Hammon may have been taken captive and his logging vessel may have been attacked by a segment of the *guarda costa* that included Florida Indians in its crew and used canoes to attack larger sloops. In this case, Hammon's elision of the Spanish would signify an awareness of the geopolitical interests of his readers. While accounts of Spanish piracy and brutality were frequently reported in British and colonial newspapers through 1753, they virtually disappeared once the North American front of the Seven Years' War erupted into conflict in 1754. Hammon, writing at the apex of this later war in 1760, would have understood that his reading public would be more interested in accounts of Indian warfare than Spanish piracy and may have transformed a multiracial crew of privateers into a band of Florida Indians.[39] Whatever the truth, those awaiting Hammon's return to Massachusetts could only scan the newspaper for clues of his fate in reports from the Yucatan and Spanish-held Florida. When he provided his own account of the disaster, years later, Hammon cast himself as the victim of an international incident, pitting Spain's Indian allies against British loggers to win the sympathy of his British master and readers.

Eating Rock Stones in Havana

In early August 1748 and after five weeks in captivity, during which time Hammon remembers that the Indians "were better to me than my Fears" and "us'd me pretty well," Romond—either released, with his sloop, from Jamaica or escaped and made captain of a second vessel—arrived to deliver Hammon from bondage (*N* 22). Anchoring offshore, Romond requested that Hammon be allowed to visit onboard his ship, at which point Romond, "knowing me very well, weigh'd Anchor and carry'd me off to the *Havanna*" (*N* 22). Hammon represents his providential delivery as a rescue mission undertaken by Romond for the sake of friendship and at the risk of aggravating Spain's Indian allies. But Spanish captains frequently took possession of British castaways who were complete strangers, and in the context of Hammon's earlier account of Indian attack and later portions of the text that clearly misrepresent well-documented historical episodes, this unlikely double encounter with a bilingual Romond raises red flags.[40] Hammon may be relating "*Matters of Fact*," but the balance of the *Narrative* forces us to consider the possibility that he is exaggerating or altering the truth. After all, Romond disappears from the *Narrative* and turns Hammon over to Don Francisco, presumably for a small fee, in the four days before his Indian captors arrive in Havana to demand his return. Enlsaved black Africans living in Cuba ran away from their masters in prodigious numbers during the 1740s, even as the demand for enslaved labor was growing; Don Francisco likely would have been eager to purchase Hammon, integrating him into a large community of enslaved and free peoples of African descent in Cuba.[41]

If, as seems likely, Romond sold Hammon to Don Francisco, Romond's apparent willingness to provoke Hammon's Indian captors almost certainly had less to do with their friendship or mutual acquaintance than with a desire for profit. However, the *Narrative* obscures Romond's disappearance, Hammon's sale, and his status as a slave. While Hammon notes that the governor paid the Indians (an additional) "Ten Dollars for me," he also records Don Francisco's offer to pay "Ten Dollars a-head" for anyone shipwrecked on the Florida coast (*N* 22). Hammon presents himself as a generic British castaway, a subject rather than a slave or foreigner. Whether Hammon's intimacy with Romond is a matter of fact or an invention of mind, their relationship in the *Narrative* rhetorically obscures Hammon's predicament as a black African sailor traveling without legal documentation attesting to his status as either a free person or an enslaved individual who belongs in Massachusetts. Hammon uses Romond's presence (rescuing Hammon) and later his absence (turning Hammon over to the governor) to erase the predicament of being a black African in the eighteenth-century Caribbean. Like Benjamin Brooks, Robin, Joseph, and Isaac, the black African sailors who shipped on the *Experience* with William Finks but remained in Spanish hands when Finks returned to Jamaica, Hammon had no way to win his freedom without documentary proof of his legal status. Rather than acknowledging and legitimizing this powerlessness, Hammon's *Narrative* emphasizes his own humanity and the strength of his empathic or diplomatic connections with others, including the governor and Romond.

Hammon apparently arrived in Cuba just weeks before the Battle of Havana in October 1748, when Knowles captured one Spanish ship of the line and destroyed a second. Knowles's victory coincided with the release, from Havana, of at least one British prisoner who described the scene when the remaining five Spanish ships limped into harbor: "they arriv'd [at Havana] in a miserable Condition, their Sails and Rigging shot to Pieces; the Legs & Arms of the wounded were bro't up in Carts & Wheelbarrows: it would have made an Englishman laugh to see how the Spaniards tawney Countenances changed."[42] Laboring for Don Francisco, Hammon might have been one of the workers assigned—perhaps with the British prisoner who provided this account—to haul away these bloody remnants of war. It is tempting to imagine that Hammon also would have been released into British custody in the wake of Knowles's triumph, if not for the Treaty of Aix-la-Chapelle in 1748, which officially ended the War of the Austrian Succession (to which the War of Jenkins' Ear was an ancillary conflict) and prevented Knowles from taking further action against Havana and the Spanish fleet. Instead, Hammon reports that he remained in the governor's service until the summer of 1749, when he "met with a Press-Gang who immediately prest me, and put me into Goal," where he languished for the next fifty-five months (*N* 22).

One of the oddest features of Hammon's *Narrative*—about which readers have said nothing—is his description of the relationship between the press-gang that imprisons him and Don Francisco, who houses him "in the Castle" and seems to have a legal claim on his person (*N* 22). Havana became a major site for Spanish shipbuilding during the mid-eighteenth century because of the beliefs that Caribbean wood "is inured, and in some Measure naturalized to the burning Rays of the [equatorial] Sun" and, therefore, that ships built from Caribbean timber would prove more durable.[43] Because the naval yards were continually producing new ships needing to be manned and because as many as three quarters of the sailors sent from Old Spain for that purpose "died of the Black Vomit" (or yellow fever), Havana press-gangs attempted to coerce every British castaway onto a Spanish ship.[44] In most cases these press-gangs seem to have acted at the behest of the governor, Don Francisco. Andrew Connel, master of a ship taken as a prize after the peace of 1748, complained in a newspaper dispatch "that it was the Governor's Orders, they must either eat Rock Stones, or enter on board the Spanish Men of War."[45] Connel's colorful description of the consequences for refusing to serve in the

Spanish navy presumably refers to confinement in a "close Dungeon" such as the one inhabited by Hammon, although his words may also refer to the scant provisions offered to inmates at the Havana prison (*N* 22). Colonial newspapers protested that British prisoners had "little or no Sustenance allow'd them," and "the governor confined [one group of inmates] 4 days without food."[46] Havana's jail was crowded with British castaways, and most seem to have been sentenced to confinement or impressment by the governor himself.

In contrast, Hammon recalls that during his time in prison, "I often made application to the Governor, by Persons who came to see the Prisoners, but they never acquainted him with it, nor did he know all this Time what became of me, which was the means of my being confin'd there so long" (*N* 22). When compared to other accounts of Havana imprisonment, Hammon's experience seems unusual in two respects. First, while other prisoners complained that the governor was slow to hear their petitions, most received an audience with him within a few days or at most within months of their confinement. Hammon's racial identity may have dissuaded the governor's interpreter, Michael Britt, from presenting his case for liberty as forcefully as he did on another occasion, when the *Public Advertiser* announced he saved sixteen British castaways from jail and impressment by "movingly sollicit[ing] in their Behalf," but even in a bustling port city of 50,000 people it seems unlikely that an enslaved person legally the property of Don Francisco could be seized by press-gangs working for him and then languish in prison for more than four years without the governor's knowledge.[47] Whatever the historical truth, Hammon's insistence that Don Francisco did not know of his confinement and that he would have liberated Hammon from prison if he had known perpetuates the *Narrative*'s earlier insistence that indviduals of all nationalities empathize and identify with Hammon. Construing his imprisonment as a moment of misunderstanding rather than an economically motivated or racially sanctioned act allows Hammon to preserve his dignity and insist on his humanity.

A second odd feature of Hammon's experience is that the press-gang accepted his refusal to work in the navy and allowed him to serve time in prison, fed at the Crown's expense. Many British sailors chose impressment over eating "Rock Stones," but when two of Connel's men "would not enter as Volunteers on Board their Men of War, they were forced on Board them, and sent Prisoners to Spain."[48] Hammon spent more time in the Havana gaol than any other British sailor I have identified: most "were *put* on board Spanish Vessels bound for Old Spain, to work their Passages home there, before they could be discharged." Briton Hammon's remarkable ability to resist impressment and his willingness to endure years of brutal living conditions rather than serving in the Spanish navy suggest an ardent British nationalism befitting his first name and explicitly celebrated in later portions of the *Narrative*.[49] Hammon uses markers of national allegiance, and not racial status, as his primary mode of self-identification.

When, through the advocacy of an expatriate named Betty Howard and an anonymous British captain visiting Havana, Hammon finally emerged from prison during the winter of 1753–54, he turned his attention to escape. On multiple occasions British ships in the Caribbean picked up a canoe with a handful of enslaved black Africans escaping from Havana, but Hammon never seems to have considered that option.[50] Instead, he repeatedly attempted to stow away on board British ships making port calls in the Havana harbor. On his first attempt, Hammon

> got on board of Captain *Marsh*, an *English* Twenty Gun Ship, with a Number of others, and lay on board conceal'd that Night; and the next Day the Ship being under sail, I thought myself safe, and so made my Appearance upon Deck, but as soon as we were discovered the Captain ordered the Boat out, and sent us all on Shore—I intreated the Captain to let me, in particular, tarry on board, begging, and crying to him, to commiserate my unhappy Condition, and added, that I had been confin'd almost five Years in a close Dungeon, but the Captain would not hearken to my Intreaties, for fear of having the Governor's Displeasure, and so I was obliged to go on Shore. (*N* 22–23)

If Hammon's Captain Marsh is Henry Marsh of the twenty-four-gun *Shoreham*, this is the first point in Hammon's *Narrative* where outside sources could corroborate his account. The *Shoreham* visited Havana only once, in 1756, and no mention of Hammon or other stowaways survives in its log.[51] Marsh came to its captaincy in December 1754 after the *Shoreham*'s previous master, Julian Legge, was court-martialed "for some extraordinary Expences charged on him," and with that immediate reminder that captains could be held accountable for their actions, Marsh may have been reluctant to provoke hostilities with Spain by facilitating the escape of Don Francisco's human property.[52]

About a year after his attempt to stow away aboard the *Shoreham*, Hammon writes, he spent seven months carrying the Catholic Bishop Pedro Agustín Morell de Santa Cruz through the Cuban countryside on a litter. Bishop Morell left Havana on a tour of the island's churches on July 21, 1755.

His account of this journey, *La Visita Ecclesiastica* (1757), fails to mention Hammon and the other seven men who apparently carried him in a sedan chair across the countryside; in describing his movements from one town to another, Morell notes merely that he "walked 4 leagues" or that he "arrived at the city of Saint Philip and Santiago: one league further south from the previous town." In the countryside, as Hammon remembers, Morell proceeded "to confirm the old People, baptize Children, &c. for which he receives large sums of money" (*N* 22). After a brief sojourn, excessive rainfall forced Morell to return to Havana in September 1755, where he spent two months before setting out again in November; this second leg of his trip lasted fifteen months, from November 1755 until the end of February 1757.[53] Hammon recalls that during his service to Morell, "I lived very well," and Morell has been praised by some scholars for integrating Afro-Cuban social organizations into the fabric of the Catholic Church (*N* 23). In Morell, Hammon might have found a master who acknowledged his humanity, a man as interested in the state of his soul as in the strength of his back.[54]

While Hammon's experiences with Marsh and Morell represent welcome opportunities to contextualize the *Narrative*, his encounters with these men represent a problem of chronology. Hammon dates his escape to the *Shoreham* in the winter of 1754–55, approximately one year after his release from prison. His tour of duty with Morell came a year later and lasted, he claims, for seven months. The potential problems with Hammon's chronology are threefold. First, logbooks show that Marsh made only one voyage to Havana, in 1756, a visit which took place more than a year after Hammon reportedly stowed away onboard the *Shoreham*. Second, Morell left Havana—without returning—for periods of two months and fifteen months; if Hammon actually carried the bishop through the countryside, he seriously misremembered the duration of his service. Finally, and more problematically, Hammon almost certainly *cannot* have had both of these experiences. Beyond the relatively minor temporal inconsistencies (how long Hammon carried Morrell, Hammon's claim that he boarded Marsh's *Shoreham* almost two years before Marsh made port in Havana), there is the more pressing problem that Hammon's travels with Morrell and his adventure aboard the *Shoreham* seem to be mutually exclusive: Marsh's 1756 port call occurred during the fifteen months Morell was out of Havana, traveling through the countryside. If Morell's diary and Marsh's logbook—both recorded in the moment, unlike Hammon's *Narrative*—are accurate, Hammon either stowed away on the *Shoreham*, or he carried Morell; he cannot have done both.

While the troubling aspects in Hammon's account of American Indian violence might easily be attributed to the interference of sensationalistic editors, this apparent inconsistency seems much more likely to originate with Hammon himself. Editors might easily exaggerate the violence involved in an encounter with Indians, but no Massachusetts publisher would have known that Marsh visited Cuba and that Morell toured the countryside—only Hammon could have supplied the information in these conflicting accounts. But if he could not both meet with Marsh and carry Morell, where did his information come from? One possibility is that Hammon learned about the bishop's travels from another source, perhaps an enslaved person he met at one of the numerous clubs in Havana where Afro-Cubans gathered to socialize on the weekend. In listening to the tale of a fellow sufferer, Hammon may have come to identify with aspects of another man's service under Morell, internalized his account, and taken the story as his own—just as enslaved individuals later came to identify with and appropriate biblical stories of bondage as their own. Later, relating his experiences in Cuba to a New England audience wary of popish practices and immersed in a war against Catholic France, Hammon would have had ample reason to describe Morell's excesses, even if he had not personally observed them. Stories that emphasized the traits of greed and sloth in a Catholic bishop undoubtedly evoked sympathy and outrage from his audience, and Hammon may have consciously chosen to cultivate those emotions in the men, women, and publishers to whom he told his story. His familiarity with Morell and Don Francisco also placed Hammon in proximity to the power brokers of the age, reinforcing his centrality to important public figures in the eighteenth-century Atlantic.

Fighting for Britain

After more than a decade in Cuba, Hammon writes, he escaped from Havana in December 1758 with the aid of Edward Gascoigne, commander of the *Beaver*, an eighteen-gun man-of-war. After the ship's lieutenant smuggled Hammon on board, Spanish officials "came alongside the *Beaver*, and demanded me again, with a Number of others who had made their Escape from them, and got on board the Ship, but just before I did; but the Captain, who was a true *Englishman*, refus'd them, and said he could not answer it, to deliver up any *Englishman* under *English* Colours" (*N* 23).[55] Tensions between the British and Spanish had cooled significantly since the early 1750s, when Spanish *guarda costas* continued to search and seize British merchantmen they suspected of violating the treaty of 1748, but editorials in colonial newspapers still raged against the practice, and Gascoigne's defiant speech, as reported by Hammon, captures the tone of writers complaining about *"the Men obliged to work for nothing as Prisoners and Servants to Old Spain; there to get home as they could.... Or, are the English resolved to let the Spaniards always treat them as Gallenas, as they call us, and at our Hands take no Wrong, nor do no Right? ... Must not all indifferent Persons think we are indeed the Dupes of those People? And can any Man who ever suck'd one Drop of British Milk, or have one Drop of British Blood in his Veins, hear this without the utmost Indignation?"*[56] In his rendering of Gascoigne's speech, more than anywhere else in the *Narrative*, Hammon foregrounds his allegiance to the Crown, and Karen Weyler argues that he establishes himself "as first and foremost a Protestant Englishman."[57] His identities as a *"Negro Man"* and as the chattel of Don Francisco are subsumed in the national affiliation that doubled as his given name.[58] Appropriately, then, when Briton Hammon enlisted aboard the *Beaver*, he was known as "Britain" in the muster book.[59]

Hammon definitely sailed from Havana on the *Beaver*, but his account of the showdown between Gascoigne and Spanish officials differs markedly from that preserved in the ship's log. That record gives the date of Hammon's escape as November 4, 1758. As the *Beaver's* sailors prepared to celebrate Guy Fawkes Day, or Pope's Day as it was often called, on November 5th, feelings of British and Protestant nationalism were likely running high. Gascoigne may well have given the stirring, patriotic speech that Hammon recounts in his *Narrative*. However, if he did speak defiantly to a group seeking the return of runaways, the captain probably did not think that his defense of Englishmen and English rights applied to Hammon. The ship's log only notes, "came from the shore 5 Negroes and 2 Englishmen at 7 A.M. sail'd a Spanish 64 Gun Ship Rec'd from the Spanish Admiral a Launch of Water."[60] Gascoigne seemed to have enjoyed a relatively cordial relationship with Spanish officials, who resupplied him with water the same day Hammon arrived, so his defiance may be one of the *Narrative*'s rhetorical flourishes, meant to signal Hammon's allegiance to Britain. But even if Hammon's recollection of the speech is wholly accurate, Gascoigne's words likely referred to the two "Englishmen" who arrived with Hammon and four other "Negroes." The *Beaver's* log suggests that Gascoigne never thought of Hammon as an Englishman; that was a title reserved for persons who were not "Negroes." Hammon might have misunderstood Gascoigne, but it seems more probable that he invented or deliberately misrepresented the captain's message in an attempt to stress his allegiance to Britain.

From Havana, Hammon departed with Gascoigne for Jamaica, where he stayed until leaving for London on February 5, 1759. The *Beaver* guarded a convoy of between twenty-four and thirty ships across the Atlantic, arriving in the first week of April.[61] On May 10, 1759, after a month in port—which the *Narrative* suggests he spent aboard another vessel, the *Arc-en-Ciel*—the *Beaver's* muster book shows that Hammon was discharged in Chatham. Because the *Arc-en-Ciel* was in disrepair, newspapers reported that its crew—including Hammon, presumably—was "turn'd over to the Hercules, lately built at Deptford. The Sandwich and Mercury are rigging as fast as possible."[62] "On board the *Sandwich*," Hammon writes, "I tarry'd 6 Weeks, and then was order'd on board the *Hercules*" (*N* 23). Presumably Hammon spent time preparing the *Sandwich* to make sail before leaving harbor with the *Hercules*, a newly built third-rate ship of the line, in late June 1759, for a cruise that would last, by Hammon's reckoning, three months. But while independent sources confirm most of Hammon's claims regarding his time aboard the *Beaver*, almost none of his assertions regarding the *Hercules* seem to be true.

For 1760 readers, Hammon's service aboard the *Hercules* would have been the most important section of the *Narrative* because it represents his recent contribution to the ongoing Seven Years' War, a conflict that Boston newspapers covered closely. Hammon recalls that after being

> order'd on board the *Hercules*, Capt. *John Porter*, a 74 Gun Ship, we sail'd on a Cruize, and met with a *French* 84 Gun Ship, and had a very smart Engagement, in which about 70 of our Hands were Kill'd and Wounded, the Captain lost his Leg in the Engagement, and I was Wounded in the Head by a small Shot. We should have taken this Ship, if they had not cut away the most of our Rigging; however, in about three Hours after, a 64 Gun Ship, came up with and took her—I was discharged from the *Hercules* the 12th Day of *May* 1759 (having been on board of that Ship 3 Months) on account of my being disabled in the Arm, and render'd incapable of Service, after being honourably paid the Wages due to me. (*N* 23)

A footnote inserted in the original *Narrative* by Hammon's editors reminded readers that "a particular Account of this Engagement, has been Publish'd in the *Boston* News-Papers" (*N* 25). Despite this notice, few of Hammon's readers probably took the time to fact-check his account against reports given in a January edition of *The Boston News-Letter* and a March edition of *The Boston Evening-Post*. Indeed, it seems unlikely that Hammon's publishers bothered to do so, because if they had, they never would have directed readers to a source that so obviously contradicts Hammon's *Narrative*. Here, as in the conflicting reports of his escape to Marsh and his service under Morell, Hammon seems responsible for the *Narrative's* ahistorical claims.

The first and most obvious problem is the chronology of Hammon's claim that he was discharged from the *Hercules* on May 12, 1759, after three months of service. Since the *Hercules* left the shipyards on March 15, it had not even been afloat for three months by that date, and Carretta notes that Hammon's "name does not appear on any of the ship's muster lists through December 1759" (*N* 25, note 20). Perhaps Hammon confused his discharge from the *Beaver* on May 10, 1759, with a later discharge from the *Hercules*. But other contradictions likewise suggest that Hammon either never served on the *Hercules* or had already left the ship long before its confrontation with the French man-of-war *Souverain* on October 10, 1759. The *Narrative* explains that Hammon convalesced from injuries suffered aboard the *Hercules* in a hospital, but there is no record of his admission to the British navy's Greenwich Hospital, where he would have been taken. Following his recovery, Hammon writes that he "ship'd myself a Cook on board Captain *Martyn*, an arm'd Ship in the King's Service. I was on board this Ship almost Two Months, and after being paid my Wages, was discharg'd in the Month of *October*"—at the same time the battle in which he claimed to have been injured took place (*N* 23). Hammon's service under Captain Martyn through the months of August, September, and into October fits, chronologically, with his May discharge from the *Beaver* and a June discharge from the *Sandwich*, but it is wholly incompatible with his account of service under Captain Porter of the *Hercules*, which left port on May 21, 1759, well before Hammon would have finished his six weeks aboard the *Sandwich*.

The second major problem with Hammon's claim is his account of casualties suffered at sea. The *Hercules* was captained by Jervis Porter, and Porter's official report of the action, penned just days after the battle, clearly contradicts Hammon's account: "At ½ past 10, we was so unlucky as to have our main topmast head shot away . . . and having all our sails and rigging very much shattered (at which the enemy only aimed) we left off the chase and wore ship—having one man killed and two wounded, including the captain, who was shot in the head and has lost the use of his right leg by the wind of a shot."[63] The most significant discrepancy between the two accounts has to do with the number and the nature of the casualties resulting from the *Souverain's* attacks. Hammon numbers the casualties at seventy; Porter states that there was only one fatality and two men wounded, of which he was one, meaning that Hammon overstates the body count by a factor of twenty.[64] The *Narrative* omits any mention of Porter's head wound but, quite interestingly, states that Hammon himself suffered an analogous injury during the action, when he was "Wounded in the Head by a small Shot." Even if readers were to disregard Hammon's questionable chronology and accept that he was on-board the *Hercules* when it engaged the *Souverain* on October 10, 1759, the odds that he was the only one of six hundred hands to be wounded and that he suffered the same wound attributed to the ship's captain in newspaper ac-counts are astronomically low; it seems much more likely that Hammon read the newspaper or heard about the encounter from other readers and assigned himself one of the two injuries reportedly suffered by Porter. We may not ever be able to ascertain whether Hammon was telling the truth with regards to his Indian captivity, his double encounter with Romond, his time with Bishop Morell, or Gascoigne's speech, but we can be fairly certain that he misrepresented his service onboard the *Hercules*.

At least two factors might have motivated Hammon to claim, falsely, that he had fought and been wounded in the *Hercules'* attack on the *Souverain*. First, by participating in the engagement, Hammon made himself a part of the decisive naval battle of the Seven Years' War. The *Hercules* encountered the *Souverain* during a blockade of French seaports that culminated in the Battle of Quiberon Bay; this British victory crippled the French navy and was widely celebrated in Boston during the spring of 1760.[65] By self-identifying as one of the men wounded in the Crown's service at this critical juncture, Hammon placed himself at the center of foreign affairs, as a hero. Second, Hammon's participation in the *Hercules'* battle and his account of resisting impressment in the Spanish navy while imprisoned in Cuba would have been particularly interesting—and gratifying—to the man who claimed him as property, General John Winslow. By 1760, Winslow's military career was al-ready over, although he may not have known it at the time, after service in the Cartagena expedition (1740), King George's War, and a number of engage-ments on the North American front of the Seven Years' War.[66] Hammon, hoping to win the favor of "*my good Master*," might have falsified aspects of an oral report to Winslow that later became the basis for his *Narrative* by exag-gerating the extent of his military service in their shared struggle against Brit-ain's enemies (*N* 24). By placing himself at the center of a famous naval battle and exaggerating his involvement in other international exchanges, Hammon might reasonably have hoped for an amelioration of the conditions of his en-slavement or even for emancipation.

By claiming the head wound of Jervis Porter in his *Narrative*, Hammon thrust the suffering of his enslaved black African body into the spotlight of global affairs. As previously noted, the War of Jenkins' Ear—a conflict whose politics justified Hammon's detainment in Cuba and allegedly inspired black African arsonists in New York—began with a disagreement between Britain and Spain over the *assiento*, a contract granted by the Spanish government to Britain and other foreign entities permitting the importation of black African slaves into Spanish American ports. Daniel Baugh suggests that the Seven Years' War likewise stemmed from a French desire to ensure their continued control over the labor of enslaved black Africans in the West Indies.[67] Ownership of black African bodies and the ability to harm them, in other words, lay at the heart of Atlantic naval and military conflicts during the period covered in Hammon's *Narrative*, but public accounts of these wars perversely valorized wounds suffered by the white bodies of Porter and other officers whose sacrifices for King and country were celebrated in the newspapers. To paraphrase Sari Edelstein's description of Harriet Jacobs, Hammon "takes a newspaper that has served as a vehicle for oppression and misinformation and transforms it into a source of unintended knowledge, a tool for liberation, and the basis for a fiction about [his] whereabouts."[68] By claiming Porter's head injury for his own, Hammon recenters eighteenth-century Atlantic wars and politics around the wounds of slavery and the humanity of black African laborers, foregrounding the rational faculties that directed enslaved bodies and inviting a sympathetic identification with his suffering.[69] More than any other moment in the *Narrative*, Hammon's claim to the head wound of Porter signifies his status as an enslaved individual and an invisible victim of global power imbalances, as well as his dissatisfaction with that condition—it is the moment when Hammon's "*Mind*" emphatically rejects slavery and other unjust "*Matters of Fact.*"

The Plasticity of History and Identity

When Carretta first discovered the baptismal record and muster book indicating Equiano may have falsified aspects of his *Narrative*, he buried that information in a footnote to his Penguin edition of the text, apprehensive that some scholars might question the impartiality of his conclusions. While many have hailed the care with which Carretta has documented Equiano's life, the fears that prompted his caution were well-grounded, as other scholars have made allegations of racial profiling. Carretta, who published the first scholarly edition of Hammon's *Narrative* in 1996, has likely long been familiar with historical inconsistencies related to Hammon's service aboard the *Hercules* but may have refrained from questioning the authenticity of this account for the same reason that he initially relegated his discovery of Equiano's baptismal certificate to a footnote. The restoration of historical truths surrounding Hammon's transatlantic travels has been delayed for too long. Acknowledging that Hammon bent the truth need not diminish our regard for him or his *Narrative*; if anything, the rhetorical sophistication with which he demonstrated his allegiance to England should only heighten our appreciation of his storytelling prowess.

When Briton Hammon returned to Marshfield in June 1760, he found the Winslow home substantially altered; among other improvements, Winslow renovated the drawing room and installed a new fireback that year. A complete restoration of the house, undertaken in 1919 by the Historic Winslow House Association, identified this improvement and noted that portions of the house's woodwork lay under thirty-four coats of paint.[70] Stripping away each layer of paint to reveal the underlying wood required precision; dig too deep and the wood itself would be marred. Reclaiming an understanding of Briton Hammon's life and *Narrative*, as well as a sense of where the two may have diverged, requires a similarly painstaking and perilous process of historical reconstruction, particularly because Hammon's account conflates fact and fiction so seamlessly.

One of the most persuasive critiques of Carretta's conclusions regarding the historicity of Equiano's description of life in Africa and the Middle Passage suggests that autobiographies are generally either entirely true or entirely false. Responding to Carretta, Adam Hochschild contends that "it seems somewhat improbable that [Equiano] invented the first part of his life story when the rest of it, to use Carretta's words, is 'remarkably accurate whenever his information can be tested by external evidence.' There is a long and fascinating history of autobiographies that distort or exaggerate the truth. . . . But in each of these cases, the lies and inventions pervade the entire book. Seldom is one crucial portion of a memoir totally fabricated and the remainder scrupulously accurate; among autobiographers, as with other writers, both dissemblers and truth-tellers tend to be consistent." In Hammon we find a precedent for Equiano's inconsistently truthful *Narrative* and an exemplary case in what Natalie Davis calls "the problem of truth and doubt: of the difficulty in determining true identity in the [eighteenth] century and of the difficulty in the historian's quest for truth in the [twenty-first]."[71] Hammon's enlistment onboard the *Beaver*, his recollection that a twenty-gun man-of-war commanded by Henry Marsh docked in Havana during the 1750s—these are historically verifiable aspects of his account. But by insisting upon his participation in the *Hercules'* engagement with the *Souverain*, Hammon also included at least one crucial, demonstrably false account in his *Narrative*, and several others seem suspect. Rather than the rigidity Hochschild attributes to autobiographical narratives, the accounts of Hammon and Equiano manifest what Jean Viviès refers to as textual plasticity, moving fluidly from history to fiction and back again.[72]

The approach of enslaved black Africans to international conflicts and foreign affairs might also be described as plastic, as they shifted fluidly from an allegiance to one power or another according to their circumstances. In 1741, a number of New York's black residents apparently decided that they were more likely to win their freedom by fighting against the British and for the coalition of French and Spanish troops they hoped would come to occupy the city. While he was in Cuba, Hammon strove for familiarity with the governor, Don Francisco, but when he saw an opportunity to escape from enslavement and join the British navy as a freeman, he leapt at the opportunity. Black Africans living in the Atlantic world and traveling far from their native countries lacked the protections and privileges accorded to the subjects of European princes; their best recourse was to select a state and declare allegiance to its interests, as Briton Hammon did in his *Narrative*, and as the *"Spanish Negroes"* at the center of Horsmanden's plot to burn New York allegedly tried to do through acts of arson. Identifying a nation and a constituency that might be sympathetic to professions of allegiance by black Africans required the enslaved to think of themselves in the terms of global politics. Only by carefully considering the domestic and personal implications of foreign news and international affairs could the enslaved know which political and martial postures might provide them with an opportunity for freedom or with increased respect and improved living conditions.

The manipulations of history in Hammon's *Narrative* reflect his keen awareness of geopolitics and emphasize his self-conception as a patriotic British subject, a man who would merit the respect of Winslow and others complicit in his enslavement. When he arrived home, near the conclusion of the Seven Years' War, he was celebrated as a hero, and an account of his adventures was published to commemorate his loyalty to the Crown. In contrast to Hammon, the enslaved black Africans who purportedly attempted to burn down New York City and gave their allegiance to Spain were treated with cruelty and put to death. Picking the winner in an ongoing international conflict was a matter of life and death, but so were many other decisions for the enslaved, and this decision, at least, offered the hope of advancement and emancipation. Hammon's story of surviving violence has often been called the first slave narrative and is sometimes identified with the genre of Indian captivity narratives, but its personal perspective on global affairs and cross-cultural exchanges might better be compared to the letters so frequently published in newspapers, by foreign correspondents who had lived through extraordinary events. Slavery, captivity, and redemption are, in Hammon's *Narrative*, functions of war and diplomacy. To refer to it as the first slave narrative is, then, to acknowledge the genre's roots in a concept of slavery that had largely disappeared by the nineteenth century, a concept of slavery rooted in international law rather than racism. To refer to it as a slave narrative is to acknowledge that much shorter accounts of enslaved life preserved in eighteenth-century newspapers and court records which underscore similar themes are also part of the slave narrative tradition. To refer to it as a slave narrative is to see enslaved black Africans as they saw themselves in the eighteenth century: as strangers in a strange land, seeking safety and security through acts of allegiance.

CHAPTER FIVE

Narratives of Slavery and the Stamp Act

Dickinson and Crèvecoeur Debate the
Racial Limits of a Genre

When Briton Hammon's *Narrative* was published, in the middle of the Seven Years' War, the colonial residents of Massachusetts would have considered his self-identification as an Englishman and his expressions of allegiance to England patriotic. But in the aftermath of the Seven Years' War, Parliament attempted to raise revenue and pay for debt incurred on its North American front, in the French and Indian War, by taxing the American colonies. Attitudes toward England quickly shifted in Massachusetts and other colonies as a result, and protestors began to characterize England's oppressive tax policies as a form of slavery. As Bernard Bailyn notes, North American Whigs borrowed this conception of slavery from their eighteenth-century counterparts in England and popularized its figurative use during debates over the Stamp Act, Townshend Duties, and subsequent crises.[1] In 1764, while Prime Minister George Grenville was still formulating the specific provisions of the Stamp Act, the governor of Rhode Island, Stephen Hopkins, anticipatorily objected that "they who are taxed at pleasure by others, cannot possibly have any property, can have nothing to be called their own; they who have no property, can have no freedom, but are indeed reduced to the most abject slavery."[2] Representations of involuntary taxation and political oppression as forms of bondage proliferated in the decade that followed. Colonists opposed to the Stamp Act reported a public discourse "filled with exclamations against Slavery and arbitrary Power," and declamations against the British imposition of slavery persisted in colonial newspapers long after the duty had been repealed.[3]

Among the many colonial voices objecting to British taxation were those of two enslaved black African poets: Caesar, a writer hitherto unknown to scholars, and Phillis Wheatley Peters.[4] Peters's double-voiced verse is widely admired, and her poem "America" deploys the imagery and language of slavery to criticize English governance of her North American colonies.[5] Figuring England as a mother and America as her only child, Peters writes that England "laid some taxes on her darling son" and punished him with "many

Scourges" until America "weeps afresh to feel this Iron chain" (lines 11, 15, 31).[6] Peters condemns England for its oppressive and tyrannical policies in fairly conventional language, but because of her own legal status as a human chattel held in bondage by the slaveowners John and Susanna Wheatley, this invocation of whips and fetters functions as a reminder of colonists' complicity in systems of oppression. In articulating the distress of white colonists, Peters also gave voice to enslaved black Africans who were regularly infantilized by the men and women who thought of them as property, rather than persons. Crucially, Peters refuses to refer to the colonists as slaves, insisting upon a fundamental difference between her own status and that of property owners subject to taxation without representation. Even as she creates an affiliative link of the sort described by Caroline Wigginton, between herself and the white colonists surrounding her, she suggests that there are limits to this affinity. Although Peters believed that "infringing on another's freedom, either for political or economic reasons, is an act of tyranny and cruelty," she also knew that not all acts of tyranny and cruelty are equivalent.[7] Peters deploys slavery as a metaphor for British taxation in her poetry, but she does so with an awareness of the difference between her own status as a human chattel and that of colonists subjected to the decrees of a distant Parliament.

Caesar, an enslaved young man of black African descent who delivered the *Boston Evening-Post* for the Fleet family, also described English governance with the figurative language of slavery, but because his poems were published anonymously, modern readers have never appreciated the irony of his verse. Every New Year's Eve, from 1764 to 1770, subscribers to the *Boston Evening-Post* received a special, poetic supplement to the newspaper bearing some variation of the 1764 title, "The News-BOY's *Christmas* and *New-Years* VERSES." (Each of these seven poems is republished in the Appendix.) Scholars encountering them in the twentieth and twenty-first centuries have dismissed these poems as anonymous and largely unremarkable pleas for supplemental income, but the men and women to whom they were addressed in the eighteenth century clearly found them persuasive and entertaining; the regularity with which they appeared is a testament to the enthusiasm with which they were received. Unlike their twenty-first-century counterparts, eighteenth-century readers likely knew that Caesar was the author of these poems.[8] They had known his father, Black Peter, who carried the *Post* in the 1730s and 1740s, and his brothers, Robin and Pompey, who had carried the newspaper in the 1750s. Members of Caesar's family had been collecting a Christmas bonus from *Post* subscribers for decades, so when these supplements first arrived, readers knew that their support would provide spending money to an enslaved young man without ready access to cash.[9] They knew, also, that when Caesar discussed slavery, he spoke from personal experience.

The first of Caesar's seven surviving New Year's Eve poems, published in 1764, speaks of England from the same patriotic perspective as Hammon's *Narrative* and alludes to the challenges of slavery only obliquely.[10] Reflecting with gratitude on the victorious conclusion of the French and Indian War, Caesar expresses his desire that "the Noise of War henceforth cease, / And British Realms be hush'd in Peace" (lines 58–59). Caesar's expression of hope, that "nothing Britain's Peace annoy," evinces no awareness that Massachusetts colonists would be the empire's primary annoyance in the year to come (line 61). There is no talk of England oppressing or enslaving its American subjects, but Caesar's poem does suggest a keen awareness of and struggle with his own subordinate legal status. The very first stanza notes that everyone he meets must be addressed as "Mistresses and Masters" whom he must seek "to please" (lines 3, 17); the phrase appears twice more, as he explains how he, "To please, spar'd no Toil nor Pain," and how he "Has strove to please you all the Year" (line 31, 53). This plaintive, repetitive acknowledgment of his obligation to gratify others rather than himself gets at the heart of what it means, to Caesar, to be enslaved. He writes to the newspaper subscribers from whom he hopes to earn a small gratuity of "Experience woful" and "a tedious Year of Pain" (lines 34, 50). Dressing up these laments "in Rhime, ding, dong," for the entertainment of his oppressors, presents his pain and his brain as the only forms of capital left to him by enslavement (line 15). Caesar grieves the circumstances of his life in bondage even as he reminds his enslavers of their fortunate circumstances, free to enjoy peace and prosperity under the benevolent rule of "*great George our King*" (line 56).

Of course, by the time Caesar wrote again to the subscribers of the *Post*, in December 1765, he and his readers had come to see their metropolitan overseers in different, and much less flattering, terms. During the intervening year, Caesar had helped to set type for a new edition of Jeremiah Dummer's *A Defence of the New-England Charters* (1721), in which Dummer both expresses contempt for enslaved black Africans and alleges that England seeks to make each of its colonists comparably "miserable, and a slave."[11] He also helped to publish and distribute Benjamin Church's poetic objection to the Stamp Act, "The Times: A Poem," written to unmask that "greatest of blessings the S—p A—t" as a tool of "hypocrisy, slavery and tyranny."[12] (line 2) Like Dummer and Church, Caesar writes "(In spite of *Stamps*)" to describe "Fair Freedom" pirouetting "in graceful Dance, / One foot on *Spain* and one on *France*" (lines 54, 10–12). Questions of freedom and enslavement, in other words, are relative to international politics. When England took prisoners from foreign powers in the Seven Years' War, it did so in the service of freedom; when taxes were levied on colonial newspapers and other paper goods, Caesar asked, "Will *British* Steel in GEORGE's Reign, / Bend for to form a Subject's Chain?" (lines 17–18). Like Peters, Caesar may still have found the colonial claims of enslavement a touch hyperbolic. He also refused to use the words *slave* or *slavery* in his 1765 poem, even though they were regularly inserted into comparable political expressions.

One year later, Caesar expressed a more jaded perspective on British governance in a 1766 poem featuring a number of double-voiced passages criticizing both imperial overreach and colonial hypocrisy. Describing the message sent to England by colonial protests that led to the Stamp Act's repeal, Caesar declares that now parliamentarians "know, thro' every Vein, / The British Blood flows with Disdain, / Of such oppress'd Condition" (lines 22–24). This declaration recalls the popular refrain of "Rule, Britannia!" suggesting that Britons—especially the British colonists for whom Caesar writes—never, never, never will be slaves. However, Caesar's invocation of this wholly conventional sentiment also recalls the disdain he and other enslaved black Africans had frequently felt as a result of their own oppressed conditions. The same words that signified colonists' scorn for tyranny also signified their scorn for the enslaved black African men and women to whom they, themselves, were tyrants.

In 1766 Caesar still felt obliged, as in earlier years, "To please you Gentlemen," but his "pleasing Task," or the task of pleasing the *Post*'s subscribers, could not keep him from self-expression (lines 60, 52). Thus, his call to take up Dummer's work "and Defend, / Your Constitution" is preceded by a stanza that implicitly castigates both Parliament and the colonists as enslavers (lines 37–38). Caesar writes,

> Freedom shall still inhabit here,
> Her Mansions free from slavish Fear,
>   Protected by her Friends;
> Unnat'ral Wretches they! who strive
> To bury her whilst yet alive,
>   This ne'er shall serve their Ends. (lines 25–30)

Upon the indefinite pronoun *they* hangs the import and sense of the stanza. For readers predisposed to regard Parliament and its advocates as "Unnat'ral

Wretches," Caesar's meaning is clear. But the exclamation point dividing *they* from the parenthetical description, "who strive / To bury her whilst yet alive," works to identify the colonists as both "Friends" and "Wretches." Because of the exclamation point and preceding semicolon, the pronoun might plausibly—and even preferentially—refer backward, to the colonists, rather than forward, to parliamentary overseers who bury freedom alive. As Molly Perry reminds us, it was protesting colonists and not British officials who held mock funerals for Freedom; they also buried alive a royal stamp collector.[13] Caesar's verse indicts both English governance and the colonial hypocrites who claim to love liberty but bury it alive and consign black Africans to a lifetime of bondage. This newsboy poem acknowledges the grievances of colonists but insists, reciprocally, that colonists acknowledge their own participation in systems of oppression.

The biblical metaphor at the heart of his 1767 poem is a similarly double-edged sword. Although he wrote almost two years after the Stamp Act's repeal, Caesar continued to invoke that piece of legislation as emblematic of England's "*enslaving* Design" (line 23). He compares this tax to the "*Imposts in Silver and Gold*" levied by Egypt in the book of Genesis (line 18), when a famine led the household of Israel to seek food in foreign lands: "And Judah and his brethren came to Joseph's house; for he was yet there [in Egypt]: and they fell before him on the ground."[14] England, Caesar writes, seeks to "drain us as *Joseph*—the *Egyptians* of Old, / That our *Substance & Persons* like *theirs* might be sold" (lines 19–20). This biblical simile is all too easy to misread: England is Egypt, enslaving, the colonists are Israel, enslaved; the moral arithmetic is clear. But that is not at all what Caesar writes; it is the Egyptians who are enslaved in his poem, not the Israelites, and they are enslaved by Joseph, the prince of Israel. Those who identify with Joseph and with biblical Israel, as Massachusetts colonists did, are the actual instruments of oppression, enslaving the inhabitants of northeast Africa. In other words, Caesar muddies the moral waters by identifying Joseph, who was sold into slavery by the other sons of Israel, as a figure of oppression; he is both master and chattel, enslaved and enslaving. So, too, the white colonists around him, who self-identify as chattels but enslave persons like Caesar. Caesar seems to give voice, in his verse, to the complaints of colonists. He seems to validate their claims of victimhood but actually insists that they recognize the role they play in victimizing the black Africans they hold captive.[15] Like Joseph and his brothers, white colonists occupy a moral middle ground as prosperous slavers whose prospective enslavement is hypothetical and the problem of future generations.

With Peters, Caesar offers a double-voiced perspective on the Stamp Act. Their poetic narratives of slavery were well received by colonists in North

America, but the most famous objection to colonial enslavement via the Stamp Act was made by a white writer: John Dickinson.[16] "The Voice of Freedom," a 1773 poem sometimes attributed to Peters, characterizes Dickinson as the "Immortal Farmer" because in the winter of 1767–68, he published a series of twelve letters in the *Pennsylvania Chronicle* that were reprinted in nineteen of twenty-three extant North American English-language newspapers and then issued as a pamphlet entitled *Letters from a Farmer in Pennsylvania*. Peters warns, in "The voice of Freedom," that unless colonists unite in opposition to their English oppressors, "Base *slaves* you'll live, like *malefactors* die!" (20).[17] More than any other writer, Dickinson popularized the belief that "*those* who are *taxed* without their own consent, expressed by themselves or their representatives, are *slaves*. We are taxed without our own consent, expressed by ourselves or our representatives. We are therefore— SLAVES" (D 53). These words were consumed silently and read aloud in public spaces, as Wigginton attests.[18] In just two years Dickinson's letters to the *Pennsylvania Chronicle* ran through seven different pamphlet editions, proving so successful that Milton Flower argues, "Until Thomas Paine's *Common Sense* was published early in 1776, no other document earned the acclaim given the *Farmer's Letters*; none reached a wider public. Until the year of Independence, John Dickinson, apart from Benjamin Franklin, was probably the American known to more colonists than any other."[19] Dickinson and his ubiquitous *Letters* taught colonial readers to think of oppressive parliamentary governance as a form of slavery, paving the path to revolution. It was the white Dickinson, not Peters or Caesar or Hammon, who popularized narratives of enslavement in the late eighteenth century.

Not everyone who read Dickinson's *Letters* found the simile appropriate or thought that he had a moral right to castigate British officials as slavers. In 1769 J. Hector St. John de Crèvecoeur began drafting the epistles that would eventually be published as *Letters from an American Farmer* (1782), in response to Dickinson's critique of parliamentary power and his accompanying representation of colonists as slaves.[20] Although he first put pen to paper at the height of Dickinson's considerable renown, when Dickinson was the most famous of Crèvecoeur's "famous lawyers," the relationship between these two texts has remained concealed over the centuries, for two reasons.[21] First, Crèvecoeur did not find a publisher for his work until he reached England, in 1782, when Dickinson's fame had faded and the questions of taxation underlying both collections of letters had been eclipsed by military matters; parallels that would have seemed obvious and inflammatory to readers of colonial American newspapers in the 1760s and early 1770s failed to

excite English readers in the 1780s.[22] Second, modern readers have long resisted treating Crèvecoeur's epistles as the letters they purport to be.[23] As
Elizabeth Cook notes, the text's "epistolarity—its generic context and codes—is
almost always ignored."[24] That Crèvecoeur responds to or, given the genre,
corresponds with Dickinson and other eighteenth-century newspaper editorialists would have been obvious if we had treated the title of *Letters from an
American Farmer* as a serious generic claim: "correspondence consists in re-
ciprocal letters" (*C* 18).

Reading Dickinson and Crèvecoeur in tandem transforms their letters
into a debate over the racialization of the slave narrative. In the ninth epistle
to readers of the *Pennsylvania Chronicle*, Dickinson asked, "Is it possible to
form an idea of a slavery more *compleat*, more *miserable*, more *disgraceful*,
than that of a people, where *justice is administered, government exercised*, and a
standing army maintained, AT THE EXPENCE OF THE PEOPLE, and yet WITH-
OUT THE LEAST DEPENDENCE UPON THEM?" (*D* 69). Dickinson claims
that his narration of the historical sufferings and imagined future miseries
brought on by imperial coercion and taxation without representation constitutes a slave narrative (*the* slave narrative, even). But when Crèvecoeur responds
in his ninth letter with a portrait of black Africans toiling in a slavery more
complete, more miserable, more disgraceful than the state of Dickinson's colonists, he rejects this Whiggish equation between involuntary taxation and
slavery, adopting the Royalist strategy so well documented by Peter Dorsey:
critiquing "the slavery metaphor as a means of discrediting the patriots'
cause."[25] With Caesar and Peters, Dickinson and Crèvecoeur wrote to determine what forms of oppression constitute slavery and which experiences
authorize the composition of a slave narrative. Crèvecoeur's epistolary argument with Dickinson, as to whether the Stamp Act had enslaved American
colonists, thus represents one of the earliest attempts to theorize and delimit
the racial boundaries of the slave narrative, a generic debate grounded in the
conventions of newspaper editorials and epistolary culture. Peters and Caesar were willing to validate colonial complaints of enslavement in the hope
that white colonists might, in turn, regard enslaved black Africans with empa-
thy; however, Crèvecoeur rejected the equation entirely, denouncing Dickinson and other disaffected editorialists as foolish rebels, not slaves.

Silk and Stamps and Kingbirds

While many readers of Crèvecoeur's *Letters* have focused on the volume's discussion of revolutionary-era violence in Letter XII, most of Crèvecoeur's

preceding epistles consider the philosophical disagreements that preceded war, especially the legitimacy of Whiggish principles undergirding Dickinson's use of the slave metaphor. As David Carlson helpfully suggests, a "dehistoricization of the text" has led to readings of Crèvecoeur "focused too exclusively on the *manifest* social upheaval ... in Revolutionary America, rather than on the deeper ideological issues and debates of the period."[26] Until 1776 Dickinson, like Crèvecoeur, accepted and even advocated British governance of the colonies. Both considered themselves loyal British subjects, though they disagreed as to whether Dickinson's aggressive challenge to the exercise of imperial powers and his invocation of slavery were consistent with fealty to the Crown. The editorials of Dickinson and the letters of Crèvecoeur are more concerned with finding an appropriate metaphor for the fiscal relationship between imperial metropole and colonial outpost—with inscribing a poetics of taxation—than with revolutionary violence.[27]

Dickinson's letters to the *Pennsylvania Chronicle* objected to the Stamp Act and Townshend Duties on two grounds. First, he condemns taxation for the purpose of "raising a revenue"—as opposed to taxes regulating trade, "imposed *with design* to restrain the commerce of one part [of the empire], that was injurious to another, and thus to promote the general welfare"—and warns that these new taxes will lead to "a state of the most abject slavery" (*D* 8–9, 69). Second, he rejects Parliament's allegation that the acts are meant to finance debt incurred while protecting colonists during the French and Indian War, insisting the taxes are self-serving and meant to create new revenue streams that will continue after war debt has been repaid, by expanding British rule over "*the conquered provinces of Canada and Florida, and the* British *garrisons of* Nova Scotia," which "do not deserve the name of colonies" (*D* 56). Colonists will eventually find themselves unable to support this new and unconstitutional tax burden, Dickinson argues, because rates can be raised at any time, without justification; he predicts that taxes will "regularly encrease ... till at length the inattentive people are compelled to perceive the heaviness of their burthens" (*D* 87). Dickinson prophesies that if England can tax its North American outposts for the sole purpose of raising money, British levies will soon "sink them into slaves" (*D* 39).

Whereas Dickinson complains that British taxes are an insupportable burden, Crèvecoeur contends that colonial taxes are negligible, that a beneficent British Parliament unites colonists "from Nova Scotia to West Florida" (*C* 41). Farmer James, Crèvecoeur's narrative persona, insists that the British "government ... requires but little from us. I owe nothing but a pepper-corn to my country, a small tribute to my king" (*C* 25). And in the Nantucket letters,

Farmer James turns to this theme repeatedly.[28] James writes that the colonies pay only "the trifling duties which this community owe to those who protect them, and under the shadow of whose wings they navigate to all parts of the world" (C 107). Later, Farmer James praises the British tax code, noting that the "principal benefit it confers is the general protection of individuals, and this protection is purchased by the most moderate taxes, which are cheerfully paid, and by the trifling duties incident in the course of their lawful trade (for they despise contraband)" (C 136). These lines, written about an island off the Massachusetts coast at a time when groups promoting Dickinson's Whiggish invocation of slavery were busily importing contraband goods to evade British duties, are more than a little ironic. Crèvecoeur's utopian island—knowingly placed at an inaccurate latitude and longitude—is less a reality than an expression of his desires, a place where the acceptance of parliamentary tax policies has produced prosperity and peace.

If Crèvecoeur's encomiums on Nantucket reflect a willful disregard of dissatisfaction with the Stamp Act and the active resistance prompted by Dickinson's Pennsylvania Farmer, so too does his well-known third letter. In language that any colonist living in the 1760s and 1770s would have found deeply ironic but that modern readers regularly accept at face value, Farmer James writes that Americans "are a people of cultivators, scattered over an immense territory, communicating with each other by means of good roads and navigable rivers, united by the silken bands of mild government, all respecting the laws, without dreading their power, because they are equitable" (C 41; see also 108). Ironically, by making colonial unity conditional on a belief in equitable laws and the "silken bands of mild government," Crèvecoeur satirically characterizes Dickinson's editorial war on the Stamp Act and Townshend Duties, which united colonists as never before, as divisive and disruptive, suggesting that British taxes better resemble the silk collars of high society than the iron manacles of an enslaved black African.

During the decade between the Stamp Act's passage and the shots fired at Lexington and Concord, silk became a symbol of both imperial oppression and parliamentary support. Because the Townshend Duties assessed taxes on imported silk, colonial newspapers called for farmers to plant mulberry trees. Until domestic silk production could begin in earnest, newspaper editorials instructed women to wear homespun fabrics and warned, "[I]f we meet any of the said Female Sex, dressed in Foreign Silks, and Laces &c. we will pass by them, as persons that have been too free with some Merchant, and are Adulteresses forsaking the interest of their Country."[29] In the interval before the Revolution, individuals who wore silk were presumed to be

Tories, while Whigs flaunted their homespun. Crèvecoeur's description of governance both praises the lenient policies of London and implicitly casts the blame for colonial divisions at the feet of Dickinson and other writers, whose newspaper editorials have allegedly torn the continent apart over trifling duties on silk.

Lest his readers miss the symbolic significance of these "silken bands," Crèvecoeur's third letter follows this praise of British tax law with a more explicit encomium on the Stamp Act. After describing the transformation of poor European immigrants into prosperous American farmers, Crèvecoeur asks:

> By what invisible power hath this surprising metamorphosis been performed? By that of the laws and that of their liberty. The laws, the indulgent laws, protect them as they arrive, *stamping* on them the symbol of adoption: they receive ample rewards for their labours: these accumulated rewards procure them lands: those lands confer on them the title of freemen, and to that title every benefit is affixed which men can possibly require. This is the great operation daily performed by our laws. Whence proceed these laws? From our government. Whence that government? It is derived from the original genius and strong desire of the people ratified and confirmed by the crown. (C 43; my emphasis)

Crèvecoeur could not be more clear: the Stamp Act and other imperial laws governing the colonies are a source of prosperity, without which North America would falter. British tax law affixes the status and benefits of freemen to colonists just as imperial stamps were to have affixed value and legality to colonial paper.

Later, when the third letter considers American Indians in contact with European colonists, Crèvecoeur simultaneously defends the constitutionality of the Stamp Act and argues that laws of this sort are the primary factor differentiating colonists from their "savage" indigenous neighbors. Comparing the "tender minds" of Indian children with "Europeans, who have not that sufficient share of knowledge they ought to have, in order to prosper: people, who have suddenly passed from oppression, dread of government, and fear of laws, into the unlimited freedom of the woods," Crèvecoeur warns that both groups will "grow up a mongrel breed, half civilized, half savage, except nature *stamps* on them some constitutional propensities" (C 52; my emphasis). In combination with a reminder of colonists who fear government and dread its laws, Crèvecoeur's use of the word *stamp* suggests that he regards Dickinson's crusade against imperial coercion and involuntary taxation as a degenerative influence that will strip colonists of civility and leave them racialized savages rather than freemen; for Crèvecoeur, as Jeff Osborne suggests, "citizenship requires the domination of multiple social segments" through imperial legislation.[30] In Crèvecoeur's *Letters*, it is the question of whether or not colonists accept the Stamp Act and parliamentary power that will determine whether they are savage Creoles or English gentlemen.[31] Dickinson repeatedly describes the Stamp Act and the Townshend Duties on goods such as paper, glass, lead, and silk as a form of "slavery" designed to raise a general revenue (*D* 13); just as often, Crèvecoeur construes the taxes as an ennobling and civilizing pittance gladly paid for protection from racialization, as well as from domestic and foreign enemies that might otherwise overrun the colonies.

Parliament regularly denied that the Stamp Act was intended to raise general-purpose funds, presenting the tax as a way of recovering British expenses incurred while protecting colonists during the French and Indian War. Dickinson disagreed. In response to the British insistence that colonists should reimburse London for the costs of military protection from French and American Indian attacks, Dickinson calls the late conflict "a war *undertaken solely for* [Britain's] *own benefit. The objects of it were, the securing to herself the rich tracts of land on the back of these colonies, with the Indian trade; and Nova-Scotia, with the fishery. These and much more, has that kingdom gained; but the inferior animals, that hunted with the lion, have been amply rewarded for all the sweat and blood their loyalty cost them, by the honor of having sweated and bled in such company*" (*D* 57). Rejecting the English pretense of "defending, protecting and securing" the colonies, Dickinson describes both colonists and king as animals cooperating in an offensive hunting venture (*D* 56). He condemns imperial taxation with a metaphor that characterizes colonial cooperation as the voluntary association of admittedly inferior animals—perhaps wolves, snakes, or other less impressive predators—with a royal lion reminiscent of George III. If the colonies are inferior, Dickinson insists that they are nonetheless independent entities whose cooperative hunting venture with the lion has yielded few tangible benefits.

When Crèvecoeur refers metaphorically to the British navy as protective "wings" overshadowing colonial commerce, he replies to Dickinson's animal allegory with one of his own, inviting readers to reconsider an anecdote describing the protection kingbirds provide Farmer James by preserving his fields "from the depredation of crows" (*C* 29). In his second letter, James acknowledges practical benefits derived from the oversight of kingbirds, but he also complains that these guardians regularly kill and eat the bees that pollinate his fields. When hundreds of bees unite and attack a kingbird, Farmer James watches them drive the predator off, only to disband soon after. Seeing its assailants separate, the kingbird returns and eats dozens of the bees. Farmer James, for his part, kills the kingbird, cuts open his stomach, and watches in amazement as fifty-four of the swallowed bees return to life, lick themselves clean, and fly back to their hive. Given Crèvecoeur's later, explicit connection between moderate tax rates, British protection, and wings, this anecdote about kingbirds preserving colonial fields from marauding crows clearly serves, as Christine Holbo once speculated it might, "as an allegorical apology for British rule, pointing out that the crown ('our king-birds') earns the taxes owed it by protecting the colonies against outside invasion."[32] As John Cox notes, the "meaning of these stories becomes clearer in the following paragraph when James explicitly compares himself to the colonial legal system, which, he points out, should protect those who are unable to take care of themselves."[33]

Crèvecoeur, like Dickinson before him, converts the debate over who should pay for the French and Indian War into an allegory involving animals that hunt. Crèvecoeur's kingbird, like Dickinson's lion, is a regal predator credited with protecting colonial property, but Crèvecoeur's allegory differs from Dickinson's in three notable respects. First, Crèvecoeur reaffirms the British perspective of the French and Indian War as a conflict fought to protect colonial prosperity (Farmer James's fields) rather than an attempt to enlarge British dominion, as Dickinson alleged. Second, Crèvecoeur dramatically exaggerates the inferiority of colonial "animals." Whereas Dickinson insists that colonists participated cooperatively in the lion's pursuit of prey, Crèvecoeur suggests that colonists are more likely to become prey themselves than to join in the kingbird's fight against the crows. Third, Crèvecoeur implies that the colonies, far from being the inferior but independent and autonomously governed animals suggested by Dickinson's comparison, are merely parts of the British body politic.[34] The kingbird eats the bees precisely because they belong inside of his body, and as Crèvecoeur's allegory suggests, incorporation within the British body politic does not necessarily result in death: a third of the ingested bees continue to live and function within the kingbird's craw.[35] Dickinson's editorials rail against taxation as a form of slavery and use animals symbolically to illustrate the injustice of British claims to reparation for costs incurred during the French and Indian War; Crèvecoeur's letters respond with a new animal allegory, downplaying the impact of British taxes and praising the crown's protection of colonial interests.

Notwithstanding the violence of these allegories, both Dickinson and Crèvecoeur yearned for peace. But Dickinson warns that colonists can never enjoy that peace until Parliament stops attempting to tax colonial wealth, or property, without consent. Quoting from the millennial prophecies of Micah, Dickinson argues "that their property, acquired with so much pain and hazard, should be disposed of by none but themselves—or to use the beautiful and emphatic language of the sacred scriptures, 'that they should sit *every man* under his vine, and under his fig-tree, and NONE SHOULD MAKE THEM AFRAID'" (*D* 34). Dickinson looks forward to a paradisiacal reprieve from oppressive tax policies. Like Dickinson, Crèvecoeur references the millennial promise of Micah; unlike Dickinson, Crèvecoeur suggests that colonists already "enjoy the fruit of their labour under the peaceable shade of their vines and fig trees" (*C* 87). Because the British tax burden is trifling, a mere peppercorn, Crèvecoeur contends that colonists retain "the full rewards of their industry" and that Dickinson's divisive colonial rhetoric is the only real obstacle to peace and prosperity in North America (*C* 87). The colonists of Nantucket already enjoy "peace," Crèvecoeur reminds his readers, precisely because they are not affected by "the political commotions which sometimes agitate our continent!" (*C* 138). He acknowledges Dickinson's complaint by quoting Micah but rejects the premise that British taxes deprive colonists of their property. Here, as in other instances, Crèvecoeur has clearly read Dickinson's letters to the *Pennsylvania Chronicle* and composes his own epistles in reply, challenging the Whiggish logic that equates taxation and heavy-handed parliamentary governance with slavery.

Machiavelli, Ministers, and Natural Slaves

In crafting his response to Dickinson, Crèvecoeur labors to link his *Letters* to the Pennsylvania Farmer even as he simultaneously works to undermine Dickinson's use of the slave metaphor. He does so by drawing distinctions between himself, in the rustic guise of Farmer James, and an urbane Dickinson, whom Crèvecoeur casts as a lawyer hypocritically invoking the specter of slavery to undermine social hierarchies for personal gain. An avaricious attorney and slave owner like Dickinson, Crèvecoeur suggests, supports oppressive systems far more unnatural and burdensome than imperial governance and the Stamp Act.[36]

Beyond the topical correspondences already noted and obvious similarities in the two collections' titles, Crèvecoeur ties his work to Dickinson by describing himself—indistinguishable, at this point, from Farmer James—as "a farmer in Pennsylvania" (C 1). This statement is, as several have previously noted, factually inaccurate; Crèvecoeur owned and cultivated land in Orange County, New York—not Pennsylvania. Crèvecoeur's geographical red herring is, in part, a commercial calculation.[37] Dickinson's Pennsylvania Farmer was a newspaper persona familiar to all of Crèvecoeur's eighteenth-century American neighbors and most British citizens across the Atlantic. Nearly every literate colonist had read Dickinson's syndicated letters, and his Farmer reached illiterate Americans through oral tributes and attempts to merchandize his likeness. As Frank Mott recalls: "[T]own-meetings and grand juries commended the Farmer; songs were written in his honor; his likeness was engraved and printed for sale at a shilling, or 'glazed and framed' at five shillings; the College of New Jersey made him a Doctor of Laws. In the lists of toasts at patriotic meetings in the late sixties and seventies—those lists which begin 'The King; The Queen' and run on to a score or more—'The Farmer' was sure to appear not too late in the enumeration."[38] When Crèvecoeur began writing his *Letters*, Dickinson's editorials were universally known, recently published, and internationally relevant. In describing himself as a Pennsylvania farmer, Crèvecoeur undoubtedly hoped that his readers would associate this second set of letters from a second farmer in Pennsylvania with Dickinson's earlier, famous contributions to the *Pennsylvania Chronicle*.

Having begun by tying his *Letters* to Dickinson, Crèvecoeur moves to distinguish himself from his predecessor by foregrounding the agricultural authenticity of his own authorial persona. In the summer of 1768, after the public learned that Dickinson had penned the pseudonymous editorials, some—aware that Dickinson was first and foremost a Philadelphia lawyer, whose property lay in Maryland and Delaware—attacked his credibility. As Jeffrey Pasley explains, by "disclosing the real identities of newspaper writers," Tories "made the Revolutionary agitation appear to be the illegitimate machinations of a handful of conspirators," and Dickinson's critics launched a concerted attack on his character.[39] Capitalizing on Dickinson's new celebrity, newspapers throughout the colonies republished excerpts from his previous pamphlet against the Stamp Act, *An Address to the Committee of Correspondence in Barbados* (1766), and Philadelphia editorialists worked to discredit Dickinson by accusing him of lying in the earlier *Address*. A "BARBADIAN" suggested that in composing the *Address* and then permitting its resurrection in newspapers, "the author of the *Farmer's Letters*" acted contrary to "common *justice* . . . and if such are his notions of that *divine virtue*, I am sure *he* shall never be my *lawyer*." And "*A COUNTRY Farmer*" called attention to the deceitfulness of Dickinson's legally minded "*City-Farmer*" by contrast.[40]

In *Letters from an American Farmer,* Crèvecoeur adopts a strategy from Dickinson's earlier newspaper critics—castigating the urbane, slaveholding lawyer with the voice of a more authentic "*COUNTRY Farmer*"—and it seems all but certain that he either participated in or read and received inspiration from these editorial exchanges, whose rhetorical strategies he adopts at other moments, as in his attempts to link lawyers like Dickinson to Machiavelli (on which more soon).[41] Indeed, Crèvecoeur calls attention to the avidity with which colonial cultivators such as Farmer James consumed the newspapers that published epistles by Dickinson, his critics, and supporters: "[T]hey will carefully read the newspapers, enter into every political disquisition, freely blame, or censure, governors and others. As farmers, they will be careful and anxious to get as much as they can, because what they get is their own" (*C* 46). Crèvecoeur prefaces his *Letters* with a declaration of authenticity that implicitly contrasts the private epistles of Farmer James with the putatively promotional and deceptive productions of the "*City-Farmer*" Dickinson: "*The following Letters are the genuine production of the American Farmer whose name they bear. They were privately written, to gratify the curiosity of a friend; and are made public, because they contain much authentic information, little known this side of the Atlantic*" (*C* 3). Dickinson's critics alleged that he adopted the persona of a farmer and wrote his letters to the *Pennsylvania Chronicle* only in order to campaign for public office.[42] By claiming to be an actual farmer who writes without any desire for a public readership—or public office—Crèvecoeur disavows the corruption so often associated with publicity in colonial America and positions Farmer James as a more credible correspondent than Dickinson's politically minded Pennsylvania Farmer.[43]

Throughout the *Letters,* as Carlson and others have noted, Crèvecoeur repeatedly contrasts farmers and lawyers, exalting the former and criticizing the latter. Describing his "family and farm" in the third letter, Farmer James asks, "Is it not better to contemplate, under these humble roofs, the rudiments of future wealth and population, than to behold the accumulated bundles of litigious papers in the office of a lawyer?" (*C* 63). Throughout his Nantucket letters, Farmer James blames lawyers for economic inequality, characterizing them as scheming practitioners who cheat farmers of their labor's rewards:

> Lawyers are so numerous in all our populous towns, that I am surprised they never thought before of establishing themselves here: they are plants that will grow in any soil that is cultivated by the hand of others; and, when once they have taken root, they will extinguish every other

vegetable that grows around them. The fortunes they daily acquire, in every province, from the misfortunes of their fellow citizens, are surprising! The most ignorant, the most bungling, member of that profession, will, if placed in the most obscure part of the country, promote litigiousness, and amass more wealth, without labour, than the most opulent farmer with all his toils. (C 135)

In the context of newspaper editorials castigating Dickinson for masquerading as a farmer to win political office and generate wealth, this portrait of attorneys who take root in the country and mismanage the surrounding soil seems particularly pointed. Legal fees burden Crèvecoeur's cultivators far more grievously than the taxes of which Dickinson's Pennsylvania Farmer complains, and Crèvecoeur suggests that attorneys like Dickinson would do well to leave agriculture and rural politicking to Farmer James or other, more experienced husbandmen.

When James later journeys to Charlestown and sees the atrocities that this lawyerly love of money has induced slave owners to commit, he discovers attorneys at the root of slavery's evils also. Lawyers, he laments,

are more properly law-givers than interpreters of the law, and have united here, as well as in most other provinces, the skill and dexterity of the scribe with the power and ambition of the prince: who can tell where this may lead in a future day? The nature of our laws, and the spirit of freedom which often tends to make us litigious, must necessarily throw the greatest part of the property of the colonies into the hands of these gentlemen. In another century, the law will possess in the north what now the church possesses in Peru and Mexico. (C 152–53)

By accusing attorneys of acting with "the power and ambition of the prince," Crèvecoeur echoes the language of the same newspaper editorials that criticized Dickinson the lawyer for masquerading as a farmer. In the eighteenth century, princely power and ambition were widely associated with *The Prince* of Machiavelli, and one of Dickinson's harshest editorial correspondents adopted the sobriquet "Machiavel"; this anonymous writer suggested that Dickinson was attempting to establish himself as an American emperor after the model of Octavius. Forecasting a political alliance between Dickinson, Boston lawyer James Otis, and the anonymous author of *Considerations upon the Rights of the Colonists* (1766), Machiavel warns readers of the *Pennsylvania Chronicle* that the three will form a new triumvirate: "The Author of the Considerations, is *Anthony*; the Author of the Farmer's Letters, *young Octavius*; and the Author of the Riots at *Boston* (Mr. O—s) is *Lepidus*."[44] When Crèvecoeur wrote, in the voice of a Pennsylvania country farmer, of lawyers profiting politically from slavery and pursuing Machiavellian schemes in order to seize power, he reformulated accusations made against Dickinson, the original Pennsylvania Farmer. A greedy lawyer and slave owner like Dickinson, Crèvecoeur implies, has fostered forms of bondage far worse than the putatively burdensome taxes of the Stamp Act; Dickinson's syndicated editorials, and not parliamentary power or oppressive tax laws, have transformed white colonists into slaves.

Dickinson, for his part, blamed Grenville, Great Britain's former prime minister, for enslaving the colonists, and his editorials caution that the Stamp Act's repeal has not freed them from the threat of bondage. His ninth epistle warns that "if Mr. *Greenville*, setting his fertile fancy again at work, can, as by one exertion of it he has stript us of our *property* and *liberty*, by another deprive us of so much of our *understanding* ... we may bow down our necks, with all the stupid serenity of servitude" (*D* 69–70). Colonists blamed Grenville, often described simply as "the minister," for their fiscal oppression more frequently even than they censured Parliament, because they knew that radical members, such as John Wilkes, espoused the colonial cause. Indeed, colonial rhetoric often reflected Wilkes's insistence that "he was always ready to take any dutiful, humble or submissive measure, with respect to the King, which should be hinted to him, was agreeable, but would never make an application to any present or future minister." The same patriotic toasts that lauded Dickinson's Farmer began with a tribute to "our rightful sovereign GEORGE the Third" before proceeding to jeers at the Stamp Act, which was described as a "'meerly ministerial' Mandate" or the "Mandates of a minister."[45] In 1768 Grenville, the minister jeered at in these toasts, may have been the least popular person in North America.

Dickinson blamed Grenville for the deteriorating relationship between London and the colonies and, in an argument that Crèvecoeur would respond to, suggested that the problem was epistolary in nature. In a portion of the *Address* widely reprinted by colonial newspapers after Dickinson's authorship of *Letters* had been revealed, he portrays British ministers as power mongers seeking to construe colonial letters of protest as a rebellion against the monarchy:

> The *British* nation is *wise* and *generous*. They can distinguish between a disgust to *government* and to the *administration* of it; a distinction, which bad ministers are continually striving to confound. *They* set up *their*

passions for the *interest of their king and country*; and then, whoever is offended with *their* conduct, is convicted by a very plain deduction of *ministerial* logic, of being an enemy to his *king* and *country*. No farmer dislikes the sun; but if it collects such thick clouds as too much intercept its beams, surely the poor man who sees all his hopes sickening and withering, may very innocently dislike the gloom and wish the reviving rays may be felt again.

The farmer of Dickinson's *Address*, here conflated with his Pennsylvania Farmer by colonial newspaper editors, blames a deteriorating relationship with England (the sun) on ministerial interference (the clouds) and specifically accuses the ministry of mishandling colonial correspondence. He complains, "Many of our colonies sent home petitions; others ordered their agents to make proper applications on their behalf. What was the effect? *They were rejected without reading.* . . . The language of the ministry was, that '*they* would teach the insolent *North-Americans*, the respect due to the laws of their mother country."[46] Ministers, Dickinson suggests, have sought to destroy the transatlantic relationship between king and colonists by ignoring American letters.

In the first of his own letters, Crèvecoeur rebuts Dickinson's complaint by making a figure known only as "Minister" the indispensable intermediary who facilitates an epistolary exchange between Farmer James and his English correspondent, Mr. F. B. (C 14–16).[47] Crèvecoeur positions Farmer James as a well-traveled, representative colonist (albeit a firm supporter of king and Parliament), and his correspondent, "a great European man, who hath lived abundance of time in that big house called Cambridge" studying science and "never in his life done a single day's work," shares many qualities with George III, who did not attend Cambridge but did live in a palace, study science intensively, and live a life free of physical toil (C 12). Like the relationship between king and colonists, James's relationship with his aristocratic correspondent is mediated by Minister, who "lives upward of twenty mile distant" but solicitously visits James often, despite his other, pressing affairs (C 12). When James's wife discourages him from replying to F. B., Minister encourages James to write and assures him that F. B. "will read your letters with pleasure" (C 13). James, for his part, respectfully accepts Minister's instruction and even asks for more: "Do go on. I always love to hear you talk" (C 14). Minister urges James to "begin this correspondence, and persevere. Difficulties will vanish in proportion as you draw near them" (C 20); furthermore, he warns James that this correspondence is necessary because "[i]t is good for

American farmers to have friends even in England" (*C* 17). Whereas Dickinson accused British ministers of ignoring colonial communications and working to damage American relations with the king, Crèvecoeur's Minister works to improve relations between both sides of the Atlantic and teaches James how to compose effective letters. The benefits of this colonial correspondence with royalty are only reaffirmed in Letter XI, when Crèvecoeur details John Bertram's correspondence with George III and Queen Ulrika of Sweden.

In Crèvecoeur's *Letters*, it is the farmer's Quaker wife—not ministers, as in Dickinson's *Address*—who seeks to prevent communication between James and his correspondent, and here, too, Crèvecoeur jabs subtly at Dickinson, who, although not a member of the Society of Friends, was a public advocate of Quaker views and often mistaken for a Quaker.[48] James's wife objects that F. B. cannot seriously desire a letter from James and, in words that Crèvecoeur's modern interpreters would do well to heed, insists that James "read this letter over again, paragraph by paragraph, and warily observe whether thee can'st perceive some words of jesting; something that hath more than one meaning" (*C* 13). Crèvecoeur's warning that letters often contain multiple meanings invites readers to think more carefully about his own prose and, in particular, about James's wife, who persists in discouraging James's correspondence with F. B. She objects that if James writes, "[s]ome would imagine that thee wantest to become either an assembly-man or a magistrate" (*C* 21), and rather than James come to be known as "the scribbling farmer," she would prefer that the public pay attention to the condition of the enslaved black Africans working their land: "Better hear them, as usual, observe. . . . Look how fat and well clad their negroes are" (*C* 22). By diverting attention from the authorship of a farmer's letters to the status of his enslaved black Africans (prosperous here, sapping the Whiggish political metaphor of its potency) so that others do not construe his writing as an attempt to win political office, and by working to sever epistolary relations between England and North America, James's wife conforms to newspaper editorials maligning Dickinson. In Letter I Crèvecoeur casts American Whigs generally—and Dickinson, more specifically—in the role of James's wife.[49]

From Crèvecoeur's perspective, American Whigs and the Quaker "Farmer" who purportedly leads them have inappropriately censured king and minister, their social, political, and economic superiors; he emphasizes their improper relationship with London by effeminizing Whiggish firebrands like Dickinson and allowing James's outspoken wife to advocate a rupture with England.[50] James, of course, ignores his wife's dire warnings—just as Crèvecoeur hoped colonists would ignore Dickinson.[51] Anticipating Washington Irving's shrewish Dame Van Winkle by more than thirty years, Crèvecoeur implies that rebellious colonies are an inferior partner in the political marriage between England and her North American outposts, using entrenched eighteenth-century gender hierarchies to reinscribe colonial subordination.

By effeminizing Dickinson and his allies, Crèvecoeur might even hint that those who characterize the exercise of parliamentary power as enslavement are themselves natural slaves in an Aristotelian sense. Describing the relationship between husband and wife, Aristotle insists that "the male is by nature superior, and the female inferior; and the one rules and the other is ruled; this principle, of necessity, extends to all mankind. Where then there is such a difference as that between soul and body, or between men and animals (as in the case of those whose business is to use their body, and who can do nothing better), the lower sort are by nature slaves, and it is better for them as for all inferiors that they should be under the rule of a master." Aristotle identifies two categories of slavery: slavery by law and slavery by nature.[52] In his newspaper critique of the Stamp Act and Townshend Duties, Dickinson insists that tax-burdened colonists have been made slaves by law; Crèvecoeur counters that claim by implying that slavery is a natural state for colonists whose effeminate lack of reason leads them to disregard the advantages of a transatlantic correspondence and the arguments posed by Crèvecoeur's Minister. Dickinson, Crèvecoeur suggests, has forgotten his place, and *Letters from an American Farmer* works to restore social order by reminding readers that wives ought not attempt to control their husbands, that lawyers ought not farm, and that colonists ought not criticize their king or his ministers.[53]

Race and the Limits of Metaphor

In condemning Dickinson's invocation of slavery, Crèvecoeur spoke for the minority. Most colonists identified with the Pennsylvania Farmer's editorial critique of parliamentary oppression, and in the 1770s, the same newspapers that printed Dickinson's *Letters* also adopted and adapted Benjamin Franklin's rattlesnake with its accompanying mottoes ("Join, or Die" and "Don't Tread on Me") as a symbol of the colonies' collective resistance to British tax policy. (See figures 5.1 and 5.2, following page.)

In his tenth letter Crèvecoeur draws on that rattlesnake imagery to demonstrate, in another animal allegory, the dangers of inflammatory Whiggish rhetoric: "A Dutch farmer of the Minisink went to mowing, with his negroes, in his boots, a precaution used to prevent being stung. Inadvertently he trod on

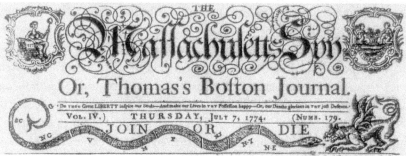

FIGURES 5.1 AND 5.2 Benjamin Franklin published the "Join, or Die" woodcut now celebrated as the first American political cartoon in *The Pennsylvania Gazette* on May 9, 1754. This image became a symbol of colonial unity and was modified by other newspapers that republished it, including *The Massachusetts Spy*, which added the rattlesnake to its masthead. Images courtesy of the Library of Congress.

a snake, which immediately flew at his legs, and, as it drew back in order to renew its blow, one of his negroes cut it in two with his scythe. They prosecuted their work and returned home: at night the farmer pulled off his boots and went to bed, and was soon after attacked with a strange sickness at his stomach; he swelled, and, before a physician could be sent for, died" (C 167–68). Crèvecoeur's words—"he trod on a snake"—specifically recall the colonial cry for unity, "Don't Tread on Me." This farmer from the Minisink, a township in Orange County, New York, where Crèvecoeur farmed, might represent Crèvecoeur himself and, more generally, his perception of the Loyalist cause. His death from rattlesnake poison—the inflammatory Whiggish rhetoric of Dickinson and the radicalized woodcut of Franklin—foreshadows Crèvecoeur's twelfth letter, where Farmer James describes the horrors of revolution. Crucially, however, the rattlesnake that bites this farmer also dies, sliced in two; here, as in his earlier description of the conflict between kingbirds and bees, mutual destruction ensues.[54] Crèvecoeur warns that Franklin and other Patriots will suffer from the Revolution, as will Loyalist farmers like himself.

That an enslaved black African should slice Crèvecoeur's rattlesnake in two seems appropriate, given Dickinson's divisive claim that an oppressive Parliament will enslave American colonists, and it is in these last four letters that Crèvecoeur directly rejects Dickinson's characterization of taxation as slavery and his right to author a slave narrative. Even more than in his letters to the *Pennsylvania Chronicle*, Dickinson's poetic trope for taxation reached the ears and voices of common people through the chorus of his popular "Liberty Song." After its publication in several July 1768 newspapers, colonists across the continent regularly gathered to sing:

> In FREEDOM we're BORN, and in FREEDOM we'll LIVE
> Our Purses are ready,
> Steady, Friends, Steady,
> Not as SLAVES, but as FREEMEN our Money we'll give.[55]

Thus, when Crèvecoeur answers Dickinson's challenge to present "an idea of a slavery more *compleat*, more *miserable*, more *disgraceful*" than that endured by colonial taxpayers, he begins by describing the tortured and enslaved bodies of black Africans in South Carolina, rejecting the notion that considerations of genre or politics justify Dickinson's decision to write a slave narrative (*D* 69).

Indeed, in Letter IX Crèvecoeur offers a haunting portrait that implicitly damns Dickinson for his cavalier usage of slavery as a metaphor. While walking through a South Carolina forest, Farmer James

> perceived . . . something resembling a cage, suspended to the limbs of a tree, all the branches of which appeared covered with large birds of prey. . . . I fired at them; they all flew to a short distance, with a most hideous noise: when, horrid to think and painful to repeat, I perceived a negro, suspended in the cage, and left there to expire! I shudder when

I recollect that the birds had already picked out his eyes; his cheek bones
were bare; his arms had been attacked in several places, and his body
seemed covered with a multitude of wounds. From the edges of the hollow sockets, and from the lacerations with which he was disfigured, the
blood slowly dropped, and tinged the ground beneath. No sooner were
the birds flown, than swarms of insects covered the whole body of this
unfortunate wretch, eager to feed on his mangled flesh and to drink his
blood. (*C* 163–64)

The sufferer begs first for water and then for death, but Farmer James embar-
rassedly explains that he can satisfy only his thirst and departs for a dinner
appointment with the slaver who had devised the suffering man's torment.

In this arresting scene, painted to answer the Pennsylvania Farmer's dare,
Crèvecoeur shapes his correspondence with Dickinson into a debate over the
meaning of slavery and the right of colonists to invoke the tortured bodies of
kidnapped black Africans as a moral justification for rebellion against the
Crown. At stake is the question of whether distress induced by an oppressive
Parliament authorizes the overburdened colonist to narrate an account of
slavery. Dickinson conceives of himself and his fellow colonists as slaves
pressed into bondage by British duties; his anticipation of stolen labor and
colonial suffering in the *Pennsylvania Chronicle*, when considered from this
perspective, might be described as one of the first North American slave narratives: an account in which one who is "master of my time" experiences an
inversion of power and is subjected "to any drudgery, which our lords and
masters shall please to command" (*D* 1, 70). Of course, Dickinson's farmer
does not even till the soil; he reads in the library while "servants" tend his
crops, and "a little money at interest" provides a fund for books (*D* 1). But the
absence of present labor only heightens the horror of his prospective enslavement when, coerced by parliamentary masters, Dickinson's farmer will lose
his own privileged position and join his servants in the fields. So the Pennsylvania Farmer spends his days synthesizing the narrative of his own future
slavery from the foreign reports in newspapers and accounts in his books, a
patchwork story of vassals "in wooden shoes, and with uncombed hair"
(*D* 15); of Romans suffering under "the cruel and rapacious NERO" (*D* 49); of
starving Sardinians; and of "dutiful children, who have received unmerited
blows" (*D* 22). Dickinson's composite slave is a curious conflation of those
enslaved by nature (children) and by law (Sardinians), and his Farmer seems
helpless to redirect the pseudomasochistic bent of an imagination committed
to vicariously enduring the horrors of matted hair and uncouth footwear. He

denounces enslavement by parliamentary coercion as a fate equivalent to death (*D* 16) but flounders for anecdotes and illustrations that adequately communicate the gravity of his plight. To compile this synthetic story of bondage from fragmented narrative accounts that inspire little sympathy or anguish is to depend on the associative and imaginative powers of colonial readers, assuming that they will supply their own knowledge of chattel slavery, which Dorsey reminds us was "an intimate reality, a common reference point, and thus a unifying experience for those whose economies, climates, and ways of life were frequently quite diverse."[56] Suffering black African bodies, such as the one discovered by Farmer James, are implicitly present in the white spaces of Dickinson's editorials; they *must* be imported by his readers, or the Farmer's dire warnings of enslavement amount to little more than a laughable forecast of impending bad fashion.[57]

Dickinson never acknowledges the suffering of enslaved black Africans, perhaps because—as the largest slave owner in the Delaware Valley at the time he wrote his letters to the *Pennsylvania Chronicle*—he knew that this most obvious comparison would undermine the moral authority of his claims. The examples of slavery that Dickinson references by way of comparison are always classical or feudal: peoples ruled by Carthaginian masters or, in news from Europe, by French and Polish lords. But Crèvecoeur refuses to let Dickinson's omission obfuscate the fact that slavery, in eighteenth-century North America, almost always referred to the bondage of black Africans like Caesar, Peters, and Hammon. Dickinson introduces the metaphor of slavery and the condition of European peasants as a demonstration of that condition in his second letter; Crèvecoeur responds, in his own second letter, by acknowledging that he has received and rejected Dickinson's message. Farmer James thanks "God that my lot is to be an American farmer, instead of a Russian boor or a Hungarian peasant. I thank you kindly for the idea, however dreadful, which you have given me of their lot and condition. . . . Hard is their fate to be thus condemned to a slavery worse than that of our negroes" (*C* 24). This mention of contrasting experiences of slavery is the only point in *Letters from an American Farmer* when James discloses the content of epistles received from F. B. and is, thus, the moment when Crèvecoeur reveals the underlying theme of his correspondence with Dickinson. Crèvecoeur places the servitude of Dickinson's European vassals within the context of chattel slavery, and while Farmer James writes, here, of enslaved black Africans as a relatively privileged class, he will come to reconsider that position after his encounter with the gibbeted man in Letter IX. No matter how often Dickinson references classical or distant models of slavery, Crèvecoeur suggests, colonial readers like Farmer James will always associate the term with contemporary, local practice; he calls Dickinson to task for evading the most obvious meaning of his metaphor and for exploiting the horrors of eighteenth-century American slavery in the minds of his readers without explicitly acknowledging the suffering of enslaved black Africans.

Crèvecoeur rejects the metaphorization of slavery because the realities of that condition, as illustrated by his account of the caged man, are so troubling that he implies the term cannot be ethically or accurately used to describe any state that does not involve a direct bodily compulsion to labor and to suffer against one's will. An eighteenth-century slave narrative, Crèvecoeur insists, can take as its subject only the plight of brutalized black Africans or those whose bondage entails bodily suffering similar to that endured by the gibbeted man of his ninth letter. When the gunshot of Farmer James drives birds of prey away from the caged man, Crèvecoeur reveals the black bodies so carefully concealed in the white space of Dickinson's newspaper editorials, recentering slavery and the newspaper slave narrative around the pain of a confined "negro" body rather than the political distress of a white mind reading the international news.

After revealing the unspoken premise of Dickinson's tirade against slavery, Crèvecoeur presents a portrait of liberated black Africans, freemen whose relationship to their employer, John Bertram, better represents his understanding of the connection between Crown and colonists. In the process of depicting Bertram's happy freemen, Crèvecoeur's eleventh epistle also foregrounds the generic significance of the letter as a medium of imperial and interpersonal reconciliation. Whereas James is the narrative voice in every other epistle, this letter is written to James by a Russian named Iwan, whose visit to Bertram foregrounds the sympathetic bonds forged by correspondence. Bertram engages in "extensive correspondence . . . with the most eminent Scotch and French botanists," with George III, and with a Swedish queen (C 173); Iwan's visit is anticipated with pleasure because of "a letter from Philadelphia" (C 175), and Bertram assures him that he is "no stranger" (C 178). Holbo suggests that by including Iwan's epistle, "Crèvecoeur abandons James's unifying and limiting perspective"—the perspective of a Dickinsonian farmer in Pennsylvania—"to emphasize what we might call the 'letterness' of the letters: the fact that correspondence creates ties of sympathy among people. . . . By thus presenting these communities, Crèvecoeur suggests a model for an ideal American identity, one in which limited and local communities are directly allied with global communities."[58] Letters like his own, Crèvecoeur hopes, might facilitate the reconciliation of local, colonial interests with imperial, British interests: the barrier between colony and Crown is one of communication, not taxation, and feelings of subjugation or enslavement might be mitigated by placing individuals in a broader global context.

By reframing the problem as a matter of correspondence both here and in his earlier portrayal of the understanding Minister, Crèvecoeur underscores the political work done by his own letters and, more broadly, by all the letters that flooded sympathetic newspapers in response to Dickinson's editorials. If the British government would only subscribe to the *Pennsylvania Chronicle*, Crèvecoeur seems to suggest, it would perceive that a strong chorus of colonial voices had joined together in support of the Stamp Act and in willing subjection to British authority. If those legally or figuratively enslaved could only see themselves in a global context and help their enslavers to see them similarly, oppression might diminish and even disappear.

Once cordial communications have been restored "by this management" of letters, Crèvecoeur implies, Dickinson and the American Whigs who promoted Dickinson's editorials, like Bertram's happy, formerly enslaved black Africans, will "become a new set of beings" who once again "do their work with the cheerfulness of white men" (C 182). Indeed, a peaceful transition from slave to relative, from colonial Creole to English gentleman is implicit in the sympathetic intercourse—both textual and sexual—of Bertram's freed black African laborers; formerly enslaved "women breed in our families; and we become attached to one another" (C 183). Before James's descent into revolution, Crèvecoeur provides a last model of appropriate colonial communication and "subordination" as a peaceful alternative to Dickinson's narrative of slavery (C 183). Communicating a desire to obey British laws and respect parliamentary authority, Crèvecoeur promises, will purge colonists of the racializing influence of Dickinson's rhetoric and accompanying acts of resistance, such as the nighttime raids against Stamp Act supporters conducted in blackface.[59] Inspired, perhaps, by Iwan's epistle, Farmer James finally decides to free the enslaved Africans living on his farm: "I intend to say to my negroes,—In the name of God, be free, my honest lads; I thank you for your past services; go, from henceforth, and work for yourselves." However, this act of emancipation is not to be conflated with support for American independence and the Whiggish use of slavery; James explains, "Lest my countrymen should think that I am gone to join the incendiaries of our frontiers, I intend to write a letter" indicating otherwise (C 207). The letter, which has induced James to follow Bertram's example and free his slaves, is optimistically touted in Crèvecoeur's conclusion as a relational genre that stimulates sympathy and cultivates new forms of community; it does the work that

Peters and Caesar hoped their poetic reflections on the Stamp Act might do in real life.

Of course, while Crèvecoeur's last two epistles stress correspondence, in its double meanings of equivalence and intercourse, his earlier letters acknowledge that the genre can also reify and legitimize the relational hierarchies that enable slavery as an institution. At the beginning of Letter X, Farmer James, who has previously and pliantly insisted that F. B. is "to give me my subjects, and on no other shall I write, lest you should blame me for an injudicious choice," complains that the demands of his correspondent have effectively enslaved him (C 22). When F. B. requests a letter on snakes—symbols of slavery, as I have argued earlier and elsewhere—James asks, "Why would you prescribe this task? you know that what we take up ourselves seems always lighter than what is imposed on us by others" (C 166). The letter, in this context, enacts social control, and Crèvecoeur makes visible the ways in which epistles consolidate "covert power significant for its very *invisibility.*" As Konstantin Dierks contends, correspondence cultivates "a *prescriptive force of letter writing* whereby authors in print and especially writers of letters defined the meanings of communication and expression, of personal identity and agency, and of social order and change."[60] Farmer James characterizes the epistolary power wielded by F. B. as a form of bondage, and so, too, did the earliest writers describing the New World for a European elite. At the beginning of the sixteenth century, when Peter Martyr d'Anghiera wrote of Columbus's voyages in a letter to Cardinal Luigi d'Aragona, he expressed dismay that "you haue layde this burden on my backe, in whose power it is to commaunde me to take vppon me more then I am wel able."[61] As it places two parties in relation, the letter works to instantiate power as well as sympathy, and it is this element of the genre that makes the letter an ideal vehicle for accounts of bondage— for narratives of slavery.

The slave narrative, as we now understand it, is concerned primarily with making visible and critiquing the various forms of relational authority wielded by white masters in subjugating racialized peoples; the genre performed a function, in the nineteenth-century United States, similar to that of many newspaper editorials in the eighteenth century, when the colonial inhabitants of North America came to be considered Creoles by those living in the imperial centers of Europe. Like eighteenth-century editorials, slave narratives are "intensely political documents" meant to challenge, as Dickson Bruce argues, the "philosophical underpinnings" of "arbitrary power."[62] In other words, the project of a slave narrative is not only to castigate the obvious and visible injustices of chattel slavery through biography but also to reveal the prescriptive force of traditions—such as liberalism, letter writing, or Whiggish political metaphors—that invisibly or circuitously facilitate, shield, and perpetuate the institution of slavery.[63] *Letters from an American Farmer* unveils the ways in which a letter's generic codes and contexts can enact coercion and anticipates the conclusion of Patricia Bradley, that the figurative use of slavery "gave first evidence that the issue of real slavery was not to have a part in the revolution."[64] In recentering Dickinson's artificial, conglomerate pseudo–slave narrative around the bleeding bodies of black African laborers, Crèvecoeur theorizes the limits and functions of the slave narrative while bridging the gap between two genres more closely connected than we have hitherto supposed.

And yet: although Crèvecoeur vehemently opposed Dickinson's description of parliamentary coercion and unjust taxation as a form of slavery, he does not write in anticipation of modern voices decrying that equation as a divisive racialization of politics. Crèvecoeur and other Tories, as much as Dickinson and his compatriots, eagerly embraced inflammatory racial rhetoric as a weapon in their epistolary war for colonial hearts and minds; Alan Gilbert reminds us that "we see enough casual racism and social and racial condescension on both sides to subvert any claims to absolute 'good' or 'bad.'"[65] Just two months after Dickinson's "Liberty Song" had been released, Tory poets responded with "A Parody upon the Well Known Liberty Song," which was published in the *Boston Evening Post* and delivered to subscribers by Caesar:

> In Folly you're born, and in Folly you'll live,
> To Madness still ready,
> And stupidly Steady,
> Not as Men but as Monkies the Tokens you give.[66]

Read in opposition to the Liberty Song's final line ("Not as SLAVES, but as FREEMEN our Money we'll give"), this anonymous poet's representation of Dickinson and Whigs as lower-order primates is far more racially fraught than Dickinson's characterization of taxation without representation as slavery. Dickinson's "SLAVES" have been replaced with "Monkies," implying that black Africans who have been kidnapped and brought to the Americas, like Peters and the parents or grandparents of Caesar, are more simian than human. If, as Dickinson alleges, tax-strapped colonists are slaves, his anonymous adversary suggests that mere animals do not deserve their freedom— that both black Africans and rebellious white colonists are animals whose enslavement, from an Aristotelian perspective, is natural. Tories generally,

and Crèvecoeur in particular, were less concerned about the racial implications of Dickinson's metaphor than with defusing its rhetorical charge. Crèvecoeur objects to Dickinson's characterization of slavery because it is politically
expedient and not necessarily or even primarily because he conceives of the
institution as inherently evil. From a modern perspective, Crèvecoeur's utili-
zation of slavery's horrors may be just as repugnant as Dickinson's, perhaps
even more so, since he seems fully conscious that employing the language of
slavery exploits human suffering for political gain.

Thus, to recover Crèvecoeur's forgotten critique of revolutionary rhetoric
is not to rebrand him as a forebear of contemporary liberals or to unleash a
facile (but centuries-old and therefore venerable!) literary attack on the continuing use of Dickinson's tax metaphors by conservative politicians and pun-
dits. In fact, Crèvecoeur's resistance to the equation of slavery and involuntary
taxation might just as easily be deployed against the agenda of progressive
thinkers like Walter Benn Michaels, who seeks to redirect attention and resources away from calls for reparations for slavery to a more broadly based
redistribution of wealth through tax reforms.[67] Rather, reading Crèvecoeur's
Letters from an American Farmer in the context of Dickinson's *Letters from a
Farmer in Pennsylvania* speaks to the casuistic and contingent nature of both
political rhetoric and public morals, whether in the eighteenth century or the
twenty-first. Language linking taxation and slavery was a political problem
for revolutionaries because Loyalists exploited the suffering associated with
human trafficking to label them hypocrites. Neither side considered questions of racial appropriation significant outside the crucible of imperial politics, and because the War of American Independence had largely concluded
by the time Crèvecoeur's *Letters* was published, his advocacy for racializing
the slave narrative was largely ignored. Instead of sparking a debate over the
definition of slavery or the right of Dickinson and the Whigs who promoted
his *Letters* to self-identify as slaves, Crèvecoeur's correspondence with Dickinson languished in relative obscurity.

After the War

By the end of the War of American Independence, slavery was no longer
a productive metaphor for the white inhabitants of North America, and
so they largely stopped self-identifying as victims of foreign oppression
and enslavement. This shift may have resulted, at least in part, from an
unwillingness to invoke the just-war theory of slavery as a pretext for enslaving prisoners during the conflict. When a Scottish Loyalist was taken as a

prisoner of war and an American officer ordered that he "be coupled to one of his Black Brother Soldiers with a pair of Handcuffs," Cole Jones writes that the order was rejected; victory in war was no longer considered an acceptable pretext for the enslavement of prisoners—unless, of course, those prisoners were black Africans.[68] If white soldiers could not be enslaved, or even bound to a black African soldier, when they had been captured and placed in actual chains by the enemy, it was hardly reasonable to pretend that they might be enslaved after the war's conclusion, by a tax hike. Whatever else it accomplished, the War of American Independence established that slavery was a product of racialization, not war.

Accordingly, the use of slavery as a metaphor for taxation and political oppression declined precipitously in the late 1770s and 1780s. Unfortunately, for enslaved black Africans like Caesar and Phillis Wheatley Peters, shedding the status of slaves was a matter of law and not merely rhetoric. British rule and imperial oversight had ended, but humans continued to be held as property in the new United States, whose inhabitants could no longer pretend—as Thomas Jefferson had, in the draft Declaration of Independence he first presented to the Continental Congress—that George III was solely or primarily responsible for the kidnapping and continuing enslavement of black Africans.[69] Peters wrote, obliquely, that "'twas mercy brought me from my *Pagan* land" (line 1), but that "mercy" arrived in the form of Peter Gwinn, a British colonist who captained the brig *Phillis*, after which Peters was subsequently named.[70] Gwinn's voyage and his purchase of Peters was financed by Timothy Fitch, a Boston merchant whose shifting business interests reflect this evolution in the attitudes and engagement of white North Americans with respect to slavery.

Thanks to his engagement in the transatlantic Triangle Trade, Fitch prospered throughout the 1750s and 1760s. He converted Boston goods—rum, bread, pork, beef, turpentine, flour, and other commodities—into the captive bodies of enslaved black Africans; sold those human chattels for Caribbean sugar; then imported sugar and other goods into Massachusetts, to begin the cycle all over again. But during the War of American Independence, Fitch "met with several losses and retired from business" to live in Medford.[71] The commodities he had once exchanged for human chattels were vital to the war effort, and the state legislature regulated every export so that even a modest 1779 voyage to Connecticut required the legislature's approval, "That the said Timothy Fitch have liberty to ship on board the sloop Boston-Packet, Shubael Killey master, ten barrels of rum, two hogsheads of sugar, two barrels of coffee, one barrel of oil, and a quantity of earthen ware."[72] New constraints on the "liberty" of Fitch, to dispose of property such as rum and sugar, led indirectly to his divestment from the transatlantic slave trade, and he was relegated to petitioning the Board of War for permission to scavenge stoves and other metal from "the Wreck of the Vessels lately lost in the unfortunate Expedition to Penobscot."[73] Reduced from international businessman to domestic scavenger, Fitch found a more constrained focus for his commercial interests as a result of the War of American Independence.

Neither Fitch's divestment nor the revolutionaries' rhetorical shift away from metaphors of enslavement were prompted by a recognition of the essential humanity of enslaved black Africans, but the War prodded him and others, however unwillingly, to adopt new policies and attitudes towards slavery and those previously dismissed as human chattels. Peters was emancipated in 1773, twelve years after her arrival aboard Fitch's schooner. Caesar realized his freedom seven years later, when the 1780 Constitution of Massachusetts abolished slavery with its first seven words: "All men are born free and equal."[74] However, liberty was no guarantee of either equality or prosperity, as Peters soon discovered; although her husband, John Peters, owned £150 of real estate in 1780 and became a yeoman landowner in Middleton, that property was lost in a series of lawsuits, and she died prematurely and in financial distress four years later—before her second volume of poems could be published.[75] Caesar, for his part, seems to have taken rooms with Prince Hall, the famous black African abolitionist and activist, when he was emancipated in 1780; Boston tax records for that year list his name immediately after those of Prince Hall and Primus Hall.[76] He still owned no real estate in 1784, and after that year, Caesar disappeared from the historical record.

But the absence of archival evidence is not evidence of absence, and Caesar may well have lived on in the margins of history, as he lived for so many years in the margins of the *Boston Evening Post*, his New Year's Eve addresses, and other works published by the Fleet family. If he was still alive in 1788, at age forty, Caesar might well have been one of the "greet Number of Blacks freemen of this common welth" that his friend Prince Hall represented in a petition to the Massachusetts General Court protesting the kidnapping of free black Africans, both on the docks of Boston and on the shores of Africa. Hall wrote to criticize the state's renewed participation, after the War of American Independence, in the coastal and transatlantic slave trades. Lamenting the precarity of his liberty and the liberty of others, in Africa, Hall mourns "that your Petetioners have for Sumtime past Beheald Whith Greaf Ships Cleared out from this Herber for Africa and there thay other steal or case others to steal our Brothers & Sisteres fill there Ships holes full of unhappey Men & Women crouded together, then set out to find the Best market. Seal them there like Sheep for the Slarter and then Returne hear like Honest men; after haven sported with the Lives and Lebeties Fello men and at the same time call themselves Christians."[77] The pernicious Massachusetts "mercy" that led to Peters's enslavement still operated after the War of American Independence, as the pious successors of Timothy Fitch persisted in buying and selling human chattels. However, free black Africans like Hall and Caesar could now petition for political redress from a domestic power whose foundational Declaration of Independence proclaimed their right to liberty, property, and the pursuit of happiness.

Happily, the legislature responded to Hall's petition with an act banning the slave trade on March 26, 1788. Black Africans in Massachusetts no longer needed to petition a foreign government for their freedom, as Ayuba Suleiman Diallo had, or to self-identify as British nationals in order to secure preferential treatment, as Briton Hammon had. Instead, they could participate directly in domestic political debates, as Dickinson and Crévecoeur did, claiming rights guaranteed them by the state constitution. The stories told by black Africans in North America changed accordingly; after 1788, their narratives increasingly emphasized local and national politics, and black African writers consistently self-identified as Americans in order to claim the rights of citizens. By the time that Peters and Caesar disappeared from the historical record, there was no longer a need to write poetry protesting the threat of enslavement by foreign powers across the Atlantic, or to situate themselves and their experience of bondage within an international conflict between American colonists and British officials. From this point forward, narratives of the African American experience frequently communicated a sense of racial solidarity, displacing an awareness of the distinctive nations and linguistic groupings that led Fitch to send the *Phillis* to Senegambia rather than Guinea or Gold Coast.[78] Slavery was no longer a foreign affair but a domestic concern, and the newspaper's primacy as a source for public narratives of enslavement would be challenged by the rise of cheap print and the proliferation of separately bound auto/biographies featuring African American authors and subjects.

After Equiano

The Medium and the Message

The Massachusetts state legislature was forced to prohibit the slave trade in 1788 because delegates to the Constitutional Convention of 1787 inserted a compromise, protecting until 1808 the "Importation of such persons as any of the States now existing shall think proper to admit," into the final text of the United States Constitution (I.9).[1] For those who endured the Middle Passage or a voyage north from the Caribbean during that twenty-year window, the story of enslavement was still shaped by foreign affairs and diplomacy.[2] But there was a widespread expectation in the United States that Congress would abolish the international slave trade at the first moment permitted by the Constitution, and it did so on January 1, 1808. After the ratification of the Constitution in March 1789, then, those narrating the experience of enslavement in North America generally situated their accounts and their views on this tragic institution within a domestic, rather than a diplomatic, context. The story of enslavement in the United States would no longer be that of black Africans whose bondage was rationalized with the language of just wars and international law but of African Americans whose bondage was justified only by racism and heredity. Accordingly, narratives of enslavement began to communicate a new message about the abolition of slavery itself, and not merely the emancipation of specific individuals wrongfully taken or held as chattels.

Because it was one of the first book-length autobiographies penned by a black African man, *The Interesting Narrative of the Life of Olaudah Equiano, or Gustavus Vassa, the African* (1789) is often presented, in the classroom, as the first in a series of American slave narratives. However, Equiano's autobiography, which was written as part of a campaign to end Britain's participation in the international slave trade and which reflects a sophisticated awareness of global events, grew out of an earlier textual tradition that characterized slavery as a foreign affair; it is an end or inflection point, not a beginning. Published in 1789, the year that the Constitution of the United States was implemented and slavery became an institution whose future in North America would be determined by domestic politics, the *Interesting Narrative* marks a turning point in the arc of African American literature.

Equiano announces the political designs of his autobiography in its open-ing pages. Addressing Parliament, he declares that his "chief design ... is to excite in your august assemblies a sense of compassion for the miseries which the Slave Trade has entailed on my unfortunate countrymen. . . . May the god of Heaven inspire your hearts with peculiar benevolence on that important day when the question of Abolition is to be discussed!"[3] Equiano's intent in narrating his experience of bondage is clear; he tells his story to intervene in international trade, as Ayuba Suleiman Diallo and William Ansah Sessara-koo did before him.[4] Appropriately, then, *The Interesting Narrative* commences with an account of African polities, as theirs did. He begins, like Diallo, by describing the borders of the nation from which he was kidnapped, explain-ing that "the kingdom of Benin ... is situated nearly under the line and ex-tends along the coast about 170 miles, but runs back into the interior part of Africa to a distance hitherto I believe unexplored by any traveller; and seems only terminated at length by the empire of Abyssinia, near 1500 miles from its beginning."[5] Drawing the borders of a country and naming its neighbors was an exercise made expedient by the still-extant belief that slavery is a func-tion of warfare and foreign relations.[6]

Although he described himself as an African, Equiano also came to iden-tify with the British during the Seven Years' War. When he left Virginia, Equi-ano worried that his white captors might "kill and eat me"; the customs of the Englishmen with whom he associated were apparently so alien that Equiano was willing to believe them cannibals. But as his mastery of the language grew and as he was transferred from one ship to another, Equiano increasingly thought of his white companions in the first person plural. Aboard the *Indus-trious Bee*, just after his departure from Virginia, Equiano conceived of his shipmates as "the captain and people." But by the time he shipped aboard the *Namur* four years later and joined an expedition to expel the French from Fort Louisbourg, Equiano thought in terms of "our men and the enemy."[7] A common, foreign enemy helped Equiano to feel a sense of kinship with the individuals holding him as a chattel; situating himself within a broader geopolitical context allowed Equiano to construct, for himself, a hybrid iden-tity that would reduce the mental and physical burden of his legal status as human property. Like Briton Hammon before him, Equiano narrated his ex-perience of the Seven Years' War in a way that emphasized his naturalization as a British subject and his allegiance to the British Crown.

In these and other respects, *The Interesting Narrative* clearly echoes the themes of earlier, eighteenth-century accounts of enslavement. It is a text ex-tending prior approaches to the story of bondage and the black African experience in North America more than a harbinger of what was to come. The slave narrative proper, with its emphasis on individual rights and authorship, on domestic politics, and on the injustice of heritable enslavement, would come later—displacing the fragmented texts, global perspective, and international conflicts that distinguished narratives of slavery before Equiano.

After Equiano published his *Narrative*, starting in the 1790s, black Africans living in the United States who had endured the Middle Passage began to narrate their experience of bondage with reference to U.S. politics and cultural norms. Venture Smith describes foreign policy as the reason for his enslavement, yet the subtitle of his 1798 autobiography makes it clear that although he is "*A NATIVE OF AFRICA*," his life story reflects that he was "*resident above sixty years in the United States of America*."[8] As James Horton writes, his narrative "is an American story of the struggle for freedom. Yet Venture struggled against a powerful American institution, the institution of slavery. The capture and enslavement of this one African in eighteenth-century America before the North American British colonies began their own freedom struggle, which led ultimately to national independence, illustrate the young nation's most fundamental contradiction."[9] As a self-made man, Venture writes a slave narrative that is paradigmatically American, defined not by diplomacy or war but by commerce and domestic legal struggles. By the end of his autobiography, Venture's identity as a native of Africa has been subsumed by his status as a resident in the United States of America.

Similarly, the memories of Boyrereau Brinch, recorded by a white amanuensis, begin with an account of his kidnapping in Africa but were published in 1810 for the express purpose of influencing domestic politics. Benjamin Prentiss, Brinch's amanuensis, declares that "in *America*, that spirit of liberty, which stimulated us to shake off a foreign yoke and become an independent nation, has caused the New-England states to emancipate their slaves, and there is but one blot to tarnish the lustre of the *American* name, which is permitting slavery under a constitution, which declares that 'all mankind are naturally and of right ought to be free.'" Brinch likewise situates his story within the larger framework of U.S. politics and culture, noting that he risked his life in the Revolutionary War as "a slave for five years fighting for liberty . . . my services in the American war, having emancipated me from further slavery, and from being bartered or sold." Clarifying why he wishes to share his story, Brinch explains, "I have concluded it my duty to myself, to all Africans who can read, to the Church, in short to all mankind, to thus publish these my memoirs, that all may see how poor Africans have been, and perhaps now are abused by a christian and enlightened people . . . it is my anxious wish that this simple narrative may be the means of opening the hearts of those who hold slaves and move them to consent to give them that freedom which they themselves enjoy, and which all mankind have an equal right to possess."[10] In this sentence, as in the larger autobiography, Brinch begins as an African but ends as a citizen of the United States, reflecting on American politics and liberty. He is no longer a foreigner but an African American seeking the rights due to every one of the nation's residents.

This desire for citizenship and its associated rights became a through line that shaped the slave narrative and African American literature more broadly in the early nineteenth century. Black writers used a variety of print forms to make their case for inclusion and equality in the fledgling nation, including the medium that had publicized and politicized eighteenth-century narratives of slavery: the newspaper. As Martha Jones notes, black "ideas about the terms of national belonging were expressed in newspapers and political conventions." Because the discourse of republican citizenship was still plastic, unencumbered by volumes of legal precedent, the print forms through which African American writers argued for their incorporation into the body politic needed to be correspondingly nimble. Derek Spires observes that, "aesthetically and formally, black theorizing and citizenship practices surfaced in black writers' experimentation with implicitly ephemeral forms such as the sketch, with popular forms such as the convention, pamphlet, or ballad, and with collaborative venues such as newspapers."[11] The Industrial Revolution lowered the fiduciary risk of publishing books written by unproven authors, including the formerly enslaved, but newspapers continued to be a popular venue for narratives detailing the experience and perspective of the enslaved, the emancipated, and their freeborn descendants as they collectively sought the rights of citizenship.

Over the decades nineteenth-century newspapers began to shift away from eighteenth-century precedents, even as they continued to document the impact of slavery on Americans of African descent. The number of newspapers in circulation increased with every year, as more and more cities began to print a local paper, and coverage of regional affairs or national politics progressively displaced the foreign dispatches that had occupied so much space in colonial newspapers. Thus, when Boyrereau Brinch died, in 1827, his passing was announced in newspapers across the country, which followed the trajectory of his as-told-to biography, from foreign body to naturalized citizen. Brinch, the papers announced, "was taken from Africa by a party of white kidnappers, when about 16 years old; was with Gen. Wolf at the siege of Quebec, and served in the American revolutionary army, for which we believe he received a pension from our government."[12] His story, in its movement from a distant continent to a British military engagement in Canada to the pension he received from a new federal government in Washington, D.C., tracks changes both to narratives of slavery and to newspapers, as the medium conveying those narratives; newspapers and the stories told about slavery shifted in scope together, from the global to the national, between the eighteenth and nineteenth centuries. This proliferation of newsprint addressing local and national issues for more specific audiences made possible, in 1827, the rise of *Freedom's Journal*, the first newspaper published by and for African Americans. Writers for *Freedom's Journal* paid more attention to Africa and Haiti than correspondents writing for other newspapers, but the paper's focus was still on the domestic plight of free and enslaved African Americans seeking the rights readily afforded to white men.[13] The work accomplished by *Freedom's Journal*, in cultivating a national black consciousness, was revolutionary; but it was also an extension of the work performed by Black Peter, on the *Boston Evening-Post* and on the woodcuts he carved, as he advocated for the acknowledgment of black Africans' humanity and their positive contributions to colonial British life.

Only recently have critics devoted substantial attention to the role that *Freedom's Journal* and other African American newspapers played in developing a shared, national sensibility among black readers. The scholarly preference for extended narratives penned by individual authors has cultivated a belief in the importance of books, as indices for and influences on popular opinion, that is disproportionate to their readership, relative to popular and ephemeral forms of print such as newspapers. For this reason, Eric Gardener argues, "Literary historians in particular need to reevaluate what they read (and why) much more thoughtfully, especially given recent recognitions that both the circumscribed demands of white abolitionists and the exclusionary practices of 'mainstream' white print culture regularly made the nineteenth-century Black press the best—and often the *only*—outlet for many Black authors."[14] The labor of recovering both black periodicals and representations of black speech or narrative in other periodicals is ongoing, and *Before Equiano* might be thought of as a companion or prequel to the literary histories of Gardener, Jacqueline Bacon, and Benjamin Fagan. Like this study, their work develops a fuller picture of antebellum African American literature, a field in which our collective focus on the book object and a romantic conception of authorship has too often relegated newspapers, and the writers whose stories are preserved in them, to the margins of literary history.[15]

Even the book-length nineteenth-century slave narratives to which scholars most frequently turn attest to the continuing importance of newsprint in
shaping African American literature and a collective black consciousness.
Frederick Douglass, in his *Narrative*, famously attributes his understanding of
the word *abolition*, and its significance within his own quest for freedom, to the
newspaper. "I got one of our city papers," Douglass writes, "containing an account of the number of petitions from the north, praying for the abolition of
slavery in the District of Columbia, and of the slave trade between the States.
From this time I understood the words *abolition* and *abolitionist*, and always
drew near when that word was spoken, expecting to hear something of importance to myself." A consciousness of the liberating potential and forma-
tive influence of newsprint led slaveholders like Sophia Auld to snatch
periodicals from the enslaved whenever they were found together. Douglass
remembered, "Nothing seemed to make her more angry than to see me with
a newspaper."[16] His first sense of the great political struggle to which he
would devote the remainder of his life was revealed to him in the pages of a
newspaper.

So, too, Harriet Jacobs attests to the crucial role that newspapers played in
developing an awareness, among enslaved black men and women, of their
relationship to the nation that had endorsed their status as human chattels.
Those who knew she could read would ask Jacobs "if I had seen any thing in
the newspapers about white folks over in the big north, who were trying to
get their freedom for them. . . . One woman begged me to get a newspaper
and read it over. She said her husband told her that the black people had sent
word to the queen of 'Merica that they were all slaves." Later, after Jacobs had
escaped from her North Carolina oppressors, she "examined the newspapers
carefully" every evening, and "kept close watch of the newspapers" for word
of her former enslaver's arrival in the North, to preserve her hard-won independence after passage of the 1850 Fugitive Slave Act by the Thirty-First Congress of the United States.[17] We read Jacobs and Douglass and the authors of
other nineteenth-century slave narratives for their perspective on the African
American experience in the antebellum United States as well as the beauty
and persuasive force of their prose. But we rarely read the newspapers that
nurtured their political sensibilities, their vocabularies, their sense of personal
security, and their understanding of themselves as "black people." The newspaper's format, contents, and language influenced narratives of slavery long before Douglass or Jacobs was even born, and it continued to do so throughout
the nineteenth century, in ways that we have only begun to appreciate.

FIGURE 6.1 "Five children of Pomp Hall, Negro tenant farmer, studying their lessons by lamplight. Creek County, Oklahoma," February 1940 photograph by Russell Lee. Image courtesy of the Library of Congress, reproduction number LC-DIG-fsa-8b23849.

The relationship of the newspaper to the slave narrative and to African American literature generally might best be represented by a 1940 photograph, composed by Russell Lee for the Farm Security Administration, that documents a textual practice originating in the nineteenth century.[18] In the photograph, four of Pomp Hall's five children each hold a book; the fifth is reading from a stack of papers. The books that they hold are clearly the focus of their study and attention. However, newsprint surrounds the children, plastered on the walls of their home and spread across the table on which their books are resting, as a disposable tablecloth. Newsprint dominates this image and, even more than the books in their hands, identifies Hall's children as readers; it supplies the visual context within which the study of individual books takes place. No matter how frequently Hall's children had read the books in their hands, they would have been far more familiar with the text surrounding them—the newspaper stories and advertisements that were always in their peripheral vision, even when they were not consciously engaged in reading their words. The books in this image can only properly be understood as literary objects within the framework of a home environment where newsprint was always subtext: the text literally under and behind the words being read. Similarly, the slave narrative and other works of early African American literature must be considered in context, as products of an environment saturated with the language and stories of newspapers.

In our efforts to understand antebellum black Americans as readers and writers and thinkers, we have devoted the bulk of our time and attention to the books that they wrote and not enough time to their consumption of and contributions to the occasional, ephemeral, collaborative texts that were far more common in their lives. We have missed the forest for the tree, the newspaper for the book. Recovering the literary presence of black Africans in eighteenth-century newspapers is an especially important endeavor because their textual footprint in other publications and manuscripts from that period is so limited. But our understanding of the slave narrative and nineteenth-century African American literature will also remain incomplete until we take the newspaper more seriously, as a print form that shaped the language, political orientation, and narrative arc of books that we love.

Appendix

The Poetic Works of Peter and Caesar

Peter

(1733)

Advice from the Dead to the Living:

OR, A

Solemn Warning to the World.

Occasioned by the untimely Death of

poor Julian,

Who was Executed on *Boston* Neck, on *Thursday* the 22d. of *March*, 1733. for the Murder of Mr. *John Rogers* of *Pembroke*, the 12th of *September*, 1732.

Very proper to be Read by all Persons, but especially young People, and Servants of all Sorts.

THIS Day take warning young and old,
By a sad Sight we here behold,
Of one whom Vengeance in his Chase
Hath taken in his sinful Race.

Here we behold amidst the Throng,
Condemned *Julian* guarded strong,
To Gallows bound with heavy Heart,
To suffer as his just Desert.

Where we for Warning may observe
What cruel Murder doth deserve,
Also the sad procuring Cause
Why Sinners die amidst their Days.

Here now we have a lively View,
Of *Cain's* vile Action fresh and new,
That old Revenge is by Permit
Prevailing in our Natures yet.

Revenge is sweet, we often hear,
How bitter now doth it appear?
It leads to Ruine, Death and Fate,
And bitter Mourning when too late.

We often hear Men to complain,
Their Punishment like guilty *Cain*,
Which justly falleth to their Share,
Is great, and more than they can bear!

The Prisoner owns the bloody Act,
And faith the Sentence on his Fact,
Was pass'd on him impartially,
And therefore doth deserve to die.

By his Account he first was sold,
When he was not quite three Years old;
And by his Master in his Youth,
Instructed in the Ways of Truth.

Was also taught to Write and Read,
And learn'd his Catechise and Creed,
And what was proper (as he faith)
Relating to the Christian Faith.

His pious Master did with care,
By Counsels warn him to beware
Of wicked Courses, that would tend
To his Destruction in the End.

When Twenty Years were gone and past,
By his Account he took at last

To Drinking and ill Company,
Which prov'd his fatal Destiny.

No timely Warnings would he hear,
From kind Reproofs he turn'd his Ear,
Provoked God for to depart,
And leave him to an harden'd Heart.

Since he despis'd the Ways of Truth,
And good Instruction in his Youth,
God then withdrew restraining Grace,
And let him run his wicked Race.

From Sin to Sin advancing thus,
By sad Degrees from bad to worse,
He did at length commit the Crime,
For which he dies before his Time.

He prays his sad untimely Fall,
May be a Warning unto all,
That they no such like Steps do tread,
Nor lead such Life as he has led.

That Children and all Servants they
Would in their Stations all obey,
Parents and Masters every one,
And not to do as he has done.

Obey them with a willing Mind,
Be always honest, just and kind,
And pray to God to give them Grace,
To do their Duty in their Place.

He thanks good Preachers heartily,
For all their Helps of Piety,
Which to his Soul they did extend,
To fit him for his latter End.

So here we leave his pitious Case,
In tender Arms of sov'reign Grace,
Altho' his Crimes are great and sore,
Grace can abound and pardon more.

Now may the Congregation hear,
This awful Voice, and stand in fear,
And being timely warn'd thereby,
may do no more so wickedly.

FINIS.

BOSTON: Printed and Sold at the *Heart* and *Crown* in *Cornhill*.

Note. There being a foolish Paper printed, called *Julian's Advice to Children and Servants*, said to be published at his Desire, this may certify, that the said Paper is false and spurious, and disowned by the said *Julian* in the Presence of three Persons.

Advice from the Dead to the Living;

OR, A

Solemn Warning to the World.

Occasioned by the untimely Death of

poor Julian,

Who was Executed on *Boston* Neck, on *Thursday* the 22d. of *March*, 1733. for the Murder of Mr. *John Rogers* of *Pembroke*, the 12th of *September*, 1732.

Very proper to be Read by all Persons, but especially young People, and Servants of all Sorts.

THIS Day take warning young and old,
By a sad Sight we here behold,
Of one whom Vengeance in his Chase
Hath taken in his sinful Race.

Here we behold amidst the Throng,
Condemned *Julian* guarded strong,
To Gallows bound with heavy Heart,
To suffer as his just Desert.

Where we for Warning may observe
What cruel Murder doth deserve,
Also the sad procuring Cause
Why Sinners die amidst their Days.

Here now we have a lively View,
Of *Cain's* vile Action fresh and new,
That old Revenge is by Permit
Prevailing in our Natures yet.

Revenge is sweet, we often hear,
How bitter now doth it appear?
It leads to Ruine, Death and Fate,
And bitter Mourning when too late.

We often hear Men to complain,
Their Punishment like guilty *Cain*,
Which justly falleth to their Share,
Is great, and more than they can bear!

The Prisoner owns the bloody Act,
And saith the Sentence on his Fact,

Was pass'd on him impartially,
And therefore doth deserve to die.

By his Account he first was sold,
When he was not quite three Years old;
And by his Master in his Youth,
Instructed in the ways of Truth.

Was also taught to Write and Read,
And learn'd his Catechise and Creed,
And what was proper (as he saith)
Relating to the Christian Faith.

His pious Master did with care,
By counsels warn him to beware
Of wicked Courses, that would tend
To his Destruction in the End.

When Twenty Years were gone and past,
By his account he took at last
To Drinking and ill Company,
Which prov'd his fatal Destany.

No timely Warnings would he hear,
From kind Reproofs he turn'd his Ear,
Provoked God for to depart,
And leave him to an harden'd Heart.

Since he despis'd the Ways of Truth,
And good Instruction in his Youth,
God then withdrew restraining Grace,
And let him run his wicked Race.

From Sin to Sin advancing thus,
By sad Degrees from bad to worse,
He did at length commit the Crime,
For which he dies before his Time.

He prays his sad untimely Fall,
May be a Warning unto all,
That they no such like Steps do tread,
Nor lead such Life as he has led.

That Children and all Servants they
Would in their Stations all obey,
Parents and Masters every one,
And not to do as he has done.

Obey them with a willing Mind,
Be always honest, just and kind,
And pray to God to give them Grace,
To do their Duty in their Place.

He thanks good Preachers heartily,
For all their Helps of Piety,
Which to his Soul they did extend,
To fit him for his latter End.

So here we leave his pitious Case,
In tender Arms of sov'reign Grace,
Altho' his Crimes are great and sore,
Grace can abound and pardon more.

Now may the Congregation hear,
This awful Voice, and stand in fear,
And being timely warn'd thereby,
may do no more so wickedly.

FINIS.

BOSTON: Printed and Sold at the *Heart* and *Crown* in *Cornhill*.

Note. There being a foolish Paper printed, called *Julian's Advice to Children and Servants*, said to be published at his Desire; this may certify, that the said Paper is false and spurious, and disowned by the said *Julian* in the Presence of three Persons.

(1741)

Ad. *Vernon*   Ad. *Ogle*, Com. *Leftock*.   *Carthagena*.

Some Excellent VERSES

On Admiral VERNON's taking the Forts and Castles of *Carthagena*,

In the Month of *March* last.

(1.)

ATTEND all Nations round about,
  Who dwell on ev'ry Shore;
Where e'er old *Neptune*'s Waves can float,
  Or *Britain*'s Cannons roar.

(2.)

I found great VERNON's spreading Fame,
  Round Heav'n's expanded Arch;
Who thund'ring on the *Spaniards* came
  On the last Ninth of *March*.

(3.)

Four Ships against two Forts sail'd on,
  And took them as they stood;
Tho' both the Forts were built of Stone,
  And th' Ships were made of Wood.

(4.)

St. *Philip* gone, and *Terra-Bomba*,
  (Was ever seen the like—O!)
Resolv'd to cut the *Spaniards* Comb—a,
  They fir'd at *Boco-Chico*.

(5.)

The *Spaniards* star'd at the loud Ring,
  As at a Rod stares Dunce;
Like frighted Pidgeons they took Wing,
  And vanish'd all at once.

(6.)

Castle *Legrand* to guard the Boom,
  Stood threat'ning far and wide;
Two Men of War did boldly come
  And pour'd a whole Broad-side.

(7.)

But, gen'rous, give the Foes their due,
  There was no Sign of Fear;
VERNON *fire on, a Fig for you!*
  For not a Man was there.

(8.)

This Castle was their greatest Strain,
  Don *Blass* concluded right;
He ran away with all his Men,
  And left the Fort to fight.

(9.)

Into his Ship the Hero got,
  Then sail'd away to Town,
Then bid them fire, then bid them not,
  Then run, then stop'd, then run.

(10.)

So a young Lady in new Stays
  Tail-nestling keeps a Rout;
And so a Maggot in a Cheese
  Rolls wriggling round about.

(11.)

You said, Don *Blass*, you'd drink a Glass
  With VERNON, could you catch him;
He's coming on, why do you run?
  Pray can't you stay to pledge him?

(12.)

Fastned in *Carthagena* close,
  No further can he fly;
Armies by Land, or Fleets let loose
  Will catch him by and by.

(13.)

How dolefully with eighty Guns,
  Don *Blass*'s Ship was seen!
Taken from Seventy *Spanish* Dons,
  By Five and Twenty Men.

(14.)

In haste they sunk Three Men of War,
  To stop the Channel up;
The rest amaz'd they set on Fire,
  Each Ship, and Snow, and Sloop.

(15.)

Don *Blass* beheld, he sobb'd and whin'd,
  His huge black Whiskers tore;
And had he not fear'd to be sin'd,
  He would have curs'd and swore.

(16.)

While these brave Things were done at Sea,
  Our Soldiers work'd for Blood,
Built on the Land a Battery,
  Behind a hideous Wood.

(17.)

Wentworth commands, down go the Trees,
  With horrible Report;
Agast, the trembling *Spaniard* sees
  The Negroes and the Fort.

(18.)

Our Picture shows all this with Art,
  (Was ever Work so pretty!)
And soon you'l see the second Part,
  When we have took the City.

Sold at the *Heart* and *Crown* in Cornhill. 1741

Some Excellent VERSES

On Admiral VERNON's taking the Forts and Castles of *Carthagena*,

In the Month of *March* last.

(1.)

ATTEND all Nations round about,
   Who dwell on ev'ry Shore;
Where e'er old *Neptune*'s Waves can float,
   Or *Britain*'s Cannons roar.

(2.)

I found great VERNON's spreading Fame,
   Round Heav'n's expanded Arch;
Who thund'ring on the *Spaniards* came
   On the last Ninth of *March*.

(3.)

Four Ships against two Forts sail'd on,
   And took them as they stood;
Tho' both the Forts were built of Stone,
   And th' Ships were made of Wood.

(4.)

St. *Philip* gone, and *Terra Bomba*,
   (Was ever seen the like—O!)
Resolv'd to cut the *Spaniards* Comb—a,
   They fir'd at *Boco Chico*.

(5.)

The *Spaniards* star'd at the loud Ring,
   As at a Rod stares Dunce;
Like frighted Pidgeons they took Wing,
   And vanish'd all at once.

(6.)

Castle *Legrand* to guard the Boom,
   Stood threat'ning far and wide;
Two Men of War did boldly come
   And pour'd a whole Broad-side.

(7.)

But, gen'rous, give the Foes their due,
   There was no Sign of Fear;
VERNON *fire on, a Fig for you*!
   For not a Man was there.

(8.)

This Castle was their greatest Strain,
   Don *Blass* concluded right;
He ran away with all his Men,
   And left the Fort to fight.

(9.)

Into his Ship the Hero got,
   Then sail'd away to Town,
Then bid them fire, then bid them not,
   Then run, then stop'd, then run.

(10.)

So a young Lady in new Stays
   Tail nestling keeps a Rout;
And so a Maggot in a Cheese
   Rolls wriggling round about.

(11.)

You said, Don *Blass*, you'd drink a Glass
   With VERNON, could you catch him;
He's coming on, why do you run?
   Pray can't you stay to pledge him?

(12.)

Fastned in *Carthagena* close,
   No further can he fly;
Armies by Land, or Fleets let loose
   Will catch him by and by.

(13.)

How dolefully with eighty Guns,
   Don *Blass*'s Ship was seen!
Taken from Seventy *Spanish* Dons,
   By Five and Twenty Men.

(14.)

In haste they sunk Three Men of War,
   To stop the Channel up;
The rest amaz'd they set on Fire,
   Each Ship, and Snow, and Sloop.

(15.)

Don *Blass* beheld, he sobb'd and whin'd,
   His huge black Whiskers tore;
And had he not fear'd to be fin'd,
   He would have curs'd and swore.

(16.)

While these brave Things were done at Sea,
   Our Soldiers work'd for Blood,
Built on the Land a Battery,
   Behind a hideous Wood.

(17.)

Wentworth commands, down go the Trees,
   With horrible Report;
Agast, the trembling *Spaniard* sees
   The Negroes and the Fort.

(18.)

Our Picture shows all this with Art,
   (Was ever Work so pretty!)
And soon you'l see the second Part,
   When we have took the City.

Sold at the *Heart* and *Crown* in Cornhill.

Caesar

(1764/65)

THE
NEWS-BOY's
Christmas and *New-Year's* VERSES.

Humbly Address'd

To the Gentlemen and Ladies to whom he carries the *Boston Evening-Post*, published by T. & J. FLEET.

THE *Boy* who Weekly Pads the Streets,
With all the freshest *News* he meets,
His Mistresses and Masters greets.

The flying Year is *almost* past :
Unwearied Time, which runs so fast,
Has brought the welcome Day at last.

This Time of Joy to all Mankind,
Your *News-Boy* humbly hopes to find,
The Bounty of each generous Mind.

Christmas and *New-Year*, Days of Joy,
The Harvest of your Carrier Boy,
He hopes you'll not his Hopes destroy.

But cheer him as he trips along,
And kindly listen to his Song,
Which runs so smooth in Rhime, ding, dong.

He begs you now to re-explore,
His Zeal to please you heretofore,
That may be never thought of more.

The great Events which mark'd the Year,
Whose final Hour approaches near,
Within his *Papers* did appear.

He search'd the Earth and Air and Skies,
For all the Curiosities,
That Time produces as it flies.

How often has he run or flew,
Loaded with all the NEWS he knew,
And given all he had to You.

He ran, he flew from Street to Street,
Thro' Winds, & Storms, & Snow, & Heat,
And never spar'd his Shoes nor Feet.

To please, he spar'd no Toil nor Pain,
Not now the Labors of his Brain,
Let him not Toil nor sing in vain.

He by Experience woful knows,
When Fancy's Current's almost froze,
Verse hardly from low Spirits flows.

But when the chearful Heart's at Ease,
As freely as the Western Breeze
It plays, and never fails to please.

And 'tis asserted by the Wise,
That *Wealth* and *Spirits* sympathize,
And with each other fall and rise.

If so, what pure poetic Fire
His generous Patrons may inspire,
By filling up his Pockets higher !

And, since they can, he hopes they will,
Inspiring Zeal to please, and Skill ;
With *New-Year's Gifts* his Pockets fill.

This is his only Day of Gain,
To cheer a tedious Year of Pain,
Oh let his Hopes not prove in vain.

Let him who in an humble Sphere,
Has strove to please you all the Year,
Your *Favor* now and *Bounty* Share.

Then will your humble News-Boy sing,
And pray,---*God bless great* George *our King* !
Long from his Reign may Blessings spring.

May the Noise of War henceforth cease,
And British Realms be hush'd in Peace,
And Wealth and Happiness increase.

May nothing Britain's Peace annoy,
May *New-Year* prove a Year of Joy,
To every honest Man---and Boy.

The *News-Boy* hopes you ne'er may know,
The want of *Something* to bestow,
And richer for your *Gifts* may grow.

December 31. 1764.

THE

News-BOY's

Christmas and *New-Year's* VERSES.

Humbly Address'd

To the Gentlemen and Ladies to whom he carries the *Boston Evening-Post*, published by T. & J. FLEET.

THE *Boy* who Weekly Pads the Streets,
With all the freshest *News* he meets,
His Mistresses and Masters greets.

The flying Year is *almost* past;
Unwearied Time, which runs so fast,
Has brought the welcome Day at last.

This Time of Joy to all Mankind,
Your *News-Boy* humbly hopes to find,
The Bounty of each generous Mind.

Christmas and *New-Year*, Days of Joy,
The Harvest of your Carrier Boy,
He hopes you'll not his Hopes destroy.

But cheer him as he trips along,
And kindly listen to his Song,
Which runs so smooth in Rhime, ding, dong.

He begs you now to re-explore,
His Zeal to please you heretofore,
That may be never thought of more.

The great Events which mark'd the Year,
Whose final Hour approaches near,
Within his *Papers* did appear.

He search'd the Earth and Air and Skies,
For all the Curiosities,
That Time produces as it flies.

How often has he run or flew,
Loaded with all the NEWS he knew.
And given all he had to You.

He ran, he flew from Street to Street,
Thro' Winds, & Storms, & Snow, & Heat,
And never spar'd his Shoes nor Feet.

To please, he spar'd no Toil nor Pain,
Nor now the Labors of his Brain,
Let him not Toil nor sing in vain.

He by Experience woful knows,
When Fancy's Current's almost froze,
Verse hardly from low Spirits flows.

But when the cheerful Heart's at Ease,
As freely as the Western Breeze
It plays, and never fails to please.

And 'tis asserted by the Wise,
That *Wealth* and *Spirits* sympathize,
And with each other fall and rise.

If so, what pure poetic Fire
His generous Patrons may inspire,
By filling up his Pockets higher!

And, since they can, he hopes they will,
Inspiring Zeal to please, and Skill;
With *New-Year's Gifts* his Pockets fill.

This is his only Day of Gain,
To cheer a tedious Year of Pain,
Oh let his Hopes not prove in vain.

Let him who in an humble Sphere,
Has strove to please you all the Year,
Your *Favor* now and *Bounty* Share.

Then will your humble News-Boy sing,
And pray,—*God bless great* George *our King!*
Long from his Reign may Blessings spring.

May the Noise of War henceforth cease,
And British Realms be hush'd in Peace,
And Wealth and Happiness increase.

May nothing Britain's Peace annoy,
May *New-Year* prove a Year of Joy,
To every honest Man—and Boy.

The *News-Boy* hopes you ne'er may know,
The want of *Something* to bestow,
And richer for your *Gifts* may grow.

December 31. 1764.

(1765/66)

The *News-Boy*

Who carries the *Boston Evening-Post*, with the greatest Submiffion begs Leave to prefent the following Lines to the Gentlemen and Ladies to whom he carries the NEWS.

ODE *on the* New Year.

WHAT Time bears on his rapid Wing,
And of the doubtful Year I fing.
Say Monarch! why thy furrow'd brow
Frowns from thy Chariot on us now?
Thy Wheels, which fometime feem'd to glide,
In fmoother Currentt than the Tide,
Now lumber heavy as my Verfe?
Why com'ft thou to us in a Hearfe?
At thy approach, when George firft reign'd,
Fair Freedom wanton'd in thy Train:
I faw her move in graceful Dance,
One Foot on *Spain* and one on *France*.
But now fhe droops, deform'd with Fear;
From her dim Eye-ball ftarts the Tear.
Whence, too, that grifly Form that bears
Bonds made for Innocents to wear?
Will *Britifh* Steel in George's Reign,
Bend for to form a Subject's Chain?
Avert it————————
Methinks a mighty Hand I fee,
That grafps thy Rein and governs thee.
Him, as in filent Pomp He rides,
No Pencil paints, no Pen defcribes:
An awful Veil his Body fhrouds;
His Head lies hid in Golden Clouds.
When Captives long have groan'd in vain,
His fingle *touch* diffolves their Chain.
He over *King* and *Senate* rules;
Oppreffors, fometimes, are his Tools.
Hail, King fupreme! thy mighty Hand,
Has, more than once, reliev'd this Land;
Defcend, and blefs the coming Year;
And humble Hope fhall banifh Fear.

Therefore————

YE Months foredoom'd to form th' enfuing Year,
With ev'ry happy Omen fraught appear:
Each Week, Day, Hour, in all the annual round,
With ev'ry profperous Event be crown'd;
Nor let one fwiftly flying Minute move,
That fhan't *New-England*'s happinefs improve:
Oppreffive Schemes let Difappointment brand,
Nor let one Tyrant in the Senate ftand:
Let Study and Experience make us wife;
And as our Years extend, our Virtues rife:
Let Reafon's Light gild Life's extremeft gloom,
And Virtue's Lamp attend us to the-Tomb;
And the Memorial that we leave behind,
To us be glorious—ufeful to Mankind.

Thus does the Carrier of your NEWS appear,
To wifh you in the New, *a happy Year!*
Time fwiftly flying, hurl'd the Year away,
And once a Week produc'd *his* running Day;
And whether wet or cold, his Tafk he ftill maintains,
(In fpite of *Stamps*) In hopes you'll now *reward him* for his
[Pains.

Vox Populi

Liberty, Property,

And *No* Stamps.

The *News-Boy*

Who carries the *Boston Evening-Post*, with the
greatest Submission begs Leave to present the
following Lines to the Gentlemen and Ladies to
whom he carries the NEWS.

ODE *on the* New Year.

WHAT TIME bears on his rapid Wing,
And of the doubtful Year I sing.
Say Monarch! why thy furrow'd brow
Frowns from thy Chariot on us now?
Thy Wheels, which sometime seem'd to glide,
In smoother Current than the Tide,
Now lumber heavy as my Verse:
Why com'st thou to us in a Hearse?
At thy approach, when GEORGE first reign'd,
Fair Freedom wanton'd in thy Train:
I saw her move in graceful Dance,
One Foot on *Spain* and one on *France*.
But now she droops, deform'd with Fear;
From her dim Eye-ball starts the Tear.
Whence, too, that grisly Form that bears
Bonds made for Innocents to wear?
Will *British* Steel in GEORGE's Reign,
Bend for to form a Subject's Chain?
Avert it————————
Methinks a mighty Hand I see,
That grasps thy Rein and governs thee.
Him, as in silent Pomp He rides,
No Pencil paints, no Pen describes:
An awful Veil his Body shrouds;
His Head lies hid in Golden Clouds.
When Captives long have groan'd in vain,
His single *touch* dissolves their Chain.
He over *King* and *Senate* rules;
Oppressors, sometimes, are his Tools.
Hail, KING supreme! thy mighty Hand,
Has, more than once, reliev'd this Land;
Descend, and bless the coming Year;
And humble Hope shall banish Fear.

Therefore——[1]

YE Months foredoom'd to form th' ensuing Year,
With ev'ry happy Omen fraught appear:
Each Week, Day, Hour, in all the annual round,
With ev'ry prosperous Event be crown'd;
Nor let one swiftly flying Minute move,
That shan't *New-England*'s happiness improve.[2]
Oppressive SCHEMES let Disappointment brand,
Nor let one Tyrant in the Senate stand:[3]
Let Study and Experience make us wise;
And as our Years extend, our Virtues rise:
Let Reason's Light gild Life's extremest gloom,
And Virtue's Lamp attend us to the Tomb;
And the Memorial that we leave behind,
To us be glorious—useful to Mankind.

    Thus does the Carrier of your NEWS appear,
    To wish you in the New, *a happy Year!*
    Time swiftly flying, hurl'd the Year away,
    And once a Week produc'd *his* running Day;
    And whether wet or cold, his Talk he still maintains,
    (In spite of *Stamps*) In hopes you'll now *reward him* for his Pains.

(1766/67)

The Boy who carries the *Boston Evening-Post*,
Presents his Compliments of Joy
On the Commencement of the Year 1767.

OFT, gen'rous Patron, to regale your Taste,
The Summer's Suns, and Winter Storms I've fac'd.
How many Annual Miles fatigu'd I've trod,
Thro' Depths of Snow, and Magazines of Mud!
Now at your Door I once again appear,
To wish all Blessings crown your HAPPY YEAR.

ONCE more I'll rouse my rustic Muse,
And as I pass from House to House,
My Customers address:
The Day now calls for plaintive Lays,
As Times are dull and Trade decays,
I must expect the less.

But as I've trudg'd thro' thick and thin,
And often have been wet to th' Skin,
And never miss'd your Door:—
I do not doubt your gen'rous Hearts
Will far exceed my just Deserts,
And I can ask no more.

November 1st, * that fatal Day,   [*1765]
Oppression's Sons design'd to play,
Their Engines of Perdition;
But now they know, thro' every Vein,
The British Blood flows with Disdain,
Of such oppress'd Condition.

Freedom shall still inhabit here,
Her Mansions free from slavish Fear,
Protected by her Friends;
Unnat'ral Wretches they! who strive
To bury her whilst yet alive,
This ne'er shall serve their Ends.

But see! the uncertain Fate of Things,
Tho' happy in the best of Kings,
Our Burthens have increas'd;
Such servile measures have of late,
Adopted been by T--ls of State,
That must our Purse have fleec'd.

New-England Sons Rouse and Defend,
Your Constitution and Contend,
With every manly Grace,
Let not your Predecessors Manes,
Be disturb'd in Elyzian Plains,
Or blame their dastard Race.

Not many Months are past and gone,
Since your poor Carrier heard the Mourn,
Of the distressed PAPERS;
Such great Complaints as then were made,
By every one concern'd in Trade,
As put me in the Vapours.

I did not then expect to bear,
These Emblems of the passing Year,
Though I was vastly willing,
But strange to tell the pleasing Task,
Still remains for me to ask,
The Gift of a few *Shillings*.

If I may find my Purse replete,
I then shall think my self as great
As is the Grand M----l;
What tho' the World in tumous is,
Nothing shall rob me of my Bliss,
Or discompose my Soul.

I with redoubled Vigor will,
Use my utmost Power and Skill,
To please you GENTLEMEN;
I will not fail to bring to you,
All Advices Fresh and New,
In hopes to get again.

I've not forgot to pay Regard,
For every Favor and Reward,
That you have been pleas'd to give;
And now GOD grant another Year,
May crown your Joys, and free from Fear,
May you contented live.

May every Pleasure still increase,
Relax'd from Cares, may you in Ease,
Enjoy of Plenty's Hoard;
May you have every dainty Dish,
Provided to your sanguine Wish,
With Friends to Crown your Board.

To me what Blessings can my Friends impart,
Last NEW-YEAR's Day how blithsome was my Heart,
My Pockets Jingled when I left the Door,
Alas! they're Empty, and they found no more!
THIS DAY—this happy Day; kind Sirs, employ,
Some Pence to bless your faithful Boy.

The Boy who carries the *Boston Evening-Post*,

Presents his Compliments of Joy

On the Commencement of the Year 1767.

Oft, gen'rous Patron, to regale your Taste,
The Summer's Suns, and Winter Storms I've fac'd.
How many Annual Miles fatigu'd I've trod,
Thro' Depths of Snow, and Magazines of Mud!
Now at your Door I once again appear,
To wish all Blessings crown your HAPPY YEAR.

ONCE more I'll rouse my rustic Muse,
And as I pass from House to House,
    My Customers address:
The Day now calls for plaintive Lays,
As Times are dull and Trade decays,
    I must expect the less.

But as I've trudg'd thro' thick and thin,
And often have been wet to th' Skin,
    And never miss'd your Door:—
I do not doubt your gen'rous Hearts
Will far exceed my just Deserts,
    And I can ask no more.

November 1st,* that fatal Day,   [*1765]
Oppression's Sons design'd to play,
    Their Engines of Perdition;
But now they know, thro' every Vein,
The British Blood flows with Disdain,
    Of such oppress'd Condition.

Freedom shall still inhabit here,
Her Mansions free from slavish Fear,
    Protected by her Friends;
Unnat'ral Wretches they! Who strive
To bury her whilst yet alive,
    This ne'er shall serve their Ends.

But see! the uncertain Fate of Things,
Tho' happy in the best of Kings,
    Our Burthens have increas'd;

Such servile measures have of late,
Adopted ben by T—ls of State,
    That must our Purse have fleec'd.

New-England Sons Rouse and Defend,
Your Constitution and Contend,
    With every manly Grace,
Let not your Predecessors Manes,
Be disturb'd in Elyzian Plains,
    Or blame their dastard Race.

Not many Months are past and gone,
Since your poor Carrier heard the Mourn,
    Of the distressed PAPERS;
Such great Complaints as then were made,
By every one concern'd in Trade,
    As put me in the Vapours.

I did not then expect to bear,
These Emblems of the passing Year,
    Though I was vastly willing,
But strange to tell the pleasing Task,
Still remains for me to ask,
    The Gift of a few *Shillings.*

If I may find my Purse replete,
I then shall think my self as Great
    As is the Grand [Mogul];
What tho' the World [tumultuous] is,
Nothing shall rob me [of] my Bliss,
    Or discompose my Soul.

I with redoubled Vigor will,
Use my utmost Power and Skill,
    To please you GENTLEMEN;
I will not fail to bring to you,
All Advices Fresh and New,
    In hopes to get again.

I've not forgot to pay Regard,
For every Favor and Reward,
    That you have been pleas'd to give;

And now GOD grant another Year,
May crown your Joys and free from Fear,
    May you contented live.

May every Pleasure still increase,
Relax'd from Cares, may you in Ease,
    Enjoy of Plenty's Hoard;
May you have every dainty Dish,
Provided to your sanguine Wish,
    With Friends to Crown your Board.

To me what Blessings can my Friends impart,
Last NEW YEAR's *Day how blithesome was my Heart,*
My Pockets Jingled when I left the Door,
Alas! They're Empty, and they sound no more!
THIS DAY—*this happy Day; kind Sirs, employ*
Some Pence *to bless your faithful Boy.*

(1767/68)

New-Year's Day, 1768.

The News BOY's Verses
Who carries the *Boston Evening-Post.*

TO give his Friends *Pleasure* the *New-Boy* with Pain,
Has labor'd this Twelve-Month—He hopes not in vain.
—If the least Breath of NEWS flew abroad, that was good,
He eagerly caught it as soon as *he* could,
And *he* spread it about, to let all the World see,
That none took more *Pains* to give *Pleasure*, than He.

But if any Thing threatned his Country with Harm,
No Watchman more ready to give the Alarm ;
Her wrongs, and her Dangers he boldly made known,
And freely for her *Safety*, ventur'd *his own.*

When the Foes of *America*, Britain, Mankind,
To *ruin*, and strip them of *Freedom* combin'd,
And had form'd the *Stamp-Act* to determine their Fate,
And Discord between King and Subject create.

When they stop'd *all our Commerce* that *Wealth* could supply,
And burden'd the *Goods* from Great Britain so high
That *Americans* had not the *Power* to buy ;
When they levy'd those *Imposts* in *Silver* and *Gold*, } * Gen.
And drain us as *Joseph*—the *Egyptians* of Old,* } 44. 14.
That our *Substance* & *Persons* like *theirs* might be sold.

These Matters, the PAPERS I carried about,
Related, and pointed the Consequence out.
Americans saw the *enslaving* Design,
And *all* in Defence of their *Liberty* join.
The Friends of *Oppression* all trembled for Fear,
But none for those *Acts* durst speak or appear.

Though of late I brought you no dire Alarms
Wars, of Sieges, Battles, Feats of Arms,
No Armies fighting, conquer'd Countries sacking,
No French Ships sunk, or Forts and Castles taking.

Yet, of *Heroes* whole *Columns* you see——A fine Sight
(I mean in the *Papers*)——who manfully fight :
All fir'd (they say) with Zeal patriotic,
In Favour (some not) of Schemes œconomic.

With Paper Wars I'd fain prolong my Verse,
Of hard-nam'd Chiefs the deathless Deeds rehearse :
But ah! the sad *Paper-Duty* cramps my Lay,
And affords me but just Room enough to pray——

1st——Generally——

May the next Year more prosperous prove,
And all unite in Bonds of Peace and Love ;
May Trade revive and each Business flourish,
Let Discord cease and baneful Faction perish.

May his Majesty (bless him) hear our suppliant Voice,
And another REPEAL make us once more rejoice ;
Our Burdens relieve, and dispel all our Fear,
And add new Occasion of Song for next *New-Year.*

2d——Particularly——

May each good Customer of mine encrease
In Wealth and Honor, Health and Ease,
And your *poor Boy*, the happy Consequence
Gladly experience,—by *an Addition of* PENCE.
And if of your *Favour* I do but obtain,
'Twill give me fresh Spirits to labour again ;
But whether I've Reason to hope or to fear,
I heartily wish you a Happy NEW-YEAR.

New-Year's Day, 1768.

The News BOY's Verses

Who carries the *Boston Evening-Post*.

TO give his Friends *Pleasure* the *New-Boy* witih Pain
Has labor'd this Twelve-Month—He hopes not in vain.
—If the least Breath of NEWS flew abroad, that was good,
He eagerly caught it as soon as *he* could,
And *he* spread it about, to let all the World see,
That none took more *Pains* to give *Pleasure*, than *He*.

But if any Thing threatned his Country with Harm,
No Watchman more ready to give the Alarm;
Her wrongs, and her Dangers he boldly made known,
And freely for her *Safety*, ventur'd *his own*.

When the Foes of *America*, Britain, Mankind,
To *ruin*, and strip them of *Freedom* combin'd,
And had form'd the *Stamp-Act* to determine their Fate,
And Discord between King and Subject create.

When they stop'd *all our Commerce* that *Wealth* could supply,
And burden'd the *Goods* from Great Britain so high
That *Americans* had not the *Power* to buy;
When they levy'd those *Imposts* in *Silver* and *Gold*,
And drain us as *Joseph*—the *Egyptians* of Old,*   *Gen.
That our *Substance* & *Persons* like *theirs* might be sold.   44.14.

These Matters, the PAPERS I carried about,
Related, and pointed the Consequence out.
Americans saw the *enslaving* Design,
And *all* in Defence of their *Liberty* join.
The Friends of *Oppression* all trembled for Fear,
But none for those *Acts* durst speak or appear.

Though of late I brought you no dire Alarms
[Of Wars], of Sieges, Battles, Feats of Arms,
No Armies fighting, conquer'd Countries sacking,
No French Ships sunk, or Forts and Castles taking.

Yet, of *Heroes* whole *Columns* you see——A fine Sight
(I mean in the *Papers*)——who manfully fight:
All fir'd (they say) with Zeal patriotic,
In Favour (some not) of Schemes œconomic.

With Paper Wars I'd fain prolong my Verse,
Of hard-nam'd Chiefs the deathless Deeds rehearse:
But ah! the sad *Paper-Duty* cramps my Lay,
And affords me but just Room enough to pray——
        1st——Generally——
May the next Year more prosperous prove,
And all unite in Bonds of Peace and Love;
May Trade revive and each Business flourish,
Let Discord cease and baneful Faction perish.

May his Majesty (bless him) hear our suppliant Voice,
And another REPEAL make us once more rejoice;
Our Burdens relieve, and dispel all our Fear,
And add new Occasion of Song for next *New-Year*.
        2d——Particularly——
May each good Customer of mine encrease
In Wealth and Honor, Health and Ease,
And your *poor Boy,* the happy Consequence
Gladly experience,—by *an Addition of* PENCE.
And if of your *Favour* I do but obtain,
'Twill give me fresh Spirits to labour again,
But whether I've Reason to hope or to fear,
I heartily wish you a Happy NEW-YEAR.

(1768/69)

To all his kind Cuſtomers,
The BOY who carries
The EVENING-POST,
W I S H E S
A Happy NEW-YEAR.
1769.

ONCE more the poor Boy who diſtributes the NEWS,
Would fain (if he could) invite forth his Muſe;
But *Clio*, more fond of a peaceable Sway,
From *Guns, Drums* and *Soldiers* has wing'd far away.

She could not have left him in any worſe Time,
Having now the greateſt Occaſion for Rhime,
To tell how he's ſtrove thro' dry aud thro' wet,
To ſerve you with all the beſt NEWS he could get.

The Matters important his PAPERS related,
At the Cloſe of the Year ſhould in Verſe be repeated;
But how harſh and unpleaſing are moſt of laſt Year!
'Twixt Parent and Offspring what Diſcords appear!

How then ſhould a poor *Muſe-forſaken* Bard
Attempt to ſing of Times ſo diſtreſſingly hard?
His Heart's full of Grief for his Country's Wrong,
His Spirits depreſs'd, and lame muſt be his Song.

When Patriots are ſtruggling in ſupport of our Laws,
And our Senate expires in Liberty's Cauſe;
When ſuch burthenſome Taxes upon us are laid,
As muſt ruin our Country——if ever they're paid.

When Duties are levy'd on Wines, PAPER, and Glaſs,
Under which poor *America* bows like an Aſs;
When Subjects moſt loyal——are *no loyaller* made
By military Farce, or by warlike Parade.

BUT quiet your Fears, for from yon Eaſtern Skies,
A Gleam of Encouragement ſeems to ariſe;
Great GEORGE our bleſs'd Sov'reign, has heard of our Woes,
HE'll ſurely relieve us, and humble our Foes.

Which may we all live to ſee ſpeedily done,
To the Joy and Content of each true Britiſh Son;
And we have abundant Occaſion to ſing,
Huzza for Old England, and GOD bleſs the *KING!*

Let the Mother and Children join Heart and Hand,
Then againſt the whole World they'll be able to ſtand:
Let Love, Peace and Concord again be reſtor'd,
And to future Ages the Bleſſing ſecur'd.

May you, my good Cuſtomers, always increaſe
In Wealth and in Honour, in *Freedom* and Eaſe;
And if I of your Bounty a *ſmall Token* obtain,
(Should I e'er ſing again) 'twill enliven my Strain.

To all his kind Customers,

The BOY who carries

The EVENING-POST,

WISHES

A Happy NEW-YEAR.

1769.

ONCE more the poor Boy who distributes the NEWS,
Would fain (if he could) invite forth his Muse;
But *Clio*, more fond of a peaceable Sway,
From *Guns, Drums* and *Soldiers* has wing'd far away.

She could not have left him in any worse Time,
Having now the greatest Occasion for Rhime,
To tell how he's strove thro' dry and thro' wet,
To serve you with all the best NEWS he could get.

The Matters important his PAPERS related,
At the Close of the Year should in Verse be repeated;
But how harsh and unpleasing are most of last Year!
'Twixt Parent and Offspring what Discords appear!

How then should a poor *Muse-forsaken* Bard
Attempt to sing of Times so distressingly hard?
His Heart's full of Grief for his Country's Wrong,
His Spirits depress'd, and lame must be his Song.

When Patriots are struggling in support of our Laws,
And our Senate expires in Liberty's Cause;
When such burthensome Taxes upon us are laid,
As must ruin our Country—if ever they're paid.

When Duties are levy'd on Wines, PAPER, and Glass,
Under which poor *America* bows like an Ass;
When Subjects most loyal—are *no loyaller* made
By military Farce, or by warlike Parade.

———————————

But quiet your Fears, for from yon Eastern Skies,
A Gleam of Encouragement seems to arise;
Great GEORGE our bless'd Sov'reign, has heard of our Woes,
HE'll surely relieve us, and humble our Foes.

Which may we all live to see speedily done,
To the Joy and Content of each true British Son;
And we have abundant Occasion to sing,
Huzza for Old England, and GOD bless the *KING!*

Let the Mother and Children join Heart and Hand,
Then against the whole World they'll be able to stand:
Let Love, Peace and Concord again be restor'd,
And to future Ages the Blessing secur'd.

May you, my good Customers, always increase
In Wealth and in Honour, in *Freedom* and Ease;
And if I of your Bounty a *small Token* obtain,
(Should I e'er sing again) 'twill enliven my Strain.

(1769/70)

JANUARY 1. 1770.

A New Year's Addreſs

OF THE

Printer's BOY

Who carries the *Boſton Evening-Poſt*.

Revolving Time, bleſs'd Year-renewing Time,
   Forth calls me again to exhibit in Rhime,
And as is the Cuſtom, befure I'll not fail,
(*A la mode de Sir F——s*) to tell my own Tale.

How faithful I am, and how well you're ſerv'd,
How much I've endur'd, and what I've deſerv'd;
Each MONDAY alert, NO Weather reſtraining,
To bring you my PAPERS, the *freſheſt containing*.

But ah! the Muſe indignant, ſtill diſdains
To aid my Verſe, while fell Contention reigns,
Oppreſſive, peace-deſtroying Arms abhors,
And, ſullen, from th' enthralled Town withdraws.

But, thanks to Heaven, ſome Hope yet appears,
When, remov'd each Grievaance, baniſh'd all Fears,
And thoſe who have wrong'd us meet their Reward,
We ſoon ſhall ſee Peace and Union reſtor'd.

May you my good Cuſtomers always obtain
The Favor of Heaven (the higheſt of Gain)
And all earthly Bleſſings long may you enjoy,
And e'er be diſpos'd to reward the poor BOY.

Whoſe *weekly* Taſk is to bring you the NEWS,
Your Minds to inform, inſtruct or amuſe ;
And begs you'll with-hold not your *annual* Favors,
Which gladden his Heart, and excite new endeavors.

JANUARY 1. 1770.

A New Year's Address

OF THE

Printer's BOY

Who carries the *Boston Evening-Post*.

Revolving Time, bless'd Year-renewing Time,
Forth calls me again to exhibit in Rhime,
And as is the Custom, before I'll not fail,
(*Ala mode de Sir F——s*) to tell my own Tale.

How faithful I am, and how well you're serv'd,
How much I've endur'd, and what I've deserv'd;
Each MONDAY alert, NO Weather restraining,
To bring you my PAPERS, the *freshest containing.*

But ah! the Muse indignant, still disdains
To aid my Verse, while fell Contention reigns,
Oppressive, peace-destroying Arms abhors,
And, sullen, from th'enthralled Town withdraws.

But, thanks to Heaven, some Hope yet appears,
When, remov'd each Grievance, banish'd all Fears,
And those who have wrong'd us meet their Reward,
We soon shall see Peace and Union restor'd.

———————————

May you my good Customers always obtain
The Favor of Heaven (the highest of Gain)
And all earthly Blessings long may you enjoy,
And e'er be dispos'd to reward the poor BOY.

Whose *weekly* Task is to bring you the NEWS,
Your Minds to inform, instruct or amuse;
And begs you'll with-hold not your *annual* FAVORS,
Which gladden his Heart, and excite new endeavors.

(1770/71)

A
New Year's WISH,

OF THE

Printer's Boy

Who carries the *Boston Evening-Post*.

OLD Time again has run the circling Year,
   With Wings unwearied, in a swift Career:
And brings the *New Year*, happy to our view,
When *Printer's Boys* in humble Strains do sue,
And with best Wishes hail you on *this Day*,
While, as in Duty bound, for you they ever pray.

ALL hail! *Kind Sirs*, unto another Year,
The Old One's gone, may newer Scenes appear:
May Trade revive, and Commerce flourish more,
Than in this Country they did e'er before!
May you, once more, see happier change of Time,
And I with joyful Stories tell my Rhimes.

THUS does the Carrier of your News appear,
To wish you in the *New*, a happy Year!
Time swiftly flying, hurl'd the Year away,
And once a Week produc'd *his* running Day;
And whether wet or cold, his Task he still maintains,
In hopes you'll now *reward him* for his Pains.

Thus wishing you a happy Year,
   Success, and much good News;
The Courtesy of generous Minds
   We ask, and won't refuse.

A

New Year's WISH,

OF THE

Printer's Boy

Who carries the *Boston Evening-Post*.

OLD Time again has run the circling Year,
With Wings unwearied, in a swift Career:
And brings the *New Year*, happy to our view,
When *Printer's Boys* in humble Strains do sue,
And with best Wishes hail you on *this Day*,
While, as in Duty bound, for you they ever pray.

ALL hail! *Kind Sirs*, unto another Year,
The Old One's gone, may newer Scenes appear:
May Trade, revive, and Commerce flourish more,
Than in this Country they did e'er before!
May you, once more, see happier change of Time,
And I with joyful Stories tell my Rhimes.

THUS does the Carrier of your News appear,
To wish you in the *New*, a happy Year!
Time swiftly flying, hurl'd the Year away,
And once a Week produc'd *his* running Day;
And whether wet or cold, his Task he still maintains,
In hopes you'll now *reward him* for his Pains.

Thus wishing you a happy Year,
Success, and much good News;
The courtesy of generous Minds
We ask, and won't refuse.

Notes

Introduction

1. Harriet Beecher Stowe, *Uncle Tom's Cabin*, ed. Elizabeth Ammons, 2nd edition (New York: W. W. Norton, 2010), 80–81.

2. Stowe was particularly indebted to the *Narrative* of Frederick Douglass, whose story she adapts in the second half of the novel. See Zachary McLeod Hutchins, "Rejecting the Root: The Liberating, Anti-Christ Theology of Douglass's *Narrative*," *Nineteenth-Century Literature* 68.3 (2014): 300–3.

3. For examples of the fragmentary newspaper narratives from which she drew inspiration for the vividly human characters of her novel, see *A Key to* Uncle Tom's Cabin (1853).

4. The archive is available online at http://docsouth.unc.edu/neh/ (accessed January 21, 2022). Throughout this book, I use the phrase *African American* only when describing individuals of African descent living in North America after the American Revolution; to describe the same group in colonial times, I use the phrase *black African*. Whereas *African* became an adjective describing black Americans after the founding of the United States, its use as a noun in colonial times signifies their foreign status in the British colonies. Of course, those I refer to as black Africans had little sense of the continental identity ascribed to them by white colonists. "Initially seeing themselves as Temne, Igbo, or Mandinka or as members of even smaller ethnolinguistic, familial, or village-based groups," John Catron writes, "the newly enslaved had only a thin understanding of their supposed identities as Africans," so I do not capitalize the word *black* except when using well established terms such as *Black Atlantic* or when describing the sense of racial identity that consolidated among African Americans in the nineteenth century; in many and perhaps most cases I discuss, a diasporic sense of racial solidarity had not yet displaced identification with ethnolinguistic or national groups. See John W. Catron, *Embracing Protestantism: Black Identities in the Atlantic World* (Gainesville: University Press of Florida, 2016), 4.

5. See Frances Smith Foster, *Witnessing Slavery: The Development of Ante-bellum Slave Narratives* (Westport, CT: Greenwood Press, 1979); Marion Wilson Starling, *The Slave Narrative: Its Place in American History* (Boston: G. K. Hall, 1982); *The Art of the Slave Narrative: Original Essays in Criticism and Theory*, ed. John Sekora and Darwin T. Turner (Macomb: Western Illinois University, 1982); William L. Andrews, *To Tell a Free Story: The First Century of Afro-American Autobiography, 1760–1865* (Urbana: University of Illinois Press, 1986); Joanne M. Braxton, *Black Women Writing Autobiography: A Tradition within a Tradition* (Philadelphia: Temple University Press, 1989); Frances Smith Foster, *Written by Herself: Literary Production by African American Women, 1746–1892* (Bloomington: Indiana University Press, 1993); Sterling Lecater Bland Jr., *Voices of the Fugitives: Runaway Slave Stories and Their Fictions of Self-Creation* (Westport, CT: Greenwood Press, 2000); Helen Thomas, *Romanticism and Slave Narratives: Transatlantic Testimonies* (Cambridge: Cambridge

University Press, 2004); Dwight A. McBride, *Impossible Witnesses: Truth, Abolitionism, and Slave Testimony* (New York: New York University Press, 2001); and John Ernest, *Liberation Historiography: African American Writers and the Challenge of History, 1794–1861* (Chapel Hill: University of North Carolina Press, 2004).

6. Nicole N. Aljoe, "Introduction: Remapping the Early American Slave Narrative," in *Journeys of the Slave Narrative in the Early Americas*, ed. Nicole N. Aljoe and Ian Finseth (Charlottesville: University of Virginia Press, 2014), 6; Eric Gardener, *Unexpected Places: Relocating Nineteenth-Century African American Literature* (Jackson: University of Mississippi Press, 2009), 10.

7. Charles E. Clark, "Periodicals and Politics," in *A History of the Book in America*, vol. 1, *The Colonial Book in the Atlantic World*, ed. Hugh Amory and David D. Hall (Chapel Hill: University of North Carolina Press, 2007), 355.

8. Cassander L. Smith, *Black Africans in the British Imagination: English Narratives of the Early Atlantic World* (Baton Rouge: Louisiana State University Press, 2016), 178–79, 2. Karen Weyler documents the power accrued through authorship to persons in marginalized groups after 1760, noting that "they saw authorship as a means to empower themselves"; work such as hers is, implicitly, the scholarship to which Smith responds. But marginalized individuals could also gain power through their mere presence in print, whether or not they held a pen and wrote the accounts documenting their lives. Authorship was not a binary construct in the eighteenth century but a sliding scale of responsibility for the distribution of information and ideas. Almost every enslaved person in eighteenth-century North America knew that flight would result in the publication of a runaway slave advertisement. We might ask: does it matter whether runaways penned the actual advertisement, if they determined what would ultimately be written? They chose the clothes they wore during an escape; they chose the companions with whom they fled; they chose the destinations rumored for their flight. Enslaved persons in the eighteenth century would have been familiar with the textual output that accompanied escape—these advertisements circulated widely and were often read aloud so that the illiterate or those without the funds to buy a paper could keep abreast of the news. Runaways knew, when they fled, that the words, "Ran-away from his master," would be printed and distributed, following them on their journey. Their formulaic publication was preordained the moment escape was discovered. Might we not, thus, argue that the runaways authored these texts when they chose to flee and that composition was in this case a matter of literal, physical feet rather than the metrical feet we point to in Phillis Wheatley Peters's account of the Middle Passage? See Karen A. Weyler, *Empowering Words: Outsiders and Authorship in Early America* (Athens: University of Georgia Press, 2013), 2.

9. Eighteenth-century correspondence between Whitehall and Boston attests to the circum-Atlantic distribution of these early New England newspapers; an October 1705 issue of the *Boston News-Letter* caused a minor uproar in England, where readers objected to its characterization of Quaker life and business. See *Calendar of State Papers, Colonial Series, America and West Indies*, vol. 23, ed. Cecil Headlam (London: 1916), 43.

10. Srividhya Swaminathan and Adam R. Beach, "Introduction: Invoking Slavery in Literature and Scholarship," in *Invoking Slavery in the Eighteenth-Century British Imagination*, ed. Srividhya Swaminathan and Adam R. Beach (Burlington, VT: Ashgate, 2013), 1–2.

11. Many of the most interesting passages uncovered in this comprehensive examination have now been published in an anthology I coedited with Cassander L. Smith, *The Earliest*

African American Literatures: A Critical Reader (Chapel Hill: University of North Carolina Press, 2021).

12. Lisa A. Lindsay and John Wood Sweet, "Introduction: Biography and the Black Atlantic," in *Biography and the Black Atlantic*, ed. Lisa A. Lindsay and John Wood Sweet (Philadelphia: University of Pennsylvania Press, 2014), 1; Randy Sparks, *Africans in the Old South: Mapping Exceptional Lives across the Atlantic World* (Cambridge, MA: Harvard University Press, 2016), 3. Robert Desrochers offers an excellent analysis of slave-for-sale advertisements in Massachusetts, for example, but his reading identifies trends (e.g., "more than nine out of ten notices announced private sales, not auctions") rather than examining individual lives. See Robert E. Desrochers Jr., "Slave-for-Sale Advertisements and Slavery in Massachusetts, 1704–1781," *The William and Mary Quarterly* 59.3 (2002): 629.

13. Jessica Marie Johnson, "Markup Bodies: Black [Life] Studies and Slavery [Death] Studies at the Digital Crossroads," *Social Text* 137 36.4 (2018): 70–71.

14. Marisa J. Fuentes, *Dispossessed Lives: Enslaved Women, Violence, and the Archive* (Philadelphia: University of Pennsylvania Press, 2016), 4. As Fuentes suggests, the archive itself can be a site of violence, as its composition—preserving the papers of the wealthy while rejecting, discarding, or ignoring material evidence of marginalized populations—contributes to the erasure of black Africans and other racialized peoples from literary history. Reclaiming the stories of such individuals places the scholar and the archive in an antagonistic position: "History is produced from the what the archive offers. It is the historian's job to substantiate all the pieces with more archival evidence, context, and historiography and put them together into a coherent narrative form. The challenge this book has confronted is to write a history about what the archive does not offer" (146). Similarly *Before Equiano* attempts to retell stories whose inclusion in the archive is incidental or accidental and thus relies upon contextual imagination to fill in gaps left through violence done to and through the archive. On various approaches to how the enslaved might be located within or posed against the archive, see also Simon Gikandi, "Rethinking the Archive of Enslavement," *Early American Literature* 50.1 (2015): 81–102.

15. Julie Sievers, "Drowned Pens and Shaking Hands: Sea Providence Narratives in Seventeenth-Century New England," *The William and Mary Quarterly* 63.4 (2006): 748. Although Frances Smith Foster insists that her "decision to eliminate the anthologies of slave autobiographies, the third person accounts, and those that were obviously 'fictionalized' was pragmatic," few scholars have seen fit to give those anthologized accounts significant attention in the years since. Frances Smith Foster, "Introduction to the Second Edition," *Witnessing Slavery: The Development of Ante-bellum Slave Narratives*, 2nd ed. (Madison: University of Wisconsin Press, 1994), xxi–xxii.

16. William L. Andrews, "The First Fifty Years of the Slave Narrative, 1760–1810," in *The Art of the Slave Narrative: Original Essays in Criticism and Theory*, 8.

17. Joseph Addison, *The Tatler*, September 14, 1710, in *The Works of Joseph Addison*, vol. 3 (New York: 1868), 67. Clearly not all readers approached the mundane matter in newspapers with Addison's relish. Henry David Thoreau complained, "I am sure that I never read any memorable news in a newspaper. If we read of one man robbed, or murdered, or killed by accident, or one house burned, or one vessel wrecked, or one steamboat blown up, or one cow run over on the Western Railroad, or one mad dog killed, or one lot of grasshoppers in the winter,—we never need read of another. One is enough. If you are acquainted

with the principle, what do you care for a myriad of instances and applications?" But the popularity of newspapers throughout the eighteenth and nineteenth centuries suggests that most readers *did* want to read and think about variations on the standard story of a deserting seaman, a runaway servant, or a sunk slave ship. See Henry D. Thoreau, *Walden*, ed. Jeffrey S. Cramer (New Haven, CT: Yale University Press, 2006), 100.

18. Addison, *The Tatler*, 68.

19. *Boston Gazette*, July 28, 1729.

20. Henry Louis Gates Jr., *Figures in Black: Words, Signs, and the "Racial" Self* (New York: Oxford University Press, 1987), 123. Because slavery, as a legal system, was predicated on historical narratives preserved in the texts this book examines, our rejection of slavery and the racism that undergirds it must be grounded in new narratives that foreground the subjectivity of narrative and the fictionality of history, acknowledging that all selves and institutions are in one sense or another fictive constructs. As Michel-Rolph Trouillot writes, "To state that a particular narrative legitimates particular policies is to refer implicitly to a 'true' account of these policies through time, an account which itself can take the form of another narrative. But to admit the possibility of this second narrative is, in turn, to admit that the historical process has some autonomy vis-à-vis the narrative. It is to admit that as ambiguous and contingent as it is, the boundary between what happened and that which is said to have happened is necessary. It is not that some societies distinguish between fiction and history and others do not. Rather, the difference is in the range of narratives that specific collectivities must put to their own tests of historical credibility because of the stakes involved in these narratives." See Michel-Rolph Trouillot, *Silencing the Past: Power and the Production of History* (Boston: Beacon Press, 1995), 13–14.

21. *New-England Courant*, Oct. 1, 1722. (Subsequent in-text citations to this newspaper appear as "*NEC* 1722/10/1.") This advertisement, which I can find no hint of in another newspaper, may have circulated as a broadside, or it may have been entirely fictional. Describing the arrival of a prophet from England, it suggests both the imaginative interest with which back-of-the-paper materials were read and written as well as the reality that this content was occasionally of greater interest than the news itself.

22. *Boston News-Letter*, April 26, 1708. Subsequent in-text citations to this newspaper appear as "*BNL* 1708/4/26."

23. Nathaniel Hawthorne, *The Scarlet Letter*, ed. John Stephen Martin, 2nd ed. (Toronto: Broadview, 2004), 101.

24. Matthew P. Brown, *The Pilgrim and the Bee: Reading Rituals and Book Culture in Early New England* (Philadelphia: University of Pennsylvania Press, 2007), xii.

25. Roland Barthes, "The Death of the Author," in *Image, Music, Text*, ed. and trans. Stephen Heath (New York: Hill and Wang, 1977), 146–47.

26. This claim builds on the groundbreaking work of David Waldstreicher, who argued that "runaway advertisements, in effect, were the first slave narratives," broadening the scope of material that might have prompted Black Peter and other invested readers to an expansive view of fairly narrow texts. See David Waldstreicher, "Reading the Runaways: Self-Fashioning, Print Culture, and Confidence in Slavery in the Eighteenth-Century Mid-Atlantic," *The William and Mary Quarterly* 56.2 (1999): 247.

27. A second Boston school "for the Instruction of Negro's in Reading, Catechizing, & Writing if required" was advertised in 1728. *The New-England Weekly Journal*, April 1, 1728,

and April 8, 1728. (Susbequent in-text citations to this newspaper appear as *"NEJ* 1728/4/1.") For additional information on efforts to educate black Africans in colonial North America, see E. Jennifer Monaghan, *Learning to Read and Write in Colonial America* (Amherst: University of Massachusetts Press, 2005), 241–72.

28. Jared Hardesty, "An Angry God in the Hands of Sinners: Enslaved Africans and the Uses of Protestant Christianity in Pre-Revolutionary Boston," *Slavery & Abolition* 35.1 (2014): 73.

29. For an account of the school opened in Charleston by Alexander Garden, see Edward E. Andrews, *Native Apostles: Black and Indian Missionaries in the British Atlantic World* (Cambridge: Harvard University Press, 2013), 108–12.

30. *American Weekly Mercury*, Feb. 12, 1723. Subsequent in-text citations to this newspaper appear as *"AWM* 1723/2/12."

31. As quoted in John C. Van Horne, "The Education of African Americans in Benjamin Franklin's Philadelphia," in *"The Good Education of Youth": Worlds of Learning in the Age of Franklin*, ed. John H. Pollack (New Castle, DE: Oak Knoll Press, 2009), 95.

32. Adam Beach notes that our familiarity with the sufferings of enslaved Africans and their descendants on Caribbean and Southern plantations sometimes obscures the different manifestations of slavery endured by a variety of groups in the late seventeenth and early eighteenth centuries, arguing that "we have some work to do to recapture a more developed picture of global slave practices in the period and a more nuanced delineation of early-modern English understandings of slavery." See Adam R. Beach, "Global Slavery, Old World Bondage, and Aphra Behn's 'Abdelazer,'" *The Eighteenth Century*, 53.4 (2012): 414.

33. Brett Rushforth, *Bonds of Alliance: Indigenous and Atlantic Slaveries in New France* (Chapel Hill: University of North Carolina Press, 2012), 8. That American Indians enslaved and sold human beings is often forgotten in accounts of New World slavery, but Rushforth points out that some three million Indian slaves were traded between the fifteenth and nineteenth centuries, "most of whom were initially enslaved by other Native peoples" (9). Among the many black Africans whose bondage is recounted in this study, only Briton Hammon, the subject of chapter 4, was taken captive by Indians.

34. A slave trader who trafficked in Indians, Moore likely attacked in anticipation of personal gain. A colleague estimated that military action against the Spanish in Florida might improve the Carolina Indian trade by several thousand pounds annually. Moore's contemporary, John Ash, derided the expedition, incredulous that "Two Thousand Pounds were raised to equip his Honour and his Comrades out for their beloved Exercise of Plundering, and Slave-catching." See Fred Lamar Pearson Jr., "Anglo-Spanish Rivalry in the Chattahoochee Basin and West Florida, 1685–1704," *The South Carolina Historical Magazine* 79.1 (1978): 58; John Ash, "The Present State of Affairs in Carolina, by John Ash, 1706," in *Narratives of Early Carolina, 1650–1708*, ed. Alexander S. Salley Jr. (New York: Scribner and Sons, 1911), 272. See also Charles W. Arnade, "The English Invasion of Spanish Florida, 1700–1706," *The Florida Historical Quarterly* 41.1 (1962): 29–37.

35. Many of the best-known narratives of enslaved white Americans in North Africa have been collected in *White Slaves, African Masters: An Anthology of American Barbary Captivity Narratives* (Chicago: University of Chicago Press, 1999). Nineteenth-century readers thought Riley's narrative of enslavement relevant to their understanding of chattel slavery in the United States, and its influence on Abraham Lincoln's decision to emancipate enslaved

African Americans has been much discussed. See R. Gerald McMurtry, "The Influence of Riley's *Narrative* upon Abraham Lincoln," *Indiana Magazine of History* 30.2 (1934): 133–38.

36. On the experience and representation of white captivity, see Michael Guasco, *Slaves and Englishmen: Human Bondage in the Early Modern Atlantic World* (Philadelphia: University of Pennsylvania Press, 2014), 121–54; Gillian Weiss, *Captives and Corsairs: France and Slavery in the Early Modern Mediterranean* (Stanford, CA: Stanford University Press, 2011); Giles Milton, *White Gold: The Extraordinary Story of Thomas Pellow and Islam's One Million White Slaves* (New York: Farrar, Strauss and Giroux, 2004); Nabil Matar, "Introduction: England and Mediterranean Captivity, 1577–1704," in *Piracy, Slavery, and Redemption: Barbary Captivity Narratives from Early Modern England*, ed. Daniel J. Vitkus (New York: Columbia University Press, 2001), 1–54; and *White Slaves, African Masters: An Anthology of American Barbary Captivity Narratives*, ed. Paul Baepler (Chicago: University of Chicago Press, 1999).

37. Paul Baepler, "The Barbary Captivity Narrative in Early America," *Early American Literature* 30.2 (1995): 114.

38. See David Waldstreicher, *Runaway America: Benjamin Franklin, Slavery, and the American Revolution* (New York: Hill and Wang, 2004); Daniel Meaders, *Dead or Alive: Fugitive Slaves and White Indentured Servants before 1830* (New York: Garland, 1993); and John Van Der Zee, *Bound Over: Indentured Servitude and American Conscience* (New York: Simon & Schuster, 1985).

39. Slavery may also have been a condition occasionally imposed upon white criminals as a punishment. Although the records are more suggestive than conclusive, colonial officials seem to have sold some few convicted criminals into slavery. Thus, the Council of Trade and Plantations wrote to Governor John Seymour in 1706, "we do not well understand what you write, Aug. 28 [1705], that you had consented to sell two of the criminals to some of the Islands for the country's good. We desire therefore that you would explain who those criminals are, and by what authority they are sold." *Calendar of State Papers, Colonial Series, America and West Indies*, vol. 23, ed. Cecil Headlam (London: 1916), 40–41.

40. Katherine Howlett Hayes, *Slavery Before Race: Europeans, Africans, and Indians at Long Island's Sylvester Manor Plantation, 1651–1884* (New York: New York University Press, 2013), 3.

41. "Index from manuscript by Arthur Trader, Chief Clerk in the Maryland Land Commission, 1917," in *The Early Settlers of Maryland: An Index to Names of Immigrants, Compiled from Records of Land Patents, 1633–1680*, ed. Gust Skordas (Baltimore: Genealogical Publishing, 1968), 320; Thomas Scharf, *Delaware, 1609–1888*, vol. 2 (Philadelphia: 1888), 1256; Edwin Jacquett Sellers, *Supplement to Genealogies* (Philadelphia: 1922), 66.

42. Jodi Schorb's brief discussion of Colson's narrative, placing it in the context of other dying confessions by women, is the exception to this rule, but Schorb's focus is on Colson's sexuality, not her experience as a black African. Another reason that Colson's life story may not have received the attention it deserves is the tendency noted to "dismiss the gallows genre as fictive or ventriloquized"—mediated. See Jodi Schorb, "Uncleanliness Is Next to Godliness: Sexuality, Salvation, and the Early American Women's Execution Narrative," in *The Puritan Origins of American Sex: Religion, Sexuality, and National Identity in American Literature*, ed. Tracy Fessenden, Nicholas F. Radel, and Magdalena J. Zaborowska

(New York: Routledge, 2013), 79–81; and Jodi Schorb, *Reading Prisoners: Literature, Literacy, and the Transformation of American Punishment, 1700–1845* (New Brunswick, NJ: Rutgers University Press, 2014), 8.

43. Nicole Aljoe has recently proposed that relations such as Colson's, which have been edited or transcribed by others, may not belong in the slave narrative genre at all. In her examination of slave narratives from the British West Indies (which does not treat Colson's "Account"), Aljoe suggests that such narratives belong to the genre of *testimonio*, a syncretic form that relates communal experience rather than the individual triumph over conditions of bondage. See Nicole N. Aljoe, *Creole Testimonies: Slave Narratives from the British West Indies, 1709–1838* (New York: Palgrave Macmillan, 2012), 14–18.

44. Catherine Adams and Elizabeth Pleck identify Colson as an indentured servant. See Catherine Adams and Elizabeth H. Pleck, *Love of Freedom: Black Women in Colonial and Revolutionary New England* (New York: Oxford University Press, 2010), 40.

45. The notice of Hono's execution goes on to state that he shared the gallows with "a White Married Woman" who "sat upon the Gallows with a rope about her Neck for having been delivered with a Negro Child, being Whipt several times between the Gallows and Town-house, which we hope will be a sufficient Warning to all White Women to keep clear of Negro's, for the future" (*BNL* 1721/5/29). This invective against miscegenation demonstrates the precariousness of Colson's position as a biracial individual; interracial sex is represented as a more egregious offense in this report than extramarital sex.

46. The institution of slavery continued in practice, if not in name, for many African Americans in Massachusetts, as the case of Pomp—a black man executed in 1795 after being denied his freedom—demonstrates. See Jonathan Plummer, *Dying Confession of Pomp* (Newburyport, MA: 1795). For a discussion of Walker's transition from slave to freeman, see William O'Brien, "Did the Jennison Case Outlaw Slavery in Massachusetts?" *The William and Mary Quarterly* 17.2 (1960): 219–41; Robert Spector, "The Quok Walker Cases (1781–1783)—Slavery, Its Abolition and Negro Citizenship in Early Massachusetts," *Journal of Negro History* 53.1 (1968), 12–32; Emily Blanck, "Seventeen Eighty-Three: The Turning Point in the Law of Slavery and Freedom in Massachusetts," *The New England Quarterly* 75.1 (2002): 24–51; and Douglas R. Egerton, *Death or Liberty: African Americans and Revolutionary America* (New York: Oxford University Press, 2009), 93–121. Sojourner Truth's transition to freedom was recorded by an amanuensis in her autobiography. See Olive Gilbert, *Narrative of Sojourner Truth* (Boston: 1850), 39–55.

47. Jordan Alexander Stein, "Early American #BlackLivesMatter," *Common-place* 16.2 (2016), http://common-place.org/book/early-american-blacklivesmatter/, accessed January 24, 2022.

48. *History of Weymouth, Massachusetts*, vol. 3 (Boston: 1923), 166–67.

49. *History of Weymouth, Massachusetts*, vol. 4 (Boston: 1923), 506–7, 570.

50. *Historic Homes and Institutions and Genealogical and Personal Memoirs of Worchester County Massachusetts*, ed. Ellery Bicknell Crane (New York: Lewis Publishing, 1907), 253.

51. Just months after Colson's execution, in Connecticut, "an Indian Woman at New London, was deliver'd of a Child when alone, which she hid in her Masters Barn, and at times went to its relief, but was not discover'd till about Ten Days after, (she being about her Work as usual) when the Child was heard to cry by some that pass'd by the Barn, and upon their searching found the Child, and carry'd it in to the guilty Mother, and surprized

Houshold" (*NEJ* 1727/9/25). Although Colson expresses regret for the "*Sin of Fornication*," her sexual experiences seem voluntary rather than coercive or violent, as is so typical in the slave narrative. See Frances Smith Foster, "Ultimate Victims: Black Women in Slave Narratives," *Journal of American Culture* 1.4 (1978): 845–54; and "'In Respect to Females . . .': Differences in the Portrayals of Women by Male and Female Narrators," *Black American Literature Forum* 15 (1981): 66–70.

52. Katherine Fishburn, *The Problem of Embodiment in Early African American Narrative* (Westport, CT: Greenwood Press, 1997), 11.

53. Adams and Pleck, *Love of Freedom: Black Women in Colonial and Revolutionary New England*, 43. See also Peter C. Hoffer and N. E. H. Hull, *Murdering Mothers: Infanticide in England and New England, 1558–1803* (New York: New York University Press, 1983), 47–48; and Randolph H. Roth, "Child Murder in New England," *Social Science History* 25.1 (2001): 117.

54. Terri L. Snyder, *The Power to Die: Slavery and Suicide in British North America* (Chicago: University of Chicago Press, 2015), 10, 65.

55. *Maryland Gazette*, Feb. 11, 1729.

56. The governor of Massachusetts at the turn of the eighteenth century, Joseph Dudley, believed black African runaways would "alway's run to the Southward for warme Weather" because "the cold is disagreeable to them." *Documentary History of the State of Maine*, vol. 9, ed. James Phinney Baxter (Portland, ME: 1907), 282.

57. *Boston Evening-Post*, Aug. 25, 1735. (Subsequent in-text citations to this newspaper appear as "*BEP* 8/25/1735.) Isaiah Thomas, an eighteenth-century publisher who would go on to found the American Antiquarian Society, wrote that Peter "worked at the printing business, both at the press and at setting types; he was an ingenious man, and cut, on wooden blocks, all the pictures which decorated the ballads and small books of his master." See Isaiah Thomas, *The History of Printing in America*, in *Transactions and Collections of the American Antiquarian Society*, vol. 5 (Worcester, MA: 1874), 99.

58. The Maroon communities of Jamaica might have been regarded, in some sense, as English spoils of war—and not simply runaways. As David Gaspar notes, they were founded by enslaved individuals who escaped in 1665, when England invaded the island and wrested control of its land and inhabitants from Spain. Thus, many of the "Rebellious Negroes" of this notice were the descendants of people originally subject to Spain who gained a measure of self-determination and self-rule during a war; they were not English in any sense but foreigners. See David Barry Gaspar, "'Rigid and Inclement': Origins of the Jamaica Slave Laws of the Seventeenth Century," in *The Many Legalities of Early America*, ed. Christopher L. Tomlins and Bruce H. Mann (Chapel Hill: University of North Carolina Press, 2001), 80.

59. As Michael Guasco explains, "Englishmen encountered Africans in Africa as members of identifiable communities with territorial and political integrity. The Africans they met in the Americas, however, appeared to be rootless and moveable. They could be exploited because they had nobody to protect them." See Michael Guasco, *Slaves and Englishmen: Human Bondage in the Early Modern Atlantic World*, 232.

60. Stephanie M. H. Camp, *Closer to Freedom: Enslaved Women and Everyday Resistance in the Plantation South* (Chapel Hill: University of North Carolina Press, 2004), 14.

61. Pass laws regulating the movement of impressed seamen and individuals experiencing other forms of unfreedom were also, occasionally, instituted (*BNL* 1708/12/27).

62. Even white bodies arriving in a new city or town were treated as foreigners in colonial North America (though not immediately, as racialized and therefore identifiably foreign bodies were). Thus, Massachusetts law stipulated that all nonresidents who spent twenty or more nights in a particular municipality were required to "give an Account" of their lives and circumstances to the selectmen or town clerk of that town (*BEP* 1736/2/2). In other words, a foreign identity necessitated the constant production and reproduction of an auto/biography. Foreign status necessitated a narration of self, so it is small wonder that eighteenth-century colonial narratives of enslavement often foregrounded the foreign status of black African men and women.

63. Black African bodies were always foreign, even after individuals self-identified as English or American. As Geneva Cobb Moore attests, the committee of eighteen white men who authenticated Phillis Wheatley Peters's poetry denied her "the status of even a cultural hybrid," refusing to acknowledge "her as anything other than a *foreign* body in the national body politic." See Geneva Cobb Moore, *Maternal Metaphors of Power in African American Women's Literature: From Phillis Wheatley to Toni Morrison* (Columbia: University of South Carolina Press, 2017), 17.

64. See *A Report of the Record Commissioners of the City of Boston, Containing the Boston Records from 1700 to 1728* (Boston: 1883), 174.

65. As Jill Lepore notes, prosecutors alleged that the entire episode was attributable to foreign influence, the work of Spanish and Catholic agents. Concern that the arsonists might have ties to foreign powers is evident in the court's record of interrogations. According to the testimony of an enslaved man named York, the ringleader, John Hughson, "told them at his house, that the Spaniards knew better than York negroes how to fight, and they were all to stand by one another and assist the French and Spaniards, they were to wait for them some time, if they did not come, they were to do all themselves." Among other allegations, witnesses testified that the accused black Africans spoke Dutch when plotting; that they intended to leave for Mohawk country after burning New York to the ground; and that they bought firearms with Spanish pieces of eight. Chapter 4 offers a lengthier discussion of these arson attacks and their foreign connections. See Jill Lepore, *New York Burning: Liberty, Slavery, and Conspiracy in Eighteenth-Century Manhattan* (New York: Vintage, 2006), 196; and Daniel Horsmanden, *The New-York Conspiracy, or a History of the Negro Plot, with the Journal of the Proceedings against the Conspirators at New-York in the Years 1741–2* (New York: 1810), 170.

66. All of Fleet's woodcuts were done by Peter because "there were few persons in Boston who could 'cut' on wood or type metal. . . . Fleet had a negro who illustrated his ballads by cuts." Peter, the "negro" referenced here, left his initials on a woodcut for "The Prodigal Daughter," which was reprinted by Thomas Fleet and his sons throughout the century. See Benjamin Franklin Thomas, *Memoir of Isaiah Thomas, by His Grandson* (Boston: 1874), 11.

67. Fittingly, this victory was the inspiration for naming the Washington family estate Mount Vernon. Both the plantation and the military success in Cartagena were predicated on black labor, but in both cases, a white military leader is the figure by which each was remembered.

68. Peter's years of service in a printing shop certainly familiarized him with poetry, and I present evidence in chapter 5 that one or more of his sons was a poet. We cannot know whether Peter wrote "Some Excellent VERSES," but because his artistic vision

demonstrably influenced its composition and because he likely set the type himself, I would argue that this is a black African poem, whether or not he originally penned the words. As it predates Lucy Terry's "Bars Fight" by five years, it might well be celebrated as the *first* poem in English by a black African in North America.

69. "*Advice from the Dead to the Living*; or, a Solemn Warning to the World. Occasioned by the untimely Death of poor Julian" (Boston: 1733), lines 29–30.

70. *Weekly Rehearsal*, Sep. 4, 1732.

71. Herman Melville, *Parthenope*, in *The Writings of Herman Melville*, vol. 13, *Billy Budd, Sailor and Other Uncompleted Writings*, ed. Harrison Hayford et al. (Evanston, IL: Northwestern University Press, 2017), 147.

72. Ezra Pound, *ABC of Reading* (New York: New Directions, 2010), 29. Sean Moore has done much to illuminate the presence of black Africans in early American libraries and print shops, showing that the colonial consumption and production of literature was funded by enslaved labor and a trade in human capital. The poetry and novels composed by white writers for white readers are implicitly, then, enmeshed in narratives of slavery, and a black African literary presence between 1619 and 1760 might be restored to the early American literature classroom strictly through the study of book history. But to this implicit, economic presence should be added the stories told by and about those black Africans, and that is the work of *Before Equiano*. See Sean D. Moore, *Slavery and the Making of Early American Libraries: British Literature, Political Thought, and the Transatlantic Book Trade, 1731–1814* (New York: Oxford University Press, 2019).

73. Charles Dickens, *Our Mutual Friend* (New York: Modern Library, 2002), 192.

Chapter One

1. Samuel Sewall, *The Selling of Joseph: A Memorial*, in *The Diary of Samuel Sewall, 1674–1729*, ed. M. Halsey Thomas, vol. 2 (New York: Farrar, Straus and Giroux, 1973), 1117. On the links drawn between Eden and slavery by Sewall and others, see Zachary McLeod Hutchins, *Inventing Eden: Primitivism, Millennialism, and the Making of New England* (New York: Oxford University Press, 2014), 222–30.

2. John Greenleaf Whittier, "The Prophecy of Samuel Sewall," in *The Complete Poetical Works of John Greenleaf Whittier* (Boston: Houghton, Mifflin & Co., 1904), 82.

3. John Saffin hinted as much in his reply to *The Selling of Joseph*, asking, "doth it follow, that it is altogether unlawful for Christians to buy and keep Negro Servants (for this is the thesis) but that those that have them ought in Conscience to set them free, and so lose all the money they cost (for we must not live in any known sin) this seems to be his opinion; but it is a Question whether it ever was the Gentleman's practice?" In an investigation of Saffin's intimations, Sidney Kaplan acknowledged that Sewall employed two black freemen named Boston and Scipio (who lived in Sewall's house), but concluded, "There is, in fact, no evidence in *Diary* or *Letter-Book*, before or after *The Selling of Joseph*, that Sewall owned slaves—and much to the contrary." See John Saffin, *A Brief and Candid Answer to a Late Printed Sheet*, in *History of the Negro Race in America, 1619 to 1880*, vol. 1, ed. George W. Williams (New York: 1883), 215; and Sidney Kaplan, *American Studies in Black and White: Selected Essays*, ed. Allan D. Austin (Amherst: University of Massachusetts Press, 1991), 17. Among modern scholars Lawrence Towner first noted that Sewall participated in the slave

trade, although he mistakenly thought the vendor was the judge's nephew (also named Samuel). See Lawrence W. Towner, "The Sewall-Saffin Dialogue on Slavery," *The William and Mary Quarterly* 21.1 (1964): 41.

4. Merchants Row was located at the foot of the Long Wharf; Sewall's warehouse (mentioned only once in the Diary, in 1708, before the Long Wharf was constructed or these advertisements published) was generally identified by one of these two landmarks. His home was located near the corner of Winter Street and Newbury Street, just a stone's throw from the Boston Common; all three landmarks were used to identify the Sewall home. Sewall's nephew, sometimes erroneously identified as the merchant named in these advertisements, lived in Brookline.

5. *Boston News-Letter*, Sep. 13, 1714. Subsequent in-text citations to this newspaper appear as "BNL 1714/9/13".

6. *Boston Gazette*, Aug. 19, 1723. Subsequent in-text citations to this newspaper appear as "BG 1723/8/19."

7. Elisabeth Ceppi, *Invisible Masters: Gender, Race, and the Economy of Service in Early New England* (Hanover, NH: Dartmouth College Press, 2018), 142.

8. Sewall's casuistic approach is characteristic of both antislavery and proslavery treatises of the late seventeenth century. See Philippe Rosenberg, "Thomas Tryon and the Seventeenth-Century Dimensions of Antislavery," *The William and Mary Quarterly* 61.4 (2004): 609–42.

9. Sewall, *The Selling of Joseph*, 1118, 1120. The *Body of Liberties* stipulates, in its discussion of the *"Liberties of Forreiners and Strangers,"* that "there shall never be any bond slaverie, villinage or Captivitie amongst us unles it be lawfull Captives taken in just warres, and such strangers as willingly selle themselves or are sold to us. And these shall have all the liberties and Christian usages which the law of god established in Israell concerning such persons doeth morally require. This exempts none from servitude who shall be Judged thereto by Authoritie." See the *Body of Liberties* in *American Historical Documents, 1000–1904*, ed. Charles W. Eliot, in *The Harvard Classics*, vol. XLIII (New York: 1910), 79. A history of the concept of "just war" in early New England is traced in Matthew Steven Muehlbauer, "Justice and Just War: A History of Early New England, 1630–1655" (PhD diss, Temple University, 2008).

10. John M. Lund, "The Contested Will of 'Goodman Penn': Anglo-New England Politics, Culture, and Legalities, 1688–1716," *Law and History Review* 27.3 (2009): 583.

11. Marion Wilson Starling, *The Slave Narrative: Its Place in American History* (Boston: G. K. Hall and Co., 1981), 50. Records relating to Adam's suit for freedom were printed in *Publications of the Colonial Society of Massachusetts*, vol. 1 (Boston: 1895), 84–114.

12. Frances Smith Foster, *Written by Herself: Literary Production by African American Women, 1746–1892* (Bloomington: Indiana University Press, 1993), 2; see also France Smith Foster, *Witnessing Slavery: The Development of Ante-bellum Slave Narratives*, 2nd ed. (Madison: University of Wisconsin Press, 1994), 30–33

13. John Sekora, "Black Message/White Envelope: Genre, Authenticity, and Authority in the Antebellum Slave Narrative," *Callaloo* 32 (1987), 502.

14. Sewall, *The Selling of Joseph*, 1120.

15. Sewall, *Letter-Book of Samuel Sewall*, vol. 2 (Boston: 1886), 182.

16. Whiting shared her research in 2015, at the joint conference of the Omohundro Institute of Early American History and Culture and the Society of Early Americanists, in

Chicago. Her paper was entitled, "*The Selling of Joseph*: Slavery, Freedom, and Black Family Life in Samuel Sewall's Neighborhood at the Turn of the Eighteenth Century" and is part of a work in progress, *African Families, American Stories: Black Kin and Community in Early New England.*

17. Sewall, *The Diary of Samuel Sewall, 1674–1729*, vol. 1, 408, 443.

18. Sewall, *Letter-Book of Samuel Sewall*, 1.157.

19. Sewall, *The Diary of Samuel Sewall, 1674–1729*, vol. 1, 157. See also Sewall, *Letter-Book of Samuel Sewall*, 1.28, 34, 38, 45, 49, 76–77, 112. The connection between Sewall's correspondence with Ive and his subsequent publication of *The Selling of Joseph* was first noted by Lawrence W. Towner, *Past Imperfect: Essays on History, Libraries, and the Humanities*, ed. Robert W. Karrow Jr. and Alfred F. Young (Chicago: University of Chicago Press, 1993), 25–26.

20. Sewall, *Letter-Book of Samuel Sewall*, 1.201, 205, 207, 271–72, 278–79. Sewall also participated in the effort to redeem Anthony Haywood, but he was not engaged on Haywood's behalf so consistently (284–85). Mather's pastoral letter was published; see Cotton Mather, *A Pastoral Letter to the English Captives in Africa* (Boston: 1698). As Nabil Matar notes, the efforts of Sewall and Elizabeth Thatcher were part of a broader movement attempting to sway governments in London and Algiers throughout the seventeenth century: "from the 1620s on thousands of destitute wives and dependents repeatedly took to the streets with petitions on behalf of their captured kinsmen. In 1653 commercial and naval overseers unsuccessfully attempted to ransom all the captives in North Africa because 'the country wants their services.'" See Nabil Matar, "Introduction: England and Mediterranean Captivity, 1577–1704," in *Piracy, Slavery, and Redemption: Barbary Captivity Narratives from Early Modern England*, ed. Daniel J. Vitkus (New York: Columbia University Press, 2001), 5; 23–32.

21. Cotton Mather, *The Glory of Goodness* (Boston: 1703), 2.

22. Sewall, *The Selling of Joseph*, 1119.

23. Throughout the seventeenth century, Tripoli, Algiers, and Tunisia were separate regencies held at the pleasure of the Porte of the Ottoman Empire. They gained significant additional autonomy in 1711 but remained titular subjects of the Porte during the eighteenth century. Tunisian galleys operated primarily in the Adriatic Sea, while the privateers of Tripoli often attacked Maltese and Neapolitan vessels; the corsairs of Algiers sailed more widely, into the North Atlantic as well as the Mediterannean. The infamous *Sallee Rovers* sailed from the Atlantic coast of Morocco, which was an independent kingdom that occasionally pursued anti-Ottoman policies.

24. Mather, *The Glory of Goodness*, 32–33.

25. Matar, "Introduction: England and Mediterranean Captivity, 1577–1704," 17.

26. Paul Baepler, "The Barbary Captivity Narrative in Early America," *Early American Literature* 30.2 (1995): 114.

27. In June 1705 the General Court passed a "RESOLVE FOR ALLOWING AND PAYING OUT OF THE PROVINCE TREASURY TO BERNARD TROTT ELEVEN POUNDS PER ANNUM FOR FIVE YEARS, IN PART COMPLIANCE WITH AN ORDER OF THE GENERAL COURT IN 1677, FOR HIS SERVICES AND EXPENSES IN REDEEMING AND RETURNING FROM FAYAL TWO INDIANS STOLEN AND SOLD INTO SLAVERY." Sewall helped Trott receive his promised reimbursement. See *The Acts and Resolves, Public and Private, of the Province of the Massachusetts Bay*, vol. VIII (Boston: 1895), 123; see also 484–86.

28. Sewall, *The Selling of Joseph*, 1120. In a remarkable but still largely unknown argument transcribed in 1754, a black African man named Greenwich living in Canterbury, Connecticut, offered exegesis on the idea of a just war and on the circumstances by which Abraham acquired his slaves. Greenwich denounces any attempt to justify slavery by references to the biblical patriarch, as though in answer to Sewall, and insists, "Justise must Take Plase therefore I will I shou you how Abraham came by his servents in the 15 Chapt of Genesis 18 wher the Lord Covenant with Abraham saying unto thy seed have I given this Land from the river uf eupherates and the kenites and the kenizites and the kadmonites and also in the 17 Chap of Genesies and 8 vers and I will give unto the[e] and to thy seed after the Land wherein thou art a stranger all the Land of Canaan for an everlasting possession and I will be the[i]r God and In the 12 vers and he that is eight days old shall be circumsized among you every man child In your Generation he that Is born In thy house or bought with mony of any strangers which Is not of thy seed and now bretherin cast your eyes upon the fase of the earth how god hath set the bounds to the nation and that non[e] shold impose upon another nation." Greenwich, "Negrow Grinning of Canterbury," in Erik R. Seeman, "'Justise Must Take Plase': Three African Americans Speak of Religion in Eighteenth-Century New England," *The William and Mary Quarterly* 56.2 (1999): 411.

29. Sewall, *Letter-Book of Samuel Sewall*, 1.322–23, 2.39. See Leonard W. Cowie, *Henry Newman: An American in London, 1708–43* (London: SPCK, 1956). Sewall, who studied eschatology avidly, understood the conversion of black Africans as a necessary prerequisite to the biblical end times. Slavery's end and the conversion of black Africans to Christianity were, Sewall thought, predicted by the progress of wars in Europe between the Holy Roman Empire and the Ottoman Empire. News of enslaved Christians from Hungaria and other eastern European countries being released by the Turks as part of peace negotiations was understood by Sewall in apocalyptic terms: "God will rescue the miserable Sons and Daughters of Adam in Asia and Africa from that palpable Darkness and Death into which they are plunged. The remarkable Beating of the Turk, and the taking of Belgrade, are I hope comfortable Indications that the second Wo is passing away, whatsoever hardships and sorrows the Reformed of Hungaria or other parts may in the mean time undergo." Sewall, *Letter-Book of Samuel Sewall*, 2.80. News of enslaved Christians taken or released by Turkish forces appeared regularly in the newspapers; in the two years prior to Sewall's comment about Hungaria, he would have read a half dozen reports of Turkish slavery. See *BNL* 1715/9/12; *BNL* 1716/2/27; *BNL* 1716/3/5; *BNL* 1716/3/5; *BNL* 1716/11/26; and *BNL* 1717/1/21. On Sewall's apocalypticism, see Mukhtar Ali Isani, "The Growth of Sewall's *Phaenomena Quaedam Apocalyptica*," *Early American Literature* 7 (1972): 64–75.

30. See, for example, Margaret Ellen Newell, *Brethren by Nature: New England Indians, Colonists, and the Origins of American Slavery* (Ithaca, NY: Cornell University Press, 2015), 244–45.

31. Frederick Douglass, *Narrative of the Life of Frederick Douglass*, ed. John W. Blassingame, John R. McKivigan, and Peter P. Hinks (New Haven, CT: Yale University Press, 2001), 38.

32. Samuel Sewall, *Probate Court Records, 1715–1728*, Massachusetts Historical Society, http://www.masshist.org/collection-guides/digitized/fa0242/s171-3-10#1, 41 (accessed January 25, 2022).

33. *American Weekly Mercury* June 1, 1727. Subsequent in-text citations to this newspaper appear as "*AWM* 1727/6/1."

34. *The Acts and Resolves, Public and Private, of the Province of the Massachusetts Bay*, vol. IX (Boston: 1902), 469.

35. Like many, Sewall followed the discourse of slavery in stories about the Pretender with interest. When he wrote to Edward Taylor in January 1723, Sewall "Inclosed the Gazett of Jany 7th that [*had*] His Majs Speech to the Parliament." In that speech, George I reportedly scoffed that the Pretender should "*hope to perswade a free People, in full Enjoyment of all that's dear and valuable to them, to exchange Freedom for Slavery, the Protestant Religion for Popery*" (BNL 1723/1/14). Sewall, *The Diary of Samuel Sewall, 1674–1729*, vol. 2, 1004.

36. *New-England Weekly Journal* May 8, 1727. Subsequent in-text citations to this newspaper appear as "*NEJ* 1727/5/8."

37. In this communication, British officials insist that the daughter of John Williams—whose captivity narrative helps define the genre—is enslaved, not simply ransomed. This passage, perhaps better than any other, illustrates the extent to which generic differentiation between Barbary captivity narratives, Indian captivity narratives, and slave narratives is an outgrowth of modern scholarship that elides the essential sameness of these conditions in the minds of American colonists.

38. Sewall, *Letter-Book of Samuel Sewall*, 1.387.

39. I intentionally conflate Basilio—an enslaved Spanish speaker—with the unnamed Spanish slave described in two entries of Sewall's diary from January 1709. I cannot prove that the two Spanish-speaking enslaved persons awaiting a declaration of freedom from the General Court are the same individual, because the minutes of the governor's council for 1709 are missing from the Massachusetts State Archives, but that is the simplest and most likely explanation.

40. Sewall, *The Diary of Samuel Sewall, 1674–1729*, vol. 2, 613.

41. Sewall, *The Diary of Samuel Sewall, 1674–1729*, vol. 2, 614.

42. Sewall, *The Diary of Samuel Sewall, 1674–1729*, vol. 1, 595.

43. The logic of this argument against enslaving black Africans is consonant with Sewall's own line of questioning, in *The Selling of Joseph*, as to "whether all the Benefit received by *Negro* Slaves, will balance the Accompt of Cash laid out upon them." Sewall, *The Selling of Joseph*, 1119.

44. Discussion of the *assiento* and its importance to French interests is recurrent in correspondence between colonial governors and government officials in England. Many British traders sold human chattels illegally to French and Spanish traders. See, for example, *Calendar of State Papers, Colonial Series, America and West Indies*, vol. 23, ed. Cecil Headlam (London: 1916), 17–18, 24–25. (Subsequent citations to this publication are abbreviated as follows: "*CSP* 23.17–18, 24–25.") British acknowledgment of the West Indies' centrality to the war and the French need for human chattels is evident in the number of troops allocated to the islands. When the French began raiding the islands for slaves in 1704, the number of British troops assigned to the West Indies rose by 400 percent, from 599 in 1703 to 3,102 in 1704. See John B. Hattendorf, *England in the War of the Spanish Succession: A Study of the English View and Conduct of Grand Strategy, 1702–1712* (New York: Garland, 1987), 173.

45. Because the French were continually trying to secure enslaved persons for sale, British correspondents regarded the seizure of French slaving vessels as a key to the war effort—thus the celebration in Faial, in July 1706, when "two of Her Majesty's Ships, the *Chester* and *Pool* were arrived there from the Coast of *Guinea*, who had taken two *French* Ships upon

that Coast, one whereof was a Ship of 30 Guns, who had on board 300 Slaves" (*BNL* 1706/8/19).

46. *CSP* 23.117.

47. This newspaper account neglected to mention that enslaved black Africans initially aided the French in their attacks on the island's English inhabitants. Colonel George Burt reported from Nevis that the French, "with ye revolting negroes robbed ye planters as ye women and ye familyes left their houses, and plundered more than 3 parts of ye houses in ye Island. The negroes betooke themselves to ye mountaines with their plunder and there defend themselves, some that were nearest ye enemy went to them and were strip't of what they carryed off, as they deserved" (*CSP* 23.184–85). These individuals followed the script of a 1690 rebellion on the neighboring island of St. Christopher's, when enslaved black Africans took advantage of fighting between the English and French to win their autonomy with a retreat to the mountains (*CSP* 23.146). Stripped of their chattels and other wealth, the white inhabitants of Nevis complained that they themselves "must inevitably perish or become slaves with our wives and children to the enemy." Pierre d'Iberville, the commanding French officer, insisted "they were used but as prisoners of warr," but since prisoners of war were often sold into slavery, the distinction between slave and prisoner was tenuous and sometimes difficult to articulate (*CSP* 23.142–43).

48. Charles F. Nunn, *Foreign Immigrants in Early Bourbon Mexico, 1700–1760* (New York: Cambridge University Press, 1979), 36. English ships also made port in New Spain, but those voyages seem to have been more rare than those undertaken by the French. In 1708 Governor Thomas Handasyd of Jamaica wrote to the Council of Trade and Plantations, "Nine trading sloops will go out within this day or two to the Spanish coast, but I am very apprehensive, so many will spoil one another's trade." Officials in Whitehall were surprised that English vessels would be received there but encouraged the trade (*CSP* 23.675, 750).

49. On the selling of French prisoners held at Port Royal, see Emerson W. Baker and John G. Reid, *The New England Knight: Sir William Phips, 1651–1695* (Toronto: University of Toronto Press, 1998), 86–109.

50. A fuller account of this skirmish is given in *CSP* 23.248–54.

51. Thus, when an English "Pilot-Boat" hailed a French prize that still looked like a British vessel, the French seized "an Indian Slave that belong'd to the Pilot, then put one of the [white] Prisoners into the Pilots Boat and left her" (*BNL* 1707/8/18). Race was the difference between being claimed as property and being released as a prisoner of war.

52. Sewall, *The Selling of Joseph*, 1120.

53. Sir Edward Northey, Attorney General for England and Wales, objected to a 1703 act "*for the better Government of negroes and other slaves*" in Nevis; that law governed the treatment of "white slaves, who may fairly become slaves by their own contracts" as well as "persons stole in England and sold there." See *CSP* 23.126.

54. This copy of the *News-Letter* is held by the American Antiquarian Society.

55. Sewall's copy of the *News-Letter* is held by the Massachusetts Historical Society.

56. Governor John Seymour of Maryland was similarly "alarm'd by the French squadron and privateers that have infested the West Indies . . . and tooke care to putt the Country into the best posture of defence I could." See *CSP* 23.197.

57. Letter of May 19, 1707, from Joseph Dudley to Benjamin Colman, in the *Benjamin Colman Papers, 1641–1806*, Massachusetts Historical Society, Box 1, Folder 3,

http://www.masshist.org/collection-guides/digitized/fa0288/b1-f3-i3#1 (accessed January 26, 2022).

58. Jared Hardesty, "An Angry God in the Hands of Sinners: Enslaved Africans and the Uses of Protestant Christianity in Pre-Revolution Boston," *Slavery & Abolition* 35.1 (2014): 67.

59. Matar, "Introduction: England and Mediterranean Captivity, 1577–1704," 21.

60. Cotton Mather, *A Letter Concerning the Terrible Suffering of Our Protestant Brethren, on Board the French Kings Galleyes* (Boston: 1701); Sewall, *Letter-Book of Samuel Sewall*, 1.324. Mather translated several French narratives of enslavement, highlighting tropes common to the genre. See Ruth Whelan, "Turning to Gold: The Role of the Witness in French Protestant Galley Slave Narratives," *Seventeenth-Century French Studies* 32.1 (2010): 3–18.

61. See *BNL* 1713/12/18, *BNL* 1714/5/10, *BNL* 1716/9/10, *BNL* 1716/12/31, *BNL* 1717/2/11, *BNL* 1717/4/8, *BNL* 1717/4/15, *BNL* 1717/5/20, *BNL* 1718/2/10, *BNL* 1718/9/15, *BNL* 1719/4/6, *BNL* 1721/5/29, *BNL* 1721/8/7, *BNL* 1722/4/9, *BNL* 1724/1/9, *BNL* 1724/8/20; *AWM* 1720/12/13, *AWM* 1724/5/14, *AWM* 1724/11/19, *AWM* 1725/8/5; *BG* 1721/2/27, *BG* 1721/1/16, *BG* 1721/7/31, *BG* 1722/1/29; and *New-England Courant*, Mar. 15, 1725. Subsquent in-text citations to this newspaper appear as "*NEC* 1725/3/15."

62. The *American Weekly Mercury* printed selections from *The Sailors Advocate*, a 1728 pamphlet arguing against impressment published in London. The anonymous author asks, "How can it be expected, that a Man should fight for the Liberty of others, whilst he himself feels the pangs of Slavery, or expose his Life to defend the property of a Nation, where his dearest pledges, his Wife and Children, are pining away with Want?" (*AWM* 1728/7/25). On the problem of manning naval vessels and impressment more generally, see Denver Brunsman, *The Evil Necessity: British Naval Impressment in the Eighteenth-Century Atlantic World* (Charlottesville: University of Virginia Press, 2013).

63. Teate complains of a shrinking complement in letters to the Admiralty dated March 10, 1709; August 4, 1709; and October 25, 1709; see ADM 1/2573, The National Archives.

64. *Documentary History of the State of Maine*, vol. 9, ed. James Phinney Baxter (Portland, ME: 1907), 241.

65. Teate to the Admiralty, December 10, 1709; see ADM 1/2573, The National Archives.

66. See Alden T. Vaughan, *Transatlantic Encounters: American Indians in Britain, 1500–1776* (New York: Cambridge, 2006), 113–36. Aware that Teate might not welcome his Indian guests, Dudley wrote to London requesting that since these passengers "will occasion him some considerable expence, *pray* that he may be considered, *etc.*" See *CSP* 25.40.

67. David Waldstreicher, "Reading the Runaways: Self-Fashioning, Print Culture, and Confidence in Slavery in the Eighteenth-Century Mid-Atlantic," *The William and Mary Quarterly* 56.2 (1999): 244–45.

68. Douglass, *Narrative of the Life of Frederick Douglass*, 13.

69. Gregory E. O'Malley, *Final Passages: The Intercolonial Slave Trade of British America, 1619–1807* (Chapel Hill: University of North Carolina Press, 2014), 7.

70. See Joseph Calder Miller, *Way of Death: Merchant Capitalism and the Angolan Slave Trade, 1730–1830* (Madison: University of Wisconsin Press, 1988), 543.

71. Miller explains that this confidence would have been misplaced, if only because "slaves' final ports of embarkation gave only the roughest indication of their origins." In the

Angola region, John Thornton writes, "while Kongo rulers did participate in the slave trade, they generally did not export their own subjects." The kingdom imported slaves, and the majority of those sold were, reportedly, "purchased from the Gentiles" in interior African states. Miller, *Way of Death: Merchant Capitalism and the Angolan Slave Trade, 1730–1830,* 225; John Thornton, "Demography and History in the Kingdom of Kongo, 1550–1750," *The Journal of African History* 18.4 (1977), 528.

72. Walter Rodney places the tactics of Charles in a broader context, emphasizing his attempts to bypass Luso-African middlemen and trade directly with the Bullom and Susu of Sherbro. See Rodney, *A History of the Upper Guinea Coast, 1545–1800* (New York: Oxford University Press, 1970), 213–15.

73. Phyllis M. Martin, "The Cabinda Connection: An Historical Perspective," *African Affairs* 76.302 (1977): 51.

74. Sewall, *The Selling of Joseph,* 1120.

75. For an overview of the attack on Hereford and the Royal African Company at Cabinda, see Alicia Marie Bertrand, "The Downfall of the Royal African Company on the Atlantic African Coast in the 1720s," Masters thesis, Trent University, 2011, http://www.collectionscanada.gc.ca/obj/thesescanada/vol2/002/MR81097.PDF, 60–66 (accessed January 26, 2022).

76. Hugh Thomas, *Slave Trade: The Story of the Atlantic Slave Trade, 1440–1870* (New York: Simon & Schuster, 1997), 365. Loss of the fort at Angola in 1722 was later blamed for the Royal African Company's demise; see *An Antidote to Expel the Poison* (London: 1749), 15–16.

77. These events were later recounted by an English slave, Thomas Pellow, in a Barbary captivity narrative. For fuller accounts of this conflict, see Thomas Pellow, *The History of the Long Captivity and Adventures of Thomas Pellow* (London: 1740); and *Muhammad al-Qadiri's Nashr al-Mathani: The Chronicles,* ed. and trans. Norman L. Cigar (London: Oxford University Press, 1981).

78. Those crimes included nine instances of murder, twelve acts of piracy, six thefts, nine cases of arson, and five instances of rape or infanticide.

79. Those four positive notices are as follows: in 1721 the *New England Courant* described a "Wedding of Two Africans" celebrated with "unaccustom'd Magnificence" and attended by prominent citizens (*NEC* 1721/12/25); the black African widow of James Carlington was carried to her grave and "magnificently interr'd" in a procession suggesting her good standing in the community (*NEC* 1723/7/29); the *New England Weekly Journal* reported on the death of "a Negro Freeman named **Boston**" who was followed to the grave by "about 150 Blacks, and about 50 Whites, several Magistrates, Ministers, Gentlemen, &c." (*NEJ* 1729/2/24); and "a Negro named Papaw" living in Virginia reportedly "discovered a certain Remedy for the Venereal Disease," earning his freedom and an annuity from the colonial government (*NEJ* 1729/12/22). Notably, all four of these positive reports appeared in the city's alternative newspapers, venues that thumbed their noses at the government and the status quo.

80. Sewall, *The Diary of Samuel Sewall, 1674–1729,* vol. 2, 1007.

81. See Wendy Warren, *New England Bound* (New York: W. W. Norton, 2016), 199–206; and John Ballantine, *Diary of John Ballantine,* transcribed by Joshua D. Bartlett, American Antiquarian Society, mss octavo vols. B.

82. The cry "*A Bite, a Bite*" was likely an attempt to characterize this offer of reward as a trap. A *bight* is a loop of rope such as that used in a noose. Thus, the cry warned that any who accepted the offer risked death for themselves and others.

83. As quoted in *The New England Historical and Genealogical Register* 14 (1860): 36. I am indebted to Michael Weisenburg for heping me to locate this record of the sermon in Dexter's diary.

84. Joseph Sewall, *Two Sermons, Joseph Sewall*, held by the Hatfield Historical Museum, https://archive.org/details/twosermonsjosephoosewa, p. 14 (accessed January 26, 2022). I am deeply indebted to Debra Ryal for identifying this book of sermons by Sewall as the repository of his 1723 address.

85. Sewall, *Two Sermons, Joseph Sewall*, 16.

86. Sewall, *Two Sermons, Joseph Sewall*, 14.

87. Sewall's perspective on the spiritual potential of black African men and women is similarly expressed in a 1741 sermon, in which he condescends "to exhort our *Indians and Negroes to submit to Christ, and stand on his Side*. Your Names indeed are not reckoned in our Muster-Rolls; but tho' our Lord needs none, he alone is able to subdue the Enemy, and whatever Instruments are used by him, his is the Power and the Victory; yet I say, He condescendeth to accept the Service of the meanest, who are willing heartily to epouse his Cause. Now then, that God has bro't you out from the dark Places of the Earth, where Satan had his Seat, to a Land of Gospel-Light, where it is declared that the Son of God was manifest in the Flesh, and hath *redeemed a People to God by his Blood, out of every Kindred, and Tongue, and People, and Nation*; seeing this is the happy State of Things, despise the Slavery of the Devil, shake off the Chains of Darkness in which you have been bound, and cry to your Saviour, that you may be *delivered from the Bondage of Corruption*, into the *glorious Liberty* of the Children of God." Joseph Sewall, *The Holy Spirit Convincing the World of Sin, of Righteousness, and of Judgment* (Boston: 1741), 130.

88. Enslaved black Africans were valued at thirty pounds apiece in BNL 1706/6/10. This valuation is in keeping with the average price paid by Paul Dudley, Attorney General of Massachusetts Bay and the son of Governor Dudley, for two enslaved persons in 1706. Because the governor oversaw the sale of these two, who were taken on board the pirate *John Quelch*, one John Coleman questioned the legality of the sale and the valuation of a black African boy or "pennyworth" at 20*l*. Dudley responded by acknowledging "that the price of Negroes differs from 10*l*. to 100*l*. in the market," but insisted that "if Mr. Coleman had offered 1*s*. more, he might have had the rich pennyworth himself." In 1708, Dudley estimated that prices "are usually between £15 and £25 per head." See *CSP* 23.236–39, 262; 24.110.

89. Sewall, *Two Sermons, Joseph Sewall*, 26, 22.

90. Phillis Cogswell, "[P]hillis Cogswell, Negro," in Erik R. Seeman, "'Justise Must Take Plase': Three African Americans Speak of Religion in Eighteenth-Century New England," *The William and Mary Quarterly* 56.2 (1999): 413; and Flora, "The Confession of Flora Negro," in Erik R. Seeman, "'Justise Must Take Plase': Three African Americans Speak of Religion in Eighteenth-Century New England," 407.

91. Phillis Wheatley Peters, "On the Death of the Rev. Dr. Sewell. 1769," in *Complete Writings*, ed. Vincent Carretta (New York: Penguin, 2001), 13–15.

92. Sewall, *The Diary of Samuel Sewall, 1674–1729*, vol. 2, 983.

93. *A Report of the Record Commissioners of the City of Boston, Containing the Boston Records from 1700 to 1728* (Boston: 1883), 172–75.

94. Sewall, *The Diary of Samuel Sewall, 1674–1729*, vol. 2, 762.

95. Newell, *Brethren by Nature: New England Indians, Colonists, and the Origins of American Slavery*, 242; see also Towner, "The Sewall-Saffin Dialogue on Slavery," 41.

96. Sewall, *The Diary of Samuel Sewall, 1674–1729*, vol. 1, 611.

97. Sewall, *The Diary of Samuel Sewall, 1674–1729*, vol. 2, 765.

98. Sewall, *Probate Court Records, 1715–1728*, http://www.masshist.org/collection-guides/digitized/fa0242/s171-3-10#1, 23 (accessed January 26, 2022).

99. Sewall, *The Diary of Samuel Sewall, 1674–1729*, vol. 2, 985, 998.

100. Sewall, *The Diary of Samuel Sewall, 1674–1729*, vol. 2, 1028, 1065.

Chapter Two

1. *Boston News-Letter*, March 19, 1716. (Subsequent in-text citations to this newspaper appear as "*BNL* 1716/3/19.") This copy of the *Boston News-Letter* is held by the American Antiquarian Society.

2. This copy of the *Boston News-Letter* is held by the Massachusetts Historical Society.

3. See, for example, Robert E. Desrochers Jr., "Slave-for-Sale Advertisements and Slavery in Massachusetts, 1704–1781," *The William and Mary Quarterly* 59.3 (2002): 623–64.

4. *New-England Weekly Journal*, Jan. 1, 1728. Subsequent in-text citations to this newspaper appear as "*NEJ* 1728/1/1."

5. See Kelly Wisecup, "African Medical Knowledge, the Plain Style, and Satire in the 1721 Boston Inoculation Controversy," *Early American Literature* 46.1 (2011): 25–50.

6. See *American Weekly Mercury*, Dec. 13, 1720; and *Boston Gazette*, Jan. 16, 1721. Subsequent in-text citations of these newspapers appear as "*AWM* 1720/12/13" and "*BG* 1721/1/16."

7. *Maryland Gazette*, Dec. 31, 1728. Subsequent in-text citations to this newspaper appear as "*MG* 1728/12/31."

8. Joe's head was cut off before he was killed, and then his body, like that of his brother Cora, was put on display as a warning to the local black African community.

9. See David Waldstreicher, "Reading the Runaways: Self-Fashioning, Print Culture, and Confidence in Slavery in the Eighteenth-Century Mid-Atlantic," *The William and Mary Quarterly* 56.2 (1999): 243–72.

10. Essays that take runaway slave advertisements as their primary subject matter include Simon P. Newman, "Runaway Bodies," in *Embodied History: The Lives of the Poor in Early Philadelphia* (Philadelphia: University of Pennsylvania Press, 2003), 82–103; Antonio T. Bly, "A Prince among Pretending Free Men: Runaway Slaves in Colonial New England Revisited," *Massachusetts Historical Review* 14 (2012): 87–118; Matthew J. Clavin, "Runaway Slave Advertisements in Antebellum Florida: A Retrospective," *The Florida Historical Quarterly* 94.3 (2016): 426–43; Rebecca Schneider, "'He Says He Is Free': Narrative Fragments and Self-Emancipation in West Indian Runaway Advertisements," *European Romantic Review* 29.4 (2018): 435–47; and Robert B. Winans, "Black Musicians in Eighteenth-Century America: Evidence from Runaway Slave Advertisements, in *Banjo Roots and Branches*, ed. Robert B. Winans (Urbana: University of Illinois Press, 2018), 194–213. In addition to the numerous digital databases of runaway slave advertisements, scholars have published a

number of print collections: *Runaway Slave Advertisements: A Documentary History from the 1730s to 1790*, 4 vols., ed. Lathan Windley (Westport, CT: Greenwood, 1983); *Blacks Who Stole Themselves: Advertisements for Runaways in the Pennsylvania Gazette, 1728–1790*, ed. Billy G. Smith and Richard Wojtowicz (Philadelphia: University of Pennsylvania Press, 1989); *"Pretends to Be Free": Runaway Slave Advertisements from Colonial and Revolutionary New York and New Jersey*, ed. Graham Russell Hodges and Alan Edward Brown (New York: Garland, 1994); and *Escaping Bondage: A Documentary History of Runaway Slaves in Eighteenth-Century New England, 1700–1789*, ed. Antonio T. Bly (Lanham, MD: Lexington Books, 2012).

11. Seven of the runaway slave advertisements published between 1704 and 1730 announce the disappearance of an enslaved man named Caesar; only Jack (ten advertisements) was a more popular name among these early runaways.

12. *New-England Courant*, June 14, 1725.

13. "The withholding of closure," Felicitas Meifert-Menhard suggests, "triggers readerly conjecture rather than complacency," engaging an audience. This open-ended narrative format is characteristic, as John Ellis argues, of television series, which have often drawn their cues from "the news bulletin, endlessly, updating events and never synthesizing them." Runaway slave advertisements and similar narrative fragments were in a real way—as Addison implies—the minidramas or soap operas of the eighteenth century. See Felicitas Meifert-Menhard, *Playing the Text, Performing the Future: Future Narratives in Print and Digiture* (Boston: de Gruyter, 2013), 104.

14. Peter's enslaver was a shipbuilder and the father and namesake of the much more famous William Pepperell (1696–1759), who would go on to marry Samuel Sewall's granddaughter and be elevated to a baronetcy for his part in capturing the French fort at Louisburg in 1745. For a brief reading of Peter's escape, see Ian K. Steele, *The English Atlantic, 1675–1740: An Exploration of Communication and Community* (New York: Oxford University Press, 1986), 132–33.

15. My conjecture about Peter's slit ear is informed by the example of Philip Ludwell II. Fifteen years after his father, the governor of South Carolina, caught Peter and sent him back to Maine, Ludwell II bored the ears of his enslaved coachman after he ran away the first time and advertised the fact as an aid to identification when John ran a second time: "a Small hole made in the upper part of each Ear, made with a short punch when he ran away before" (*AWM* 1720/9/29). John seems to have had more success in his second attempt and remained free for at least fourteen months. He ran away on July 4, 1719, and was still unaccounted for in September 1720.

16. Lisa A. Lindsay and John Wood Sweet, "Introduction: Biography and the Black Atlantic," in *Biography and the Black Atlantic*, ed. Lisa A. Lindsay and John Wood Sweet (Philadelphia: University of Pennsylvania Press, 2014), 4.

17. Mitch Kachun, "Slave Narratives and Historical Memory," in *The Oxford Handbook of the African American Slave Narrative*, ed. John Ernest (New York: Oxford University Press, 2014), 23; and James Olney, "'I Was Born': Slave Narratives, Their Status as Autobiography and as Literature," in *The Slave's Narrative*, ed. Charles T. Davis and Henry Louis Gates Jr. (New York: Oxford University Press, 1985), 151.

18. Martin Klein, "Understanding the Slave Experience in West Africa," in *Biography and the Black Atlantic* (Philadelphia: University of Pennsylvania Press, 2014), 64–65.

19. Newport Historical Society, mss box 43, Folder 6.

20. See Mary L. F. Power, "The Quakers in Scituate," in *Old Scituate* (Boston: 1921), 75.

21. Augustine Jones, "Nicholas Upsall," *The New England Historical and Genealogical Register* 34.1 (1880): 29.

22. William Sewel, *The History of the Rise, Increase and Progress, of the Christian People Called Quakers*, 3rd edition (Burlington, NJ: 1774), 255. The resolve of Cassandra Southwick was immortalized by the Quaker abolitionist poet John Greenleaf Whittier in an eponymous ballad, "Cassandra Southwick." See *The Complete Poetical Works of John Greenleaf Whittier* (Boston: 1904), 22–25.

23. As Evan Haefeli argues, religious difference preceded—and may have helped to create—racial difference as a category justifying the enslavement of foreign bodies. In Protestant colonies, he writes, "religious difference had come to serve the purpose of distinguishing between those who deserved freedom (Christians) and those who could be enslaved (heathens, pagans). . . . For example, when a Scottish aristocrat compiled a list of the population of various parts of America in the mid-seventeenth century, he divided it into 'souls' (i.e., Europeans), 'negroes,' and 'indians.' The idea that Europeans were 'white' and Africans 'black' can be found on Barbados as early as the 1640s, but religion remained the primary marker of European difference until the 1680s." Evan Haefeli, *Accidental Pluralism: America and the Religious Politics of English Expansion, 1497–1662* (Chicago: University of Chicago Press, 2021), 35.

24. George Bishop, *New England Judged* (London: 1661), 75.

25. See *American Historical Documents, 1000–1904*, ed. Charles W. Eliot, in *The Harvard Classics*, vol. XLIII (New York: 1910), 79.

26. Bishop, *New England Judged*, 160–63.

27. An enslaved black African named Jack reportedly received one hundred blows from his Massachusetts enslaver, Samuel Wolcott, on multiple occasions; the penalty is that of an enslaved individual, rather than a recalcitrant colonial subject. See *Colonial Justice in Western Massachusetts, 1639–1702: The Pynchon Court Record*, ed. Joseph H. Smith (Cambridge, MA: Harvard University Press, 1961), 298.

28. Newport Historical Society, mss box 156.

29. Edward Wanton, "Statement," Rhode Island Historical Society, mss 9003, vol. 10, box 9.

30. See Rhondda Tobinson Thomas, *Claiming Exodus: A Cultural History of Afro-Atlantic Identity, 1774–1903* (Waco, TX: Baylor University Press, 2013).

31. Something similar happened twenty years earlier in Barbados, where "one Harrison, a Planter (being much in debt) (notwithstanding the strictest orders given to the fforts), run off in a sloop with above 60 negros, leaveing his land to the creditors." See *Calendar of State Papers, Colonial Series, America and West Indies*, vol. 23, ed. Cecil Headlam (London: 1916), 580. Subsequent citations to this source appear as "*CSP* 23.580."

32. Jessica Marie Johnson, *Wicked Flesh: Black Women, Intimacy, and Freedom in the Atlantic World* (Philadelphia: University of Pennsylvania Press, 2020), 12.

33. "Petition of Jethro Boston for Divorce, 1741," in *The Earliest African American Literatures: A Critical Reader*, ed. Zachary McLeod Hutchins and Cassander L. Smith (Chapel Hill: University of North Carolina Press, 2021), 89.

34. John D'Emilio and Estelle B. Freedman, *Intimate Matters: A History of Sexuality in America*, 3rd edition (Chicago: University of Chicago Press, 2012), 34.

35. Cotton Mather, *Warnings from the Dead* (Boston: 1693),

36. Massachusetts State Archives, vol. 40, *Judicial, 1683–1724*, 624. At this time, the calendar year changed in March, rather than January.

37. *Acts and Laws, of His Majesty's Province of the Massachusetts-Bay in New-England* (Boston: 1726), 187.

38. Samuel Deane, *History of Scituate, Massachusetts* (Boston: 1831), 314. White and Newell were fined by the Plymouth County Sessions Court for engaging in premarital intercourse, but their sentence was similar to that received by white couples convicted of fornication. In 1698 another interracial couple—the white Sarah Curtice and Jo, "a Negro servant to William Holbrooke of Scituate"—were fined for fornication when Curtice delivered a black baby. See *Plymouth Court Records 1686–1859*, ed. David Thomas Konig, vol. 1 (Wilmington, DE: Michael Glazier, 1978), 200; and Jeremy Dupertius Bangs, *The Seventeenth-century Town Records of Scituate, Massachusetts*, vol. 3 (Boston: New England Historic Genealogical Society, 1997), 505.

39. The children of Newell and White hardly enjoyed a carefree life. Because of the 1706 law forbidding interracial marriage, apparently only one—James—married. And in 1758 Jerusha Newell, then a sixty-seven-year-old woman, was raped by a white man. See *Vital Records of Scituate, Massachusetts to the Year 1850*, vol. 2 (Boston: 1909), 216; and *Plymouth Court Records, 1686–1859*, vol. 3 (Wilmington, DE: 1978), 94

40. For an excellent overview of the case, see Wendy Warren, *New England Bound: Slavery and Colonization in Early America* (New York: W. W. Norton, 2016), 221–45.

41. John Saffin, *A Brief and Candid Answer to a Late Printed Sheet, Entituled,* The Selling of Joseph, in Abner C. Goodell, "John Saffin and his Slave Adam," in *Publications of the Colonial Society of Massachusetts*, vol. 1 (Boston: 1895), 108.

42. "The Will of Walter Briggs, of Scituate, Mass," in Samuel Briggs, *The Archives of the Briggs Family* (Cleveland, OH: 1880), 234

43. L. Vernon Briggs, *History and Genealogy of the Briggs Family, 1254–1937*, vol. 1 (Boston: 1938), 179, 181.

44. See *Vital Records of Scituate, Massachusetts to the Year 1850* (Boston: 1909), 435; and *Plymouth Court Records 1686–1859*, ed. David Thomas Konig, vol. 5 (Wilmington, DE: Michael Glazier, 1978), 68.

45. Saffin's smuggling activities are documented by Albert Von Frank. Maria, in 1706, was well into her forties; that she birthed two children after that date is at least somewhat surprising. Briggs, for his part, was just trying to avoid paying for Maria's maintenance after her most productive years of labor had passed. See Albert J. Von Frank, "John Saffin: Slavery and Racism in Colonial Massachusetts," *Early American Literature* 29.3 (1994): 256–57.

46. Joseph F. Cullon, "Colonial Shipwrights and Their World: Men, Women, and Markets in Early New England," (doctoral dissertation, University of Wisconsin-Madison, 2003), 79–80. On the implications of Quaker grammar in colonial New England, see Zachary McLeod Hutchins, *Inventing Eden: Primitivism, Millennialism, and the Making of New England* (New York: Oxford University Press, 2014), 175–77.

47. Power, "The Quakers in Scituate," 76.

48. As Brycchan Carey and Geoffrey Plank note, "Fox's plea for benevolent slaveholding accorded with the official stance of Quaker meetings throughout the British Empire well into the eighteenth century. . . . Indeed, between 1681 and 1730, slaveholders and occasional

slave traders occupied most of the positions of leadership within the Delaware Valley's Quaker meetings." Brycchan Carey and Geoffrey Plank, Introduction to *Quakers and Abolition* (Urbana: University of Illinois Press, 2014), 3.

49. Cullon, "Colonial Shipwrights and Their World: Men, Women, and Markets in Early New England," 86, 134.

50. L. Vernon Briggs, *History of Shipbuilding on North River, Plymouth County, Massachusetts* (Boston: 1889), 246–47.

51. See, for example, Gretchen Martin, *Dancing on the Color Line: African American Tricksters in Nineteenth-Century American Literature* (Jackson: University Press of Mississippi, 2015).

52. The destinations of vessels built in the Wanton Shipyard can be traced through the newspaper, but citations of, for instance, the Hopewell's journeys to and from Pennsylvania (*BNL* 1706/3/11; *BNL* 1706/8/19; *BNL* 1707/1/20; *BNL* 1707/3/10) are so numerous that providing documentation for each of the above destinations would be more cumbersome than helpful.

53. On the importance of Barbados as a source of enslaved labor for other British colonies, see the *CSP* 24.59, *CSP* 24.110, *CSP* 24.171. According to Christy Clark-Pujara, Rhode Island slavers imported 948 human chattels from Africa between 1701 and 1725, while all other colonies brought in a total of 1,047; from 1726 through 1750, Rhode Island imported 16,195 human chattels, while all other colonies brought in a total of 5,792. See Christy Clark-Pujara, *Dark Work: The Business of Slavery in Rhode Island* (New York: New York University Press, 2016), 18.

54. See *Records of the Colony of Rhode Island and Providence Plantations in New England*, ed. John Russell Bartlett, vol. 4 (Providence: 1859), 31; *Records of the Colony of Rhode Island and Providence Plantations in New England*, ed. John Russell Bartlett, vol. 3 (Providence: 1858), 491; see also *BNL* 1704/4/24; *BNL* 1706/6/10; *BNL* 1707/4/21.

55. Benjamin Franklin, *Benjamin Franklin's Autobiography*, ed. J. A. Leo Lemay and P. M. Zall (New York: Norton, 1986), 10, 6.

56. Land Evidences Collection, Rhode Island Historical Society, mss 527, pp. 354–56.

57. Newport Historical Society, box 43, folder 6.

58. The relative value and prestige of a steersman, carpenter, and captain in the eighteenth-century Atlantic is manifest in the ransoms demanded by Algerian pirates. Correspondents in Algiers reported "that the Barbarians have enhanced the Ransom Money for Christian Slaves, 2000 Dollars being demanded for a Dutch Skipper, 1200 for a Steersman, and 1500 for a Carpenter" (*BNL* 1722/8/6).

59. Masters seem to have expected servants, sailors, and slaves to run away occasionally and were often willing to overlook the disappearance of runaways without punishment, provided they returned in a timely fashion. Thus, when Arthur Savage announced the desertion of "*Charles Parris*, a tall black thin Visage fellow . . . *Peter Riggin*, a thick short black fellow" and their three companions, he also stipulated that for several of the men, if they "return to their Service on Board said Ship in 8 days they shall be freely Pardoned and their Wages fully run on as if not deserted" (*BNL* 1713/1/4). This distinction between runaways who sought only a short break from slavery or a change in working conditions and runaways who sought their freedom is better known in studies of Caribbean and South American slavery, where scholars have distinguished between *petit marronage* (in which the

enslaved left their masters for a brief period) and *grand marronage* (in which the enslaved sought their emancipation). For recent scholarship on the subject, see Marjoleine Kars, "Maroons and Marronage," *Oxford Bibliographies Online* www.oxfordbibliographies.com (accessed January 31, 2022).

60. John Ballantine, *Diary of John Ballantine*, transcribed by Joshua D. Bartlett, American Antiquarian Society, mss octavo vols. B.

61. See *BNL* 1704/5/15, *BNL* 1707/4/21, *BNL* 1707/12/1, *BNL* 1708/5/24, *BNL* 1708/5/31, *BNL* 1708/12/13, *BNL* 1710/3/5; and *CSP* 24.469–71, 24.520–21.

62. See *CSP* 24.175.

63. See Kris E. Lane, *Pillaging the Empire: Piracy in the Americas, 1500–1750*, 2nd edition (New York: Routledge, 2015), 181–97.

64. *The Acts and Resolves, Public and Private, of the Province of Massachusetts*, vol. 2 (Boston: 1874), 119.

65. Trevett called Williams by the name Pompey, and on August 6, 1724, he published an advertisement in the *Boston News-Letter* announcing that Pompey had escaped: "*Ran-away from his Master Capt. Richard Trevett of Marblehead, A Negro Man Named Pompey, about Twenty-two Years of Age, a Lusty, Tall Fellow: He had on when he went away, a striped home-spun Jacket, Cotton & Linen Shirt, dark coloured Kersey Breeches, grey yarn Stockings, round To'd Leather-heel Shoes, and Felt Hat. Note, He deserted his Masters Service in the Shallop Ann, at Plymouth. Whoever shall apprehend the said Run away, and him safely convey to his said Master at Marblehead, or to Mr.* Francis Miller *in* Boston, *near the Green Dragon, shall have Fifty Shillings Reward and all necessary Charges paid.*" Notably, Trevett used the naval language of desertion to characterize Pompey's offense, as well as the standard accusation of running away.

66. "John Williams and the Atlantic World, 1724," in *The Earliest African American Literatures: A Critical Reader*, 172.

67. "John Williams and the Atlantic World, 1724," 170, 168. Williams persuaded Hastie that "he was Deluded away" by Moffatt and "kept four Days in the Country hid" while Trevett's representatives searched the *Morehampton*, but Moffatt and his crew swore they had no knowledge of Williams's location on board the vessel until they discovered him two days after they left port (169).

68. "Titus in the Caribbean, 1714–1716," in *The Earliest African American Literatures: A Critical Reader*, 164–65.

69. Between 1714 and 1716, at least three different carpenters tried to escape by finding employment on a vessel: Daniel, Caesar (*BNL* 1715/5/9), and "An Indian Man Named *Nim*, he lately belonged to Mr. *James Moore*, he is about One and Twenty years of Age, and is a short broad shouldred Fellow, his Hair hath been lately cut off, he has a swelling on the back of his right hand, and can do something at the Carpenters Trade, he hath with him two new Shirts, a new Waste-Coat and Breeches of white course Linnen, and the same of Blew striped: a home-spun Coat, wears a Hat, Shoes and Stockings; it is believed he endeavours to get on board some Vessel" (*BNL* 1716/7/30).

70. See Peter Linebaugh and Marcus Rediker, *The Many-Headed Hydra: Sailors, Slaves, Commoners, and the Hidden History of the Revolutionary Atlantic* (Boston: Beacon Press, 2000), 162–67.

71. *CSP* 23.86.

72. Rhode Island Historical Society, mss box 191, p. 2.

73. Rhode Island Historical Society, mss 9001-s.

74. Rhode Island Historical Society, mss 554, in *Mason's Newport*.

75. Rhode Island Historical Society, mss 9001-s.

76. Ralph Waldo Emerson, *Emerson's Prose and Poetry*, ed. Joel Porte and Saundra Morris (New York: Norton, 2001), 59.

Chapter Three

1. *Boston News-Letter*, July 13, 1713. Subsequent in-text citations of this newspaper appear as "*BNL* 1713/7/13."

2. See Christopher Storrs, *The Spanish Resurgence, 1713–1748* (New Haven, CT: Yale University Press, 2016), 4–5.

3. Hugo Grotius, the seventeenth-century father of modern international jurisprudence, held up Roman custom as the relevant precedent in these cases: "In the law of the Romans it was a maxim, that nations, which had not entered into terms of amity, or into treaties with them were not to be considered enemies. But if any thing belonging to the Romans fell into their hands, it became theirs; or any citizen of Rome, taken by them, became a slave; and the Romans would treat any person belonging to that nation, in the same manner." Hugo Grotius, *The Rights of War and Peace*, trans. A. C. Campbell (Washington: 1901), 169; see Mary Nyquist, *Arbitrary Rule: Slavery, Tyranny, and the Power of Life and Death* (Chicago: University of Chicago Press, 2013), 218–24.

4. Thomas Hobbes, *Leviathan*, ed. C. B. Macpherson (New York: Penguin, 1968), 276, 273.

5. For a detailed account of the *Kalabalik*, as the skirmish at Bender has come to be known, see R. M. Hatton, *Charles XII of Sweden* (New York: Weybright and Talley, 1968), 350–64.

6. For a detailed account of this failed revolt see Daniel Szechi, *1715: The Jacobite Rebellion* (New Haven, CT: Yale University Press, 2006).

7. See *New-England Weekly Journal*, Aug. 23, 1737, and Sep. 13, 1737; *BNL* 1738/1/12.

8. John Ballantine, *Diary of John Ballantine*, transcribed by Joshua D. Bartlett, American Antiquarian Society, mss octavo vols. B.

9. See Table I.2, in the Introduction. The vast majority of entries in the "Foreign Relations" category of that table, which accounts for a majority of references to slavery in early colonial newspapers, describe the bondage of Christians captured by Muslims, either in open battle between the Ottoman and Holy Roman Empires or in naval conflicts between European nations and Morocco or the Ottoman regencies of Algiers, Tripoli, and Tunisia.

10. To wit: when two Armenian princes began attending Protestant services in Dresden, *The American Weekly Mercury* expressed hope "they will shortly renounce Paganism and embrace the Protestant Religion." Similarly, when the presumptive heir to the Ottoman Empire was sent abroad, correspondents expressed their expectation of new "Regulations throughout his Dominions for the advantage of the Christians in their Privileges and Commerce" (*BNL* 1722/5/14). The potential conversion of a prince to the Protestant faith was a cause for celebration because his conversion was understood as both an expansion of freedom and a victory in the apocalyptic conflict between Protestants and their adversaries.

See *The American Weekly Mercury*, July 23, 1724. Subsequent in-text citations to this newspaper appear as "*AWM* 1724/7/23."

11. Wylie Sypher, "The African Prince in London," *Journal of the History of Ideas*, 2.2 (1941), 237. Barry Weller notes that the royal status of an enslaved prince "constitutes a claim to attention. It anticipates and attempts to answer the indifference of the reader to a socially marginalized, outcast, and degraded subject or speaker." See Barry Weller, "The Royal Slave and the Prestige of Origins," *The Kenyon Review*, 14.3 (1992), 66.

12. Herman Bennett points out that the ecclesiastical and diplomatic roots of the slave trade have largely been ignored. He writes, "Church-state relations, though rarely attended to in standard histories of black studies, figure prominently in Europe's history with Africa and Africans." There has been, he continues, "little recognition of how sovereignty, political traditions, or politics on the African side shaped how Europeans interacted with Africans in order to lubricate the trading mechanism of the slave trade. When the focus turned to wars, diplomacy, or political economy (wealth in people), the scholarly perspective merely rendered them as facets of trade thereby overlooking the existence and importance of African sovereignty"—and sovereigns. See Herman L. Bennett, *African Kings and Black Slaves: Sovereignty and Dispossession in the Early Modern Atlantic* (Philadelphia: University of Pennsylvania Press, 2018), 12.

13. William Andrew Pettigrew, *Freedom's Debt: The Royal African Company and the Politics of the Atlantic Slave Trade, 1672–1752* (Chapel Hill: University of North Carolina Press, 2013), 193.

14. I stress the voluntary participation of these African princes in the slave trade to acknowledge their agency more fully and to prevent the romanticization of these narratives of enslaved royalty and not in any way to cast blame for the transatlantic slave trade onto African shoulders—which would only recycle early modern justifications for slavery. As James Campbell has observed, "Defenders of the [slave] trade, facing rising opposition in the late-eighteenth and early-nineteenth centuries, would place great stress on African complicity. Their arguments quickly assumed the quality of a catechism: slavery was endemic to Africa, a land wracked by perpetual war and unspeakable savagery; those imported to America were in fact the lucky ones, for their labor was light and they enjoyed the blessings of Christianity and 'civilization.' Even at the time, such rationalizations could not stand close scrutiny. While slavery certainly existed in Africa prior to the Europeans' arrival (as it did in virtually every other civilization known to history), the opening of the transatlantic trade radically transformed the institution's scale and character, sparking a vast new demand for slaves and precipitating centuries of war and political upheaval. European traders actively fomented conflict, most notably by offering guns and powder in exchange for slaves. The pistol that figured so prominently in Ayuba's story was not manufactured in Africa; it was one of the nearly twenty million guns exported to Africa by Europeans during the centuries of the slave trade. Great Britain alone, in a single decade at the peak of the traffic, exported more than one and a half million small arms to West Africa. In such circumstances, Africans who declined to trade with Europeans could quickly find themselves among the traded." See James T. Campbell, *Middle Passages: African American Journeys to Africa, 1787–2005* (New York: Penguin, 2006), 9.

15. John Towgood, "Memorial of September 1720 to the Court of Directors of the East India Company," British Library, IOR/E/1/11 ff. 326–328v.

16. The brothers were introduced to the SPCK as James Maquillan Mussoom and John Chaung Mussoom, and it is possible that these alternate middle names represent an African legacy otherwise erased, but I use the names given by Brent Sirota in his gloss of their lives for the sake of consistency. See Brent S. Sirota, *The Christian Monitors: The Church of England and the Age of Benevolence* (New Haven: Yale University Press, 2014), 240; for the SPCK record of their names, see *Minutes of the S.P.C.K. General Meetings*, vol. 9, p. 195, October 5, 1721. *S.P.C.K. Early 18th Century Archives*, microfilm edition, reel 3. Ira J. Taylor Library, Iliff School of Theology, Denver.

17. Towgood, "Memorial of September 1720 to the Court of Directors of the East India Company." White's ship is not listed in Kevin McDonald's index of slave ships visiting Madagascar during the seventeenth and eighteenth centuries. Marmaduke Penwell, who accompanied John Mastoon on his return to Delagoa, met with an anonymous ship captain who had known the Mastoons prior to their departure with White and who contradicted Towgood's claim to the EIC, "in telling them that he was a Prince & brought Elephant teeth and ambergreece from Delagoa, for it was false & that Coll. Towgood knew better, but that he had a mind to make a hand of them." See Kevin P. McDonald, *Pirates, Merchants, Settlers, and Slaves* (Berkeley: The University of California Press, 2015), 136; and Marmaduke Penwell to John Perceval, May 21, 1722, letter in the Egmont Papers, *Letterbook of John Perceval*, British Library Add MS 47029.

18. "Jamaica Appendix" in Part III of *Report of the Lords of the Committee of Council Appointed for the Consideration of All Matters Relating to Trade and Foreign Plantations . . . Concerning the Present State of the Trade to Africa, and Particularly the Trade in Slaves* (London: 1789), 8–11.

19. Towgood, "Memorial of September 1720 to the Court of Directors of the East India Company."

20. *Calendar of State Papers, Colonial Series, America and West Indies*, vol. 24, ed. Cecil Headlam (London: 1922), 210.

21. Towgood, "Memorial of September 1720 to the Court of Directors of the East India Company."

22. John Towgood, "Memorial of November 1720 to the Court of Directors of the East India Company," British Library, IOR/E/1/11 ff. 326–328v.

23. *Official Letters of the Secretary—Newman's Draft Correspondence*, vol. 11, pp. 18–19, August 18, 1721. *S.P.C.K. Early 18th Century Archives*, microfilm edition, reel 21. Ira J. Taylor Library, Iliff School of Theology, Denver.

24. Sirota exposes the superficiality of the SPCK concern for the princes' welfare in his account of the guidelines given to their spiritual mentor, Marmaduke Penwell, who was to "Appear at all times to delight in their company" and to "avoid at all costs the mysteries and subtleties of religion." This emphasis on appearances and avoidance of deep engagement with theological questions, together with detailed instructions on how Penwell was to assess the socioeconomic conditions of Delagoa, suggest that the princes were valued more as a point of entry into this foreign land, rather than as individual converts. See Sirota, *The Christian Monitors: The Church of England and the Age of Benevolence, 1680–1730*, 241.

25. *Official Letters of the Secretary—Newman's Draft Correspondence*, vol. 11, pp. 18–19, August 18, 1721. *S.P.C.K. Early 18th Century Archives*, microfilm edition, reel 21. Ira J. Taylor Library, Iliff School of Theology, Denver.

26. "The Royal African Company: Minutes of the Committee of Trade," *Documents Illustrative of the History of the Slave Trade*, ed. Elizabeth Donnan, vol. 2 (Washington D. C.: Carnegie Institution, 1931), 263.

27. Although Towgood verbally protested, to the RAC, that "the Expences he has been at on their account has been from no private view nor other motive but in pure compassion to their unhappy Circumstances, till he could find some means of getting them sent home to their own Country, which if the Company agrees to do, he expects no reimbursement from them of the charges he has hitherto been at," his written memorial clearly expresses an expectation of compensation—which he received. See "The Royal African Company: Minutes of the Committee of Trade," 262.

28. *Minutes of the S.P.C.K. General Meetings*, vol. 9, p. 195, October 5, 1721. *S.P.C.K. Early 18th Century Archives*, microfilm edition, reel 3. Ira J. Taylor Library, Iliff School of Theology, Denver.

29. Edward E. Andrews, *Native Apostles: Black and Indian Missionaries in the British Atlantic World* (Cambridge, MA: Harvard University Press, 2013), 80. In *A Proposal For the Better Supplying of Churches in our Foreign Plantations* (1725), George Berkeley proposed the establishment of a Bermudian college where these kidnapped youth would be educated until they could be sent to England for indoctrination. Thomas Bray, who helped establish the SPCK, opposed Berkeley's plan, but Sirota notes that John Perceval—who was the SPCK member most closely engaged with the Mastoons' Christian education—supported it. See Sirota, *The Christian Monitors: The Church of England and the Age of Benevolence*, 245.

30. *Minutes of the S.P.C.K. General Meetings*, vol. 9, p. 196, October 5, 1721. *S.P.C.K. Early 18th Century Archives*, microfilm edition, reel 3. Ira J. Taylor Library, Iliff School of Theology, Denver.

31. John W. Catron, *Embracing Protestantism: Black Identities in the Atlantic World* (Gainesville: University Press of Florida, 2016), 5.

32. Marmaduke Penwell to John Perceval, May 21, 1722, letter in the Egmont Papers, *Letterbook of John Perceval*, British Library Add MS 47029. One of the men who shunned James Mastoon was a Captain Hill, who had previously had custody of the brothers. Apparently the Mastoons struggled with Hill's oversight; when they were released from his care through the intervention of William Wake, the Archbishop of Canterbury, Newman wrote to Wake, "The African Princes are very thankfull for Your Graces Good Offices in getting them remov'd from Captn Hill to Captn Sherow." See Henry Newman to William Wake, September 9, 1721, in *Draft Letters*, vol. 11, p. 25, in *S.P.C.K. Early 18th Century Archives*, microfilm edition, reel 21, at the Ira J. Taylor Library, Iliff School of Theology, Denver.

33. Henry Newman to William Wake, May 10, 1722, in *Draft Letters*, vol. 12, p. 16, in *S.P.C.K. Early 18th Century Archives*, microfilm edition, reel 22, at the Ira J. Taylor Library, Iliff School of Theology, Denver.

34. Marmaduke Penwell to John Perceval, May 21, 1722, letter in the Egmont Papers, *Letterbook of John Perceval*, British Library Add MS 47029.

35. Terri L. Snyder, *The Power to Die: Slavery and Suicide in British North America* (Chicago: The University of Chicago Press, 2015), 16.

36. See W. K. Lowther Clarke, *A History of the S.P.C.K.* (London: S.P.C.K., 1959), 97–98.

37. Marmaduke Penwell to John Perceval, November 30, 1722, letter in the Egmont Papers, *Letterbook of John Perceval*, British Library Add MS 47029.

38. Grant writes that Oglethorpe "redeemed Job either 'out of Tenderness, or thinking he might be usefull.'" Grant, *The Fortunate Slave: An Illustration of African Slavery in the Eighteenth Century*, 159.

39. Diallo's story was fleshed out in great detail by Grant, in 1968, but has rarely been discussed since, except in discussions of William Hoare's 1733 portrait of him. See Douglas Grant, *The Fortunate Slave: An Illustration of African Slavery in the Early Eighteenth Century* (New York: Oxford University Press, 1968); and Marcia Pointon, "Slavery and the Possibilities of Portraiture," in *Slave Portraiture in the Atlantic World*, ed. Angela Rosenthal and Agnes Lugo-Ortiz (New York: Cambridge University Press, 2013), 41–70.

40. For example, Anna Mae Duane acknowledges that Venture's "decision to purchase a slave—and his surprise and hurt when the man runs away to gain his freedom—offers one of the more problematic moments in the text," but she largely shies away from a discussion of what his participation in the slave trade means. Duane is not unique; Vincent Carretta and others mention his brief experiment in slaveholding, only to illustrate that Venture "appears to see slavery as bad for individuals, especially himself and members of his family, without attacking the system of slavery directly." See Anna Mae Duane, "Keeping His Work: Money, Love, and Privacy in the Narrative of Venture Smith," and Vincent Carretta, "Venture Smith, One of a Kind," in *Venture Smith and the Business of Slavery and Freedom*, ed. James Brewer Stewart (Amherst: University of Massachusetts Press, 2010), 198, 176.

41. Campbell, *Middle Passages: African American Journeys to Africa, 1787–2005*, 2.

42. Thomas Bluett, *Some Memoirs of the Life of Job, the Son of Solomon the High Priest of Boonda in Africa* (London: 1734), 16.

43. Bluett, *Some Memoirs*, 13.

44. Bluett, *Some Memoirs*, 17. The number of cows is given in Grant, *The Fortunate Slave: An Illustration of African Slavery in the Early Eighteenth Century*, 67.

45. Bluett, *Some Memoirs*, 17–18.

46. Grant, *The Fortunate Slave: An Illustration of African Slavery in the Early Eighteenth Century*, 69.

47. Thanks to Diallo's advocacy and the Duke of Montagu's generosity, Yoai would also be redeemed. After taking leave of Diallo, Bluett returned to Maryland and purchased his freedom, sending him on to England and, eventually, Africa. See Grant, *The Fortunate Slave: An Illustration of African Slavery in the Eighteenth Century*, 195–96.

48. James Campbell describes the conditions Diallo would have endured on the Middle Passage: "If his experience was a typical one, he and Yoai would first have had the initials RAC branded onto their left shoulders, marking them as property of the Royal Africa Company, the chartered corporation that enjoyed a monopoly on the British slave trade. They would then have been chained together at wrist and ankle and loaded into a low compartment, perhaps three feet high, crammed with hundreds of other men. (Women and children were generally housed in separate compartments from men.) Aside from periods of enforced exercise on deck, they would have spent the next six to eight weeks in the hold, rank with the smell of seasickness and the overflowing 'necessary tubs,' subsisting on rice and thin gruel, unappetizing fare but adequate to sustain life. Slave-ship captains well appreciated the value of their involuntary passengers and made every effort to keep them alive. They installed netting along the rails to prevent captives from hurling themselves overboard. Those who refused to eat were force-fed, often using a *speculum oris*, a mechanical

device invented for patients with lockjaw but quickly adapted for use on slave ships. Despite such precautions, somewhere between 10 and 20 percent of the captives on a typical voyage perished before reaching the Americas. If a ship were stricken with disease—smallpox, cholera, amoebic dysentery ('bloody flux,' in the parlance of the time)—mortality was much higher." See James T. Campbell, *Middle Passages: African American Journeys to Africa, 1787–2005* (New York: Penguin, 2006), 3–4.

49. Bluett, *Some Memoirs*, 19.

50. Grant, *The Fortunate Slave: An Illustration of African Slavery in the Eighteenth Century*, 83.

51. Bluett, *Some Memoirs*, 21–22.

52. Bluett, *Some Memoirs*, 22.

53. Grant, *The Fortunate Slave: An Illustration of African Slavery in the Eighteenth Century*, 85.

54. The rule and social standing of a prince was supposedly a matter of immutable and divine will transcending the temporary circumstance of his enslavement. Thus, Philip V of Spain explained his claim to the throne by declaring, "I succeeded to the Possession of the whole Monarchy, by virtue of the undeniable Rights which God was pleas'd to transmit into my Royal Veins," notwithstanding English & Dutch protest (*BNL* 1710/3/19). Similarly, English commentators noted that "the Bastards of our Kings are Princes by their Birth, and have been always placed above the Dukes and Peers, whose Dignity, how great soever it has been render'd by the favour of our Monarchs, is limited within some Bounds, and cannot raise a Gentleman to the degree of a Prince, and give him Rank above the Natural Children of our Kings" (*BNL* 1718/4/21). Thus, an enslaved prince or an enslaved member of the ruling class would have been identified first and foremost as an individual of noble birth, whatever their social circumstances; Diallo and other enslaved princes were nobles who happened to be enslaved, rather than slaves who happened to be noble.

55. Grant, *The Fortunate Slave: An Illustration of African Slavery in the Eighteenth Century*, 101.

56. Bluett, *Some Memoirs*, 28, 31.

57. Bluett, *Some Memoirs*, 34.

58. Francis Moore, *Travels into the Inland Parts of Africa* (London: 1738), 206–7.

59. Moore, *Travels into the Inland Parts of Africa*, 208.

60. Diallo also later claimed two slaves from the RAC in exchange for the watch he received from the monarch. See Grant, *The Fortunate Slave: An Illustration of African Slavery in the Eighteenth Century*, 198.

61. Grant, *The Fortunate Slave: An Illustration of African Slavery in the Eighteenth Century*, 108.

62. Describing a story related by Bluett, of Diallo fighting off a band of thieves while leading fifteen enslaved persons through foreign lands, Grant observes that Bluett and other Englishmen likely identified with Diallo more after hearing this account because "He, too, like themselves was one of the masters." See *The Fortunate Slave: An Illustration of African Slavery in the Eighteenth Century*, 95.

63. James Olney, "'I Was Born': Slave Narratives, Their Status as Autobiography and as Literature," in *The Slave's Narrative*, ed. Charles T. Davis and Henry Louis Gates Jr. (New York: Oxford University Press, 1985), 154.

64. Sessarakoo is identified only as Cupid in *The Royal African*, but his name—if it had been given—would have well-illustrated the connection between slavery and foreign policy. Sessarakoo was the son of Corrantee and "Eukobah (also Ekua), the daughter of Ansah Sessarakoo (Ansa Sasraku), king of Aquamboo (Akwamu), and niece of the king of Akron." His marriage to Eukobah allowed Corrantee privileged access to the interior slave trade controlled by the kings of Aquamboo, and William's name identified the prince as a living symbol of Corrantee's role as a powerbroker in the world of human trafficking. See Randy J. Sparks, *Where the Negroes Are Masters: An African Port in the Era of the Early Slave Trade* (Cambridge, MA: Harvard University Press, 2014), 38.

65. Ryan Hanley, "The Royal Slave: Nobility, Diplomacy and the 'African Prince' in Britain, 1748–1752," *Itinerario* 39.2 (2015): 335.

66. *The Royal African: or, Memoirs of the Young Prince of Annamaboe* (London: 1749), i–ii.

67. Randy Sparks has identified the slaver who betrayed Sessarakoo as David Crichton, but Hanley argues persuasively that it was Dwyer and not Crichton. See Hanley, "The Royal Slave: Nobility, Diplomacy and the 'African Prince' in Britain, 1748–1752," 332.

68. *The Royal African*, iii–iv. Ironically, Sessarakoo's "royal" status was only attained in the weeks before or after he was kidnapped. Corantee was a trader with significant political clout in the 1730s and 1740s, but Rebecca Shumway suggests that he only rose to the position of "omanhen—a title given to the highest political authority in a town or region—of Anomabo in, or just prior to, the year 1747." See Rebecca Shumway, *The Fante and the Transatlantic Slave Trade* (Rochester, NY: University of Rochester Press, 2011), 76.

69. Pettigrew, *Freedom's Debt: The Royal African Company and the Politics of the Atlantic Slave Trade, 1672–1752*, 180.

70. *The Royal African*, vii–viii.

71. *The Royal African*, 13–4

72. *The Royal African*, 16, 19; Sparks, *Where the Negroes Are Masters: An African Port in the Era of the Early Slave Trade*, 43.

73. As Randy Sparks notes, Corrantee himself was educated by the English during a period he spent in their power, possibly as a hostage guaranteeing his father's cooperation with English traders. Thus, the proposal to educate Corrantee's sons represented an intergenerational effort on the part of European traders to sway black African leaders, by indoctrination and intimidation as well as generosity. For their part, black African traders and rulers "clearly saw the advantage of having their own eyes and ears inside the European forts where they might remain for long periods." See Sparks, *Where the Negroes Are Masters: An African Port in the Era of the Early Slave Trade*, 36–37.

74. *The Royal African*, 26, 28–29, 40.

75. Corrantee was understandably upset by Sessarakoo's sale, but he had previously kidnapped and sold others into slavery, so he likely accepted Dwyer's betrayal as a lamentable but ethical strong-arm tactic. Sparks notes that "kidnapping was widespread at Annamaboe. One trader reported that he often bought enslaved persons who were brought on board his ship during the night" and that "these slaves often were not payed for until the ship was ready to sail in case their sale was disputed." See Sparks, *Where the Negroes Are Masters: An African Port in the Era of the Early Slave Trade*, 41.

76. *The Royal African*, 43–44.

77. *The Royal African*, 43, 18.

78. *The Royal African*, 48; J. Spencer Ewary, "Colonel Edward Hamilton of the Honourable East India Company's Service," *Blackwood's Magazine* 208.1262 (1920): 773–74. As Laura Brown notes, this shift in costume also served an important function in translating the social status of black African visitors into signs legible to English observers; they were "dressed in carefully designed attire meant to signify their nobility, both of status and of nature." See Laura Brown, *Fables of Modernity: Literature and Culture in the English Eighteenth Century* (Ithaca, NY: Cornell University Press, 2001), 184.

79. *The Royal African*, 46.

80. Philip D. Curtin, ed., *Africa Remembered: Narratives by West Africans from the Era of the Slave Trade* (Madison: University of Wisconsin Press, 1967), 4–5.

81. *The Gentleman's Magazine* 29 (1759): 240.

82. See Randy J. Sparks, *The Two Princes of Calabar* (Cambridge: Harvard University Press, 2004), 130.

83. Black African princes who were not enslaved were also celebrated, inasmuch as they identified as Protestant allies: in 1791 John Frederick Naimbanna, a son of the king of Robanna in Sierra Leone, arrived in England to be educated as a Protestant. Two other sons were sent to Turkey and to Portugal for Muslim and Roman Catholic educations, suggesting the calculated and cynical nature of these diplomatic educations; even if princes sincerely converted to a new faith (and by all accounts Naimbanna's belief in Christian doctrine was genuine), the fathers who sent them for indoctrination likely did so for mercenary motives. In April 1793, word arrived in England that Naimbanna's father had died; he left England for Robanna in May and died on July 18, inspiring the publication of an undated literary memorial to his life, *The Black Prince*.

84. English sympathy for enslaved black African princes is evident in an account of Sessarakoo's attendance at a performance of Thomas Southerne's stage adaptation of *Oronooko*. Correspondents reported that the drama "strongly affected them with that generous grief which pure nature always feels, and which art had not yet taught them to suppress; the young prince was so far overcome, that he was obliged to retire at the end of the fourth act. His companion remained, but wept the whole time; a circumstance which affected the audience yet more than the play, and doubled the tears which were shed for *Oroonoko* and *Imoinda*." See *The Gentleman's Magazine* 19 (1749): 90.

85. Joseph Warton, "Ode to Liberty," in Charles Dexter Cleveland, ed., *English Literature of the Nineteenth Century* (New York: 1871), 19.

86. As quoted in James Boswell, *Life of Johnson* (London: Oxford University Press, 1953), 877–78.

87. Weller, "The Royal Slave and the Prestige of Origins," 65.

88. Sparks, *The Two Princes of Calabar*, 131.

89. Hanley, "The Royal Slave: Nobility, Diplomacy and the 'African Prince' in Britain, 1748–1752," 339.

Chapter Four

1. Ryan Hanley, "The Royal Slave: Nobility, Diplomacy and the 'African Prince' in Britain, 1748–1752," *Itinerario* 39.2 (2015), 331.

2. Gerald Horne details the foreign affiliations and imperial consciousness of enslaved black Africans in British North America living a generation after Hammon, in *The Counter-Revolution of 1776: Slave Resistance and the Origins of the United States of America* (New York: New York University Press, 2014), especially 63–87.

3. Andy Doolen and William Moses are the only scholars to treat Horsmanden's *Journal* as a literary text in the last thirty years. See William J. Moses, "Sex, Salem, and Slave Trials: Ritual Drama and Ceremony of Innocence," *The Black Columbiad: Defining Moments in African American Literature and Culture*, ed. Werner Sollors and Maria Diedrich (Cambridge: Harvard University Press, 1994), 64–76; and Andy Doolen, "Reading and Writing Terror: The New York Conspiracy Trials of 1741," *American Literary History* 16.3 (2004): 377–406.

4. Doolen casts doubt on the historicity of Horsmanden's *Journal*, but after comparing Horsmanden's *Journal* with manuscript minutes of the confessions and trials made by Governor George Clarke, Jill Lepore concluded that Clarke's notes largely "vindicate Horsmanden, whose *Journal* turns out to be exactly what he said it was: a lightly edited collection of rather conventional legal documents, or, as Clarke himself put it, 'very little more than a Copy of the Court Entries.' Because Horsmanden shaped the proceedings *as they were happening*, he had little need to doctor the written record. But he did doctor it some, and that doctoring matters." Jill Lepore, *New York Burning: Liberty, Slavery, and Conspiracy in Eighteenth-Century Manhattan* (New York: Knopf, 2005), 95–96.

5. Lepore, *New York Burning: Liberty, Slavery, and Conspiracy in Eighteenth-Century Manhattan*, 11.

6. Even texts untouched by a white editorial hand were written with an awareness of white readers and subject to self-censorship. For example, Geneva Cobb Moore explains that Phillis Wheatley Peters "engages in a double-voiced discourse, which underscores the fragile nature of her existence in colonial Boston," not because she had to accommodate white editors but because she had to write for white readers. See Geneva Cobb Moore, *Maternal Metaphors of Power in African American Women's Literature: From Phillis Wheatley to Toni Morrison* (Columbia: University of South Carolina Press, 2017), 21.

7. Daniel Horsmanden, *Journal of the Proceedings* (New York: 1744), 49, 32.

8. Horsmanden, *Journal of the Proceedings*, 64–65, 69.

9. Horsmanden, *Journal of the Proceedings*, 8.

10. On the British acquisition of the *assiento* and its role in provoking hostilities between Britain and Spain in the late 1730s, see James A. Rawley and Stephen D. Behrendt, *The Transatlantic Slave Trade: A History*, rev. ed. (Lincoln, NE: University of Nebraska Press, 2005), 59–62.

11. Doolen, "Reading and Writing Terror: The New York Conspiracy Trials of 1741," 380.

12. Vincent Carretta first republished Briton Hammon's *Narrative* in *Unchained Voices* (Kentucky UP, 1996), an anthology of black authors in the eighteenth-century English-speaking world, and his introduction suggests that Hammon was a freeman. On the question of Hammon's legal status, see Robert Desrochers Jr., "'Surprizing Deliverance'?: Slavery and Freedom, Language and Identity in the *Narrative* of Briton Hammon, 'A Negro Man,'" in *Genius in Bondage: Literature of the Early Black Atlantic*, ed. Vincent Caretta and Philip Gould (Lexington, KY: University Press of Kentucky, 2001), 153–74.

13. Other texts sometimes identified as the first slave narrative include Bluett's 1734 biography of Ayuba Suleiman Diallo discussed in chapter 3 and a 1709 transcription published

as "A SPEECH made by a BLACK of Guardaloupe, at the Funeral of a Fellow Negro," in *Caribbeana: An Anthology of English Literature of the West Indies, 1657–1777*, ed. Thomas W. Krise (Chicago: University of Chicago Press, 1999), 93–100.

14. As Julie Sievers demonstrates, editorial interference also shaped the narratives of socially disadvantaged white authors: "Though experience could authorize an unusually broad range of individuals, many of them unlettered, of low social status, or female, to tell their stories, this authority did not necessarily lend them control over the form or even the words their narratives would eventually take as recorded texts." Regarding the similarities between the texts of Brown and Hammon, which were produced by two different printers, Sekora writes, "To the trained eye, a connection of some sort between the two firms beyond the conventions of the day could be deduced from the title pages of Brown's and Hammon's narratives. Using essentially the same layout and typographical style, they give greatest emphasis to the word *Narrative* and to the name of their respective subjects. Both undergo uncommon sufferings, while Brown's deliverance is 'remarkable' and Hammon's is 'surprising.' Brown is recorded as the one '*Who returned to his Father's House the Beginning of Jan. 1760, after having been absent three Years and about eight Months.*' Although Hammon's delayed return is not given the accent of italics, it does receive certain prominence, for it was he 'who returned to *Boston*, after having been absent almost thirteen years.' Hammon, like Brown, could represent the many young men pulled from their homes who were returning in 1760. Under the heading of 'CONTAINING,' each title page provides a précis of events, with stress upon the sensational, especially torture and murder. At work here is apparently a common house style, since far more resemblance exists between Fowle and Draper and Green and Russell than between either and any other Boston printers." See Julie Sievers, "Drowned Pens and Shaking Hands: Sea Providence Narratives in Seventeenth-Century New England," *The William and Mary Quarterly* 63.4 (2006): 748; and John Sekora, "Briton Hammon, the Indian Captivity Narrative, and the African American Slave Narrative," in *Where Brer Rabbit Meets Coyote: African-Native American Literature*, ed. Jonathan Brennan (Urbana, IL: University of Illinois Press, 2003), 150–51. Frances S. Foster first noticed the similarities between Hammon's *Narrative* and colonial captivity narratives; see Frances S. Foster, "Briton Hammon's *Narrative*: Some Insights into Beginnings," *CLA Journal* 221.2 (Dec. 1977): 179–86.

15. Rafia Zafar, "Capturing the Captivity: African Americans among the Puritans," *MELUS* 17.2 (1991–1992), 27.

16. Vincent Carretta, "Olaudah Equiano or Gustavus Vassa? New Light on an Eighteenth-century Question of Identity," *Slavery & Abolition* 20.3 (Dec. 1999): 102. Responses to the records unearthed by Carretta have ranged from attacks on the reliability of the records themselves to documentation of the ways in which Equiano's account captures the essence and values of Igbo culture and considerations of the relationship between nativity and human rights. Paul Lovejoy notes that Mary Guerin, Equiano's godmother, may have provided the information recorded on the baptismal record, conjecturing that "the Guerins and Pascal [Equiano's owner at the time] wanted people to think that Vassa was creole born, and not a native African, because he had mastered English so well by then or for other reasons relating to perceived higher status for creoles." More recently, a coalition of African scholars have collectively argued that Equiano knew far more about Igbo culture than someone born in South Carolina could reasonably have learned in absentia from Africa;

that the facial features preserved in portraits of Equiano resemble those of living Igbo with the surname Ekweanuo—potential relatives; and that the oral history of the Dimori kindred in Isseke preserves the memory of a small boy named Olaude who was kidnapped. Carretta's claims have provoked charges of "ethnic profiling" from Catherine Acholonu; he has responded by calling Acholonu's scholarship "flawed" and Lovejoy's arguments "unconvincing." While both sides in the debate have emphasized the importance of establishing the historicity of Equiano's *Narrative*, the question of whether or not Equiano was born in Africa seems, to me, as to James Sweet, one of Carretta's challengers, less important than the question of why he and Hammon might have misrepresented their experiences. Rather than focusing exclusively on historicity, Sweet suggests that "[t]he more fruitful historical question is, Why was Equiano characterized as being from 'Carolina' [or, I would add, Africa] at particular moments and times?" See Paul E. Lovejoy, "Autobiography and Memory: Gustavus Vassa, alias Olaudah Equiano, the African," *Slavery and Abolition* 27.3 (Dec. 2006): 336; Acholonu, "The Igbo Roots of Olaudah Equiano," 61; Vincent Carretta, "Response to Paul Lovejoy's 'Autobiography and Memory: Gustavus Vassa, alias Olaudah Equiano, the African,'" *Slavery and Abolition* 28.1 (Apr. 2007): 119, 115; James H. Sweet, "Mistaken Identities? Olaudah Equiano, Domingos Álvares, and the Methodological Challenges of Studying the African Diaspora," *The American Historical Review* 114.2 (2009): 301; and Yael Ben-Zvi, "Equiano's Nativity: Negative Birthright, Indigenous Ethic, and Universal Human Rights," *Early American Literature* 48.2 (2013): 399–423. In the April 2007 issue of *Slavery and Abolition*, Carretta responded to Lovejoy, and then Lovejoy answered Carretta's counterargument. Their essays can be found in that issue on pages 115–19 and 121–25, respectively. For an extension of the debate between Sweet and Carretta, see "Communications," *The American Historical Review* 114.3 (2009): 886–88. Chima Korieh's edited collection of essays, *Olaudah Equiano and the Igbo World: History, Society, and Atlantic Diaspora Connections*, brings together seventeen articles examining Equiano's *Narrative* in conjunction with Igbo culture in the eighteenth century and the diaspora. Two scholars and three essays in particular address Carretta's claims: Catherine Obianuju Acholonu, "The Igbo Roots of Olaudah Equiano" (49–66); Dorothy Chinwe Ukaegbu, "Igbo Sense of Place and Identity in Olaudah Equiano's *The Interesting Narrative*" (67–92); and Ukaegbu, "Status in Eighteenth-Century Igboland: Perspectives from Olaudah Equiano's *The Interesting Narrative*" (93–116).

17. In underscoring the eighteenth-century interest in African geography and society, Roxann Wheeler implicitly suggests that the financial success of Equiano's work may have been connected to his ability to provide an authoritative account of African life. Angelo Costanzo has challenged this reconstruction of the incentives motivating Equiano and concludes that Equiano's interests—given his identity as a Christian, his hopes that the book's authenticity would boost sales, and his fears that misrepresenting his life might damage the abolitionist cause—would have prohibited him from placing "in jeopardy all the good he was trying to accomplish." Costanzo seems to presuppose that any deception on Equiano's part would have been uncovered immediately, but Brycchan Carey—a party I believe both sides would describe as a neutral mediator of this debate—acknowledges that "it is undeniable that Equiano would have known that it would be very difficult for his readers to check the truth, or otherwise, of his account." See Roxann Wheeler, "Limited Visions of Africa: Geographies of Savagery and Civility in Early Eighteenth-centure Narratives," in

Writes of Passage, ed. James Duncan and Derek Gregory (New York: Routledge, 1999), 14–48; Angelo Costanzo, "'Neither a Saint, a Hero, nor a Tyrant,'" *1650–1850* 17 (2010): 279; and Brycchan Carey, "Olaudah Equiano: African or American?" *1650–1850: Ideas, Aesthetics, and Inquiries in the Early Modern Era* 17 (2010): 243.

18. Randy J. Sparks, *Africans in the Old South: Mapping Exceptional Lives across the Atlantic World* (Cambridge, MA: Harvard University Press, 2016), 7.

19. Daniel Vollaro, "Sixty Indians and Twenty Canoes: Briton Hammon's Unreliable Witness to History," *Native South* 2.1 (2009): 141–42. Carretta first published his thesis regarding Equiano's American origins in "Olaudah Equiano or Gustavus Vassa? New Light on an Eighteenth-century Question of Identity." He elaborates on the evidence and its implications in his biography of Equiano: Vincent Carretta, *Equiano, the African: Biography of a Self-Made Man* (Athens: University of Georgia Press, 2005).

20. Jeffrey Gagnon, "'They Us'd Me Pretty Well': Briton Hammon and Cross-Cultural Alliances in the Maritime Borderlands of the Florida Coast," in *Journeys of the Slave Narrative in the Early Americas*, ed. Nicole N. Aljoe and Ian Finseth (Charlottesville: University of Virginia Press, 2014), 75.

21. Briton Hammon, *Narrative of the Uncommon Sufferings and Surprizing Deliverance of Briton Hammon, A Negro Man*, in *Unchained Voices*, ed. Vincent Carretta (Lexington, KY: University Press of Kentucky, 1996), 20. Subsequent in-text citations to this text appear as "N 20."

22. As Hayden White notes—repeatedly—history or reportorial travel and autobiographical writing, in the eighteenth century, "was still a literary enterprise" which involved the conscious imposition of literary structures (story, plot, and argument) onto the events being reported. See Hayden White, *The Fiction of Narrative: Essays on History, Literature, and Theory, 1957–2007*, ed. Robert Doran (Baltimore, MD: The Johns Hopkins University Press, 2010), 189, 112–25. See also Barbara J. Shapiro, *A Culture of Fact: England, 1550–1720* (Cornell, NY: Cornell University Press, 2000), 63–85. For the most recent extension of the White debate over the extent to which history is literature and vice versa, see *Tropes for the Past: Hayden White and the History/Literature Debate*, ed. Kuisma Korhonen (New York: Rodopi, 2006); and *Re-Figuring Hayden White*, ed. Frank Ankersmit, Ewa Domanska, and Hans Kellner (Stanford, CA: Stanford University Press, 2009).

23. We cannot know how old Hammon was when he sailed; his self-possession, apparent independence, and participation in hard labor suggest a grown man, but Desrochers Jr. has advanced the possibility that he was born in 1740, in which case Hammon would have embarked on this adventure as a very young boy indeed. Desrochers Jr. speculatively links Hammon to a black African man named Briton Nichols but does not mention that Nichols is only forty years old in 1780, when he enlisted in the Revolutionary Army. It seems unlikely to me that Hammon and Nichols are the same person, and I have treated his *Narrative* as a recollection of adult experience. For Nichols's age, see E. Victor Bigelow, *A Narrative History of the Town of Cohasset, Massachusetts* (Boston: Samuel Usher, 1898), 308.

24. *New-York Weekly Journal*, Mar. 20, 1748.

25. *New-York Gazette, or Weekly Post-Boy*, Apr. 4, 1748. Another account mentions that the slaves of French planters in the vicinity of Port Louis deserted their plantations hoping to be received into the British navy but that Knowles "return'd them to their masters . . . determin'd inviolably, and in the most sacred manner, to preserve the rights and properties

of the [French] inhabitants of Hispaniola." Like Hammon and the witnesses in Horsmanden's *Journal of the Proceedings*, these enslaved black Africans saw international conflicts as opportunities to secure their own freedom. See *The Pennsylvania Gazette*, Apr. 21, 1748.

26. *Boston Evening-Post*, Mar. 7, 1748.

27. Sievers notes that this device—rescue at sea by a captain who is revealed to be an old acquaintance—was incorporated by editors of seventeenth-century sea providence narratives; this moment, then, might plausibly represent an editorial embellishment of Hammon's *Narrative*. See Sievers, "Drowned Pens and Shaking Hands: Sea Providence Narratives in Seventeenth-Century New England," 762.

28. On the logwood industry, see Kevin P. McDonald, *Pirates, Merchants, Settlers, and Slaves* (Berkeley: University of California Press, 2015), 22–24.

29. *Pennsylvania Gazette*, Apr. 21, 1748. In November 1750, a ship laden with 400 tons of logwood anchored off the coast of Charleston, South Carolina. See *New-York Gazette*, Dec. 17, 1750.

30. Vollaro, "Sixty Indians and Twenty Canoes: Briton Hammon's Unreliable Witness to History," 139. Further complicating Hammon's report is the only near-contemporary account of piracy by Florida Indians. During the summer months of 1747, one Captain Taylor captured a sloop loaded with pitch and tar drifting in the Atlantic, with "no Body on board but two Florida Indians," who Taylor assumed "had murdered the People that belonged to her." If Taylor is correct and these two natives successfully captured a merchant ship off Florida waters by dispatching its crew, his account would seem to corroborate Vollaro's description of a depleted native population, while also confirming that even reduced communities of Florida Indians still engaged in coastal piracy. See *The Boston Weekly Post-Boy*, Sep. 14, 1747.

31. Vollaro, "Sixty Indians and Twenty Canoes: Briton Hammon's Unreliable Witness to History," 140–41.

32. *New-York Gazette*, Feb. 8, 1748; *Boston Evening-Post*, July 25, 1748.

33. *New-York Gazette*, Dec. 18, 1752, and Feb. 3, 1752; *Pennsylvania Gazette*, Apr. 26, 1753; Vollaro, "Sixty Indians and Twenty Canoes: Briton Hammon's Unreliable Witness to History," 136.

34. Vollaro, "Sixty Indians and Twenty Canoes: Briton Hammon's Unreliable Witness to History," 143.

35. *Pennsylvania Gazette*, Apr. 26, 1753; *The New-York Gazette*, Feb. 3, 1752.

36. Gagnon, "'They Us'd Me Pretty Well': Briton Hammon and Cross-Cultural Alliances in the Maritime Borderlands of the Florida Coast," 76.

37. *Boston Evening-Post*, Nov. 6, 1738. This account was published in four different Boston newspapers, so Hammon almost certainly heard about this particular voyage and the crew's "fear of the Indians of the Shore." On the Spanish/Indian defense of Fort Augustine, see *Pennsylvania Gazette*, May 15, 1740, and Apr. 2, 1741.

38. *New-York Gazette*, July 22, 1751; *General Evening Post*, Sep. 10, 1748. For another instance in which black sailors were detained by the Spanish in Havana after their white masters and shipmates had been released, see *Pennsylvania Gazette*, Mar. 20, 1753.

39. Spain, at this point, had just come under the rule of Carlos III, who was trying to maintain neutrality while brokering a peace between France and Britain; during the last year of his rule and until his death in August 1759, Ferdinand VI had become senile, so the

Spanish had largely withdrawn from international affairs. Carlos III and the Spanish would eventually enter the war on the side of France in 1762, but colonial interest in Spain likely hit its nadir in 1759–60. See Daniel Baugh, *The Global Seven Years War, 1754–1763* (Edinburgh: Pearson, 2011), 453–510.

40. All three of the encounters with Florida Indians described earlier end with the British castaways boarding a Spanish vessel. See *New-York Gazette*, Dec. 18, 1752, and Feb. 3, 1752; and *Pennsylvania Gazette*, Apr. 26, 1753.

41. On the frequent escapes by Cuban slaves during the 1740s, see Gabino la Rosa Corzo, *Runaway Slave Settlements in Cuba: Resistance and Repression*, trans. Mary Todd (Chapel Hill: University of North Carolina Press, 2003). Jane Landers describes Havana's bourgeois black community in *Atlantic Creoles in the Age of Revolution* (Cambridge, MA: Harvard University Press, 2010), 138–74.

42. *Boston Gazette*, Jan. 3, 1749. The Battle of Havana took place on October 12, 1748, which makes this letter—dated October 6, 1748—potentially suspect. Presumably, this eyewitness was released in a prisoner exchange such as the one recounted in *New-York Weekly Journal*, July 18, 1748.

43. *Public Advertiser*, Dec. 22, 1752.

44. *Boston Weekly Post-Boy*, May 18, 1752.

45. *London Evening Post*, May 14, 1751.

46. *Pennsylvania Gazette*, Mar. 20, 1753; *Boston Evening-Post*, Oct. 10, 1757.

47. *Public Advertiser*, May 26, 1753. Britt's full name is given in *Boston Weekly News-Letter*, Sep. 5, 1751. On Havana's population in 1750, see Andrea Colantonio and Robert B. Potter, *Urban Tourism and Development in the Socialist State: Havana During the 'Special Period'* (Burlington, VT: Ashgate, 2006), 89.

48. *London Evening Post*, May 14, 1751.

49. *New-York Gazette*, Dec. 25, 1752; emphasis added.

50. For accounts of "Negroes" escaping from Havana in canoes, see *Pennsylvania Gazette*, Mar. 13, 1753; and *Boston Weekly Post-Boy*, May 27, 1754.

51. PRO ADM 36/6585; 51/904. Marsh's *Shoreham* is the only vessel to which Hammon can possibly allude; according to Rif Winfield's comprehensive survey of naval records, only one Captain Marsh commanded a twenty-gun ship during the 1750s. See Rif Winfield, *British Warships in the Age of Sail, 1714–1792: Design, Construction, Careers and Fates* (St. Paul, MN: MBI Publishing, 2007), 224–72.

52. *Public Advertiser*, July 2, 1756. Legge was later fined fifty pounds and did not regain the command of a ship until 1758. Marsh might reasonably have construed the language in article 18 of the *Articles of War*, passed by Parliament in 1749, as threatening him with a fine if he harbored Hammon onboard the *Shoreham*, and Hammon was, indeed, the property of Don Francisco (and not the victim of shipwreck he claimed to be). Receiving illegal goods (an escaped slave) potentially would have left Marsh, like Legge, vulnerable to court-martial and fine, as explained in section XXIV of the *Articles*. The full text of the *Articles* can be found in Markus Eder, *Crime and Punishment in the Royal Navy of the Seven Years' War, 1755–1763* (Burlington, VT: Ashgate, 2004), 158–73. For a discussion of court-martial procedures, including the fining of commissioned officers such as Legge or Marsh, see pages 80–106 in Eder.

53. My translations of Pedro Agustín Morell de Santa Cruz, *La Visita Ecclesiastica*, ed. César García del Pino (Havana: Editorial de Ciencias Sociales, 1985), 33, 35. An

itinerary for the whole journey can be found on pages xxviii–xxix of del Pino's introduction.

54. Richard Gott notes that Morell "was so impressed by the attachment of the blacks to their African *cabildos* that he granted them the Church's official recognition in 1755, hoping in this way to facilitate and speed up their religious instruction." The *cabildos* were social organizations of free and enslaved Afro-Cubans formed along tribal or ethnic lines. Richard Gott, *Cuba: A New History* (New Haven, CT: Yale University Press, 2004), 47; see also Herbert S. Klein, "Anglicanism, Catholicism and the Negro Slave," *Comparative Studies in Society and History* 8.3 (1966): 307–8. It should also be noted that Hammon was not the only British subject who found the Cuban countryside more pleasant than Havana. Captain Charles Bardin, marooned on the west end of Cuba, described a drastic contrast in the treatment he received in the city and countryside: "the poor Country Inhabitants treated him with great Humanity and Kindness in this long and painful Journey; but, as he approached the Capital of the Island, he found Charity greatly abating, and by the Time he reached it, quite exhausted; so that he became most miserable where he expected most Relief and Assistance, and almost perished in the Midst of Plenty—for being an Heretic, and destitute of Friends or Money: That during two Months that he was at the Havannah, upwards of 40 English Sailors were obliged to abjure their Religion, and go in Spanish Ships or perish; and that this is frequently the Case, for want of an English Consul there, who, by claiming and relieving all that are taken and carried thither, or are cast away on the Coast of that Island, would save a great many Subjects to the Nation, otherways totally lost." See *Boston News-Letter*, Mar. 30, 1758.

55. Gascoigne's reported defiance, in carrying off Cuba's inhabitants despite the protest of government officials, certainly had a precedent. In 1708 a mariner named James Hammell testified that he had heard a Captain Fane, of the *Lastaff*, boast that "he would take from off Barbados all the white or black men that would leave it, in spight of the Government. William Robertson told deponent that he had sent two negroes on board the *Lastaff*, the tytle of one of the negroes being in dispute." See *Calendar of State Papers, Colonial Series, America and West Indies*, vol. 23, ed. Cecil Headlam (London: 1916), 731.

56. *New-York Gazette*, Nov. 19, 1750.

57. Karen Weyler, *Empowering Words: Outsiders and Authorship in Early America* (Athens: University of Georgia Press, 2013), 77.

58. Presumably, Havana jails were no longer crowded with British sailors waiting for impressment during the late 1750s; when Don Francisco sent home a British crew which had made their way to Havana after shipwreck, he "obliged them to bring off what English prisoners had escaped from the French to that place." That the governor did not manumit Hammon speaks to a belief that he viewed Hammon as property rather than a prisoner of war. See *Boston Evening-Post* Oct. 10, 1757.

59. ADM 36/5071.

60. ADM 51/3778. The other four "Negroes" who escaped with Hammon may also have been shipwrecked. When another vessel visited Havana in December 1758 "to claim some Slaves that had been wreck'd on the Florida Coast, taken up and carried thither," the ship's captain "was carried on shore by the King's Boat, guarded with Soldiers; conducted to the Governor with the same Soldiers, and by him informed, that the Negroes had been sent to Jamaica; then was reconducted to his Vessel by Soldiers, and ordered to depart immediately." See *New-London Summary* Feb. 23, 1759.

61. *London Evening Post*, Apr. 7, 1759.

62. *Whitehall Evening Post or London Intelligencer*, May 8, 1759.

63. As quoted in Sir Edward Hawke, *The Hawke Papers: A Selection: 1743–1771*, ed. Ruddock F. Mackay (Brookfield, VT: Gower Publishing Company, 1990), 328–29. Porter's letter to Hawke was reproduced in several London newspapers and in *Boston Evening-Post*, Mar. 10, 1760.

64. During the much larger battle at Quiberon Bay in November 1759, Hawke reports a total of two hundred forty-two casualties for a fleet of two dozen ships; that the *Hercules* should have suffered a loss of seventy sailors in a much smaller engagement—and then failed to report it—is inconceivable. The *Hercules*, after being repaired, rejoined the fleet at Quiberon Bay under the command of Captain William Fortescue and seems to have accounted for six of the two hundred forty-two casualties; according to newspaper reports, the *Hercules'* crew suffered more from scurvy than they did from the French. Porter returned to the captaincy of the *Hercules* in early 1760 and does not seem to have had his leg amputated. See Hawke, *The Hawke Papers: A Selection: 1743–1771*, 344–50; *Whitehall Evening Post or London Intelligencer*, Jan. 10, 1760, and June 10, 1760; and *Public Advertiser*, May 26, 1760. The best synthetic account of the *Hercules'* movements during late 1759 is in Geoffrey Marcus, *Quiberon Bay* (Barre, MA: Barre Publishing Company, 1963), but Marcus fails to treat the *Hercules'* engagement with the *Souverain*, an oversight rectified in Nicholas Tracy, *The Battle of Quiberon Bay, 1759: Admiral Hawke and the Defeat of the French Invasion* (South Yorkshire, England: Pen & Sword Maritime, 2010), 125–26.

65. While Hammon was writing or dictating his *Narrative* in June 1760, Boston newspapers continued to celebrate the blockade and victory at Quiberon Bay, boasting that "the Enemy's Ships in the Vilaine were retired up the River to dismantle, they having lost all Hopes of getting out. Two of them are entirely destroyed, and 'tis thought next Winter must finish the Remainder. . . . [British] Ships spread such a Distance, that very little [French] coasting Trade can be carried. The very Soldiers have been taken, going from the Main to the Islands, to relieve those who were Sick." See *Boston Weekly Post-Boy*, June 16, 1760.

66. For an account of Winslow's military service, see Fred Anderson, *A People's Army: Massachusetts Soldiers and Society in the Seven Years' War* (Chapel Hill: University of North Carolina Press, 1984). Little has been made of the fact that Winslow stopped briefly in Cuba before Edward Vernon's ill-fated attack on Santiago de Cuba in 1741. Winslow left for New England before the battle in order to recruit soldiers and settlers willing to return with him to Cuba. It is tempting to imagine that Hammon might have accompanied Winslow on his journeys to Cuba and present-day Colombia or that Winslow might have enlisted Hammon in the relief force he raised at Massachusetts. Accounts of Winslow's work in rounding up recruits can be found in William Shirley, "Last Wednesday His Excellency the Governour," *Boston Evening-Post*, Sep. 28, 1741; and John Winslow, "Advertisements," *Boston Evening-Post*, Dec. 28, 1741.

67. Baugh, *The Global Seven Years War, 1754–1763*, 5–8.

68. Sari Edelstein, *Between the Novel and the News: The Emergence of American Women's Writing* (Charlottesville: University of Virginia Press, 2014), 10.

69. As Ramesh Mallipeddi argues, "sentimental affect . . . was a resource deployed by the enslaved." Hammon's claim to have been injured worked doubly, "as an affective protest against colonial slavery and capitalist modernity, although such protest at times devolves

into allegory, as slavery becomes a metaphorical pretext for reflecting on British liberty." The invitation to personal sympathy and systemic critique was likely lost on most of Hammon's rabidly nationalistic readers. See Ramesh Mallipeddi, *Spectacular Suffering: Witnessing Slavery in the Eighteenth-Century British Atlantic* (Charlottesville: University of Virginia Press, 2016), 4, 11.

70. Thomas P. Robinson, "The Historic Winslow House at Marshfield, Massachusetts, and Its Restoration," *Old-Time New England: The Bulletin of the Society for the Preservation of New England Antiquities* 11 (1920–21): 107–12; see also John B. Hermanson, "Careswell: The Historic Winslow House in Marshfield, Massachusetts," *The Magazine Antiques* 160.3 (2001): 312–19.

71. Adam Hochschild, *Bury the Chains: Prophets and Rebels in the Fight to Free an Empire's Slaves* (New York: Mariner Books, 2006), 372; Natalie Zemon Davis, "On the Lame," *The American Historical Review* 93.3 (1988): 572.

72. In his discussion of eighteenth-century travel narratives, Jean Viviès argues that "[t]here is no dichotomous divide between the novel and the travel narrative [or, I would add, autobiography], but rather a gradation. . . . [Laurence] Sterne wrote his two principal texts at the locus of fictional autobiography, the novel and the travel journal, but neither *Tristram Shandy* nor *A Sentimental Journey* can be assigned to a firmly determined status. This plasticity of texts, with their problematic character in terms of reading and defining, presents critics with a challenge. They call for a critical discourse that should itself be open, and whose conceptual framework should be plural." See Jean Viviès, *English Travel Narratives in the Eighteenth Century: Exploring Genres*, trans. Claire Davison (Burlington, VT: Ashgate, 2002), 107.

Chapter Five

1. Bernard Bailyn, *The Ideological Origins of the American Revolution* (Cambridge, MA: Harvard University Press, 1967), 232–46. Bailyn's thesis has been refined and challenged over the years by David Brion Davis, *The Problem of Slavery in the age of Revolution, 1770–1823* (Ithaca, NY: Cornell University Press, 1975), 255–62; F. Nwabueze Okoye, "Chattel Slavery as the Nightmare of the American Revolutionaries," *The William and Mary Quarterly* 37.1 (1980): 3–28; Patricia Bradley, *Slavery, Propaganda, and the American Revolution* (Jackson: University Press of Mississippi, 1998), 1–24; Peter A. Dorsey, "To 'Corroborate Our Own Claims': Public Positioning and the Slavery Metaphor in Revolutionary America," *American Quarterly* 55.3 (2003): 353–86; and François Furstenberg, "Beyond Freedom and Slavery: Autonomy, Virtue, and Resistance in Early American Political Discourse," *Journal of American History* 89.4 (2003): 1295–330; among others.

2. Stephen Hopkins, *The Rights of the Colonies Examined* (Providence, RI: William Goddard, 1764), 16. For a synthetic account of colonial resistance to the Stamp Act, see Edmund S. Morgan and Helen M. Morgan, *The Stamp Act Crisis: Prologue to Revolution* (Chapel Hill: University of North Carolina Press, 1953).

3. *Boston Gazette*, Aug. 19, 1765.

4. Peters has long been known simply as Phillis Wheatley. For a discussion of the importance of referring to her as Peters, see Zachary McLeod Hutchins, "'Add New Glory to Her Name': Phillis Wheatley Peters," *Early American Literature* 56.3 (2021): 663–67.

5. David Waldstreicher notes that although "Phillis Wheatley has rarely been considered politically savvy, much less effective," her verse "challenged the American Revolutionaries, as well as their English counterparts, to respond to her political as well as poetic genius." John Levi Bernard suggests that we may have failed to appreciate Peters's political genius at least in part because it was "largely conveyed through the language of classicism." See David Waldstreicher, "Phillis Wheatley: The Poet Who Challenged the American Revolutionaries," in *Revolutionary Founders: Rebels, Radicals, and Reformers in the Making of the Nation*, ed. Alfred F. Young, Gary B. Nash, and Ray Raphael (New York: Knopf, 2011), 98; and John Levi Bernard, *Empire of Ruin: Black Classicism and American Imperial Culture* (New York: Oxford University Press, 2018), 25. On the larger question of Peters as a political writer, see also G. J. Barker-Benefield, *Phillis Wheatley Chooses Freedom: History, Poetry, and the Ideals of the American Revolution* (New York: New York University Press, 2018), 126–79; Jillmarie Murphy, "Maternal Fathers; or, The Power of Sympathy: Phillis Wheatley's Poem to and Correspondence with 'His Excellency General Washington,'" *Literature in the Early American Republic* 6 (2014): 37–62; Betsy Erkkila, "Phillis Wheatley and the Black American Revolution," in *Feminist Interventions in Early American Studies*, ed. Mary C. Carruth (Tuscaloosa: University of Alabama Press, 2006), 161–82; and John C. Shields, "Phillis Wheatley's Struggle for Freedom," in Phillis Wheatley Peters, *The Collected Works of Phillis Wheatley*, ed. John C. Shields (New York: Oxford University Press, 1988), 229–70.

6. Phillis Wheatley Peters, *Complete Writings*, ed. Vincent Carretta (New York: Penguin, 2001), 75.

7. Caroline Wigginton, *In the Neighborhood: Women's Publication in Early America* (Amherst: University of Massachusetts Press, 2016), 101.

8. Like the newspaper with which they were delivered, these poems may have been corporate compositions, drafted with type, in the pressroom, just before ink was applied to paper. Their poetic persona is that of the delivery boy—Caesar—and given that the Fleets allowed enslaved workers to keep Christmas tips for themselves (see the following note), he was the individual with the strongest financial incentive to produce such poems. Given the astonishment with which Bostonians reacted when the poetic talents of Peters were publicized during this same time period, it is possible that subscribers never knew about or disbelieved in Caesar's authorship of the poems. Alternatively, they may have rationalized that these verses, which adhere to conventions of other New Year's Eve addresses, were derivative or formulaic and thus dismissed Caesar's poems as unremarkable in comparison to those of Peters. I believe Caesar to be the primary author of these poems, but even if he contributed nothing of their language, Caesar still helped to author their meaning by performing enslavement, as he sold and delivered the poems, for readers who believed their own conditions comparable to his.

9. In 1743 Peter, whose work as an engraver is discussed in the Introduction, wrote a will explaining to the slaveowner Thomas Fleet, "I would not have you think that I got this money by Rogury in anything belong'd to you or any body else, I got it honestly; by being faithful to people ever since I undertook to carry ye Newspapers, Christmas-days, & New-years days, with contribution with gentlemen sometimes 3 pounds 10/s and sometimes 4 pounds 10/s and in ye years 1743, 5 pounds." Isaiah Thomas, an eighteenth-century printer and antiquarian, was familiar with Peter's work. After describing Peter's contributions to the *Post* and other products of Fleet's printing house, he wrote that "Fleet had also two

negro boys born in his house; sons, I believe, to the man just mentioned, whom he brought up to work at press and case; one named Pompey and the other Cesar; they were young when their master died; but they remained in the family, and continued to labor regularly in the printing house with the sons of Mr. Fleet, who succeeded their father, until the constitution of Massachusetts, adopted in 1780, made them freemen." Thomas's assertions, here and elsewhere, that Pompey and Caesar were trained to do the work their father had done, is the basis of my assumption that they—like Peter—helped to gather and compose and deliver the news printed in the *Post*. Because the poems' author is described as a boy, I ascribe their authorship to Caesar, rather than Pompey, who was his senior by three years. See "Last Will and Testament of Peter, 1743," in *The Earliest African American Literatures: A Critical Reader*, ed. Zachary McLeod Hutchins and Cassander L. Smith (Chapel Hill: University of North Carolina Press, 2021), 91–93; and Isaiah Thomas, *The History of Printing in America*, in *Transactions and Collections of the American Antiquarian Society*, vol. 5 (Worcester, MA: 1874), 99.

10. Each of these poems is reproduced in the Appendix, republished here for the first time in two hundred and fifty years.

11. Jeremiah Dummer, *A Defence of the New-England Charters* (Boston: Thomas and John Fleet, 1765), 23. In a passage that elides or obscures the labor of Hammon and other enslaved black Africans, Dummer writes, "It is wholly owing to the industry of the people of New-England, that this useful commodity [logwood] is reduced from 30 and 40l. per ton, which we used to pay for it to the Spaniard, to 12l. per ton" (6). Dummer's racism is plainly manifest in his complaint that the navy's enlistment and impressment of white New England sailors "so distressed the New-England merchants, that they were obliged to man their ships with Indians and Negroes" (7).

12. Benjamin Church, "The Times: A Poem" (Boston: 1765), 2.

13. Perry chronicles ceremonial funerals and an actual burial in her account of ritual opposition to the Stamp Act: "With the distributor 'flatly refusing' to resign his commission, the crowd 'told him. . . . they would bury him alive.' When he refused again, the assembly prepared a coffin, 'forced him into it, fastened on the Cover, and lowered the living Lump to the Bottom of a Grave dug for that purpose and slowly threw after it about two Bushels of Dirt.' As he lay contemplating his death by mob, the stamp distributor 'then consented to resign his odious Employment, and the People . . . drew him up, heard him re-deliver his Resignation in a more articulate Manner, gave him his LIBERTY, and heartily congratulated him on his Restoration to the fresh air.'" See Molly Perry, "Buried Liberties and Hanging Effigies: Imperial Persuasion, Intimidation, and Performance During the Stamp Act Crisis," in *Community without Consent: New Perspectives on the Stamp Act*, ed. Zachary McLeod Hutchins (Hanover, NH: Dartmouth College Press, 2016), 55–56.

14. Genesis 44:14.

15. In suggesting that Caesar validates the views of his captors, I stress an interpretive approach that goes beyond reading strictly for resistance. As Susen Hylen and Saba Mahmood have written with respect to women, "Interpreters will overlook elements of women's agency if they define agency only in terms of resistance. Mahmood's work offers an important correction to the tendency of some scholars to represent agency only as action taken in opposition to dominant cultural norms. Instead, she argues that agency is also found 'in the multiple ways in which one inhabits norms.'" Caesar and Peters both upheld the dominant view of

Revolution, casting it as a form of bondage, inhabiting the metaphor of taxation-as-slavery in their poetry even as they pushed their readers to think about slavery with greater nuance. See Susan E. Hylen, *A Modest Apostle: Thecla and the History of Women in the Early Church* (New York: Oxford University Press, 2015), 12; and Saba Mahmood, *Politics of Piety: The Islamic Revival and the Feminist Subject* (Princeton, NJ: Princeton University Press, 2005), 5–17.

16. Although the Stamp Act had already been repealed when Dickinson wrote *Letters*, he invokes its legislative specter in arguing against the Townshend Duties: "[W]hat signifies the repeal of the *Stamp-Act*, if these colonies are to lose their other privileges, by not tamely surrendering *that* of taxation?" He complains that these new laws "are as much *taxes* upon us, as those imposed by the *Stamp-Act*." After some thirty mentions throughout, the phrase "*Stamp-Act*" is also the conclusion of Dickinson's epistles, the last words of his Pennsylvania Farmer. John Dickinson, *Letters from a Farmer in Pennsylvania, to the Inhabitants of the British Colonies*, 3rd ed. (Philadelphia: William and Thomas Bradford, 1769), 4, 11. Subsequent in-text citations to this work appear as "*D* 4, 11."

17. Vincent Carretta transcribed the poem from a copybook in which Peters's poem "Hymn to Humanity" was written by the same hand as "The Voice of Freedom." The copybook, found by Randall K. Burkett, is linked to King Street, where Peters lived with the Wheatley family in Boston, but there is disagreement over whether the poem was written by Peters or in her hand. See "Appendix A," in Peters, *Complete Writings*, 195–98.

18. See Caroline Wigginton, "Letters from a Woman in Pennsylvania; or, Elizabeth Graeme Fergusson Dreams of John Dickinson," in Zachary McLeod Hutchins, *Community without Consent: New Perspectives on the Stamp Act* (Hanover, NH: Dartmouth College Press, 2016), 89–112.

19. Milton E. Flower, *John Dickinson: Conservative Revolutionary* (Charlottesville: University Press of Virginia, 1983), 69.

20. James Myers argues that Crèvecoeur worked to advance French interests—not those of the king or rebellious American colonists. I am concerned less with Crèvecoeur's personal views or aims than with the political perspective of his public *Letters*, which is staunchly Loyalist. Whatever Crèvecoeur's personal politics, *Letters* advocates Tory positions and repudiates Whiggish thought, as Myers himself seems to acknowledge. See James P. Myers Jr., "Crèvecoeur: Concealing and Revealing the Secret Self," *Early American Literature* 49.2 (2014): 368, 381. I cite the Oxford edition of Crèvecoeur's 1782 *Letters* rather than the excellent Harvard edition recently edited by Dennis Moore because, by eliding the distinction between Crèvecoeur's published and unpublished work, Moore questions the existence of an overriding artistic vision governing the selection of materials for and the organization of his 1782 volume. In this chapter and a second essay, I emphasize the unity and structural integrity of Crèvecoeur's 1782 *Letters*, an emphasis best served by citing the Oxford edition. See Dennis D. Moore, "Introduction to J. Hector St. John de Crèvecoeur," *Letters from an American Farmer and Other Essays* (Cambridge, MA: Belknap Press of Harvard University Press, 2013), xv; and Zach Hutchins, "Crèvecoeur's Miltonic Epic: Paradise Lost and the Subversive Structural Poetics of *Letters from an American Farmer*," *The Eighteenth Century: Theory and Interpretation* 61.1 (2020): 89–111.

21. J. Hector St. John de Crèvecoeur, *Letters from an American Farmer*, ed. Susan Manning (New York: Oxford University Press, 1997), 12. Subsequent in-text citations of this work appear as "*C* 12."

22. Grantland Rice notes that Crèvecoeur's contemporary readers struggled to understand his *Letters*: "In the two years after its English publication in 1782, *Letters* had been read by European critics as, variously, a portrayal of the exotic, a benign literary hoax, a contribution to the English literary canon, a colonial panegyric, an invective against the Revolution, a Tory panegyric, an immigration tract, a French Catholic deceit, a Rousseauistic conceit, and a true documentary account of the Americas." See Grantland S. Rice, "Crèvecoeur and the Politics of Authorship in Republican America," *Early American Literature* 28.2 (1993): 106.

23. Over the past twenty years, scholars have reframed them as "individual essays," "an early but sophisticated novel," a "loose collection of sketches," "an epic-like venture," "natural history," "parody," "travel narrative," "descriptive geography," a "discursive exposition of the local historian," and literary tiles in a larger "mosaic." See Rice, "Crèvecoeur and the Politics of Authorship in Republican America," 109, 93; Norman S. Grabo, "Crèvecoeur's American: Beginning the World Anew," *The William and Mary Quarterly* 48.2 (1991): 165; Eric D. Lamore, "Cultivating the Ancient Classical Tradition in Early America: Vergil and J. Hector St. Jean de Crèvecoeur's *Letters from an American Farmer*," *Atenea* 29.1 (2009): 130; Pamela Regis, *Describing Early America: Bartram, Jefferson, Crèvecoeur, and the Influence of Natural History* (Dekalb: Northern Illinois University Press, 1992), 107; Ralph Bauer, *The Cultural Geography of Colonial American Literatures: Empire, Travel, Modernity* (New York: Cambridge University Press, 2003), 211; John D. Cox, *Traveling South: Travel Narratives and the Construction of American Identity* (Athens: University of Georgia Press, 2005), 26; Yael Ben-Zvi, "Mazes of Empire: Space and Humanity in Crèvecoeur's *Letters*," *Early American Literature* 42.1 (2007): 78; Nathaniel Philbrick, "The Nantucket Sequence in Crèvecoeur's *Letters from an American Farmer*," *New England Quarterly* 64.3 (1991): 415; Ed White, "Crèvecoeur in Wyoming," *Early American Literature* 43.2 (2008): 397.

24. Elizabeth Heckendorn Cook, *Epistolary Bodies: Gender and Genre in the Eighteenth-Century Republic of Letters* (Stanford, CA: Stanford University Press, 1996), 141. Other than Cook, the most notable exception to this trend is Eve Bannet, who reads Crèvecoeur's first epistle in tandem with letter-writing manuals of the period. See Eve Tavor Bannet, *Empire of Letters: Letter Manuals and Transatlantic Correspondence, 1688–1820* (New York: Cambridge University Press, 2005), 275–87.

25. Dorsey, "To 'Corroborate Our Own Claims,'" 362. Although, as Jane Calvert argues, Dickinson was not a Whig, his political views overlapped with Whig thought. See Jane E. Calvert, *Quaker Constitutionalism and the Political Thought of John Dickinson* (New York: Cambridge University Press, 2009).

26. David Carlson, "Farmer Versus Lawyer: Crèvecoeur's *Letters* and the Liberal Subject," *Early American Literature* 38.2 (2003): 260.

27. Although Dickinson and Crévecoeur both wrote in prose, their work—with its metaphorization of politics and its engagement in the period's newspaper debates—is of a piece with the verse discussed by Colin Wells in *Poetry Wars: Verse and Politics in the American Revolution and Early American Republic* (Philadelphia: University of Pennsylvania Press, 2017).

28. By locating his commentary on the reasonableness of taxes in the Nantucket letters, Crèvecoeur may have subtly reminded Whigs that they faced an *internal* rebellion against locally assessed and administered taxes. As Jennifer Schell explains, "[D]uring both the

American Revolution and the War of 1812, Nantucketers negotiated treaties of neutrality openly and independently with the British and refused to pay taxes to the state of Massachusetts." See Jennifer Schell, "Figurative Surveying: National Space and the Nantucket Chapters of J. Hector St. John de Crèvecoeur's *Letters from an American Farmer*," *Early American Literature* 43.3 (2008): 584.

29. *Connecticut Journal*, Apr. 8, 1768.

30. Jeff Osborne, "American Antipathy and the Cruelties of Citizenship in Crèvecoeur's *Letters from an American Farmer*," *Early American Literature* 42.3 (2007): 541. This comparison between American Indians and colonial Whigs becomes the occasion for an allegorical warning against revolution in the Nantucket letters. Discussing American Indians, Crèvecoeur writes, "It is strange what revolution has happened among them in less than two hundred years! What is become of those numerous tribes which formerly inhabited the extensive shores of the great Bay of Massachusetts?" (*C* 103). Crèvecoeur lists fourteen American Indian nations and twelve English towns built on their home sites; when he describes the Indian inhabitants of Cape Cod, he lists thirteen "tribes" who live "divided into two great regions" (*C* 104). The number of Indian groups in play at any one time—thirteen or fourteen—approximates the number of English colonies in North America, and Crèvecoeur warns that these Indian nations "have all disappeared either in the wars which the Europeans have carried on against them or else they have mouldered away, gathered in some of their ancient towns, in contempt and oblivion" (*C* 103).

31. Ralph Bauer shows that this question of Creole identity troubled gentlemen farmers such as Crèvecoeur because English observers "referred to the colonials as 'natives,' 'Creoles,' and 'country-born.' As was the case in other parts of the Americas, nature's undesirable effects upon bodily 'humors' in the New World were thus seen as a plausible explanation for the 'extreme choler and passion' that seemed to characterize" colonists. Ralph Bauer, *The Cultural Geography of Colonial American Literatures: Empire, Travel, Modernity* (New York: Cambridge University Press, 2003), 183.

32. Christine Holbo, "Imagination, Commerce, and the Politics of Associationism in Crèvecoeur's *Letters from an American Farmer*," *Early American Literature* 32.1 (1997): 37.

33. Cox, *Traveling South*, 34.

34. Notwithstanding his characterization of the colonies as independent animals, Dickinson also viewed them as an essential part of the British body politic. Dreading the prospect of civil war and independence, Dickinson asks, "But if once *we* are separated from our mother country, what new form of government shall we adopt, or where shall we find another *Britain*, to supply our loss? Torn from the body, to which we are united by religion, liberty, laws, affections, relation, language and commerce, we must bleed at every vein" (*D* 21).

35. This proportion is not coincidental; as Edward Larkin notes, John Adams estimated that Loyalists constituted a third of the population in revolutionary North America. See Edward Larkin, "The Cosmopolitan Revolution: Loyalism and the Fiction of an American Nation," *Novel* 40.1–2 (2006–2007): 57.

36. Although Dickinson was one of the largest slaveholders in the Delaware Valley when he wrote his *Letters* and when Crèvecoeur began drafting his response, by the time Crèvecoeur published *Letters from an American Farmer* Dickinson had been speaking out against slavery for several years and had already begun the process of unconditionally emancipating all of the enslaved black Africans he claimed as property. Crèvecoeur's caricature of

Dickinson as slaveholding hypocrite was, thus, outdated by the time it made it into print. For this insight and other helpful suggestions throughout the chapter, I thank Jane Calvert.

37. Scholars have explained this diversion from autobiographical similarities between Crèvecoeur and Farmer James in various ways. Larkin notes that some scholars have suggested that Crèvecoeur turned "Pennsylvania into a model for the entirety of British North America." White suggests that a Pennsylvania setting represents Crèvecoeur's attempt to contrast the cultural values of New England and the Middle Colonies. White's arguments actually make more sense if Crèvecoeur's *Letters* responds to Dickinson; when Dickinson's *Letters* sparked a spirit of rebellion in New England, some Pennsylvanians angrily sought to dissociate themselves from New England. See Larkin, "Cosmopolitan Revolution," 62; and White, "Crèvecoeur in Wyoming," 393. On regional factionalism, see *Pennsylvania Gazette*, July 21, 1768.

38. Frank Luther Mott, *Golden Multitudes: The Story of Best Sellers in the United States* (New York: Macmillan, 1947), 50. An example of these toasts to "The FARMER" can be found in *Boston Evening-Post*, Aug. 22, 1768.

39. Jeffrey L. Pasley, *"The Tyranny of Printers": Newspaper Politics in the Early American Republic* (Charlottesville: University Press of Virginia, 2001), 35. On the need for anonymity in the development of the eighteenth-century public sphere, see Michael Warner, *The Letters of the Republic* (Cambridge, MA: Harvard University Press, 1990). Francis Walett helpfully reviews the editorial debates over the Stamp Act that preceded Dickinson's *Letters* and established the generic conventions which guided debate over Dickinson's *Letters* in the newspapers; see Francis G. Walett, "The Impact of the Stamp Act on the Colonial Press," in *Newsletters to Newspapers: Eighteenth-Century Journalism*, ed. Donovan H. Bond and W. Reynolds McLeod (Morgantown: West Virginia University, 1977), 157–69.

40. *Pennsylvania Chronicle*, Aug. 1, 1768, and Aug. 8, 1768. See also *Pennsylvania Gazette*, Aug. 4, 1768. Editorials from 1769 repeatedly drew a distinction between writers from Philadelphia and Delaware even though the two colonies were commonly combined, as John Munroe observes, into a single political entity. See John A. Munroe, *The Philadelawareans, and Other Essays Relating to Delaware* (Newark, NJ: University of Delaware Press, 2004), 44–46.

41. Norman Grabo first noted that Crèvecoeur's "prose is mainly that of the newspaper essayists of the time. . . . St. John assumes the same kind of dignity in his prose, an almost foreign formality of grammar and diction—long sentences, highly subordinated, heavily Latinate." Beatrice Fink, for her part, reminds us that Crèvecoeur wrote editorial epistles to New York newspapers during his service as the French consul in the 1780s and signed them "Agricola." Crèvecoeur's contributions to European newspapers are noted in his biography, by Gay Allen and Roger Asselineau. See Grabo, "Crèvecoeur's American," 160; Beatrice Fink, "Saint-John de Crèvecoeur's Tale of a Tuber," *Eighteenth-Century Life* 25 (2001): 231; and Gay Wilson Allen and Roger Asselineau, *St. John de Crèvecoeur: The Life of an American Farmer* (New York: Viking, 1987), 72, 200.

42. See *Pennsylvania Chronicle*, Aug. 22, 1768, and Sep. 19, 1768.

43. Cook, *Epistolary Bodies*, 155.

44. *Pennsylvania Chronicle*, Aug. 15, 1768.

45. *New-York Gazette, or Weekly Post-Boy*, June 20, 1768; *Boston Evening-Post*, Aug. 22, 1768.

46. John Dickinson, "Extracts, from a Pamphlet Published by the Author of the Farmer's Letters," *Boston Evening-Post*, Aug. 1, 1768.

47. The minister of Crèvecoeur's first letter is a clergyman, not an officer of government, but this distinction between civic and religious ministers collapses in the larger trajectory of *Letters*. In his well-known third letter, Farmer James explains that the profits of an American farmer cannot be "claimed, either by a despotic prince, a rich abbot, or a mighty lord. Here religion demands but little of him; a small voluntary salary to the minister" (*C* 44). Proximity conflates, in Crèvecoeur's prose, the payment to a clergyman with that which might be offered to a prince, lord, or abbot—another religious leader whose inclusion speaks to the alignment of church and state power and officials; the word *minister* slips between its civic and religious meanings.

48. Calvert, *Quaker Constitutionalism*, 16–17. As Moore notes, James's wife uses speech patterns characteristic of Quaker grammar consistently, but James only briefly adopts a Quaker dialect when speaking with his wife (*C* 17–18); furthermore, James's reliance on a minister and his ownership of slaves would be uncharacteristic of a Friend, suggesting that only James's wife is a Quaker. Dickinson, like Farmer James, married a Quaker woman and was often mistaken for a Quaker himself. See Moore, "Introduction," xiii.

49. Placing Dickinson's views in the mouth of a Quaker wife advocating separation from England is ironic, given that Dickinson's peers in the Second Continental Congress, as Calvert notes, "claimed that Dickinson's Quaker mother and wife 'were continually distressing him with their remonstrances'" and preventing him from embracing the Patriot cause. Calvert, *Quaker Constitutionalism*, 239.

50. Crèvecoeur also tweaks Dickinson for advocating aggressive behavior not in keeping with his position in the second letter, when he describes a wren who steals a swallow's nest: "The peaceable swallow, like the passive Quaker, meekly sat at a small distance, and never offered the least resistance. But, no sooner was the plunder carried away, than the injured bird went to work with unabated ardour, and, in a few days, the depredations were repaired. To prevent, however, a further repetition of the same violence, I removed the wren's box to another part of the house" (*C* 37). Crèvecoeur insinuates that Dickinson's aggression is inappropriate for a Quaker; he also suggests that Dickinson is fighting over a paltry sum easily regained "in a few days."

51. As if to reinforce the insignificance of Dickinson in his guise as a Quaker woman, Crèvecoeur offers us a second portrait of a Quaker woman ignored by her auditors in Letter XI. At the beginning of a Quaker meeting "profound silence ensued, which lasted about half an hour; every one had his head reclined, and seemed absorbed in profound meditation; when a female friend arose." This Quaker woman speaks for forty-five minutes, during which time "I did not observe one single face turned toward her; never before had I seen a congregation listening with so much attention to a public oration" (*C* 184–85). Crèvecoeur's narrator seems to suggest that her discourse is captivating, but the locutionary force of his language leads to the opposite conclusion: "so much" is the rhetorical equivalent of *so little*. Here, as throughout the *Letters*, Crèvecoeur writes sarcastically, tongue in cheek; auditors with "reclined" heads, who never look at a speaker, are hardly rapt with attention—they are sleeping!

52. Aristotle, *Aristotle's Politics*, trans. Benjamin Jowett (Oxford: Clarendon Press, 1908), 34–35.

53. As Osborne contends, Crèvecoeur's *Letters* promotes a hierarchical perspective, insinuating that "prosperity is a product of division and hierarchy . . . not of equality and interchangeability." My reading of James's wife diverges from a tradition, initiated by D. H. Lawrence and updated by James Bishop, that emphasizes her compliance; Lawrence calls her "Amiable Spouse," and Bishop emphasizes her "unwavering compliance." Anna Carew-Miller, however, has anticipated my more aggressive reading of James's wife, arguing that "[h]er assertion of authority outside her housewifely duties threatens his position in the domestic partnership." See Osborne, "American Antipathy," 532; D. H. Lawrence, *Studies in Classic American Literature* (New York: T. Seltzer, 1923), 25; James E. Bishop, "A Feeling Farmer: Masculinity, Nationalism, and Nature in Crèvecoeur's *Letters,*" *Early American Literature* 43.2 (2008): 370; and Anna Carew-Miller, "The Language of Domesticity in Crèvecoeur's *Letters from an American Farmer,*" *Early American Literature* 28.3 (1993): 249.

54. I have elsewhere suggested that by slicing the rattlesnake in two Crèvecoeur anticipates the colonies' eventual division over slavery, a reading in keeping with the division of thirteen American Indian nations in Letter IV. As Christopher Iannini notes, Crèvecoeur deeply absorbed the views of Abbé Guillaume-Thomas-François Raynal, who repeatedly prophesied slave insurrections; thus, the rattlesnake cut in two by "negroes" may also reflect fears that had less to do with a division between North and South than the possibility of a slave insurrection in the South. See Zachary McLeod Hutchins, "Rattlesnakes in the Garden: The Fascinating Serpents of the Early, Edenic Republic," *Early American Studies* 9.3 (2011): 696, 683–84; and Christopher Iannini, "'The Itinerant Man': Crèvecoeur's Caribbean, Raynal's Revolution, and the Fate of Atlantic Cosmopolitanism," *The William and Mary Quarterly* 61.2 (2004): 221–22.

55. John Dickinson, "A Song," *New-York Gazette, or Weekly Post-Boy,* July 11, 1768.

56. Dorsey, "To 'Corroborate Our Own Claims,'" 361.

57. That a "direct connection . . . was seldom drawn between chattel slavery and the slavery that Americans feared" is an insufficient reason to assert, as John Reid has, that "most commentators of the eighteenth century thought slavery the opposite of liberty without equating it with chattel slavery." Leaving that connection implicit was, rather, an unsuccessful attempt to avoid Loyalist allegations of hypocrisy. See John Phillip Reid, *The Concept of Liberty in the Age of American Revolution* (Chicago: University of Chicago Press, 1988), 45.

58. Holbo, "Imagination, Commerce, and the Politics of Associationism," 49–50.

59. On the raids against British officials conducted in blackface, see Morgan and Morgan, *The Stamp Act Crisis,* 41–53.

60. Konstantin Dierks, *In My Power: Letter Writing and Communications in Early America* (Philadelphia, PA: University of Pennsylvania Press, 2009), xii, 5.

61. Richard Eden, *The First Three English Books on America,* ed. Edward Arber (Birmingham, 1885), 73.

62. Dickson D. Bruce Jr., "Politics and Political Philosophy in the Slave Narrative," in *The Cambridge Companion to the African American Slave Narrative,* ed. Audrey Fisch (New York: Cambridge University Press, 2007), 28, 38.

63. François Furstenberg forcefully contends that liberalism, like letter writing, obscured the exercise of authority and force in chattel slavery: "The liberal tendency to individualize power trapped slaves in a double bind. It erased the power relationships embedded in chattel slavery and replaced them with the fiction that each individual *chooses* slavery or freedom,

thus shifting the moral burden of slavery onto the slave. By attributing moral agency to slaves—by holding them to standards of rational, autonomous subjectivity—it made slaves responsible for their condition. Even people born into slavery at some point made a choice to submit. At the very least they could have chosen death over slavery. This liberal formulation—by not resisting, slaves had consented to their enslavement—grounded both citizenship *and* slavery in consent." See Furstenberg, "Beyond Freedom and Slavery," 1310.

64. Bradley, *Slavery, Propaganda, and the American Revolution*, xxiv.

65. Alan Gilbert, *Black Patriots and Loyalists: Fighting for Emancipation in the War for Independence* (Chicago: University of Chicago Press, 2012), xi.

66. *Boston Evening-Post*, Sep. 26, 1768.

67. See Walter Benn Michaels, *The Trouble with Diversity: How We Learned to Love Identity and Ignore Inequality* (New York: Metropolitan Books, 2006), 122–40.

68. As Jones notes elsewhere, "At least one black prisoner, called Tom by his master, was sold into slavery in the West Indies in return for powder." And several states denied "captured African Americans the protections of prisoner of war status. When New Jersey militiamen captured an escaped slave who had gone 'over to the enemy' in July 1777, [George] Washington gave instructions 'to deliver him to his owner.' If an individual's master could not be determined, or if he were a free man, his captors often deemed him their own personal property. Similarly, black sailors could be auctioned off with the rest of a captured ship's assets. Either returned to their masters, forced to serve as privateers or laborers for the revolutionary forces, or sold into slavery, captured black soldiers and sailors were segregated from their white comrades and deemed ineligible for the 'many indulgences' white prisoners received." See T. Cole Jones, *Captives of Liberty: Prisoners of War and the Politics of Vengeance in the American Revolution* (Philadelphia: University of Pennsylvania Press, 2020), 111, 128–29.

69. Jefferson wrote, in words deleted by the Congress from the Declaration's final text, that the British monarch *"has waged cruel war against human nature itself, violating its most sacred rights of life and liberty in the persons of a distant people who never offended him, captivating and carrying them into slavery in another hemisphere, or to incur miserable death in their transportation hither. This piratical warfare, the opprobrium of INFIDEL powers, is the warfare of the CHRISTIAN king of Great Britain. Determined to keep open a market where MEN should be bought and sold, he has prostituted his negative for suppressing every legislative attempt to prohibit or to restrain this execrable commerce. And that this assemblage of horrors might want no fact of distinguished die, he is now exciting those very people to rise in arms among us, and to purchase that liberty of which he has deprived them, by murdering the people on whom he also obtruded them: thus paying off former crimes committed against the LIBERTIES of one people, with crimes which he urges them to commite against the LIVES of another."* See Thomas Jefferson, *Autobiography*, in *The Life and Selected Writings of Thomas Jefferson*, ed. Adrienne Koch and William Peden (New York: Modern Library, 2004), 26–27.

70. Peters, "On Being Brought from African to America," *Complete Writings*, 13.

71. *The New-England Historical and Genealogical Register*, vol. LV (Boston: 1901), 405.

72. *The Acts and Resolves, Public and Private, of the Province of the Massachusetts Bay*, vol. XXI (Boston: Wright and Potter, 1922), 259.

73. *Documentary History of the State of Maine*, vol. XVII, ed. James Phinney Baxter (Portland: Lefavor-Tower, 1913), 418, 444–45.

74. *The Constitution or Frame of Government for the Commonwealth of Massachusetts* (Boston: 1781), 3. See also note 9, above. The practical effect of these words, with respect to slavery, was clarified in 1783, by Chief Justice William Cushing of the Massachusetts Supreme Court, whose decision in *Jennison v. Caldwell* announced that the Constitution had abolished slavery. See William O'Brien, "Did the Jennison Case Outlaw Slavery in Massachusetts?," *The William and Mary Quarterly* 17 (1960): 219–41; Robert Spector, "The Quok Walker Cases (1781–1783)—Slavery, Its Abolition and Negro Citizenship in Early Massachusetts," *Journal of Negro History* 53 (1968): 12–32; Emily Blanck, "Seventeen Eighty-Three: The Turning Point in the Law of Slavery and Freedom in Massachusetts," *New England Quarterly* 75.1 (2002): 24–51; and Douglas R. Egerton, *Death or Liberty: African Americans and Revolutionary America* (New York: Oxford University Press, 2009), 93–121.

75. "Taking Book, 1780, Ward 2," *City of Boston Tax Records, 1780–1821*, Boston Public Library, https://www.bpl.org/archival_post/city-of-boston-tax-records-1780-1821/, p. 2. Accessed February 9, 2022. For an account of John and Phillis Peters's life from 1780 to 1783, see Cornelia H. Dayton, "Lost Years Recovered: John Peters and Phillis Wheatley Peters in Middleton," *The New England Quarterly* 94.3 (2021): 309–51.

76. "Taking Book, 1780, Ward 10," *City of Boston Tax Records, 1780–1821*, Boston Public Library, https://www.bpl.org/archival_post/city-of-boston-tax-records-1780-1821/, p. 10. Accessed February 9, 2022. Records from subsequent years identify the Prince Hall of Ward 10 as "Grandmaster of the lodge."

77. Prince Hall, "Petition of Prince Hall to the Massachusetts General Court, 27 February 1788," Massachusetts Historical Society, https://www.masshist.org/database/670. Accessed February 9, 2022.

78. As Vincent Carretta has observed, "Only toward the end of the eighteenth century would people forcibly removed from Africa begin to embrace the diasporan public social and political identity of *African*. For example, some in both Britain and America began to call themselves 'Sons of Africa.' In a sense, *Africa* did not exist as an idea rather than a place until after the antislave trade and antislavery movements began." See Vincent Carretta, *Phillis Wheatley: Biography of a Genius in Bondage* (Athens: University of Georgia Press, 2011), 4.

Conclusion

1. As David Waldstreicher and George Van Cleve have argued, the Constitution was a fundamentally proslavery document from its beginnings, as "problems of power and property raised by the definition of the Congress in Article I already had the Constitution favoring people who owned people." See David Waldstreicher, *Slavery's Constitution: From Revolution to Ratification* (New York: Farrar, Strauss, and Giroux, 2009), 5; and George William Van Cleve, *A Slaveholders' Union: Slavery, Politics, and the Constitution in the Early American Republic* (Chicago: University of Chicago Press, 2010).

2. As Jeffrey Kerr-Ritchie has demonstrated, enslaved individuals "continued to be transported on U.S. merchant ships in large numbers for decades after the abolition of the Atlantic slave trade," with more than 50,000 captives transported between 1820 and 1860. However, these sufferers were being moved from one state to another, in response to national economic pressures, rather than from one country to another, in response to war, international treaties, and other foreign affairs. See Jeffrey R. Kerr-Ritchie, *Rebellious Passage:*

The Creole *Revolt and America's Coastal Slave Trade* (New York: Cambridge University Press, 2019), 39.

3. Olaudah Equiano, *The Interesting Narrative and Other Writings*, ed. Vincent Carretta (New York: Penguin, 2003), 7–8.

4. Barry Weller noted this link between Equiano and his predecessors, contending that it may "have been inevitable that the first full-scale autobiography of an English-speaking African, *The Interesting Narrative of the Life of Olaudah Equiano, or Gustavus Vassa*, would conform to generic expectations shaped by the story of the royal slave." Barry Weller, "The Royal Slave and the Prestige of Origins," *The Kenyon Review*, 14.3 (1992): 66.

5. Equiano, *The Interesting Narrative*, 32.

6. Examining the geography and records of the slave trade in the Bight of Benin, Finn Fuglestad argues that the voluminous traffic in human beings at this location was more frequently a product of diplomacy than conflict. He contends "that the Europeans could not and would not have got anywhere without the very active collaboration of the locals (not that they ever tried), without having been invited ashore, so to speak." See Finn Fuglestad, *Slave Traders by Invitation: West Africa's Slave Coast in the Precolonial Era* (New York: Oxford University Press, 2018), 4.

7. Equiano, *The Interesting Narrative*, 64, 73.

8. Venture Smith, *A Narrative of the Life and Adventures of Venture, a Native of Africa: But Resident above Sixty Years in the United States of America*, in James Brewer Stewart, *Venture Smith and the Business of Slavery and Freedom* (Amherst: University of Massachusetts Press, 2010), 1. Venture writes that the people with whom he had lived during a brief separation from his family "had been invaded by a numerous army, from a nation not far distant, furnished with musical instruments, and all kinds of arms then in use; that they were instigated by some white nation who equipped and sent them to subdue and possess the country." His father offered shelter to refugees of this violence only to learn from them "that the invaders had laid waste their country, and were coming speedily to destroy them in my father's territories" (8–9). Taken captive by the army's scouts, Venture watched his father tortured to death before boarding a vessel bound for Barbados and then Rhode Island.

9. James O. Horton, Foreword, in James Brewer Stewart, *Venture Smith and the Business of Slavery and Freedom*, ix.

10. Benjamin F. Prentiss, *The Blind African Slave, or Memoirs of Boyrereau Brinch, Nicknamed Jeffrey Brace*, ed. Kari J. Winter (Madison: University of Wisconsin Press, 2004), 90, 166, 182.

11. Martha S. Jones, *Birthright Citizens: A History of Race and Rights in Antebellum America* (New York: Cambridge University Press, 2018), 10; Derrick R. Spires, *The Practice of Citizenship: Black Politics and Print Culture in the Early United States* (Philadelphia: University of Pennsylvania Press, 2019), 247.

12. *American Repertory*, Apr. 26, 1827. See also *Commercial Advertiser*, May 16, 1827; and *New-York Spectator*, May 18, 1827.

13. On the coverage of Africa and Haiti in *Freedom's Journal*, see Jacqueline Bacon, *Freedom's Journal: The First African-American Newspaper* (Lanham, MD: Lexington Books, 2007), 147–75.

14. Eric Gardener, *Black Print Unbound: The* Christian Recorder, *African American Literature, and Periodical Culture* (New York: Oxford University Press, 2015), 10.

15. As Fagan argues, "Book historians' tendency to overlook the black press helps explain why black newspapers remain neglected despite a renewed attention to early African American cultures of print." Brian Gabrial also contributes to this effort, but his monograph on newspaper coverage of significant rebellions against slavery actually ignores newspapers published by and for African Americans. Nor does the study undertake close readings that might interest literary scholars, as it is primarily interested in an analysis of how white southern media sources justified violence against enslaved individuals seeking their freedom through revolt. See Benjamin Fagan, *The Black Newspaper and the Chosen Nation* (Athens: University of Georgia Press, 2016), 9; Bacon, *Freedom's Journal: The First African-American Newspaper*; and Brian Gabrial, *The Press and Slavery in America, 1791–1859: The Melancholy Effect of Popular Excitement* (Columbia: University of South Carolina Press, 2016).

16. Frederick Douglass, *Narrative of the Life of Frederick Douglass, an American Slave, Written by Himself*, in *The Frederick Douglass Papers, Series Two: Autobiographical Writings, Volume I*, ed. John W. Blanssingame et al. (New Haven: Yale University Press, 1999), 36, 34.

17. Harriet Jacobs, *Incidents in the Life of a Slave Girl: Written by Herself* (New York: Penguin, 2000), 50, 214, 219.

18. In his history of the newspaper, Thomas Leonard writes, "Magazine pages filled the walls of many a black family at the end of the nineteenth century. Although the photographic record of these rooms is slender, there seems no doubt that a strong decorative sense controlled the papering. The most colorful pages, for example, often appeared above the mantel. Arthur Rothstein captured some of this living decorative tradition in a black home at Gee's Bend, Alabama. Here the quilters by the hearth face a maze of magazine pictures, and one is not sure where the cloth ends and the wall begins. A Historical Section photograph such as Russell Lee's picture of a fireplace in Transylvania, Louisiana, can easily be misread as a sign of desperation or pathos. In fact Lee has recorded a Southern heritage. This is what a home was *supposed* to look like to many rural Southerners. 'Most every room I's had I's been able to pretty up with magazine pictures,' an old black man told an interviewer from the Federal Writer's Project. Newspapers, too, were put up with pride and forethought. New black residents of a cabin in North Carolina cited the hanging of newspapers as proof that 'dis house is in tole'ble good shape.'" See Thomas C. Leonard, *News for All: America's Coming-of-Age with the Press* (New York: Oxford University Press, 1995), 106.

Appendix

1. The following stanza is a revision of an extant poem, "The New Year," published in *The London Magazine: and Monthly Chronologer* (January 1750): 41.

2. The original line reads, "That shall not Britain's happiness improve."

3. The original line reads, "Nor let one tyrant in the battle stand." It is followed by two lines that Caesar omits, "Let bigotry and persecution cease, / And sacred truth and charity increase."

Index

Indexes are traditionally organized by the surname of those mentioned in a given text. Because many of the people this book restores to our collective historical consciousness were never given a last name, never had an opportunity to choose one for themselves, or were identified by the last name of those who enslaved them, I include all such persons listed in this index under the heading "no last name given." Their inclusion is a reminder that many publication processes have worked to erase the presence of racialized or otherwise marginalized persons, including those who—like Black Peter, here Peter$_{(1)}$—helped to compose and set type.

CPSIA information can be obtained
at www.ICGtesting.com
Printed in the USA
LVHW102154180123
737471LV00006B/673